The Mid-Suffolk Light Railway

The Mid-Suffolk Light Railway

by

Peter Paye

Wild Swan Publications Ltd.

ISBN 0 906867 41 X

Designed by Paul Karau
Typesetting by Berkshire Publishing Services
Printed and bound by Butler & Tanner, Frome

Published by
WILD SWAN PUBLICATIONS LTD.
Hopgoods Farm Cottage, Upper Bucklebury, Berks.

Contents

Dr. I. C. Allen

Introduction

The Mid-Suffolk Light Railway was probably the least known of all the railways in East Anglia. Even at the last, many of the inhabitants of the county and surrounding areas were unaware of the existence of the line which had served their community with quiet efficiency for a period of almost 48 years.

Promoted after the passing of the Light Railways Act of 1896 to alleviate the effects of the agricultural depression in central Suffolk, the scheme was financed by local gentry and farmers with the backing of London businessmen. The 42 mile line authorised by the Light Railway Order of 1900 was to traverse and serve the open agricultural land with a route linking the Great Eastern Railway at Haughley and Halesworth with a branch from Kenton to the outskirts of Ipswich and the GER at Westerfield. So confident were the promoters for the success of their undertaking, that the cutting of the first sod was performed by none other than His Royal Highness the Duke of Cambridge at a large formal ceremony at Westerfield in 1902. Construction commenced the same year but financial difficulties were soon experienced and when the line opened for goods traffic in September 1904 operation was restricted to the 19 miles between Haughley and Laxfield and a short 1¾ mile section south of Kenton.

Disputes with the contractor, bankruptcy of the chairman, who had sunk a considerable amount of capital into the railway, and the blocking of loans from the Treasury and local councils culminated in the appointment of a Receiver. Further expansion ceased, leaving less than half the grandiose scheme completed. The Haughley to Halesworth section terminated at Cratfield whilst the stub end from the junction at Kenton to the outskirts of Debenham was all that existed of the Westerfield line. Passenger services commenced in September 1908 but only as far as Laxfield, an area with traffic potential of less than 12,000 people. The Debenham section was abandoned as early as 1906 whilst the freight only service beyond Laxfield to Cratfield succumbed in 1912. In the halcyon days passenger and freight traffic was fairly heavy for such a rural line. Most of the traffic flow was, however, to or from Stowmarket and Ipswich. The east to west routing of the line, with avoidance of major earthwork construction for economy reasons, weighed heavily against the railway in later years as improved roads and motor vehicles offered a direct door to door service from the villages to the two market towns.

Only after the satisfactory settlement of outstanding debts did the London and North Eastern Railway reluctantly assume responsibility for the Light Railway in 1924, and miraculously the route escaped closure in the 1930s when so many other East Anglian branches lost their passenger services. With neglible passenger traffic, great reliance was placed on freight receipts, but the slight upsurge of military traffic in World War Two did little to stem the flow of freight away from the railway and the line ultimately failed to withstand the pressures of post war competition from road transport and became a victim of the pre-Beeching era of railway closures in 1952.

With the initials MSLR, the railway was subjected to some ridicule, being harshly referred to as the 'Miserable Sinners Last Ride'. Others called it the 'Mud and Slush' or the 'Mad Suffolk'. To the regular travellers, to those who lived within sight or sound of the line, and the generations of schoolchildren who journeyed daily by train to Stowmarket Grammar School, it was affectionately known as the 'Middy'. The stories of the 'Middy' were many and, although officialdom was seen on occasions, unorthodox methods of working were the rule more than the exception. Schoolchildren were permitted to open and close the level crossing gates for the passage of the train and often received a penny reward from the driver or guard. Trains stopped midway between stations so that the train crew could pick mushrooms or vegetables from fields alongside the track, and a certain driver with his shotgun often took aim at rabbits or pheasants whilst on the move, and stopped to pick up the trophies on the return run. The railway was treated by many rather unfairly as a joke, but in truth operated as efficiently as possible with minimum capital.

The Mid-Suffolk train was as polished as its Great Eastern counterpart when standing at its own station at Haughley located to the east and at a slightly higher level than the main line station. Whilst the Great Eastern engine was deep blue, the motive power waiting at the single 'Middy' platform was a highly polished dark reddish brown 0–6–0 tank locomotive resplendent with brass dome and copper-capped chimney. The Westinghouse pump on the engine, panting lazily to restore pressure to the braking system on the two or three passenger coaches painted in the same livery of red brown, showed the affinity the smaller line had with the main line company. Behind the coaches was usually an assortment of open wagons and vans and at the end of the train a goods brake van. When the guard signalled 'right away' and the train set off on its journey, the loose-coupled wagons behind the coaches provided a jerky start as the diminutive locomotive struggled to get its train up the gradient away from the junction. If loads were heavy or rails slippery, the engine would stall and require to set back for a second or even third attempt to climb the bank, but regular travellers were accustomed to the routine.

Progress through the cornfields and arable land was sedate for the speed limit was 25 miles per hour or even less where the line bisected roads at open level crossings protected only by cattle guards. At each station the driver applied the train brakes whilst the guard skilfully operated the hand brake in his van at the rear of the train to prevent the loose-coupled wagons running into the buffers of the preceding vehicles. Wagons were frequently left or collected at intermediate stations and during the requisite shunting movements passengers were shunted in and out of the relevant sidings on the way. The countryside

In the last years Mid-Suffolk trains were diverted into the 280 ft bay platform and the back of the up main line platform at Haughley. Viewed from the footbridge on 1st September 1951, 'J15' class 0–6–0 No. 65447 has just arrived from Laxfield and is preparing to propel the two 6-wheel coaches and goods brake out of the platform to the interchange sidings. In the background are the stabling sidings built on the site of the former MSLR station, whilst beyond that the new grain silo is under construction. *H. C. Casserley*

traversed by the line was totally rural in character, farms and cottages, interspersed by moated houses or halls, the villages or hamlets snuggling against their spiritually protective churches. The names of the stations were almost melodic to the ear – Mendlesham, followed by Brockford and Wetheringsett, then Aspall and Thorndon. Next came the erstwhile junction at Kenton and, as the journey progressed, Worlingworth, Horham, Stradbroke and Wilby. Over an hour after leaving Haughley, the train completed its 19 mile journey and pulled into Laxfield where the station staff called to the passengers 'All change' at a station apparently located in the middle of fields. As most stations were rather remote from the villages they served, in the halcyon days of the railway a pony and trap met the train to convey travellers and their baggage to their final destination.

Such was the 'Middy'. I have attempted in this volume to trace the history of the Light Railway from conception to closure and, although many details have been painstakingly checked with available documents, apologies are offered for errors which may inevitably have occurred.

Peter Paye
1986

CHAPTER ONE

The Formative Years

THE county of Suffolk, sandwiched between the emptier open Norfolk to the north and metropolitan Essex to the south, is famous for its rolling landscape which stretches the fifty or so miles from the flat fenlands of Cambridgeshire to its eastern shingle shores facing the North Sea between Lowestoft and Felixstowe. At the time of Domesday, Suffolk was the most densely populated county in England with over 400 churches already established in the settlements dotted across the countryside.

Inland from the coast the topography is that of a boulder clay plateau occupying two-thirds of the county ringed by sandy clay loams in the north east, clay loams to the west, and sands and gravels to the south. The most prominent area of clay forms a plateau interspersed with river valleys and was known in the past as High Suffolk, the height varying between 100 to 200 feet above sea level with its highest point barely rising above the 400 feet contour. The term 'boulder' clay was misleading for the ice age glaciers deposited not boulders but chalk and flint.

The cultivation of this landscape by the plough has for generations been the main industry in this area of Mid-Suffolk. Agriculture was, however, dependent on good transport for the farmers and growers to get their produce to markets. The old Suffolk byways and roads were gradually improved upon and in the late eighteenth and early nineteenth centuries turnpike roads were soon established. Unfortunately, the carriers' wagons were slow and ponderous on their journey with many delays incurred during wet or adverse weather when the vehicles sank up to their axles in mud and mire. Very often produce rotted *en route* or earned poor prices at Ipswich, Norwich and other provincial markets. The advent of the railway in East Anglia gradually brought changes but, unfortunately, not all farmers and growers in Suffolk benefited initially from the new mode of transport.

As early as 1826 a project was mooted to build a rail or tramway from Ipswich to Eye, then an important market town in Mid-Suffolk. Routed via the valley of the River Gipping and Debenham, the scheme, to be known as the Port of Ipswich and Suffolk Railway, failed on the grounds that it would interfere with existing road and sea transport. The proposals for a railway were again raised in 1834 when John Braithwaite surveyed a route for the Eastern Counties Railway from Ipswich to Norwich via Debenham, Eye and Harleston to Trowse and then eastwards to Yarmouth. Because of financial problems the ECR were unable to extend their line from Shoreditch beyond Colchester.

The failure of the ECR to reach Ipswich encouraged businessmen, under the chairmanship of banker and brewer J. C. Cobbold, to finance and build their own railway. The new company, known as the Eastern Union Railway, was authorised by Act of Parliament on 19th July 1844 and the line linking Colchester with Ipswich was subsequently opened on 11th June 1846.

The first railway to bisect the area of central Suffolk, the Ipswich and Bury Railway, was incorporated in 1845 and opened for passenger traffic from Ipswich to Haughley and Bury St. Edmunds on 24th December 1846. Earlier in 1846 the company was authorised to raise £550,000 to finance the extension of the line surveyed by Joseph Locke from a junction at Haughley to Norwich where a terminal was to be built at the Victoria station. The Act also authorised a connecting line from Trowse to join up with the Norfolk Railway. From 9th July 1847 both the Ipswich and Bury Railway and the authorised line were absorbed by the Eastern Union Railway. Progress on construction was slow and, with a view to obtaining financial returns as quickly as possible, the line from Haughley was opened in sections to temporary terminals at Finningham on 7th June 1848 and extended to Burston on 2nd July 1849 with horse bus connection thence to Norwich. The final section beyond Burston was formally opened on 7th November 1849 although at the time only one line of rails was laid. Goods services began on 3rd December with passenger trains officially commencing nine days later.

In 1851 the first projected penetration east of the main line came with the scheme to build a railway along the Waveney Valley on the Norfolk-Suffolk border linking the EUR at Tivetshall with Bungay, an important market town and river terminal. The struggle to obtain the necessary finances delayed opening of the first section to Harleston until 1st December 1855, by which time the ECR was working the line. Completion to Bungay was delayed by shortage of men and materials and the applications for extension of time to build the line granted in the Acts of 1855 and 1856 were exceeded. The Waveney Valley Company was obliged in 1859 to seek a further Act permitting an extension to Ditchingham just beyond Bungay, whilst the following year the construction to Beccles and a junction with the erstwhile East Suffolk Railway, originally sanctioned in 1853, was granted. The railway was completed to Bungay and opened on 2nd November 1860 after which the local company and the ECR disagreed over the working of the line by the latter company. From 1861 therefore the WVR worked its own services until the line was absorbed into the Great Eastern Railway on 2nd March 1863, the same day as the railway was opened between Bungay and Beccles.

Meanwhile. to the east of the boulder clay area, the East Suffolk Railway was connecting Ipswich to Lowestoft and Yarmouth. This line originated with the Halesworth, Beccles and Haddiscoe Railway, incorporated in 1851 to join the river port of Beccles and Halesworth to the Reedham to Lowestoft line of the Norfolk Railway. The railway was opened for goods on 20th November 1854 and passengers on 4th December, operated by the Eastern Counties Railway which had leased the Norfolk Railway in 1848. In 1854 the Halesworth, Beccles and Haddiscoe Railway obtained parliamentary sanction to alter its title to the East Suffolk Railway. The same statute also authorised the company to raise £450,000 to extend southwards to Woodbridge to join up with the ECR planned line from Ipswich, and construct branches from Saxmundham to Leiston,

Wickham Market to Framlingham, and a short section to Snape Bridge. The ECR objected to this new line, announcing that it would effectively remove much of the traffic from the Haughley to Norwich route. The objections were overruled and the line, together with the branches, opened for traffic on 1st June 1859, although it was operated by the ECR. On the same day the section from Woodbridge to East Suffolk Junction, Ipswich, was also opened by the Eastern Counties Railway, who at the same time absorbed the East Suffolk Railway.

Having taken over the working of the Eastern Union Railway from 1st January 1854, an action that was officially approved by Parliamentary Act obtained on 7th August 1854, the ECR was now in control of both main railways in East Suffolk. The culmination of amalgamation of most of the railways in East Anglia was achieved in 1862 when the Eastern Counties, East Anglian, Newmarket and Eastern Union companies were amalgamated to form the Great Eastern Railway. The Act sanctioning the amalgamation – the Great Eastern Railway Act 1862 (25 and 26 Vic Cap CCXXIII) – obtained the Royal Assent on 7th August 1862, but took effect retrospectively from 1st July of that year.

Except for the short Framlingham branch, the only other attempt to build a railway into the triangle formed by the Ipswich-Norwich main line, the East Suffolk line and the Waveney Valley route, was the short branch from Mellis to Eye. Once an important market town with Borough status, trade in Eye declined as a result of the main line by-passing the town three miles to the west. Local businessmen quickly rectified matters and promoted the Mellis and Eye Railway, authorised on 5th July 1865 and opened to traffic on 2nd April 1867. The line was operated by the GER from the outset although it was not absorbed by the main line company until 1st July 1898. Had the one time mooted scheme to extend the line beyond Eye to Framlingham to join up with the branch thence to Wickham Market been completed, the history of railways in central Suffolk might have been very different.

For Suffolk these railways, however, did more to aid industrial development of towns such as Stowmarket, Halesworth, Ipswich and Lowestoft than to the rural communities where life was little changed. William White in his *History, Gazetteer and Directory*, first issued in 1844, gave a detailed picture of trades and occupations in the country parishes. Laxfield, like many others, was then, and indeed for many years after, almost a self-contained unit boasting three churches, parish, non-conformist and non-denominational, for spiritual requirements. For day to day needs there were shoemakers, saddlers, tailors, grocers, blacksmiths, wheelwrights, carpenters, a printer, a druggist, corn miller and various farmers. Decades later little had changed except that the agricultural depression was denuding the rural community of the population. Not only labourers left the land but tenant farmers and even some landlords. The year 1879 was particularly 'black' but the steady decline continued to the turn of the century. Laxfield had little claim to fame save that of being the birthplace of William 'Smasher' Dowsing, who was employed by the egregious Earl of Manchester to desecrate and vandalise the religious establishments. It is said that hardly a church in Suffolk escaped his treachery and acres of mediaeval stained glass was destroyed for posterity.

However, Laxfield was involved in the belated attempt to secure good transport facilities for the country people of Central Suffolk. This came as a result of a Parliamentary statute of 1896 which was designed to help the depressed state of the agricultural industry.

The Light Railways Act of 1896 was promoted to alleviate the distress of the agricultural depression by allowing inexpensive railways to be constructed in rural areas, with the proviso that those so constructed would be released from the obligation to build to the high standards laid down by the Board of Trade for main lines, and Section 5 of the Act stated that where the Board of Agriculture certified that the provision of a light railway would benefit agriculture, the Treasury might agree to aid the building of the line out of public money. Another significant feature of the statute was that application to the Light Railway Commissioners for an order could be made by the county, borough or district through which the railway would pass, or by any company or individual. The latter was particularly relevant to the proposal for a railway in rural areas and soon various railway contractors and engineers were formulating plans to spread the railway network through the country if local parties were agreeable to such schemes.

It was thus that the seeds of the Mid-Suffolk Light Railway were planted. As early as October 1898 H. L. Godden of Messrs. Jeyes and Godden, Civil Engineers of London, wrote to parish councils of several villages and the landowners in Mid-Suffolk suggesting that if the local populace would provide some money towards the promotion of a railway, they had clients who would help financially. The idea was greeted favourably, and the first meeting of interested parties was held at Debenham in February 1899. A committee was formed to further the aims in the area with J. W. Read, JP, chairman, and T. Last as secretary.

This initial meeting was followed by a further gathering at Laxfield, chaired by Doctor Bider with T. H. Bryant as secretary. Other committees were then formed as a result of various public meetings at Halesworth, Stradbroke, Stonham and Mendlesham. At this juncture, W. H. Smith, a solicitor of Gresham House, London, and an associate of Jeyes and Godden, wrote advising that a client, Mr. B. M. Kilby, also a friend of the engineers, would raise half the preliminary expenses if the local populace of Mid-Suffolk would raise the other portion. The generous offer was too valuable to turn down, and as a result of the enthusiasm generated in the district for the proposed railway, delegates from all the committees attended a central meeting at Ipswich. Lord Rendlesham, chairman of Suffolk County Council, initially chaired the meeting, and after due discussion, Francis S. Stevenson, Liberal MP for Eye, was elected chairman of the proposed company, with T. H. Bryant of Laxfield as secretary. Despite the trumpetings and social gatherings throughout Mid-Suffolk, the meeting was somewhat disappointed to learn that only £1,000 had been raised locally for the proposed line.

At a gathering of the Laxfield and District Committee of the Mid-Suffolk Light Railway, held in the local parish council office on 29th April 1899, C. W. Bider announced that as a result of a survey, the estimated returns for farm traffic, excluding cattle, which was expected to be sent by rail was roughly equal to the annual figure of half a ton per acre received and half a ton per acre despatched.

A further meeting of the Central Committee of the Mid-Suffolk Light Railway was held at Ipswich Town Hall on the afternoon of Friday, 26th May 1899. F. S. Stevenson, as chairman, told the gathering that his friend, the Marquis of Bristol, Lord Lieutenant of the County of Suffolk, agreed to the scheme and approved of his name being associated with the committee. The legalities of obtaining powers to build the line were well advanced and W. H. Smith, the solicitor, had visited the Light Railway Commissioners seeking advice. It was hoped they would hold their enquiry into the proposed railway in July, if not their next meeting would be September. The members then learned that 296 persons had helped raise £990 8s 6d towards the legal costs, with amounts varying between 1/- and £1. Only one parish council, that at Mendlesham, had objected to the proposed line. Against this the promoters had the backing and full support of the East Suffolk Road Construction and Bridge Committee as well as six Rural District Councils and forty Parish Councils. The secretary then presented statements received from the various District Committees of the MSLR showing the amount of expected annual goods traffic which would be conveyed on the line.

District Committee	*Goods Tons Received*	*Goods Tons Despatched*	*Cattle Trucks*
Debenham	11,894	7,509	400
Stonham	13,276		large number
Laxfield	6,528	4,530	200
Halesworth, Southwold and District	1,262	140	–
Stradbroke	639	3,452	300
Mendlesham	1,870	1,495	218

Most of these figures were based on the Board of Trade agricultural returns for the previous ten years.

At the conclusion of the meeting the solicitor was paid the £900 to progress the Light Railway Order, although local committees were urged to seek further monetary donations to boost the coffers by another £1,000.

The application for a Light Railway Order was made to the Light Railway Commissioners in May 1899, signed by Francis S. Stevenson MP and Bernard Mancha Kilby requesting a total of 50¾ miles of railway. Before the necessary authority could be given it was, however, necessary for the enquiry to be held.

The Light Railway Commissioners' enquiry into the proposed Mid-Suffolk Light Railway was duly held in the Town Hall, Ipswich, on Thursday, 6th July 1899. The commissioners were represented by the Earl of Jersey, chairman, with Mr. Gerald A. R. Fitzgerald and Colonel Boughey RE. The Light Railway promoters were represented by Mr. W. F. H. Smith of W. H. Smith and Sons, the solicitors, whilst Mr. C. C. Hutchinson represented the Great Eastern Railway. Mr. Mullins, a solicitor of Halesworth, represented Blyth Rural District Council and the River Commissioners, and Mr. F. J. Wood, the Woodbridge Urban District Council.

Smith, presenting the case for the Light Railway, told the gathering that the scheme had been carefully worked out over a period of time, not by the proprietors for their own benefit but by the residents of the large area of Suffolk as yet untapped by rail communication. So keen had been the interest when the railway was first mooted that local committees were set up based on Laxfield and District, Halesworth and District, Mendlesham, Stradbroke and Stonham. A central committee was also formed to consolidate the findings and opinions of these local committees and to prepare and present the case for the Mid-Suffolk Line to the authorities. It was hoped that the enquiry would conclude by agreeing to the scheme which would alleviate hardship and provide a much needed service to the agricultural community after the depressed years.

Details of the proposed railway were then advised. The line was to be some 50 miles in length and as a rider, Smith rather optimistically quoted it as being 'the most important Light Railway scheme to be brought before the Commissioners since the Light Railway Act of 1896.' Included within this mileage was:

Railway No. 1 from Haughley to Halesworth, 27½ miles long with 13 stations.

Railway No. 2 from a point on railway No. 1, 9 miles from Haughley at Bedingfield to Debenham, 3 miles, one station at Debenham.

Railway No. 3 commencing at a junction with Railway No. 2 at Debenham and terminating at Westerfield on the north side of the GER station, over 11 miles in length with 5 stations.

Railway No. 4 commencing at a junction with Railway No. 2 in the parish of Debenham and terminating in the parish of Needham Market on the east side of the GER line, 8 miles in length, 3 stations.

Railways Nos. 5, 6, 7 and 8 were notified as all short connecting lines between the MSLR and the GER.

Smith then stated that certain clauses regarding junctions and interchange of traffic had been agreed between the Mid-Suffolk and GER companies. Over 300 landowners and others were affected by land purchase and of these 276 actually had the proposed railway running through their land. Only one or two dissenters had voiced their opposition to the scheme whilst 101 had already agreed subject to satisfactory compensation. The only dissenting area, according to Smith, was Mendlesham where many of the residents were opposed to the building of the railway. Elsewhere, where villages were located up to 12 miles from the nearest railway, total agreement had been voiced to the scheme. Concluding his evidence to the committee, the solicitor thought that the estimated cost of the railway was £240,000.

H. L. Godden, of the firm of Jeyes and Godden, then advised the gathering of the engineering aspects of the proposed light railway. The line would service an area of some 700 square miles, all totally enclosed within existing GER lines but devoid of good access and transport for the conveyance of goods to and from the local markets and indeed the rest of the country. The majority of objections raised by landowners concerned the severance of fields and pasture land from farms and dislocation of water supplies.

Godden reiterated that any such severance or damage would be made good by the construction of occupational crossings and culverts and would also be subject to adequate compensation. One objection against the Haughley to Halesworth line was purely on sentimental grounds whilst a farmer at Cookley resisted the railway because the formation was routed too near his farm and stockyard.

Civil engineering details were then given. Railway No. 1 was to have 17 bridges including one over the River Blyth near Halesworth, whilst the steepest gradient enountered was 1 in 66. On Railway No. 2 there were two steep gradients of 1 in 50 and 1 in 51. On the third line the heaviest gradients were encountered between Otley and Westerfield especially where the proposed railway crossed the Fynne Valley, although all grades were within 1 in 50. On the Needham Market line there was to be one bridge over the River Gipping although some objections had been raised by the Stowmarket Navigation Company regarding freedom of movement of river traffic. On being questioned as to the cost of the venture, Godden replied that excluding the price of land, the railway was estimated to cost £4,410 10s 8d per mile. The sum of £4,000 had been laid aside for accommodation works and water supplies whilst works at the 22 stations was estimated at £10,000. The Mid-Suffolk country was not considered difficult to cross and the allowance for land purchase set aside by the proprietors was £40 per acre, three times the agricultural value of the property.

When asked about the competition the line might have with the GER between Halesworth and Westerfield, Godden advised that the mileage by the Mid Suffolk was 33 against the 28½ by the main line East Suffolk route. The company was not in direct competition against the GER although rather optimistically Godden admitted the Light Railway 'might carry some GE passengers'. The engineer said the GER was favourable to the scheme if the junctions between the two companies were laid and maintained as agreed and paid for by the MSLR Company.

Mr. Hutchinson, representing the GER, said initially his company had been sceptical of the plans for the light railway. They had no wish to object to the scheme and indeed looked upon the proposed Mid-Suffolk line operating as a feeder to their system by providing additional traffic to and from the Great Eastern. He confirmed that all junctions and physical connections between the two railways would have to be agreed between the respective engineers whilst all traffic movements at the junctions were to be under the control of the GER. Hutchinson was also adamant that the MSLR company was to finance all alterations or new works incurred in installing the physical junctions between the two systems.

Mr. Wood, representing Woodbridge UDC, questioned the engineer as to how the company proposed protecting the many level crossings. Godden replied that if the crossing was adjacent to a station, gates would be provided to be opened and closed by station staff. At other important level crossings gates would also be provided and at others cattle guards would protect open crossings. It was not the intention of the promoters to build houses by the gated level crossings but huts would be provided for the protection of the level crossing keepers employed. In response Wood thought that gates and gatemen should be provided at each crossing to provide full protection to the public. The chairman, however, interjected and said it would be a pity to hamper a scheme that was of benefit to a large proportion of the local community by providing such costly protection for such lightly used roads. If cattle guards and warning signs were provided, the public were not at risk.

Colonel Boughey questioned the need for the first few miles of Railway No. 1 from Haughley if Railway No. 4 was constructed. Goddard thought the Debenham to Needham Market route was essential for the conveyance of special traffic, notably barley to the large maltings at Needham. J. W. Read JP of the Hall, Debenham, an owner and occupier of 242 acres, gave evidence in support. The proposed line crossed his land, his own house was only 8-9 miles from Needham and certainly 9 miles to the market. The railway could take his produce to such markets at Needham or Stowmarket within an hour instead of the 6-7 hours by road as at present. On cross-examination Read admitted the two towns were not as useful for the sale of commodities as Ipswich where high prices were obtained. Other doubts were expressed about the viability of the line before Francis Stevenson, chairman of the promoters, admitted that the construction of Railway No. 4 was an afterthought. It had been included in the general scheme because of the special class of traffic which would be conveyed to the maltings.

Other supporters of the Light Railway then voiced their reasons for backing the scheme before F. S. Stevenson spoke of the many gentry who wished to associate their names with the Mid-Suffolk line. Mr. Smith concluded by handing the chairman a petition signed by 4,141 inhabitants of villages to be served by the railway approving of the scheme. The one note of caution against the proposal was given by Mr. G. Barnes of Mendlesham, who volunteered to voice the thoughts of the local parish council. His retort that the village was only 3½ miles from the nearest railway, which the council believed was near enough to railway accommodation, was lightly dismissed by the Chairman.

After some deliberation, the Earl of Jersey, chairman of the committee, stated that the Commission approved in principle the scheme for the Light Railway on condition that only one line was built from the GER either at Haughley or Needham but not both. In reply Stevenson said no instant decision could be made and it would be the decision of the Central Committee of the Light Railway as to which route was abandoned. The chairman stated that on receipt of a decision the Board of Trade approval would be sought.

After further local meetings and consultations, the promoters advised the Light Railway Commissioners that it had been decided to abandon the proposed Stowmarket/Needham to Stonham line. At an adjourned meeting the Commissioners duly passed the Light Railway order for the Mid-Suffolk Railway. The Light Railway Commissioners forwarded the order for the remaining 42¾ miles of route to the Board of Trade on 28th December 1899.

After the formal local enquiry, the Light Railway Commissioners issued the Mid-Suffolk Light Railway Order on 5th April 1900. The order stipulated that the first ordinary meeting of the company was to be held 6 months after the issue of the statute. The number of directors was nominally fixed at five, although this could vary between three and seven, the qualification for directorship being a £200 share holding in the company. The initial directors of the Mid-Suffolk Light Railway were to be Francis S. Stevenson MP, Bernard Mancha Kilby and three others.

The Light Railway Order authorised the construction of:

Railway No. 1
27 miles 6 furlongs 1 chain in length commencing in field No. 2 in the Parish of Haughley adjoining and at the east of Haughley GER station and passing thence in a northerly direction through the said field and in a north easterly direction keeping to the north of the villages of Old Newton and Gipping, thence in an easterly direction, keeping south of the villages of Mendlesham and Wetheringsett-cum-Brockford and through the parishes of Rishangles, Bedingfield, Aspall and Kenton, thence in a north easterly direction through the parishes of Bedingfield, Southolt and Worlingworth passing through Southolt Green and Shop Street and in a northerly direction through the parish of Athelington and to the east of the village of Horham, thence passing in an easterly direction through the parish of Stradbroke by Wootten Green and the parish of Wilby to the south of Hoxne Union Workhouse and to the north of the village of Laxfield thence in a north easterly direction keeping to the south of the village of Cratfield and through the parishes of Huntingfield and Linstead Magna north of Huntingfield village, thence in an easterly direction through the parish of Cookley and to the north of the village of Walpole and through the parish of Wenhaston, thence passing in a northerly direction through the parish of Holton into the parish of Halesworth and terminating in a field numbered on the Plan 506 in the parish of Halesworth on the west side of the Great Eastern Railway Company's East Suffolk Line.

Railway No. 2
2 miles 7 furlongs or thereabouts in length commencing by a junction with Railway No. 1 in the field numbered on the Plan 182 in the parish of Bedingfield at a point about 9 miles 7 furlongs from its commencement running thence in a south westerly direction through the parishes of Kenton and Aspall and on the west side of the village of Debenham and terminating in the field numbered on the Plan 56 in the parish of Debenham by a junction with Railway No. 3 at its commencement.

Railway No. 3
11 miles 2 furlongs 2 chains or thereabouts in length commencing by a junction with Railway No. 2 at its termination running thence in a southerly direction through the parish of Winston and in a south easterly direction through the parish of Pettaugh and through the village of Framsden thence in a southerly direction through the parish of Helmingham to the west of Otley village to the east of the villages of Swilland and Witnesham and to the west of the village of Tuddenham thence in a south westerly direction into the parish of Westerfield and terminating in the field numbered on the Plan 202, in the parish of Westerfield on the north side of the GER Westerfield Station.

Railway No. 5
9.20 chains or thereabouts in length wholly situated in the parish of Haughley commencing by a junction with Railway No. 1 near its commencement in the field numbered on the Plan 2, in the parish of Haughley and terminating by a junction with a siding to be constructed by the Company adjoining the Ipswich and Norwich line of the Great Eastern Railway Company at a point near Haughley Station.

Railway No. 6
3 furlongs or thereabouts in length wholly situated in the parishes of Holton and Halesworth commencing by a junction from Railway No. 1 near its termination and terminating by a junction with a siding to be constructed by the company adjacent to the East Suffolk Line of the GER at a point south of Halesworth Station.

Railway No. 7
1 furlong 1 chain or thereabouts in length wholly situated in the parish of Westerfield commencing by a junction with Railway No. 3 near its termination and terminating by a junction with a siding on the East Suffolk Line of the GER at or near Westerfield Station.

Three years were allowed for the compulsory purchase of land and five years for the completion of works. Clause 17 of the LRO advised that the Company were not permitted to purchase or acquire ten or more houses which on 15th December 1899 were occupied wholly or partly by working classes except with the consent of the Local Government Board, this stipulation being relevant to each parish.

Clause 22 stipulated that the railway was to construct bridges to cross roads in the following parishes:

Road	*Parish*	*Height*	*Span*
91	Mendlesham	14 ft	25 ft
366	Laxfield	14 ft	25 ft
450	Cookley	16 ft	25 ft
460	Walpole	16 ft	25 ft
25	Debenham	16 ft	25 ft
42	Debenham	16 ft	25 ft
51	Debenham	16 ft	25 ft
47	Framsden	16 ft	25 ft

In each case the clear height of the arch was to be not less than 12 feet above the road surface. The company was also to construct road bridges over the various railways as under:

Road	*Parish*	*Width of Roadway*
15	Old Newton	25 ft
109	Wetheringsett-cum-Brockford	25 ft
265	Horham	25 ft
468	Walpole	25 ft
43	Framsden	25 ft

On the subject of level crossings Clause 24 (2) ordered the Light Railway Company on the approach to Halesworth to agree with the GER for a joint level crossing where road No. 491 bisected the East Suffolk line and the proposed railway in the parish of Wenhaston, both crossings being under the control of the GER.

Although the proposed line was authorised as a Light Railway, Clause 24 (3) stipulated that the company was to erect and maintain gates at level crossings across the following public roads:

Road No.	*Parish*
21	Old Newton
72	Mendlesham
84	Mendlesham
116	Wetheringsett-cum-Brockford
120	Wetheringsett-cum-Brockford
136	Wetheringsett-cum-Brockford
160	Thorndon
185	Bedingfield
215	Worlingworth
221	Worlingworth
261	Horham
288	Stradbroke
315	Wilby
339	Laxfield
354	Laxfield
374	Laxfield

395	Cratfield
401	Cratfield
425	Huntingfield
488	Wenhaston
491	Wenhaston
37	Debenham
45	Debenham
11	Winston
31	Pettaugh
81	Otley
107	Otley
111	Otley
177	Westerfield

Unless otherwise permitted by the Board of Trade, the company was to employ crossing keepers at all gated crossings. All other public ungated level crossings were to be equipped with cattle guards and Clause 25 stipulated that the company erect posts 5 feet high with a notice advising the speed limit thereon at a point 300 yards in advance of each crossing. Similarly on each road approach to an ungated level crossing a notice was to be erected at a distance 50 yards from the railway cautioning the public to beware of trains.

Where Railway No. 1 crossed the River Blyth near Halesworth the company was empowered to erect a substantial bridge with the abutments so placed as to allow the width of the waterway to be no less than 20 feet. The river bank was to remain straight and there was to be no blockage of the towpath, the work to be completed to the satisfaction of the River Blyth Commissioners.

Clause 29 of the LRO listed the various provisions to be made by the Light Railway for connections with the GER with due protection of the interests of the main line company.

1. Lines 5 and 6 to be connected by a junction with sidings to be constructed by the MSLR.
2. Line 7 to form a junction with the GER by using the existing siding on the north side of the GER Westerfield Station.
3. The MSLR Company at their own expense to provide and construct such sidings at or near Haughley and Halesworth stations for the purpose of connecting Railways Nos. 5 and 6 with the GER.
4. The GER to grant the MSLR easement.
5. The GER may construct works and junctions on their own land but any work so executed to be paid for by the MSLR. The GER may alter junctions if they deem it necessary.
7. The MSLR to maintain the junctions at their sole expense and keep them in good order.
8. The MSLR to pay the expenses of any GER staff employed whilst the junctions are being installed and make good any losses incurred by the GER.
10. The MSLR to bear and on demand pay to the GER the cost of any alterations or additions at Haughley, Halesworth and Westerfield rendered necessary by railways No. 5, 6 and 7 and their junctions. In addition the MSLR to provide their own land for junctions 5, 6 and 7.
12. During the course of construction of the junctions the MSLR Company must not stop or hinder any GER traffic.

The Light Railway Order stipulated that the railway was not to open to the public for passenger services without the necessary Board of Trade Authority. If the company were in default they were liable to a fine of £20 for each day so operated.

Clause 32 specified the MSL Company was not to use locomotives with a greater axle loading than 12 tons. If, however, rails were not less than 60 lbs per yard in weight, an axle loading of 14 tons was permissible. Because of its status as a Light Railway, the line was restricted to a speed limit of 25 miles per hour and a lower limit of 10 miles per hour around curves of 9 chains radius and under. The ten miles per hour restriction was also imposed within 300 yards of all ungated level crossings.

If anything other than steam traction was used as motive power, the consent of the Board of Trade was required. If electrical power was utilized, the company was required to:

1. provide either insulated returns or uninsulated metallic returns of low resistance.
2. take all reasonable precautions in constructing, placing and maintaining electric lines and circuits and
3. take all reasonable precautions against interference.

Telegraphic lines owned by the Post Master General were also to be protected.

The Rates and Tolls for conveyance of merchandise by passenger train on the MSLR were subject to the maximum rates and charges applicable to the GER under the Rates and Charges Order 1891.

To finance the building of the railway, the company was authorised under Clause 43 of the LRO to raise capital of £225,000 in £10 shares and a mortgage for £75,000. The sum of £25,000 could initially be borrowed when the first £75,000 capital was actually paid up.

In the schedule attached to the LRO the Commissioners noted the company intended using 56 lbs per yard rails. In such a case if flat bottom rails were utilized check rails were required on all curves of 9 chains or less.

CHAPTER TWO

Advent of the Light Railway

THE first meeting of the directors was held on Thursday, 17th May 1900 at the premises of the company solicitor, 265 Gresham House, Old Broad Street, London EC. At the meeting the following were elected directors: F. S. Stevenson MP of 5 Ennismore Gardens, SW, and Playford Mount, near Woodbridge, chairman; R. Hon. Earl of Stradbroke of Henham Hall, Wangford, Suffolk; D. Ford Goddard MP of Oak Hill, Ipswich; and J. P. Chevallier JP of Aspal Hall, Debenham, Suffolk. B. M. Kilby, however, declined. W. H. Smith and Son were appointed solicitors to the company, whilst Messrs. Jeyes and Godden were the engineers and Barclay & Co. the railway's bankers.

Before the passing of the Light Railway Order, approaches were made to several contractors and Jeyes and Godden advised that S. Pearson had offered the most favourable price for the construction of the railway. Pearson's had recently built the Lambourn Valley Railway, a similar undertaking in rural Berkshire. The new board subsequently read and considered the terms and agreed to a draft contract being prepared.

A week later, on 24th May 1900, the MSLR board discussed the best method of raising the necessary capital for the project and after a heated debate resolved that the necessary £225,000 be raised by public subscription with almost half of the total being underwritten at a commission not exceeding 7½ per cent.

By 15th June the appointment of officers was completed when Norman P. Jeffrey became temporary secretary, F. H. Bryant local secretary in Suffolk, Faithfull, Bogg and Company brokers, and Weldon Jones and Company auditors. The new board were evidently not satisfied with the draft contract with S. Pearson and Son, and agreement was deferred so that the engineers could carry out further investigations. As a result of updated information, it was decided to have only £50,000 instead of £100,000 underwritten at 7½ per cent whilst a prospectus offering £100,000 debentures issue was to be prepared. An obvious target for such literature were Great Eastern Railway shareholders and it was hoped that these individuals would be canvassed by 6th July 1900 with the general public eligible to purchase three days later. No prospectus was subsequently issued as there was continuing disagreement between the board and their financial advisers on the exact apportionment of share issue.

In the ensuing period the engineers negotiated with the contractor, and on 29th June 1900 the board finally approved the Draft Contract for the Construction of the Railway, S. Pearson and Son duly signing on 5th July and receiving confirmation of the award of the contract by letter on 27th July.

Several months elapsed before the directors met again on 5th November. In the intervening months the Inland Revenue office had approached the railway company for payment of share capital duty. Unfortunately, the tax officer had wrongfully predicted the company's affairs for the shares had yet to be allocated. The committee had again changed their minds on the finances and decided that the proportion of ordinary shares if issued would not exceed £75,000 with the remaining issue consisting of 4 per cent preference stock. As a result of the decision, the chairman authorised the issue of not exceeding £5,000 worth of ordinary shares to finance initially the company's affairs. The change in the capital structure necessitated the authority of the Light Railway Commissioners and application for an amendment order was made one week after the meeting.

Little progress was achieved during the winter months of 1900/01 although in March a frustrated Pearson complained of indecisions and lack of any positive instruction to commence construction work, indecision that was to bring the company future inconvenience. Equally the Mid Suffolk Company board appeared loathe to release additional ordinary shares to finance construction work until the Light Railway Commissioners had agreed the amendment order. The Mid-Suffolk Light Railway (Amendment Order) 1901 was subsequently authorised on 1st June 1901. Whilst noting the original order granted the raising of 22,500 £10 ordinary shares, the new order authorised the company to issue any portion not exceeding £112,500 as preference capital, attaching thereto such preference divided not exceeding 5 per cent per annum.

During the summer months Jeyes and Godden were engaged on the detailed surveying of the proposed routes of railway. It was considered that the Haughley to Halesworth line was the easiest to build, following for most of its course the rolling plateau of central Suffolk with few difficult river valleys to negotiate. Only at the last were problems encountered when it was discovered that the marshy land to the west of Halesworth would prove far more difficult to traverse than had originally been envisaged. The other main route through Debenham to Westerfield was bisected with minor river valleys which the engineers thought would prevent the works from progressing as quickly as the Halesworth line. The report of their finding was passed to the directors early in October.

The inactivity of the company's financial affairs continued despite the granting of the authority to issue preference stock. Dissension was rife, and frustrations and the delay in taking any positive action brought the resignations of D. Ford Goddard, a director, and Faithfull, Bogg and Company, the brokers. To fill the resultant vacancies, the London firm of Pember and Boyle were appointed brokers, whilst Mr. F. Remnant of Wenhaston Grange, Woodbridge, was elected to the board. In addition, John Cobbold of Holy Wells, Ipswich, a member of the famous brewing firm, was elected a director of the company.

At the board meeting on 23rd November 1901, the engineers explained the unsuitability of the boggy nature of the land in the vicinity of the River Blyth near Halesworth. The directors requested Jeyes and Godden to resurvey the area and recommend a diverted route into the town. A committee, consisting of Lord Stradbroke, Mr. Remnant and Mr. Cobbold, was formed to liaise between the engineers and local landowners. At the conclusion of

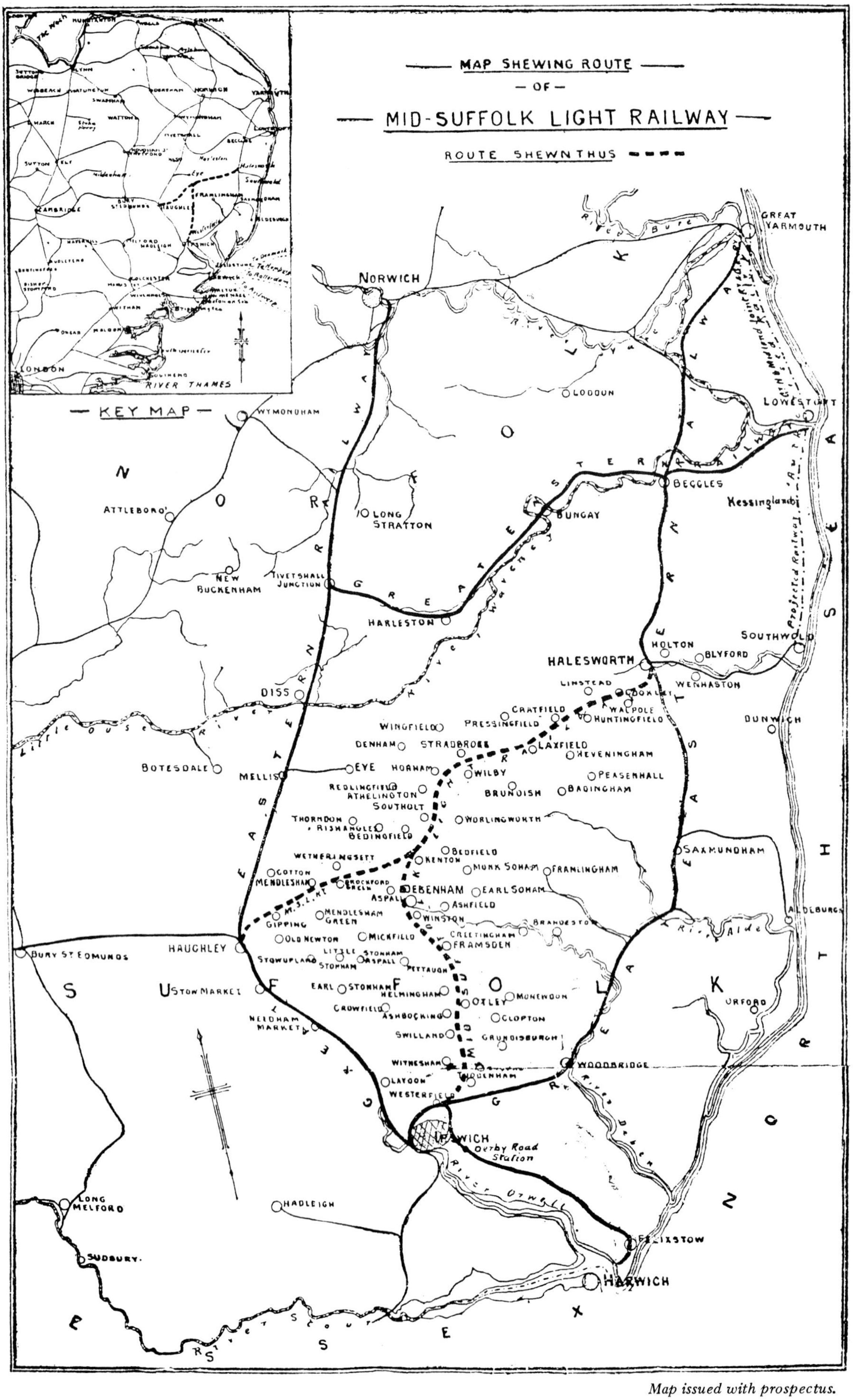

Map issued with prospectus.

the meeting, the bankers announced that they were prepared to grant an overdraft of up to £1,000 to cover the cost of additional surveys, pending the issue of shares.

The prospectus for the Mid-Suffolk Light Railway, originally drawn up in June and finally issued in December 1901, was glowing in its presentation. Prospective purchasers of shares were advised of the two main routes, the Haughley-Halesworth line being acclaimed as 'giving a direct route from Cambridge and the Midlands to the numerous popular seaside resorts on the East Coast'. The Bedingfield to Westerfield line would terminate 'within the limits of the Borough of Ipswich, which will thus be brought into direct connection with districts of Suffolk with which the means of communication have so far been absolutely inadequate'. Being a Light Railway, the average cost of construction was estimated at £5,300 per mile against the average cost of railway construction in the United Kingdom of £50,000 per mile. The new line was to have junctions with the GER at Haughley, Westerfield and Halesworth and the prospectus advised that the main line company 'have expressed their willingness to discuss the question of working arrangements as soon as the capital for the construction of the line shall have been raised'.

Once the railway was constructed, the passengers from London could be routed via Westerfield or Haughley. 'Passengers for Ipswich arriving at Westerfield (by Mid-Suffolk train) will be able either to proceed to Ipswich station by Great Eastern train or, to reach the centre of the town of Ipswich by a direct service of omnibuses which will be established'. Arrangements were also being contemplated for the collection and delivery of goods and parcels in Ipswich.

The prospectus advised of the district to be traversed by the new railway comprising some 190,000 acres with a population 'served exclusively by this railway of 40,000' most of whom lived in towns or villages 'which are at present many miles from a railway station'. The 'exceptionally rich agricultural country' to be penetrated by the proposed line was also extolled. 'It is at present one of the finest corn producing counties in the world and the soil lends itself particularly to that profitable branch of modern farming, market gardening and fruit growing'. Stock, dairy produce, eggs and poultry were also mentioned and it was confidently anticipated that the railway would convey animal foodstuffs and manures to the farmers of the district whilst 'at the same time putting him in direct communication with important markets for his produce'. The Board of Agriculture returns for the previous ten years were also quoted and showed the annual average produce and livestock approximate figures as corn 75,000 tons; roots 270,000 tons; hay, seeds, cabbages, vetches and other green crops 76,500 tons; horses and cattle 30,000 head; sheep 100,000 head; and pigs 40,000 head. The prospectus also noted that large markets of Norwich, Yarmouth and Lowestoft as well as weekly markets at Ipswich, Halesworth, Bury St. Edmunds and Stowmarket 'would be brought into communication with producing centres and rendered readily accessible by the MSLR'.

Prospective shareholders' appetites were whetted when it was reported that Messrs. Jeyes and Godden had surveyed the line and forecasted somewhat untruthfully 'no engineering difficulties'. Godden had also calculated that 'when the line is in proper working order, the average net yearly profits are likely to amount to £13,800, a sum sufficient to fully secure the payment of 4½ per cent on the 11,250 preference shares as well as interest on debentures and as much as 5 per cent on ordinary shares'. The contract for the construction of the railway had been awarded to S. Pearson and Son Ltd. who expected completion by December 1904 for the sum of £227,229, although the engineers expected this to be reduced to about £223,000.

The prospectus concluded by stating that the MSLR had power to charge 25 per cent in excess of the GER Company's maximum rates for a period of 5 years or until reduced by the Board of Trade so long as the railway was worked for the benefit of the company. Although the share capital of the company consisted of 11,250 preference shares of £10 each and 11,250 ordinary shares of £10 each, only the ordinary shares were on offer as the authorised issue of preference stock would not be made available until substantial progress had been made on the construction of the line.

The *East Anglian Daily Times*, reporting the publication of the prospectus, described the proposed railway as 'the most important enterprise, both from the commercial and agricultural point of view that has been undertaken in East Anglia for many years'. The intending investor was also wooed by a glowing description of the directors. 'It is no company promoter's swindling scheme to catch the money of misguided shareholders, the five directors are no guinea pigs or carpet baggers but men whose interests are bound up in the prosperity of the County and who have the very best reasons to make the railway a success'.

Despite the glowing recommendation to the public to buy shares in the railway, the affairs of the company further deteriorated. No sooner had the prospectus been issued than S. Pearson and Son tendered their resignation, partly because of internal problems and partly by the inactivity of the board to progress the works. Pearson had intimated his intention on many occasions beforehand and the engineers had been asked to urgently seek the services of a replacement. Thus at the board meeting held in J. C. Cobbold's office at Ipswich on 11th January 1902 the seal of the railway company was affixed to the contract with S. Jackson and Company of 81 Queen Victoria Street, London, and a cheque for £2,220 handed over as preliminary expenses. At the same meeting the engineers reported physical problems on the routeing of the Westerfield line and increasing difficulty with landowners. On recommendation the board authorised a loan of £10,000 to enable the company to seek an amendment to the Light Railway Order for the alterations, purchase of land, and other necessary additional works. A further shock awaited the directors for at the conclusion of the meeting, N. P. Jeffrey, the secretary, resigned.

Although ordinary shares were issued from December 1901, many of the payments were slipping. The reluctance to issue preference stock meant that the company had barely enough capital to continue day to day affairs. In order to rationalise, the solicitor provided a room at his premises for the board meeting on 17th February 1902 with 'one of his clerks', Ernest Messeder, acting as secretary.

At the meeting the engineer requested the provision of land beyond the site of the junction at Haughley. He also notified the board that the contractor had pegged out land at Westerfield and started preliminary work on the site.

After some discussion Jackson was requested by the engineers to commence work at the junction with the GER at Haughley and proceed 'as expeditiously as possible', on completion of the purchase of the necessary land. The MSLR board, not satisfied with the commencement of work at one point on the proposed system, rather foolishly also requested the contractor to commence work at the junction with the GER at Westerfield and proceed as far as the site of Tuddenham siding 'until further instructed' as alterations in routeing were thought necessary.

The meeting proved to be lengthy and during the proceedings Garrod Turner and Son and Robert Bond and Son were appointed valuers to the company. The board also resolved to pay the engineers £10,000 as an inclusive sum with no additional payment for alterations or modifications to the formation. The sum was to be paid proportionately as and when payments were made to the contractor for works completed.

At the conclusion of the meeting the re-routeing of the railway into Halesworth and the junction with the GER was discussed. It was thought that further investigations would have to be made before the company could apply for a Light Railway Amendment Order. Negotiations had still to be held with the GER and it was therefore not possible to include the amendment in the outstanding application to the Light Railway Commissioners.

During the first week of March 1902 the majority of Jackson's men commenced work at Haughley whilst a few were engaged clearing land at Westerfield. It was thought that time was opportune for a ceremonial cutting of the first sod and after some discussion it was agreed that the field on the north side of the GER station at Westerfield, close to Ipswich and railway connections, was the most convenient site. The directors agreed that as well as landed gentry attending, representatives from public offices, administrations and villages throughout Suffolk should be invited. The chief officers of the GER were also to be invited and Bryant, the secretary, was requested to make all the necessary arrangements.

By the end of April 1902 the contractor was preparing the ground on the east side of the GER station at Haughley ready for interchange sidings and physical connection. The brick abutments and wing walls of Haugh Lane skew underbridge were completed and the arch formed. A quarter of a mile of trackbed north of the proposed MSLR station was also under construction. The contractor had taken delivery of enough rails to lay eleven miles of track and this was being stored at Ipswich by the GER until it was possible to transfer the material to site at Haughley. At the same period the company solicitor was negotiating land purchase for 14 miles of proposed railway from Haughley and 6 miles from Westerfield. The Haughley negotiations were well advanced and the contractor was intending to lay culverts as quickly as land was handed over and fenced off.

The ceremony of the cutting of the first sod of the Mid-Suffolk Light Railway was a grandiose affair with the directors adopting a 'no expenses spared' attitude to the event as though the company was oblivious to financial problems. Certainly as chairman, F. S. Stevenson had invited representatives from every parish interested in and adjacent to the proposed line as well as the landed gentry. In order to create the impression of importance for such a small undertaking, His Royal Highness the Duke of Cambridge was to carry out the actual deed, although on hindsight it must be admitted that the 83 year old duke was only pausing to attend the event whilst travelling through Suffolk on his way to visit Captain E. G. Pretyman MP at Orwell Park.

The proceedings, as previously agreed, took place in the field to the north of the GER station at Westerfield Junction on Saturday, 3rd May 1902.

With over 600 guests attending, the GER arranged to convey as many as possible by train to Westerfield and, in order to achieve this, the 11.30 a.m. ex-Ipswich called at Westerfield at 11.37 a.m., and the 10.00 a.m. ex-Liverpool St. to Yarmouth departed Ipswich at 12.05 p.m. after taking up passengers from the Stowmarket line, with arrival at Westerfield at 12.13 p.m. A later train also departed Ipswich at 2.07 p.m.. arriving at Westerfield nine minutes later. In the up direction trains departed Felixstowe Town at 11.10 a.m. and 1.05 p.m., arriving at Westerfield at 11.37 a.m. and 1.32 p.m. respectively. From the East Suffolk line passengers were directed to the 11.59 a.m. ex-Halesworth and 12.10 p.m. ex-Framlingham, passengers off the latter changing onto the former at Wickham Market for arrival at Westerfield at 1.13 p.m. Arrangements for the receipt of guests at Westerfield station were under the direction of District Inspector Norman and Station Master H. Wilkes. The platforms at the station were decorated overall with flags whilst an archway decorated with trophies and monograms was placed over the entrance way from the platform to the field.

The prevailing wet weather threatened to dampen proceedings but shortly before 12 noon the sky cleared after a heavy downpour as a detachment of the 1st Volunteer Battalion of the Suffolk Regiment marched from Ipswich to Westerfield station where at 12.40 p.m. 100 non-commissioned officers and other ranks formed a guard of honour on the platform. The remainder joined a detachment of the 1st Suffolk and Harwich Royal Garrison Artillery Volunteers to form a guard of honour 100 strong for the duke along the interconnecting path to the tent and at other locations. In the intervening period the invited guests were taking their places in the tented pavilion to await the duke. Sharp to time at 1.20 p.m. the special train conveying HRH Duke of Cambridge, attended by Colonel Fitzgeorge, arrived at the down side platform. Alighting from the train to a salute by the guards of honour, the official party was met by the chairman and directors of the MSLR, the Marquis of Bristol and then by GER representatives, F. Gooday, general manager, H. G. Drury, superintendent of the line, F. Jackson, district superintendent, and H. Jones, district engineer.

The official party was then escorted by the chairman and directors of the Mid-Suffolk Light Railway leaving the platform and passing under the archway and across the two sidings of the goods yard which had been specially boarded

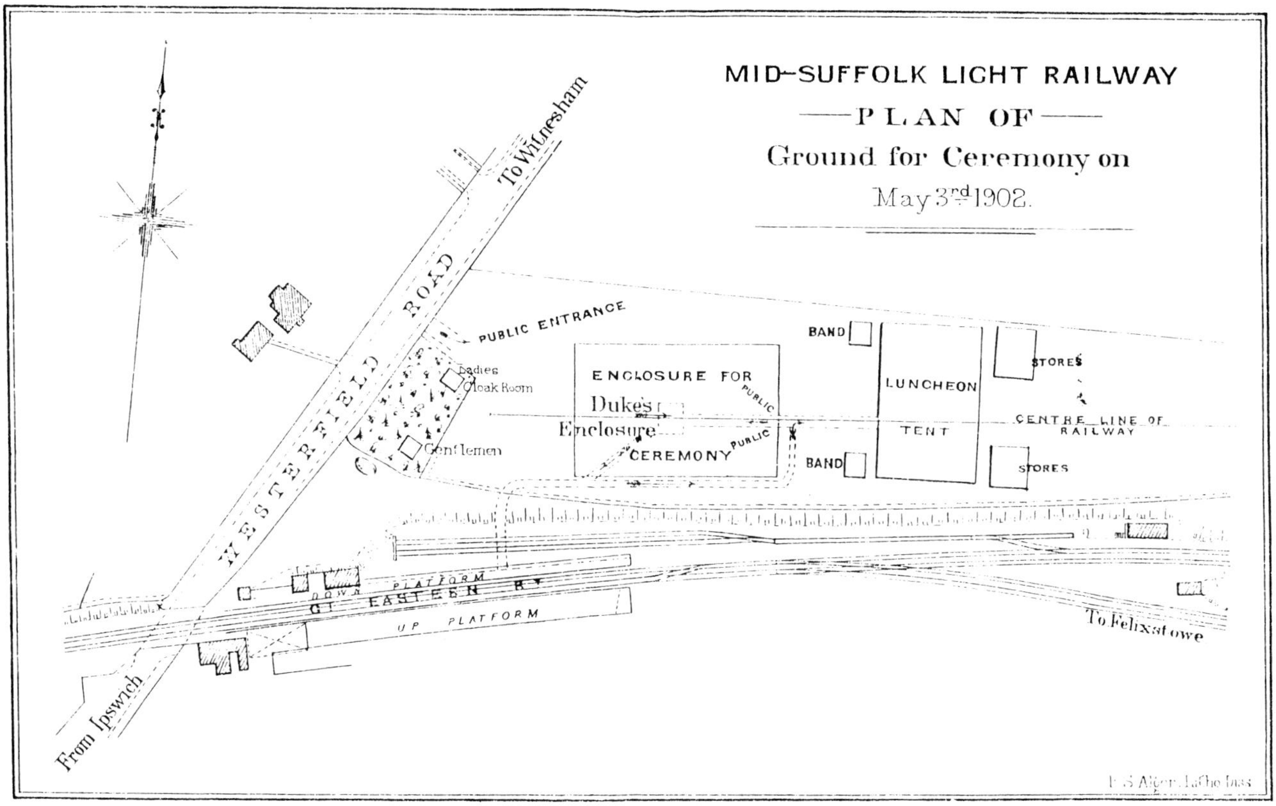

Plan accompanying the Order of Proceedings booklet for the cutting of the first sod, 3rd May 1902.

over for the occasion. The route to the pavilion, erected in the field north of the railway and east of the Westerfield Road, was lined by the 'C' Squadron of the Loyal Suffolk Hussars, 1st Suffolk and Harwich Royal Garrison Artillery Volunteers and the 1st Volunteer Battalion Suffolk Regiment. As the duke entered the luncheon pavilion, the massed bands of the 1st Volunteer Battalion Suffolk Regiment and 1st Suffolk and Harwich Royal Garrison Artillery played the National Anthem. The duke and his party then took their places centrally at the top table which faced 14 other tables at which were seated the 600 guests. Mr. W. Pipe of Messrs. Limmer and Pipe of Cornhill, Ipswich, catered for the luncheon which included as starters mayonnaise of salmon or aspic of prawns, followed by the main course of roast ribs of beef, smoked ox tongues, roast fowls, veal and ham pies, spiced beef or York ham, all served with French salad. The sweet included vanilla creams, gooseberry tarts, fruit jellies, meringues chantilly or chocolat Bavarois. Wines and spirits included claret, hock, sherry and champagne. During the the luncheon the bands of the 1st Suffolk and Harwich Royal Garrison Artillery Volunteers and the 1st Volunteer Battalion Suffolk Regiment, playing alternatively, entertained guests to a programme of music. In the meantime soldiers who had lined the entrance route from the station were moved to form a guard of honour in the special enclosure for the cutting of the first sod.

At the conclusion of the luncheon, toasts were proposed to the King, then the Queen, the Prince and Princess of Wales and other members of the royal family, coupled with the name of HRH the Duke of Cambridge. The Duke of Cambridge replying confessed that the pace of life was too rapid for an 83 year old such as he – 'we are travelling very fast, so fast that I can hardly keep pace with it. Take advice from an old man, let the changes occur as gradually as possible.' A toast was then proposed by Lord Rayleigh to the County of Suffolk and the County Borough of Ipswich. In his speech his lordship admitted his only experience of railway administration was when in 1901 he was appointed by the Board of Trade to enquire into the question of vibration caused by the Central London Railway or, as it was more popularly known, 'The Twopenny Tube'. To laughter he doubted 'whether the Mid-Suffolk Railway will seriously trouble the neighbourhood in that manner.'

Captain Pretyman MP advocated 'Success to the Mid-Suffolk Light Railway', and finally Sir Charles Dalrymple MP proposed a toast to the visitors. The toasts completed, the duke left the pavilion for the special enclosure where only those attending the luncheon with invitation 'ceremony' tickets were invited. The enclosure was covered by an awning and so great was the crush of people that few witnessed the actual cutting of the turf. The duke, using an ornate silver ceremonial spade, duly deposited the earth into a small ornate wheelbarrow to cheers from the crowd, closely watched by the Marquis and Marchioness of Bristol, Lord Claud Hamilton, chairman of the GER, Lord Huntingfield, Sir Charles Dalrymple and General Gatacre.

Afterwards the various ladies of the party were invited to cut the turf with the spade. Led by Mrs. F. S. Stevenson each sod was cut to the accompaniment of cheers. Other ladies partaking in the festivities included the Marchioness of Bristol, Countess of Stradbroke, Lady Evelyn Cobbold, Lady Stevenson and Lady Gatacre. After all had tried their hand at cutting the turf, a vote of thanks to the Duke of Cambridge was proposed by F. S. Stevenson, seconded by the Earl of Stradbroke and J. D. Cobbold. The duke then made his way by the private route back to the station which was lined as before by the 'C' Squadron of the Loyal Suffolk Hussars, 1st Suffolk and Harwich Royal Garrison Artillery Volunteers and the 1st Volunteers Battalion Suffolk Regiment. With the massed bands on the up platform playing the National Anthem, the duke departed at 3.02 p.m. by special train from the down side platform for Orwell for his visit to Orwell Park.

As earlier in the day, the GER arranged for the dispersal of guests with a train departing from Westerfield at 3.17 p.m. for Ipswich and London with passengers for East Suffolk line stations travelling via Ipswich. Felixstowe line passengers, however, had to wait until 4.29 p.m. for their return service.

The total cost of the ceremony amounted to £548 4s 7d.

For convenience, the first annual general meeting of shareholders was held on the morning of the same day as the cutting of the first sod. The gathering was informed that initial applications had been received for a total of £75,000 ordinary shares, whilst £25,000 ordinary shares were being held to issue to the contractor in lieu of cash. No preference stock had as yet been issued but 10,000 of the £10 ordinary shares had been allocated, although not all money was paid up. It was announced that Jackson, the contractor, had commenced work at Haughley in March whilst eleven miles of steel rails were available at Ipswich ready to be delivered to the work site. It was hoped that the average rate of progress would be one mile per week bearing in mind the easy terrain of the locality. However, this depended on the availability of land. W. H. Smith, acting as land agent, was negotiating for the purchase of land for fourteen miles of formation from Haughley and six miles of formation on the proposed Westerfield section.

In concluding the meeting, the directors, who were all re-elected, raised the hopes of the shareholders by announcing optimistically that 'the 66,000 population of Ipswich

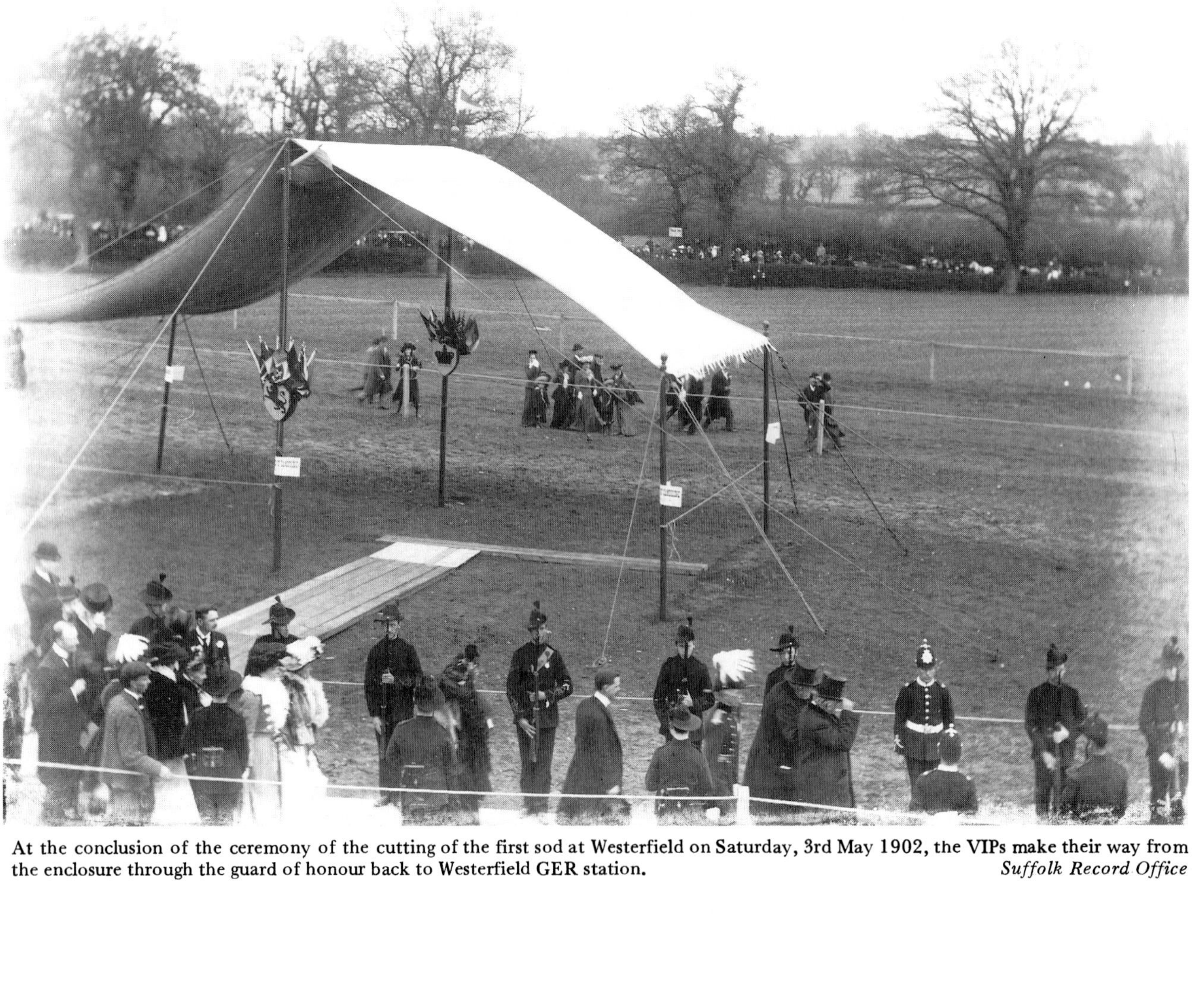

At the conclusion of the ceremony of the cutting of the first sod at Westerfield on Saturday, 3rd May 1902, the VIPs make their way from the enclosure through the guard of honour back to Westerfield GER station. *Suffolk Record Office*

would soon be within easy reach of their railway'. It was also stressed that whereas the average cost of an English railway was £50,000 per mile, the 42 miles of the Mid-Suffolk Light Railway was expected to cost a mere £5,300 per mile.

The contractor made steady progress during June and July, initially fencing off the land and then cutting the trackbed and laying the permanent way. Connections with the GER at Haughley eased delivery of equipment which had previously been held at Ipswich. At the end of July nearly four miles of permanent way was laid, although much had still to be ballasted. In contrast, no work was being carried out at Westerfield and all men had been pulled back to assist the Haughley gang.

The delayed issue of preference stock meant that the MSLR was without the vital finances to pay the contractor and engineer for the works completed. To provide the necessary capital, Barclay & Company and Bacon Cobbold & Burgoin were approached and agreed on 22nd July 1902 to the request for an overdraft of £15,000, spreading the payments over the months of July, August and September. The payment was subsequently made at an interest rate of 4½ per cent per annum pending the issue of £25,000 of debentures.

By August a recognisable railway was cutting a swathe across the Suffolk fields north-east of Haughley. A small ballast pit was opened on the south side of the line about a quarter of a mile from the terminus to provide the necessary material for the permanent way. In complete contrast, little more than staking out had been achieved at Westerfield.

The satisfactory completion of the railway to Mendlesham enabled the MSLR to receive a distinguished visitor on Tuesday, 23rd September 1902, when Lord Kitchener, hero of Khartoum, travelled for a short distance along the new line. After attending several functions and having the Freedom of Ipswich conferred the previous day, Lord Kitchener was entertained at the home of Mr. Chevallier at Aspal Hall for a reunion with his mother and other relatives. The visit proved quite a 'coup' for the Mid-Suffolk when the eminent visitor agreed to travel over the short completed section of track. After lunch at Aspall, the party travelled by car, one of the first in the district and owned by Garner of Ipswich, following as best as possible the future route of the line, passing Bentley Green, Wetheringsett and Brockford to the site of Mendlesham station where they arrived at 2.15 p.m. The bells of the local church pealed in celebration of the event whilst the advance publicity had ensured the gathering of a large crowd to watch the proceedings.

Welcoming speeches were almost inaudible in the hubbub and within minutes Lord Kitchener was escorted along the permanent way to where the special train was standing adjacent to the future road crossing. Formed of a saloon coach and passenger brake loaned by the GER, the train was hauled by a contractor's engine. In the absence of any run-round facilities, the engine had to propel the train from Haughley to the end of the line. Guests joining Lord Kitchener on the train included F. S. Stevenson MP, chairman of the MSLR, the Earl of Stradbroke, F. Remnant, Mr. Chevallier, Lady Stradbroke, Mrs. Stevenson and her daughter, Lally Stevenson. After a further speech when F. S. Stevenson announced that the company were proud to have Lord Kitchener as the 'first passenger' on the new line, the 'special' departed from Mendlesham to the cheers of the onlookers who included local schoolchildren, who had been given a day off lessons to attend the function.

The train made a sedate journey over the four miles to Haughley where it terminated at a temporary station erected especially for the event alongside the GER up side sidings. After further speeches, Lord Kitchener then joined others present in drinking a toast to the 'success of the Mid-Suffolk Light Railway' before leaving for Stowmarket by car.

The visit boosted the morale of both directors and the contractor, for the rails were soon laid beyond Mendlesham to Brockford, including a section of temporary track, complete with level crossing across the main London to Norwich main road. The Light Railway Order stipulated the provision of an overbridge to carry the road across the railway at this point but, because of ailing finances, Jackson was requested to delay the building of the structure until the monetary depression had eased.

After reporting on the general progress of works at the board meeting on 27th October 1902, the engineers gave a detailed account of the problems encountered by the marshy land west of Halesworth which effectively formed a barrier against the progress of the railway. They then advised details of the projected diversionary route by which the line would enter Halesworth from the north. Further investigation on land ownership was required before formal application could be made for the Light Railway Amendment Order. The board, whilst agreeing to further discuss the subject at a future meeting, urged the engineers to complete their case as a matter of urgency. The directors again decided to defer the issue of the preference shares from 3rd November to a later date, asking for extra calls on ordinary shares to compensate.

At the conclusion of the meeting, the engineers and directors finalised details of the diversions and alterations required on the Westerfield line. The formal application to the Light Railway Commissioners for the deviation of route and extension of time allowed to build the line as authorised in the original Light Railway Order was made during November 1902.

By 3rd December the preference share register was drawn up but again the issue was deferred. Despite their monetary difficulties, the ordinary shareholders received a three per cent dividend to the year ending, the money being paid out of the railway company's capital.

The new year brought little relief for the directors for in January 1903 the local rating assessors notified the board that the railway would be subject to the agricultural assessment of £2 for every four acres of land. In the same month the Chairman of Kenton Parish Council wrote suggesting the extension of the Mid-Suffolk Railway to Eye, Framlingham or Saxmundham where it could connect with the GER. The railway company was finding it difficult enough to build the authorised routes to Halesworth and Westerfield let alone extend to other junctions with the main line

Lady Stevenson, the Manning Wardle 0–6–0 saddle tank locomotive owned by Jackson, the contractor. She was named after the MSLR chairman's mother, and later demoted to a secondary role when the Hudswell Clarke tanks were delivered.
Collection G. F. Rice

company. After discussing the proposition at their meeting on 12th January the directors politely replied 'regretting the proposal was not acceptable'.

The Light Railway Commissioners decided that no public enquiry was necessary for the amendment order submitted in November 1902 and duly submitted the order to the Board of Trade on 16th February 1903.

Progress on construction of the railway from Haughley was proceeding steadily and March 1903 proved an expensive month for the MSLR, the contractor being paid £30,000 for works completed and £3,000 value of ordinary shares whilst the repayment of an overdrawn £20,000 was secured by the further call of £2 ordinary shares and the initial issue of preference stock. At a board meeting on 19th March the engineer was urged to report on the progress of works. He subsequently requested the board's approval for an alteration to the original layout at both Cratfield and Laxfield, a suggestion to which the directors readily approved.

By mid March Jackson had completed the line as far as Kenton Junction. The directors requested the work to continue from the junction towards Halesworth and Westerfield 'but more rapidly towards the former than the latter' as it was considered the west-east route was the higher priority. The formation of both lines was to be fenced off with the exception of the land on the approach to Halesworth for which application for a Light Railway Order had yet to be made. On this point Jeyes and Godden were consulting with Mr. Remnant. The directors also agreed to place a station at Thorndon adjacent to the level crossing where the railway bisected the Debenham to Eye road. In the same month the engineer was requested to arrange a meeting with the GER regarding the permanent junction at Haughley and the proposed junctions at Westerfield and Halesworth in an effort to conclude the positioning and working of interchange sidings.

The Mid-Suffolk Light Railway (Deviation and Amendment Order) 1903 was authorised on 1st April 1903, granting the following alterations to the original LRO. The time for completion of works was now extended to seven years instead of the five years previously granted. Under Section 24 additional level crossings were to be provided at Road 15 in the parish of Old Newton, Road 91 in the parish of Mendlesham and Road 265 in the parish of Horham as replacements for the bridges previously authorised. Subsection 4 of Section 24 was also repealed and the railway was now to consist of single track only.

Item 7 of the Deviation and Amendment Order authorised the company to deviate Railway No. 3 in the Otley, Swilland and Witnesham parishes between points 5 miles 2 furlongs 4.5 chains and 8 miles 5 chains from the commencement of the said railway. The company could also take additional land No. 187 and 188 in the parish of Kenton and No. 201 in the parish of Bedingfield and Southolt.

Subsection 4 (4) of Section 24 of the original order was also amended so that the Board of Trade at any time after the opening of the railway might, if it appeared for public safety, require the company to erect and maintain gates across the railway or conversely where already authorised require the company to remove the gates.

A further legislative procedure was enforced by this LRO so that if the company required the movement of or any change in the telegraphic lines belonging to HM Postmaster General then the provisions of Section 7 of the Telegraph Act of 1878 were applicable.

Further amendments were made to the sections applicable to the possible working of the line by electric traction. If this was ever envisaged, the company was to take all steps necessary to construct the line without alteration or amendment to Post Office telegraph lines. If any alterations were deemed necessary, the MSLR were liable to pay all costs.

Before any electric line was laid down or any act of working the railway by electricity was commenced within ten yards of the telegraphic line, the company had to give 28 days notice of intention to the Post Office. Similarly, if any railway electricity line was erected within one mile of a Post Office line and was considered dangerous, engineers were entitled to carry out tests.

About this time the contractor took delivery of an 0–6–0 saddle tank locomotive from Manning Wardle & Co. The engine, one of the manufacturer's 'L' class (maker's No. 1570), was released to traffic on 16th March 1903 and delivered to the Mid-Suffolk Railway soon after. The new acquisition was quickly put to work on construction and spoil trains, previously worked by hired locomotives or horses, and greatly assisted progress. The driver, an ex-GER man employed by Jackson, was paid two guineas per week.

F. W. Remnant and the engineers concluded their survey and enquiries into the deviated routeing into Halesworth, avoiding as much as possible the marshy land. As a result of the change in routeing, the MSLR board requested their solicitor to prepare a further submission to the Light Railway Commissioners. On 25th May 1903 the application was made requesting amendments to the Mid-Suffolk Light Railway (Deviation) Order 1903. The application was duly ratified at a board meeting on 5th June 1903 when the seal of the company was placed on the necessary order and signed by F. S. Stevenson and Mr. Chevallier. Objections were submitted to the proposal by the GER and arrangements were subsequently made for a public enquiry.

Despite bad weather in early June 1903, by the end of the month the contractors had made substantial progress on the construction work. On the Halesworth line rails were laid for a distance of 16½ miles from Haughley to a point near the Hoxne Union Workhouse, whilst the formation continued for some chains further. Ballasting of the permanent way was completed on 14 miles of the route but the engineers reported that the pits at Haughley were nearly exhausted and completion would only be carried out when fresh ballast pits became available. The railway was fenced off for a distance of 17 miles and there was sufficient materials available at the railhead to lay down a further 1½ to 2 miles of track. Jeyes and Godden, in their report of 29th June 1903 to the chairman and directors, advised 'There is still some quantity of earthwork to be done on the 16½ miles, in taking out and tipping the bank near Mendlesham and in a cutting and bank at Horham' and 'in these places a temporary road slewed to one side had been put down. The bridge at Mendlesham Ford and culverts at Horham remain to be built'. The engineers thought it inadvisable to complete the gates for public road crossings, as well as the stations and station buildings, with the exception of Haughley and sidings required by the contractor for working materials, until the work was further advanced. Jeyes and Godden, however, reported 'Mendlesham Station buildings are framed ready for erection'.

On the Kenton to Westerfield line the route of the railway was fenced off for a distance of three miles with rails laid for 1 mile 5 chains from the junction at Kenton. The contractor's men were progressing with the formation, taking out a cutting, tipping a bank and opening out the foundations for a bridge over the Aspall Road. Jackson was at this time employing nearly 200 men working in two gangs, one on the Halesworth line and the other towards Westerfield. Jeyes and Godden reported 'the progress towards Halesworth is naturally more rapid on account of the contours of the country.' Every endeavour was being made to store sufficient permanent way material at Kenton so that when work commenced on the construction of the bridge at Mendlesham, necessitating the temporary suspension of the movement of construction trains from Haughley, work on extension of the railway would not be jeopardised.

F. J. Moore, who was at this time employed by Jackson, the contractor, recollected the cuttings were hewn by hand with the navvies using picks and shovels. The resultant earth was then loaded into tip wagons which were horse-drawn. The wagons ran on 2 ft gauge track, the horse starting off at a good pace beside the rails, once the wagons were loaded. As the wagons neared the tipping point, the horse slackened pace while the driver released the swivel. The wagons then rolled past and tipped the earth as the leading vehicle struck the buffer stops. At this period a ganger earned two guineas per week, platelayers and labourers eighteen shillings per week, three shillings above a farm labourer.

The *Suffolk Chronicle and Mercury* reported 'the novelty of seeing a train in the district draws many sightseers to the lineside'. On Saturday, 11th July 1903, a train conveying navvies to site and materials from Haughley for offloading at various locations along the line also conveyed passengers. At most of the level crossings bisected by the railway spectators watched the passing of the train. Among those on board were H. Jackson Jnr., the son of the contractor, William Bowley, the contractor's general manager, and T. H. Bryant, the local secretary of the Mid-Suffolk Company. After arrival at the railhead on the borders of Laxfield, the train reversed and departed at 4 p.m., conveying the party back to Haughley.

The enquiry into the proposed deviation was held by the Light Railway Commissioners on Wednesday, 15th July 1903, at the Angel Hotel, Halesworth. Colonel Boughey was chairman, accompanied by Henry Allan Steward. The Mid-Suffolk Company case was presented by W. H. Smith, the solicitor, assisted by the Earl of Stradbroke and Mr. Remnant. The principal objector, the GER, was represented by Mr. Bodilly, counsel, Mr. Chew, solicitor, Harry Jones, district engineer, and H. G. Drury, superintendent of the line.

Opening the proceedings, Smith advised those present that the proposed deviation of Railway No. 1 commenced at a point on the intended route of the railway 23 miles 2 furlongs 2 chains from Haughley, in the parish of Huntingfield, and then ran in a north-easterly direction keeping south-east of Cookley Church, and then proceeded to Halesworth, skirting north-west of the town before terminating in a field north of the GER station on the west side of the railway. The length of this line was 3 miles 4 furlongs 4.5 chains. A further deviation of 1 furlong 5 chains was also requested in the parishes of Halesworth and Wissett, commencing by a junction with the other deviated line near the termination, and ending in a siding adjacent to the GER East Suffolk line north of Halesworth station.

The solicitor reminded the Commissioners that the length of Railway No. 1 as originally authorised was 4 miles 3 furlongs 9 chains. There were three reasons for diverting from this original route. Firstly, a mile or upward of

Lady Stevenson stands with a ballast train near Stradbroke. On the left navvies are offloading the gravel. The hybrid vehicle immediately behind the engine, wagon No. 36, has a wooden hut mounted on the flooring and when not in use by the foreman, substituted as a pay office. The sacking over the axleboxes prevented dust contaminating the oil.

marshy land on the west side and on the approach to Halesworth was forming an effective barrier against any railway construction with no firm foundation available for the trackbed. It was understood that the GER suffered from problems caused by the same marshy area and found it expensive to maintain the formation of their line in good condition. The route to be followed by the new MSLR route was more costly but ensured a good foundation on which to lay the trackbed. Secondly, the original MSLR station at Halesworth was to have been a quarter of a mile from the GER station, proving a serious inconvenience to passengers, whereas on the new line the engineer had been asked to provide a better and more convenient position for the station in relationship to the GER station. Finally, Smith explained that there was the question of expense. The original estimate for the section of line was £32,000 but with the saving of three-quarters of a mile of route, the cost was reduced to £24,000, a reduction of £8,000.

Assent for the deviated route had been given by local District and Parish Councils whilst most of the land traversed by the new route was owned by Mr. Remnant and Lord Huntingfield. The former, being a director of the Light Railway, was agreeable to the scheme and, whilst Lord Huntingfield had originally objected, he was now agreeable to the routeing of the railway on the proviso that there was a through connection for conveyance of merchandise between the MSLR and GER at Halesworth and that a station was provided on the new line near Cookley Church, together with sufficient goods sidings, with at least two trains in each direction stopping at the station each week. Smith concluded that of the other landowners affected by the new route, J. F. Button was neutral, whilst Mr. Lacroix was against. The GER also objected and would present their case.

Mr. L. Jeyes of Jeyes and Godden presented details of construction of the proposed line. The railway crossed Cookley Road by a bridge and the requested station was to be sited south of Cookley Church. Of the other public roads bisected by the line, Rockstone Lane was crossed on the level and protected by cattle guards; Chediston Road and Wissett Road were crossed by bridges. In spite of the heavier construction required, Jeyes thought the new route was a cheaper line, although he only admitted a saving of £5,000 against Smith's £8,000. At Halesworth the MSLR would have a platform close to the GER station, making it convenient for the interchange of passengers.

In answer to a question on the original scheme, Jeyes untruthfully said he had insufficient knowledge of the surveys and costings. Mr. Bodilly for the GER then asked the engineer about the proposed junction with the GER. Jeyes, rather flustered, mentioned that the siding forming the junction between the two lines was on a 1 in 86 gradient. Bodilly retorted that it was suggested the gradient was nearer 1 in 70 for the greater part, added to which the MSLR train would have to cross the up and down lines of the GER to exchange traffic and carry out shunting in the GER yard, which was situated on the up side of the line.

Next to give evidence was George Frederick Grover, an engineer employed by Jackson and Sons, the contractor. Grover explained that the condition of the marshy land was so bad that railway construction was almost impossible without a great deal of money being spent on the project.

Unfortunately, the MSLR had insufficient capital to finance such a venture, hence the application for the deviation of route.

The enquiry returned to the subject of the proposed junction. Harry Jones, the GER district engineer, said that although the grade at the commencement of the proposed junction was 1 in 86, for 500 feet or so it was at 1 in 70. Personally he had never heard of a siding being placed on a 1 in 86 or 1 in 70 gradient, and if trains were to shunt on to the main line to cross to the up side GER yard, increased use would be made of the public level crossing where gates would be closed against road traffic for longer periods each day.

H. G. Drury, the GE superintendent of the line, told Colonel Boughey that his company had no objection to the old scheme and had wanted to meet the MSLR directors on the subject. The new scheme was acceptable except for the siding on the 1 in 86 and 1 in 70 gradient which was most objectionable. Drury reiterated the point made by Jones regarding additional occupation of the level crossing. During a survey held a few days previously, 888 pedestrians and 225 road vehicles had crossed the line whilst the GE provided 22 up and 17 down trains on the East Suffolk line. Concluding, Drury said there were no objections to the MSLR having its own sidings and marshalling its own trains clear of the GER, although it would be expensive for the Light Railway Company to provide such facilities because of the undulating nature of the land.

Summing up for the GER, Bodilly said the GE ran trains of 45 wagons which stretched about 1,000 feet in length to handle such trains on a 1 in 86 or 1 in 70 gradient was wholly unacceptable. The GER objection to the deviation would, however, be withdrawn if shunting and marshalling of trains could be arranged to the satisfaction of both companies.

Before summing up, the chairman asked why Mr. Lacroix was against the building of the diversion and was told by his agent, George Durrant, that the objection was raised because the railway would take some of his land. The enquiry then closed and the Committee and representatives of both railway companies inspected Halesworth station.

The Light Railway Commissioners reserved decision pending agreement between the GER and the MSLR. This was subsequently passed to the Board of Trade on 24th August 1904.

The annual general meeting of the MSLR was held at the Ipswich Institute on 21st July 1903 when Stevenson and Chevallier resigned from the board by rotation and were duly re-elected. Those attending were informed that the declining sale of preference shares had forced the company to seek a £15,000 overdraft from Bacon Cobbold & Co. and £10,000 from Barclays Bank. It was hoped the overdrafts would be repaid by the earlier £2 calls on the ordinary shares. A further loan of £75,000 was also negotiated with the company's debenture stock bearing interest at 8½ per cent as security.

The engineers advised the gathering that 21 miles of track were now laid with steel rails from Haughley. The company was also in correspondence with the Board of Trade over suggestions to work traffic simultaneously from Haughley and Kenton. Stevenson, the chairman, ever optimistic, reiterated that as Westerfield appeared to offer more residential traffic with its resultant higher traffic returns, the company would endeavour to complete this line as quickly as possible. In order to achieve maximum receipts for minimum operating costs, thoughts had been given to operating such services with steam railcars similar to those in use on the London and South Western Railway and other lines.

At the conclusion of the proceedings, it was announced that the decision of the Light Railway Commissioners regarding the Halesworth deviation was still awaited although it was believed that the recommendation would come in the form of a suggestion for a scheme more acceptable to the GER.

During the late summer much of the heavier work was abandoned pending the provision of further capital, Jackson in the meantime utilizing his staff on tidying-up operations. On 19th October 1903 the issue of £25,000 of debentures was authorised by the board together with payment of £10,000 to the contractor for completed works, of which £4,000 was part payment for future certificates.

Complaints had been received from farmers and landowners of the inadequate fencing provided along the route of the railway, which allowed cattle to stray on the line, and the delay in providing suitable accommodation for the transit of goods at the various stations. The directors duly advised the complainants that their priority lay in completing heavy earthworks before tackling the relative minor accommodation works and stations. Work on the existing sections of the Debenham and Halesworth lines would be completed, however, before any further new construction work commenced. At this same meeting the directors finally approved the plans for the road bridge near Mendlesham.

On 31st December 1903 the financial standing of the company was £45,625 ordinary shares, £40,564 in 4% preference stock and £25,000 in 3½% debentures. During the construction of the line, interest at 3% was being paid out of capital. Bacon Cobbold & Company advised the MSLR board that at the year end they would no longer continue giving overdrafts to the company. The directors were somewhat surprised at the news but at the meeting at the 'White Horse', Ipswich, on 11th January 1904, the secretary announced that enquiries had been made with the view to obtaining an advance of £60,000 from the Treasury as permissible by the Light Railway Act of 1896. Because of the perilous financial straits of the MSLR, F. S. Stevenson arranged to meet representatives of the GER to explain the position with a view to the possible cessation of work on the junctions should no money be forthcoming.

On 18th February 1904 Ernest Messeder resigned as secretary to the company and William Warren was appointed acting secretary. It was also proposed to move the company's office from London to Ipswich as most of the monetary transactions were made and discussed in the Suffolk town.

In addition to the approach to the Treasury for a financial loan, the company secretary had written to various insurance companies seeking financial aid. Unfortunately, all replies proved negative. The Treasury later responded favourably to the request for monetary aid and arranged for a member of the Board of Agriculture, Mr. Beck, to visit and inspect the Mid-Suffolk line before confirming the transaction.

At the end of February Jeyes and Godden were instructed to communicate with the contractor and make the necessary arrangements for the speedy completion of works between Haughley and Laxfield in readiness for Board of Trade inspection, in preparation for the opening of the line to traffic. In order to make this possible, Jackson was also requested to complete the earthworks in Mendlesham cutting as a matter of urgency. Further consultation also took place to discuss the layout of a junction with the GER at Haughley.

Following satisfactory inspection of the line by the representative of the Board of Agriculture, the Treasury advised the railway company at the beginning of April 1904 that they would advance a sum of £25,000, provided the East Suffolk County Council advanced a similar sum under the terms of Section 3 sub-section (1b) of the Light Railway Order of 1896. Announcing this to the board on 21st April, the chairman reported that the Light Railway Commissioners would not require a new order covering the loans but would accept the insertion of a clause in the draft amending the Light Railway Order now before them for approval. After the meeting the East Suffolk County Council advised that they would advance £25,000 loan with interest at 3¾ per cent. They were also willing to purchase in exchange for the cash £25,000 ordinary shares and £5,000 MSLR debentures.

The engineer also reported the result of a satisfactory meeting with the GER authorities when drawings of the proposed interchange sidings between the MSLR and the main line company at Haughley, Halesworth and Westerfield were inspected and arrangements for the interchange of wagons agreed. The MSLR requested the possible use of the GER station at Haughley for their passenger services but the charges quoted proved exorbitant.

Completion of the railway was still delayed by arguments over the site of the proposed road crossing near Mendlesham. It was initially planned to provide an overbridge to carry the road over the railway, but, after negotiating with the County Council and Board of Trade, the railway company received authority in May 1904 for the bridge to be substituted by a level crossing.

In June 1904 the directors were shattered to learn that the East Suffolk County Council had voted on 31st May 1904 by 27 votes to 24 to provide assistance but, because of the failure to achieve a two-thirds majority, they had withdrawn their previous offer to advance capital and purchase shares in the company, thereby nullifying the loan from the Treasury. Crestfallen, the board attempted to find alternative sources. Stevenson and Cobbold considered the issue of further shares but, because of the delay in receiving such cash and the inherent shortage of money to settle outstanding bills, Barclays Bank were approached and finally agreed to advance an immediate loan of £7,500 to the company.

Shareholders, ever dismayed by the delays incurred in opening the railway for traffic, received support from local farmers and landowners anxious to use the railway for the conveyance of their produce to the local markets. The pressure on the board finally achieved results when the directors requested the engineer urgently to arrange completion of the works so that a goods train service could be operated from September.

On 13th July 1904 Jeyes and Godden reported to the directors on the progress of the railway in readiness for the annual general meeting. The rails were laid and permanent way completed on the 21½ miles section from Haughley to Cratfield and 1½ miles from the junction at Kenton to the Aspall Road. The formation continued beyond these points and the land was fenced off partly up to the Linstead Parish on the Halesworth line and the Otley Parish on the Westerfield route. The main work being undertaken was the cutting and bridge under the road near Brockford and the bridge over the Aspall Road near Debenham. Sufficient permanent way material was on hand to extend the railway from Cratfield to Halesworth and the Aspall Road to Debenham. The contractor had emphasised that given enough men, the line would be completed and ready for traffic to Laxfield and Debenham by early September and from Laxfield to Halesworth by February 1905.

To date the contractor had expended £119,558 5s 8d on works, although the company was withholding the usual ten per cent retention fee of £11,955 16s 7d. £800 was also paid to the GER for work completed on the physical junction between the two railways at Haughley. The engineers concluded 'the total progress made is not what it should be, chiefly on account of the difficulty the contractors have had in providing sufficient labour'.

At the Annual General Meeting held in the Lecture Hall, Ipswich, on 19th July 1904, F. S. Stevenson advised those gathered that every effort was being made to ensure the Haughley to Laxfield and Kenton to Debenham sections of line would open on or about the third week of September. As soon as the Mid-Suffolk (Halesworth) Deviation Order was received from the Board of Trade, the chairman, somewhat optimistically advised that work would be completed towards Halesworth.

The shareholders were somewhat concerned regarding the Debenham to Westerfield extension. The chairman explained the situation whereby the Treasury had offered a £25,000 advance under Section 4 of the 1896 Light Railway Act but only on condition that the East Suffolk County Council offered a similar £25,000 under section 3 of the same Act. Unfortunately, the County Council refused to give approval. With no substantial income of their own, progress on the extension depended on the receipt of the £50,000. The director hoped, however, to resurrect the arrangement in modified form in 1905. Stevenson concluded by telling the meeting that a satisfactory agreement had been reached with the GER regarding arrangements at Haughley and Halesworth including the use of the dock line to the east of the up side platform at Haughley GER station.

Reference was again made to the steam railmotor capable of conveying fifty passengers. The chairman reiterated that the company directors had agreed tentatively to adopt this method of traction to achieve an increased train service. From enquiries made of the Taff Vale Railway, the cost of operation, including trainmen's wages, was 5½d per mile, on gradients far more severe than those found on the MSLR. On a line with fairly reasonable gradients, the cost could reduce to 2¾d per mile against the 1/-d per mile for an ordinary steam locomotive.

The chairman, summing up, advised that the Halesworth Deviation had, since the last meeting, been approved by the

Lady Stevenson with the open truck containing the foreman's office near the bridge over the Aspall Road at Debenham. The engine has propelled the wagon down the branch from Kenton to the works site. The bricks in the foreground were used for the bridge. *Collection C. Scholey*

Light Railway Commissioners. On completion of the lines to Halesworth and Westerfield, the company had made arrangements to provide a covered way connecting the MSLR and GER platforms. Because of other more pressing engagements. J. D. Cobbold relinquished his directorship of the company. At the conclusion of the formal business, the question of the date of the opening of the line between Haughley and Laxfield was raised. The gathering was duly informed that work on the construction had been delayed because of neglect by the contractor, leaving the directors no alternative but to take legal proceedings against Jackson, the cost of which the railway could ill afford. As a result of this neglect in progress, the statement of the contractor was held over.

On 25th July 1904 the MSLR announced their intention of applying for change in the limits of deviation and to divert footpaths, the plans being deposited with the East Suffolk County Council and Halesworth and Wissett Parish Councils.

The months following the AGM were relatively busy. As a result of further negotiations seeking financial backing, the Scottish Imperial (Insurance) Office advised the directors that, subject to clearance from their Glasgow Headquarters, they would advance the railway company a loan of £8,000 on security of £12,000 value of debentures with 1½ per cent commission paid to their agents, Boxall and Boxall. The directors, ever keen to increase the finances of the company, agreed to the proposal on 12th September 1904.

Reporting at a board meeting on the same day, the engineer advised that the line would be opened between Haughley and Laxfield for goods only from 20th September employing only seven men. The chairman also announced that he was negotiating with the Lincoln Carriage Company for the provision of ten 8-ton trucks priced at £27 each and ten 10-ton trucks at a cost of £50 each in readiness for the service. No delivery date was, however, available and it was in the meantime the intention to hire vehicles from the GER.

As a result of the decision to open the line for goods traffic, temporary appointments were made – H. L. Godden, general manager, whilst H. J. Rednall became traffic manager at a salary of £100 per annum, with Mr. Gillingwater appointed assistant to the general manager, also at an annual salary of £100. Mr. Bryant was requested to handle all clerical work arising locally whilst Mr. Godden also offered his assistance in connection with locomotives and rolling stock matters. It was rumoured that Jackson was in financial difficulty and at the end of the meeting a pertinent question was raised regarding the possibility of the contractor paying off his men. The enquirer asked the board whether he would be justified in holding Jackson's assets in case of illegal removal by the contractor.

Tuesday, 20th September 1904, dawned bright and fair and the first official train departed Haughley at 8.00 a.m. hauled by Jackson's small 0–6–0 tank locomotive *Lady Stevenson*. There was no ordinary goods traffic to convey and *Lady Stevenson* duly departed with a train of wagons full of ballast required by the contractor further down the line. Stops were made at Mendlesham, Aspall, Kenton, Horham and Stradbroke before arrival at Laxfield at 11.15 a.m., watched by several local inhabitants. F. S. Stevenson MP, the chairman, Mrs. Stevenson, H. L. Godden, general manager, T. S. Shaw, Rector of Bedingfield, and several others watched the return train, 4.00 p.m. ex-Laxfield, gratified in the knowledge that several packages had been picked up at various stations whilst orders had been placed to receive several trucks of coal via the GER at Haughley.

Because of the rather hurried opening to traffic, the MSLR officials were only able to quote temporary rates for the conveyance of goods traffic pending full negotiations with the GER. Local farmers and merchants were notified that the MSLR would convey coal at 1½d per ton per mile, with 1/6d per ton as an average price for all stations for grain, and 3/-d per ton for ordinary goods. Parcels would be charged at 2d or 3d according to weight. At this period, in an endeavour to attract customers to use the railway, the Mid Suffolk authorities optimistically announced the probable formation of a large building society to help finance the construction of granaries at each siding along the line.

The public were officially advised that besides the ten trucks, already mentioned, a larger and more powerful locomotive was also on order to handle the goods traffic.

OPENING OF THE LINE FOR GOODS TRAFFIC.

For the convenience of the Public, and as a temporary arrangement, it has been decided to OPEN PART OF THIS LINE for ***Goods, Live Stock, and Parcels Traffic,***

On TUESDAY, September 20th, 1904,

When the following Stations will be available, viz :—

HAUGHLEY
MENDLESHAM
ASPALL
KENTON
HORHAM
STRADBROKE
LAXFIELD

Your attention is particularly directed to the fact that at present the *Stations will only be open at specified times*, as per accompanying Time Table, and that Traffic can only be dealt with at those times.

Trucks will be left at the various Stations, and can be unloaded at once.

Advise Notes of Traffic awaiting delivery will be sent to Consignees.

A List of Parcels awaiting delivery will be displayed at each Station.

Particulars can be obtained from the Officials at the time the Trains are at the various Stations, or from

Mr. H. L. GODDEN, General Manager, Framsden Stowmarket.
Mr. H. J. REDNALL, Traffic Manager, Haughley, Stowmarket.
Mr. H. R. GILLINGWATER, Assistant Manager, Haughley, Stowmarket
Mr. T. H. BRYANT, Local Secretary, Laxfield, Framlingham.

TIME TABLE.

		A.M.
HAUGHLEY,	depart	8.0
Mendlesham,	arrive	8.20
	depart	8.40
Aspall,	arrive	9.5
	depart	9.25
Kenton,	arrive	9.30
	depart	9.45
Horham,	arrive	10.15
	depart	10.35
Stradbroke,	arrive	10.42
	depart	11.0
LAXFIELD,	arrive	11.15

		P.M.
LAXFIELD,	depart	1.0
Stradbroke,	arrive	1.15
	depart	1.35
Horham,	arrive	1.42
	depart	2.2
Kenton,	arrive	2.32
	depart	2.47
Aspall,	arrive	2.52
	depart	3.12
Mendlesham,	arrive	3.36
	depart	3.55
HAUGHLEY,	arrive	4.15

CHAPTER THREE

Goods Only

Trials and Tribulations

ALTHOUGH the company opened the railway for goods traffic, work on the line was far from complete. The contractor was employing over 150 men between Haughley and Laxfield and Kenton and Debenham. Sites for the proposed stations were being cleared but construction of platforms had only commenced on a few sites. Zinc sheeting 'of a special kind' for construction of the station buildings was reported lying at Haughley in late September 1904, waiting for the contractor to collect and convey to site. Many of the level crossings were still without gates whilst a large gang of workmen were constructing the bridge near Wetheringsett to carry the Ipswich-Norwich road over the railway. The incompleteness of the structure still necessitated the provision of a temporary slewed line of track and a level crossing.

Anticipating the future passenger services, H. R. Gillingwater reported on 20th September that in addition to Haughley, Laxfield, Kenton and Debenham, stations would be provided at Halesworth, Mendlesham, Stradbroke, Horham, Brown Street (Old Newton), Brockford and Wetheringsett, Cratfield, Huntingfield, Cookley, Wilby and another proposed between Cookley and Halesworth. The hoped for extension beyond Cratfield was still in abeyance, delayed by legal problems and pending the granting of the Light Railway Order, although sufficient sleepers were on hand. It was hoped that the section from Kenton to Debenham would open to traffic within five or six weeks with the extension from Cratfield to Halesworth opening in the summer of 1905.

The Mid-Suffolk Light Railway took delivery of its first locomotive from Hudswell Clarke of Leeds at the beginning of November 1904. Typical of the firm's designs as supplied to many private owners, the 0–6–0 tank engine, numbered 1 and named *Haughley*, was painted in the company's 'Victorian brown' livery with yellow lining. On the final leg of the journey from Leeds, No. 1 was hauled 'dead' by the GER to Haughley. After examination at Haughley, the locomotive was put to work alongside *Lady Stevenson* on the freight services. Its superior tractive effort was immediately appreciated and longer goods trains were handled with ease.

To date the company had hired wagons from the GER for their freight traffic but in the autumn the first deliveries of new vehicles were received from the Lincoln Carriage and Wagon Company. At the same time a few wagons were obtained from the contractor together with a goods brake

Hudswell Clarke & Co. Ltd., official photograph of MSLR 0–6–0 tank locomotive *Haughley* (later No. 1) with the name painted on the side tanks. Typical of the Leeds firm's 'Philadelphia' or 'Canal' class supplied to private owners in the early part of the twentieth century, the locomotive, painted in a light livery with dark lining especially for the photograph, is fitted with three link couplings and has no brake pipes on the buffer beam. The builders plates attached to the bunker side plates were later removed to the front footsteps and either just before departure from Leeds or soon after arrival on the light railway, the name was obliterated from the side tanks and replaced by 'MSLR'. The number '1' was carried on brass plates on the bunker sides and painted on the front and rear buffer beams. No. 1 (makers' No. 711) was released from works on 28th November 1904. *Collection G. Rice*

The Mid-Suffolk stock of open wagons consisted of two types. In this photograph No. 4 is a representative of one of the four 8-ton 3-plank dropside vehicles purchased from Jackson the contractor. Modified with sprung buffers, they were numbered 1, 2, 3 and 4. With a tare weight of 4 tons 2 cwt, all were painted grey with black ironwork and running gear with lettering in white. With only an 8 ft wheelbase, all four were utilized for ballast and permanent way work and never ventured off the system. Coupled to No. 4 is one of the 'Middy's' two brake vans. No. 1 was ex-GER vehicle No. 25031 of 10 tons dating from 1877. As can be seen, it had no corner supports on the verandah. This vehicle was also painted grey with white lettering. *Real Photographs*

and a four wheel passenger parcels van from the GER. Pending delivery of the passenger van and the goods brake, the MSL hired a brake/third and a goods brake from the GER for £1 15s 0d and 5/-d per month respectively.

Construction work continued during the autumn of 1904 when the crossing cottages were being erected. Unfortunately, delay in the delivery of roofing material necessitated the hire of tarpaulin wagon sheets from the GER to provide protection from the elements, the main line company charging 14/-d for the loan.

A report on the operation of the Mid-Suffolk Railway since the opening for freight was presented to the directors by H. L. Godden on 7th November 1904. During the period of operation it was evident that the railway was lacking in effective leadership. To rectify the deficiency, H. R. Gillingwater was promoted to the post of general manager in the belief that he had the necessary all-round railway experience. The promotion brought Gillingwater an increase of salary to £150 per annum. At the same meeting the secretary announced the Royal Exchange Insurance Company's favourable reply to an application for monetary assistance. The offer of a £4,000 loan on security of a debenture issue of £5,000 was readily accepted by the MSLR board.

Problems with the water supply for domestic and locomotive use were raised at the end of November 1904 when a dispute arose over whether the railway should obtain supplies from local authorities or by the contractor supplying and sinking wells. After a somewhat heated discussion at a meeting on 28th November, the directors requested Godden to write to the contractor asking him to attend to the supply by sinking wells at Haughley, Kenton and Laxfield for domestic and locomotive use and at other stations for domestic use only.

The engineer, whilst readily agreeing to enter into correspondence, also claimed payment of £327 for his services to the company in the capacity of acting manager. The directors were somewhat taken aback by the claim which was far in excess of the five guineas a week originally offered on the basis of professional engineer's charges and additional travelling expenses.

At the conclusion of the meeting a contract for the supply of domestic and locomotive coal was placed with Messrs. Fosdick of Ipswich.

As goods traffic increased, the directors were confident that the expenses incurred in building the railway, albeit an incomplete system, were justified. Nine days into 1905 the board discussed the possible expansion of activities to include passenger traffic. So confident were they of early success that the proposed service of four passenger trains each way between Haughley and Laxfield weekdays only, augmented to six each way on Tuesdays (Ipswich market day) was later announced in the local press. It was optimistically thought that the working expenses of operating such a service would amount to only £35 per week.

In connection with the preparation of the line for passenger traffic, the contractor enquired of Godden details of the supply of sleepers, the number of sleepers to be provided under each length of rail and also the specification of signalling equipment required at each station. The engineer's reply regarding supplies of sleepers is not recorded although it appears there was no increase made to the number of sleepers provided under each rail length. Signalling was to be kept to a minimum with home and/or starting signals provided at Haughley Junction, Kenton Junction and Laxfield but at no other station, and a contract was subsequently placed with McKenzie and Holland Ltd.

The engineer was in great demand at this time for Mr. Remnant questioned him concerning the layout at Stradbroke station and complaints received regarding lack of siding accommodation. It was subsequently resolved to put in a longer siding for the interchange of traffic from local farms. Gillingwater also requested the provision of cattle pens at all stations. To finance the additional work, a £2,500 loan was obtained from Barclays Bank at the end of January 1905 with debentures again being offered as security.

In January the railway carried approximately 1,500 tons of goods, 30 trucks of cattle and 500 parcels. In the same month an early morning cattle train commenced running on Tuesdays only, for Ipswich market, departing Laxfield at 4.30 a.m.

By February the impression was given that work on the construction of the stations was nearing completion, so that the *Suffolk Chronicle & Mercury* had 'reason to hope the line will be open for passenger traffic by Easter'.

So keen was local interest in the new railway that late in February Gillingwater invited a reporter of the *Suffolk Chronicle & Mercury* to travel over the line by goods train to report on progress. The visitor was advised that as the GER charges for use of their station at Haughley was too high, the company was forced to build its own station on land alongside and east of the main line company's sidings. As well as the normal platform line, Gillingwater reported that the existing MSL siding had been extended by 210 feet and a new siding of 360 feet was planned. These were necessary because the company was dealing with an average of 50 wagons daily.

On reaching Mendlesham, the reporter was shown the new corrugated iron station building, as yet unpainted, containing a ladies waiting room, general waiting room and officials office. It was the intention to paint the building a dark red which was advised as the 'company's official colour'. A small goods storage shed was also provided, together with a cattle dock for livestock. The coal grounds of Thomas Moy and Fred Reason were also noted. At Brockford and Wetheringsett only the foundations of the station were laid whilst at Aspall and Thorndon similar foundations had been provided for a goods shed.

The reporter was quite impressed with the facilities at Kenton which Gillingwater advised was 'the junction for Debenham and Westerfield'. In addition to the two platform station, it was noted that the company had provided an engine shed, repair shop and steam mill, whilst a large coal store built by Mr. Harry Capon was connected to the main single line by a private siding. Passing on to Worlingworth, where the station was 'partially erected', the cattle pen provided for Mr. R. Chambers and other landowners was seen. The intention of Mr. Alfred Preston, a local auctioneer, to have a private siding was also recorded, although no reference was made to what traffic would be handled at the siding. Gillingwater also advised that the company contemplated the provision of a grain warehouse in the goods yard.

Horham station, in the course of building, was given scant mention whilst Stradbroke station was reported 'in an embryonic state'. The heavy gradients between the two places were noted as was the fact that Mr. Cole had coal allotments at Stradbroke. On the final section of line to Laxfield, the railway passed close to a large building, formerly the workhouse of the Hoxne Union, which it was thought 'might be put to industrial use now the railway runs to Laxfield'. Gillingwater concluded by explaining to the reporter that the line ran over a natural bed of hard clay on which was laid ballast from the pits at Haughley. The rails and supporting sleepers subsequently rested on the ballast. The movement of heavy goods had settled the 'road' to allow for smooth riding.

The Mid-Suffolk Company employed at this time only sixteen staff and the comradeship was close knit. Arrangements were made for the first staff dinner to be held at the Queen's Head Hotel, Stradbroke, on Saturday, 17th February 1905, when with friends and guests a total of fifty enjoyed the evening meal and entertainment.

After due deliberation, the Light Railway Commissioners finally authorised the Mid-Suffolk Light Railway (Halesworth Deviation) Order 1905 on 23rd February 1905. Under item 3 (3) the following additional bridges were permitted under Sections 22 (Bridges over Road) and 23 (Bridges over Railway) of the original order.

Public Road	*Parish*	*Height*	*Span*
5A	Cookley	16 feet	25 feet
62	Halesworth	16 feet	25 feet
73	Wissett	16 feet	25 feet

whilst the original Section 24 (2) dealing with level crossings was repealed.

Section 5 of the Deviation LRO authorised the company to abandon construction of so much of Railway No. 1 beyond 23 miles 2 furlongs 2 chains for a distance of 4 miles 3 furlongs 9 chains through the parishes of Huntingfield, Cookley, Walpole, Wenhaston, Holton and Halesworth to the termination point and also abandonment of the whole of Railway No. 6 as authorised in the 1900 order. Clause 8 of the amendment authorised the construction of Railway No. 1a (being parts of Railway No. 1 and No. 9) 3 miles 5 furlongs 7 chains or thereabouts in length, commencing in the parish of Huntingfield by a junction with Railway No. 1 at 23 miles 2 furlongs 2 chains and passing then in a north-easterly direction through the parishes of Cookley and Halesworth, thence in a north-easterly and south-easterly direction through the parish of Wissett, and terminating in the parish of Halesworth by a junction to the north of Halesworth station with the GER by means of a siding, ensuring full protection of the GER Company.

Two years were allowed for the compulsory purchase of land and seven years for the completion of works dated from the principle order issued in 1900. Clause 13 reiterated the steps to be taken by the MSLR for the avoidance of interruption of GER traffic. The Light Railway Company was authorised to construct sidings and effect a junction with the GER at Halesworth only, in accordance with the agreement dated 8th December 1904 between the MSLR and the GER. The MSLR was also permitted to divert

A specially posed photograph of MSLR 0–6–0 No. 2 shortly after delivery to the light railway in 1905. The engine is at the head of a train of GER cattle wagons on the section of line over Haugh Lane (underbridge No. 1) just north of Haughley station. In the background is the first Haughley engine shed straddling the main single line together with its adjacent water tank. The points in the foreground lead to the second Haughley engine shed. In the background is the site of Haughley ballast pit where gravel was excavated for consolidating the permanent way on the railway. The figure standing in front of the locomotive is believed to be H. R. Gillingwater. Fireman Read is standing on the running plate and driver Bennett is in the cab. *Locomotive Publishing Company*

footpaths on the diverted line in the parishes of Halesworth and Wissett.

T. H. Bryant, the local secretary, resigned on 25th February 1905 on being appointed local auditor of station accounts with a fee at £2 per station and a minimum salary of £40 per annum. On the same day Godden also approached the board with a repeated request for additional money to cover various expenses incurred during his term as temporary general manager. After some consideration, a total of £48 was paid over.

In March 1905 Hudswell Clarke and Co. supplied a second locomotive to the Mid-Suffolk line. No. 2 was smaller than the original engine constructed for the company and, being ostensibly for passenger work, was built as a 2–4–0T. It is almost certain that the wheel arrangement was changed to 0–6–0T before the locomotive left the works at Leeds. Like sister engine No. 1, the GER delivered No. 2 to Haughley and after examination she quickly entered service.

The question of the cost of the installation of private sidings was raised by the contractor in April. It was finally decided that users of sidings would be charged by payment extending over a negotiable term of years, with interest payable at 4 per cent.

By this time the company had acquired additional rolling stock. Seven 4-wheel passenger coaches from the Metropolitan Railway and modified by G. R. Turner & Co. of Langley Mill, Nottingham, for use on the light railway, were delivered in March. The same firm also built six cattle wagons to the requirements of H. R. Gillingwater, closely based on the GER design. Two horse-boxes were also bought second-hand from the GER for the increasing livestock traffic.

The poor performance of the company's two locomotives was highlighted as early as May 1905, less than two months after the delivery of No. 2 from Hudswell Clarke. Availability was not as high as expected and footplate staff complained on a number of occasions of their difficulty in handling the freight loads on the switchback gradients. In retrospect it is almost certain that the engines at this period

MSLR horse-box No. 9, formerly GER No. 408, withdrawn by the main line company on 30th June 1905. Together with a similar vehicle, numbered 10 by the MSLR in their coaching stock number series, the pair were purchased at a cost of £146. *Real Photographs*

Horham station, looking towards Laxfield in 1906. Although the station building is complete, the platform is devoid of fencing, nameboard and oil lamps and the level crossing beyond the platform is not gated. The points leading from the main line to the goods yard siding were later repositioned with the tongue of the points at the Haughley end of the platform. *Collection G. F. Rice*

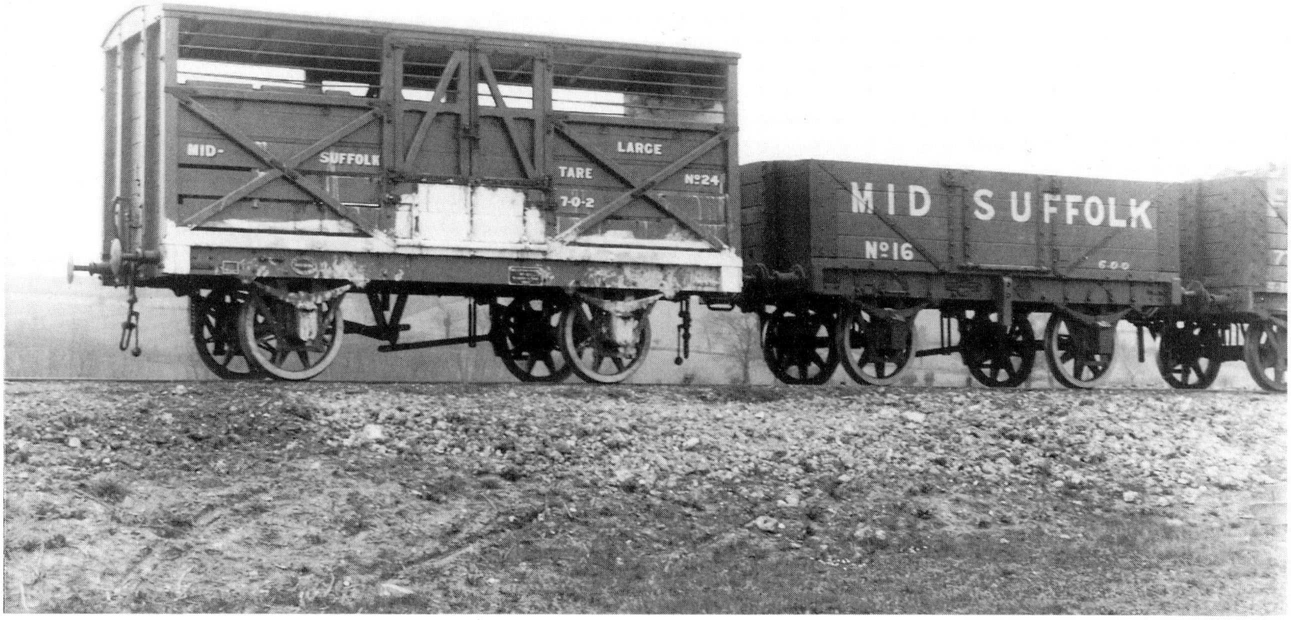

Two types of Mid-Suffolk Light Railway wagons standing at Haughley. On the left is cattle wagon No. 24, one of six built to the specification of H. R. Gillingwater by G. R. Turner of Langley Mill, Nottingham. Based closely on GER design, the wagons had a tare weight of 7 tons 0 cwt 2 qrs. and were through piped and equipped with screw couplings to enable them to work with passenger stock. They often travelled off the system to Colchester, Ipswich and Bury St. Edmunds. Alongside is an example of the sixteen 8-ton 4-plank open wagons with slightly raised ends. Built by the Lincoln Carriage Co., they were used extensively for conveyance of goods from Mid-Suffolk stations to destinations on the GER and other railway systems. No. 17 is recorded receiving repairs by the North Eastern Railway in 1919.
Real Photographs

were mishandled by inexperienced drivers whilst trains were often overloaded beyond the tractive effort of the locomotive. Fortunately, the wagon stock was standing up well to regular usage with only minimal maintenance, whilst the newly acquired coaching stock, according to Gillingwater, had yet to be fully tested.

A further £4,000 was borrowed from the Scottish Imperial Insurance Co. in the same month, but securities for this loan were taken by W. H. Smith £1,000, Gillingwater £1,000 and F. S. Stevenson £2,000.

In June the engineers advised the completion of construction work required for passenger working, including the bridge near Brockford, and application was duly made to the Board of Trade for official inspection. This took place on 2nd July 1905 when Lieutenant Colonel P. G. Von Donop visited the line. He found the portion of railway offered for inspection between Haughley and Laxfield was 18 miles 79.45 chains in length with an average formation width of 14 feet. The railway was fenced by wire strands to a height of 4 feet, supported by upright wooden posts located 6 feet apart.

Von Donop noted the steepest gradient of 1 in 50 was evident in several places whilst the sharpest curve was 20 chains radius. The deepest cutting on the line where the railway passed under the Norwich-Ipswich road bridge, was 20 feet at its maximum depth and 25 chains in length. The highest embankment of 15 feet near Horham, was 13 chains in length. Civil engineering consisted of two underbridges both constructed of semi-circular brick arch with a 15 feet span, and the Ipswich to Norwich road overbridge constructed of steel girders on brick abutments which had a span of 16 feet. The bridges were substantially constructed and standing well. Of the 35 level crossings on the line, the inspector learned that 18 were to be provided with gates shutting across the railway, 5 with gates which did not shut across the railway, whilst the remainder were open, but equipped with cattle guards. Von Donop was concerned to find that at all level crossings where the gates were capable of closing across the railway, none had been equipped. The crossings protected by cattle guards were equipped but none was provided with notices under Section 25 (b) and (c) of the Light Railway Order 1900.

A view looking west into the cutting excavated for the MSLR line to pass under the Ipswich to Norwich Road, The temporary line constructed when the railway was first built, is occupied by contractors' wagons. *Collection G. F. Rice*

Although the railway was opened for goods traffic on 20th September 1904, construction was far from complete. At a point between Mendlesham and Brockford the line crossed the main Ipswich to Norwich Road by a temporary level crossing, the alignment of the track being slewed to the north of the intended route pending the construction of an overbridge. This was accomplished by carrying the railway on 1 in 50 falling gradients through a cutting 25 chains in length to pass under the bridge. Construction was completed in June 1905, a month before the first Board of Trade inspection. In the same month a local Ipswich geological and archaeological society were offered the opportunity to visit the line, travelling at their own risk in one of the ex-Metropolitan coaches with a GER van supplied to convey equipment. In this photo members inspect the formation of the cutting near the bridge (left). Contractors' wagons are stored on the temporary track. *Collection G. F. Rice*

The reason for the Suffolk Society's special train being stabled on the temporary road near Brockford Cutting is evident in this photo for while 0–6–0 No. 2 waits with the MSLR 4-wheel coach and GER covered van, No. 1, hauling a Laxfield to Haughley freight train, pauses on the main single line for the photographer to record the event. The working of the two trains over a single line, each proceeding in a different direction, completely contravened the rules and regulations for single line working. The slack working by the MSLR is equalled by one of the occupants of the train who, with no thought for safety, has opened the carriage door in front of the locomotive.

Collection G. F. Rice

Evidently during the visit of the Ipswich Society, ballasting of the main single line was incomplete as the 56 lbs track and sleepers are laid on a raised bed of earth. Members gather round their train which is stabled on the temporary line, with the GER van and a Mid-Suffolk 4-plank open wagon nearest the camera and contractors' wagons stabled further along the temporary track. The 1 in 50 descent made by the main line through the cutting to the bridge is evident here.

Collection G. F. Rice

The eight stations at Haughley, Mendlesham, Brockford, Aspall, Worlingworth, Horham, Stradbroke and Laxfield were all provided with single platforms, each 130 feet in length, whilst the other station at Kenton was provided with a second island platform. The inspector noted the platforms were 2 ft 9 inches in height and were of sufficient width. Most stations were provided with a siding worked by a ground frame locked and unlocked by a key on the train staff. The inspector was advised that all stations were to be provided with shelters and suitable accommodation for passengers and staff, but on his visit most of the buildings were incomplete or yet to be provided.

On completion of his inspection, Von Donop advised the Mid-Suffolk Company of the following deficiencies requiring attention:

(a) At three points on the line, 8 miles 29 chains, 9 miles 18 chains and 10 miles 37 chains ex Haughley, there are reverse curves without any straight portion of line between the curves. At each place at least two chains of straight track to be provided between the reverse curves.

(b) The following temporary connections to be removed from the main single line –
1. near Haughley station leading to contractor's sheds
2. near Haughley station leading to a gravel pit
3. leading to temporary engine shed at 9 miles 40 chains.
[This connection was not removed and the engine shed was utilized until 1912.]

(c) Height of fencing alongside the cattle guards to be lowered a few inches so as not to foul carriage doors when open.

(d) Nameboards and lamps to be provided on all platforms.

(e) At several stations additional fencing is required.

(f) Arrangements at Kenton are not quite satisfactory. It has been made into a staff station but is not constructed as a crossing place. There is nothing to prevent trains approaching from either direction simultaneously.
[Von Donop recommended Kenton station to be the regular crossing place for all trains.]

(g) Cattle pen on the platform at Worlingworth station to be removed.

(h) Trap points to be provided on the main single line at the down end of Laxfield station.

Because of the incompleteness of the works, Von Donop refused to sanction the opening of the line to passenger traffic. The inspector also insisted that all the deficiencies were to be rectified before the line was resubmitted for inspection. He added a rider to the effect that the 'Company was under no obligation to provide shelter or covering at stations, but should they be provided the work must be completed before reinspection'.

The directors were crestfallen that after their five year struggle, the line was not to be opened. It must have been fairly obvious to Jeyes and Godden that with illicit pointwork, incomplete signalling and all other imperfections, the inspector would not agree to the railway being opened to passenger traffic. For this the two engineers must bear the blame by misleading the directors and advising that the line was ready for inspection. Within days the company's own detailed reinspection was in hand not only to assess the problems ahead but doubtless as part of an internal inquiry.

The epitome of Mid-Suffolk Light Railway motive power. An early photograph of the smallest of the trio of 0–6–0Ts with her regular driver Bennett on the footplate. No. 2 had 13 in x 20 in cylinders against the 14 in x 20 in of her sister and was six inches shorter in length over buffers. In an incident at Kenton, driver Bennett, who was a notable poacher, left a shotgun on the footplate of No. 2. When the locomotive was set in motion the gun accidently fired a bullet through the cab roof. *Real Photographs*

MSLR 0–6–0Ts No. 2 leading and No. 1 standing at the incomplete Haughley station in 1905 where the buildings are still under construction. Behind the locomotives are two examples of MSLR 4-plank 8-ton open wagons followed by a 3-plank open. The connecting line to the GER is in the foreground. *Locomotive Publishing Co.*

Whilst public passenger carriage was officially strictly forbidden, during the summer of 1905 members of an Ipswich historical study society were afforded a private invitation by F. S. Stevenson to visit Mendlesham, Kenton, Debenham and Aspall to view local churches and large houses in the area. More than one hundred members and guests were greeted at Haughley by the chairman before joining the Mid-Suffolk train formed of the company's new coaching stock. Departing at 10.45 a.m., the train proceeded to Mendlesham where passengers alighted to view the church. After the short visit, passengers rejoined the train and continued to the level crossing near Flemmings Hall, where a short stop enabled the members to view the building from the coaches. On arrival at Kenton the passengers left the train for a tour by road, taking in Kenton Church and Kenton Hall before luncheon was served at the Red Lion, Debenham, by courtesy of F. S. Stevenson. After lunch the party continued their tour via Debenham Church and Crows Hall before rejoining the train at Kenton for the run back to Haughley.

On 25th August 1905 the directors held a progress meeting with F. L. Jeyes, the engineer, W. H. Smith, solicitor, and Gillingwater, the general manager, also attending.

Jeyes reported to the gathering that he had requested the contractor to ease the curves and make good the permanent way defects within a fortnight. Fencing and other station work was to be attended to after completion of the trackwork. Whilst noting the remedial action, the directors questioned the engineer as to what action he had taken to put Haugh Lane underbridge No. 1 at Haughley in order, although Von Donop had made no mention of any defect. It was also mentioned that A. C. Andrews was fitting out the office at Haughley at a cost of £5 12s 0d.

A month later the permanent way was still in a bad condition at several places, despite the contractor being reminded on various occasions to maintain the road in a good condition. Gillingwater reported to the board of his difficulties with the contractor who only claimed liability for the remedial work required by the Board of Trade, the easing of curves and the provision of cattle guards at level crossings. Gillingwater was duly advised to make alternative arrangements to keep the permanent way in order and effect any remedial repairs if the contractor refused to do the work, either by using the company's own permanent way gang or by requesting the use of a GER PW gang.

For some considerable period the relationship between the railway board and the engineers and contractor had steadily deteriorated. By 25th September the directors were so disgruntled with the misleading information and ineffective performance of both Jeyes and Godden that their services were dispensed with as from that date and arrangements made for the advertising of the post of engineer.

The gathering at the Annual General Meeting held on Monday, 25th September 1905, was somewhat untruthfully advised that the company had an optimistic future. Although goods traffic was small at first, it had soon increased and by December 1904 the revenue earned was sufficient to meet working expenses. Stevenson proudly

MSLR 0–6–0T No. 1 at Haughley with two of the newly delivered 8-ton 4-plank open wagons, Nos. 18 and 14. At the rear of the formation is passenger brake van No. 1 originally GER brake/third No. 14 but converted by the main line company to a full brake before delivery to the MSLR. Driver Bennett is in the cab of Engine No. 1.
Collection G. F. Rice

boasted that only the previous week nine trucks of barley had been despatched as far afield as Burton. Staff were now appointed to each station to deal with traffic enquiries and handle goods traffic – a serious deficiency when the line first opened with only a few staff, leaving stations unmanned. The milk rates quoted were only of a temporary nature whilst the company still had no through parcels rates with the GER. These, together with through goods rates, were still being negotiated with the main line company.

The chairman advised that the railway owned 2 locomotives, 7 carriages, 2 brake vans, 18 goods wagons, 2 horseboxes and 6 cattle wagons. All rolling stock was paid for except locomotive No. 2. The passenger coaching stock had been given trial trips and all who had ridden in the vehicles had pronounced them comfortable.

As the line between Haughley and Laxfield had opened before other sections, there were continuing legal wranglings with the contractor over liabilities and maintenance. No

An early photograph of Haughley station soon after completion of construction and before painting. The platform, 185 ft in length, was longer than others on the light railway and hosted a double-ended timber-framed station building clad in zinc-coated sheets of iron in a brickwork pattern. This was later painted in a Victorian brown colour to resemble brickwork. Alongside the platform is MSLR Hudswell Clarke 0–6–0T No. 1 with two 8-ton four-plank open wagons and ex-GER full brake No. 1. The third person from the left on the platform is Vic Turner, the first station master at Haughley, with two of his staff fourth and fifth from left, Will Pleasance and Hudson Baker.
Collection G. F. Rice

Laxfield station facing east in 1906 before the completion of the final track layout and provision of the loading dock and dock siding alongside the single main line. MSLR 0–6–0T No. 2 is standing at the head of the close-coupled set of three coaches formed of brake third, third and first vehicles, delivered in 1905 for the passenger services. Following Inspector Von Donop's initial refusal to recommend the opening of the line to passenger traffic, the coaches were occasionally used for special parties and others travelling at their own risk.

Collection G. F. Rice

further progress had been made on the line to Debenham which had nearly reached the site of Debenham station. Following the lack of financial support from the Treasury and East Suffolk County Council, an approach had been made to Halesworth Urban District Council for money to help the line reach its goal. A promissory note for a loan of £5,000 was offered, to be backed by a further £5,000 from the Treasury. This arrangement, however, required the sanction of the Light Railway Commissioners by an amendment to the Light Railway Order and the proposal was disputed by the debenture holders in April 1905. By early November 1905 the directors had foolishly ignored the opposition and the draft of the application for the amendment order in respect of the monetary advance was approved. A week later the secretary forwarded the completed document to the Light Railway Commissioners.

During 1905 livestock traffic increased considerably so that by the autumn the company were embarrassed by the shortage of suitable rolling stock. To obviate the shortage of vehicles, Gillingwater approached the board on 25th November requesting the provision of cattle wagons and an additional goods brake van. The company already had a fleet of six cattle wagons and it is almost certain that here Gillingwater was asking for a further build of vehicles. The goods brake was necessary because the company was using its ex-GER 4-wheel parcels brake van as the rear vehicle on freight trains. The directors authorised the provision of the new brake van and an order was placed with Turners of Langley Mill, the brake van, numbered 2 in the MSLR wagon fleet, subsequently being delivered in the autumn of 1906. No further mention was made of the additional cattle wagons.

Jackson, the contractor, in the meantime complained of the company's treatment regarding the maintenance of the permanent way and requested an independent ruling. After arbitration the MSLR solicitor advised the directors that the contractor was completely within his rights by completing only the work required by the Board of Trade, although it was noted that he had not abided by a previous judgement.

Charles D. Szlumper was appointed the new resident engineer to the MSLR as from 1st December at a salary of £300 per annum. Szlumper was also furnished with an office on the understanding that no expenses would be incurred against the company. At the same juncture Gillingwater received an increase in salary to £175 per annum with effect from 7th November, with his post retitled as manager.

The new year brought no respite to the financial problems of the company and mounting debts made the necessity for the provision of additional capital a matter of acute importance. Thus, when the Capital and Commercial Bank of Ipswich tendered a loan of £1,250, the offer was readily accepted. Unfortunately, there were no further debentures to hand and the directors were forced to offer as security locomotive No. 1 together with surplus land, with the first charge being on the engine.

Jackson was reminded on numerous occasions to make good the deficiencies in the permanent way reported by Inspector Von Donop. On 15th February 1906, Gillingwater at the board's request gave the contractor an ultimatum that work was to be completed within three months of that date, although by 5th March it was reported that nothing had been done.

The pressures of leading a company bereft of monetary stability, heavily committed to loans and almost at the point of bankruptcy was a continuing burden on the shoulders of the directors, none more so than Francis Seymour Stevenson, the chairman, who had sunk so much of his capital in the railway. With no likelihood of early progress towards Halesworth and Westerfield and his personal affairs at crisis point, Stevenson rendered his resignation as both chairman and board member at the end of the month. The Earl of Stradbroke was asked by his fellow directors to fill the resulting vacancy as chairman of the MSLR.

This photograph has puzzled many people interested in the MSLR. It shows 0–6–0T No. 1 at Kenton in 1906 with an up freight formed of a GER open wagon with GER tarpaulin sheet, GER covered van, GER 5-plank open truck, MSLR cattle truck No. 24, MSLR van No. 9 (converted from an open wagon), another GER 5-plank open and bringing up the rear MSLR goods brake van No. 1. It was the intention to provide an island platform only between loop lines at Kenton, east of the level crossing as evidenced here. This was built and is the platform on the right of the photograph. The plan was later abandoned in favour of a crossing loop with platforms on the outer faces of the loop and consequently the down platform and building are shown in the course of construction on the left. *Locomotive Publishing Co.*

MSLR 0–6–0T No. 1 entering Stradbroke station in 1906 with a goods from Laxfield to Haughley, the contractors' hut still on site, to the left of the picture. The rolling stock on the train includes cattle truck No. 24 and a GER open wagon. The hybrid between these two is MSLR No. 9 built originally as an 8-ton, 4-plank open wagon, converted in 1906 to a covered van. *Real Photographs*

Haughley GER station viewed from the down island platform. Looking towards Ipswich c.1910. The main station buildings at the south end of the up side platform are partly concealed by the footbridge (No. 288). Mid-Suffolk 4-plank 8-ton open wagon No. 5 stands by the buffer stops at the end of the 560 ft long siding at the back of the platform. *Lens of Sutton*

The failure of the contractor to commence remedial work on the permanent way reached crisis point later in March 1906. Despite repeated pleas from the directors, Jackson remained silent and at a board meeting on 28th March the inevitable action was taken and the contract with Jackson terminated. At the same meeting the retired chairman, Stevenson, was requested to transfer the £3,000 debentures and £3,000 preference shares which he was holding in respect of monies raised on £10,000 debentures not accounted for.

The truth behind the sudden departure of Francis Seymour Stevenson from his chairmanship of the company gradually became known throughout Suffolk. The ignominy of his problems was made public on 1st May 1906, when the *London Gazette* announced that he was to appear on a charge of bankruptcy – the first hearing to be held on 10th May. At this hearing Stevenson admitted that he had been Liberal MP for the Eye constituency from 1885 until 1906 when he had been ousted in the recent election by a small majority by Harold Pearson. Until his marriage in 1889 his income was small and he had derived funds from his relatives and his stepfather's will. His income from investments in 1893 brought an annual remuneration of £2,000. The heavy financial commitment with the Mid-Suffolk Railway was only part of his sad story and at the conclusion of the private hearing, Warren, the railway secretary, advised that his company was now refusing to press claims of £3,000 against the former chairman. Because of his involvement with large amounts of public money and claims against him, Stevenson was advised that his bankruptcy case was to be held in public.

The departure of Jackson forced the company to find a small contractor to attend to level crossing works. Gates were finally erected at the level crossing adjacent to Laxfield and Stradbroke stations in May and June 1906, Robert Scott Ltd. completing the task at a cost of £15 3s 3d and £15 15s 9d respectively.

The search for a new contractor to effect the completion of the railway was now of the utmost importance. With the ever present monetary problems, the MSLR wanted no further delays than necessary, for as the months passed it became increasingly apparent that unless urgent action was taken, the company would never complete the planned railway to Halesworth let alone Westerfield. Tenders for a new contract were invited and by early June 1906 several unnamed firms were showing interest.

At a meeting on 29th June 1906, the Earl of Stradbroke met with the contractor's engineers and emphasised the urgency of pushing on from Cratfield to Halesworth and reiterating that the cost of the original deviation was so prohibitive. Optimistic of such progress, a month later a meeting was held with A. C. Pain, chairman of the Southwold Railway, to discuss the possible connection between that railway and the MSLR at Halesworth. To the chagrin of the directors the 'Middy' was already gaining an infamous reputation with contractors and no tenders were received for the construction of the extension beyond Cratfield. With matters at such a low ebb, the directors and shareholders were encouraged to learn that traffic earnings were showing a slight increase and receipts for the year ending 30th June 1906 were:

	£	s.	d.	
Parcels	80	15	5	
Goods	2234	0	3	
Collection and delivery	65	16	0	(R)
Mileage and demurrage	17	2	0	(R)
	2231	17	8	

The public examination of Stevenson's finances was held in the London Bankruptcy Court on 10th July 1906. He was said to have had gross liabilities amounting to £248,955 of which £128,476 was expected to rank for dividends, and £73,672 was due to 32 unsecured creditors. His assets totalled only £8,994 including furniture to the value of £1,800. Stevenson admitted that owing to the state of the money market when the MSLR was formed and due to the public not taking shares, he was compelled to take a larger shareholding in the company put at £73,000. In all some £95,000 of his money was lost on the line. Ordinary £10 shares were only selling at £2 17s 6d and debentures put forward at an auction were withdrawn after receiving a highest offer of £57. Stevenson also agreed to purchase £100,000 of GER stock, paying £97,125 over 2½ years with the object of improving relationships with the larger company and so arranging through rates. Unfortunately, he lost £27,667 on the deal, whilst the GER found that Stevenson had also been acquiring Midland Railway stock and were highly suspicious of his suspected double dealing. In the final years the ex-chairman was also buying jewellery on credit and pawning it the same day, which, together with interest paid to money lenders, lost him a further £45,000.

Stevenson admitted that the Mid-Suffolk Light Railway was the 'beginning and end of his troubles'. Finding his bankruptcy proven, the Official Receiver retorted 'You put all your eggs in one basket and other people's as well'. The former chairman and advocate of the 'Middy' subsequently retired a broken man to Felixstowe where he later died. It was eventually left to his father-in-law, Sir James Joicey, to clear all his liabilities on the MSLR.

The problem besetting the company came to crisis point at the end of June 1906 when the debentures became due for repayment. With all loans spent on day to day maintenance of the railway and payment to staff, no money was available to settle the debenture debt. Within days of defaulting, writs were issued against the company for immediate repayment. At a loss to find the ready cash, the directors finally, on 30th July 1906, made the first erosion into the plans of their ultimate dream by arranging for the land at Westerfield adjacent to the GER to be released to the main line company. The cash received was immediately used to repay the debts.

Despite the various ramifications at board level, the railway continued to provide a useful service to the local farming community and by this time the service had been extended operationally to Cratfield, a further 2½ miles. Anxious to gain as much publicity as possible, passengers were still occasionally permitted to ride on the goods service, although entirely at their own risk. In the summer of 1906 several members of the Ipswich Scientific Society enjoyed the privilege when they visited the line. Unfortunately, after retiring to a local hostelry for liquid refreshment, three of the party missed the return train to Haughley.

Further debentures were due for repayment on 1st October and to obviate a repeat of the problems associated with the settlement of previous debentures, representatives of the Eagle Insurance Company and others attended the board meeting on 21st September 1906. To the directors their worst fears were proved, the long fight against insolvency was finally surrendered. The Mid-Suffolk Light Railway had no ready money to repay the debenture holders, no surplus land to dispose of, no fixed assets or rolling stock they could sell without proving detrimental to the continued operation of the railway. Locomotive No. 1 was held as security and was reported as being chained to the rails at Haughley for a few days, whilst No. 2 had yet to be paid for. The inevitable was conceded and, like its former chairman, the company was declared bankrupt, with the debenture holders pressing for a receiver to be appointed. On 6th October W. Warren, the secretary of the Light Railway, assumed the role of receiver on a temporary basis pending a permanent appointment. To stabilise the affairs of the railway, H. R. Gillingwater, now titled superintendent, and W. Warren as secretary were awarded two years contracts with effect from 1st January 1907 at a salary of £200 each.

A further application was made in November for minor amendments to the original Light Railway Order and for a further deviation route into Halesworth, but strong objections were made against this latest routeing and the proposed connection with the Southwold Railway.

The financial standing of the Light Railway as at 31st December 1906 showed fully the difficulties the company

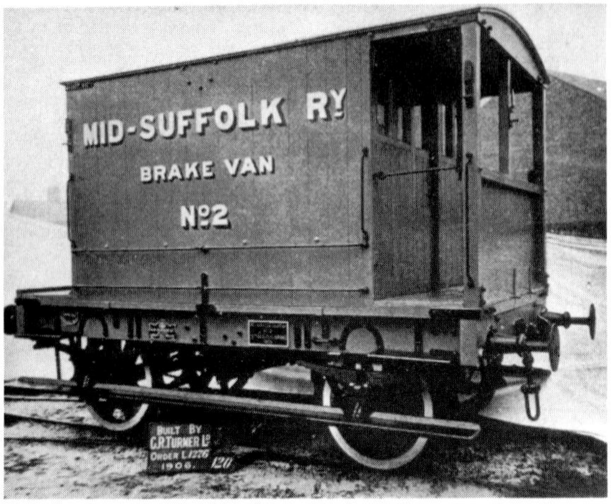

An official works photograph of Mid-Suffolk goods brake van No. 2. This 12-ton vehicle based on Midland Railway design, was built in 1906 by G. R. Turner of Langley Mill, Nottingham. Because of financial difficulties, the MSLR actually hired the vehicles until payments were completed. As No. 2 was fitted with Westinghouse brake she was painted brown bodywork with black ironwork and running gear and lettered in white.

had endured to keep the railway operating. Of the original £112,500 ordinary shares only £78,910 had been sold. An equal amount of preference stock had realised only £75,210. The shortfall had been covered by the issue of £12,500 of five per cent Lloyd's Bonds and £50,000 3½ per cent debentures.

In the first week of February 1907 William Warren relinquished his post as receiver to Major J. F. R. Daniel, a professional railway engineer of Fircliff, Portishead, near Bristol. The new man had hardly time to take stock of his new responsbilities before the Light Railway Commissioners announced the date of the hearing into the application for the further deviation of the Light Railway.

The public enquiry into the Halesworth deviation application was held in the Corn Exchange, Halesworth, on Tuesday, 26th February 1907, with the Honorable A. E. Gathorne Hardy as the chairman, assisted by Colonel Boughey. The Mid-Suffolk Company was represented by their solicitor, W. H. Smith, whilst the leading objectors, the GER, were represented by Mr. Courthorpe Monroe instructed by Mr. T. Chew, whilst H. A. Mullard represented Blything District Council, F. R. Cooper, the Southwold Harbour Co., and Mr. S. R. Paine, the Southwold Railway.

Opening for the promoters, Mr. Smith related the sad tale of the poor finances of the MSLR and how only £78,910 worth out of £112,500 value of ordinary shares had been sold, and the South African War had hindered progress. The failure of the former chairman meant £20,000 promissory notes were worthless. So desperate was the company that debenture stock had to be sought. Turning to the reasons for the application for a second deviation to the route into Halesworth, Smith agreed that the company had originally been badly advised and plans were immaturely thought out. The engineer and contractor had underestimated costs by £25,000, added to which £5,000 instead of £2,000 had to be paid to a large landowner as compensation for land purchased. The asking price for Town Lane at Halesworth was £10,000 instead of an estimated £2,000 per acre, so that instead of saving £8,000 on the scheme, the additional cost was £12,000. The company also required £5,000 to bring the completed Haughley to Laxfield section up to passenger train requirements for Board of Trade reinspection. The railway could only convey goods traffic and merchandise whilst the line was also without a contractor to carry out future work. The goods traffic conveyed was fairly successful and rendered profit of £400 to £500 per annum.

Smith was then questioned about the company debentures. He replied that the MSLR was duty bound to pay interest on the holdings but, because of poor finances, the company was unable to make any payments and subsequently applied to borrow money from the Treasury and Halesworth District Council. The debenture holders, however, opposed such a move and held a meeting in April 1905. By October 1906 the company was unable to meet the debenture interest payments and a holder of a large proportion of debentures asked for a receiver to be appointed.

The deviation now requested crossed the GER main line by a bridge and ran alongside the Southwold Railway for half a mile to terminate at a station on the south-east side of the GER Halesworth station. The estimated cost of the scheme was £29,818 and any running on the Southwold Railway was at the behest and agreement of the directors of the Southwold Railway. The only objection voiced by a local authority was that of Blything Rural District Council who objected to a level crossing where the railway bisected a road in the parish of Wenhaston. Smith concluded that the MSLR was also seeking an extension of time to 5th April 1910 for the completion of the railways authorised by the orders of 1900 aand 1903.

The question of the interchange of traffic between the GER and MSLR was raised, the MSLR representatve noting that the main line company experienced difficulty at Haughley in transferring traffic from its yard on the west side of the station to the Light Railway situated on the east of the main line. Any such movements tended to inconvenience main line traffic from the Norwich and Bury lines. The GE and MSLR authorities were aware of such problems and the GER representative advised the chairman that the MSLR had agreed to increase their siding accommodation at Haughley at a cost of £2,000 to facilitate the smooth transfer of freight traffic between the two railways.

S. R. Paine, representing the Southwold Railway, told the gathering of the MSLR approach six months previously, asking whether the two companies could work together in the interests of the district. Hederstedt, the engineer, said the Southwold Railway had powers to alter their gauge from 2 ft 6 ins to standard and if such alterations were made in Halesworth yard, the Mid-Suffolk could gain entry to the town.

The GER contingency was obviously concerned over the intended plan. Counsel for the company retorted that the directors opposed such plans as the original scheme for the Light Railway, advanced in 1900, was entirely changed. No more was the MSLR a feeder to the GER system as indeed was the Southwold Railway. The Mid-Suffolk and the Southwold combined would now provide serious competition for traffic and the amalgam of the two companies was surely a matter for Parliament to consider. The construction of a harbour at Southwold, for which the Government had given a £15,000 grant, included provision of a railway connection to link up with the Southwold line. It was known that fishing trade would increase at the port and if such traffic was sent via the Southwold Railway and the Mid-Suffolk Railway, the Lowestoft fish trade would suffer and the GER incur reduced receipts. Under these circumstances the MSLR, instead of being the feeder to the GER, would be the robber. Concluding the evidence for the GER, Walter Hyde, the assistant general manager of the main line company, stated that the MSLR scheme would create wasteful competition, whilst John Wilson, the GER engineer, estimated that the promoters' engineer would require an additional £6,000 to £7,000 above their estimates to complete the scheme.

At the conclusion of the hearing and much to the dismay of the Mid-Suffolk directors and officials, the Light Railway Commissioners announced that in their opinion there was not enough commercial justification or evidence to support the deviation. They could not consent to the alterations and proved against the scheme.

Thus the Commissioners effectively vetoed any immediate progress on the extension to Halesworth. With the Westerfield route shelved indefinitely, the grandiose schemes of the Mid-Suffolk Light Railway were rapidly receding. Much now depended on the renewal of negotiation with the GER for satisfactory conclusion in the Halesworth affair.

Little new work was carried out in the spring of 1907 and, in the absence of a contractor, now well beyond the means of the company, Gillingwater engaged local firms to carry out minor tasks.

The continuing work in bringing the line up to a standard suitable for passenger traffic and the day-to-day expenses of keeping the permanent way in order was, however, a drain on the company's resources, and the figures for the engineering function for the year ending 30th June 1907 are typical of the early years:

	£	s.	d.
Supervision	51	3	10
Platelayers Wages	318	19	1
Station Buildings	2	13	5
Station Yards and Platforms	99	3	9
Halesworth Extension	15	5	10
Construction Haughley-Cratfield	172	18	8
Gipping Siding	22	19	1
Level Crossing Gates	72	18	7
Weighing Machines	13	6	3
Tools	13	9	4
Platelayers Tools	10	4	4
Barrows	1	10	6
Brake Van No. 2 Hire	42	8	6
Less Power for PW Trains	6	0	0
	843	1	2

To counteract the expenditure, receipts for the 12 months ending 30th June 1907 were encouraging:

	£	s.	d.	
Goods	2735	4	8	
Parcels	92	12	1	
Collection and delivery	70	17	9	(R)
Mileage and demurrage	5	11	6	
	2762	10	6	

A further £1 10s 9d was expended on Gipping Siding in June 1907.

The administrative costs of running the Mid-Suffolk Light Railway also took a considerable proportion out of receipts, and the figures for years ending 30th June 1906 and 1907 make an interesting comparison:

	30 June 1906			30 June 1907		
	£	s.	d.	£	s.	d.
Salaries and Wages	332	3	8	367	4	0
Office Expenses	26	0	3	7	5	11
Advertising	2	3	6	5	14	0
Miscellaneous and Travel	54	6	0	59	4	10
Rates and Taxes	6	7	10	19	8	3
Guarantee	2	2	6		–	
Insurance	2	14	3		–	
Land Charges		–		3	2	10
	425	18	0	461	19	10

From the foregoing it was all the more crucial to the directors that the railway should open for passenger traffic at an early date. No progress, however, could be made until the legal and financial commitments had been settled. During the late summer and autumn the receiver was actively tackling those problems, at the same time investigating liabilities. In December 1907 under the Order of the Chancery Court advertisements were inserted in various local papers requesting all claims against the Mid-Suffolk Company to be submitted. The resultant claims showed heavy liabilities although it was stated they were not 'overwhelming'. Negotiations were also reopened with the GER regarding the entry of the MSLR line into Halesworth to the satisfaction of both companies.

From 31st December 1907 the statistics for the railway were produced every six months. Receipts in the last half year showed:

	£	s.	d.	
Goods	1673	5	2	
Parcels	54	1	9	
Collection and delivery	35	17	0	(R)
Mileage and demurrage	3	3	6	
	1694	13	5	

Because of the insolvency of the company and the need for consolidation, the 1907 Annual General Meeting of shareholders was held back until Thursday, 26th March 1908 at the registered offices of the company in Gresham Street. The few that bothered to attend heard that in spite of the difficulties threatening the railway, a hopeful view persisted as to the future of the line. Although only used for goods traffic, it had covered its working expenses and since opening had shown a profit of £857 11s. 7d.

The problems of the repayments on debenture was explained, as well as the requirement to appoint a receiver in October 1906. Later in the same year application was made to the courts for a receiver and manager to be appointed and although there was some dissension to this, the courts had appointed to that position Mr. J. F. R. Daniel, a railway engineer with some experience of light railways, to take charge of the company's property and complete control and management of the railway.

The board of directors were no longer responsible for the working of the line but Mr. Gillingwater was retained as superintendent to cover day to day affairs.

J. F. R. Daniel had, since taking office and with the consent of the debenture holders, obtained from the Chancery Court an order enabling him to raise the sum of £5,000 in priority of the existing debenture stock. The £5,000 was to be used to bring the existing line up to an acceptable standard for passenger train working. It was hoped that the Board of Trade would inspect and sanction the opening to passenger traffic within the next few months.

Preference shares to the value of £10,100 and £36,450 of ordinary shares had also been forfeited, reducing the capital of the company by £46,550.

Receipts for the six months ending 30th June 1908 showed a slight reduction on the previous period whilst

Right hand side view of MSLR No. 1 at Laxfield, showing the Westinghouse brake pump mounted on the side of the smokebox. The sandbox is located below the running plate in front of the leading wheels whilst the air reservoir is located behind the cab sidesteps. The side tanks held 650 gallons of water and the small bunker 1 ton 6 cwt of coal. *Collection G. F. Rice*

goods statistics were split even further to show various individual commodities.

	£	s.	d.
Parcels	47	15	5
Goods	991	11	1
Coal and Coke	213	6	6
Other Minerals	196	2	3
Livestock	163	10	9
Collection Cartage and Delivery	39	14	5
Rents	4	1	10
Mileage and Demurrage	3	13	0
	1,659	15	3

The £5,000 loan negotiated by J. R. F. Daniel was soon put to good use and during July and August 1908 the company made a concerted effort to bring the railway to the required standard for passenger traffic. Additional men were temporarily employed thoroughly overhauling and repairing level crossing gates, cattle guards, signals, stations and rolling stock ready for the Board of Trade inspector, the complete operation being supervised by Daniels and Gillingwater.

In preparation for the opening for passenger traffic, the company expended part of the loan on station equipment. Platform oil lamps were supplied by the Lamp Manufacturing Co. Ltd. at a cost of £29 17s. 2d. and £3 11s. 6d. The same firm supplied gate lamps for £18 1s. 6d. Cast iron notice plates and letters for station nameboards were obtained from Walter Macfarland Ltd. at a cost of £21 5s. 11d. and £1 4s. 8d. respectively. Enamel nameplates were manufactured by the Chromographic Enamel Company and cost £2 0s. 2d. During August ticket dating presses for stations were bought at a cost of £3 11s. 6d. whilst Bemrose and Co. supplied the tickets. The same firm had already supplied 2,000 tickets to the company. To complete the commercial supplies ticket nippers and carriage keys were also purchased.

There was considerable interest generated in the villages served by the railway when it was known that an application had been made to the Board of Trade for reinspection of the line. Many expected an earlier visit but it was universally known throughout the area that the lack of money had restricted the Mid-Suffolk Company from purchasing certain equipment and that this was the true reason for the delay. The *Suffolk Chronicle & Mercury*, announcing the possible opening to passenger traffic, was somewhat overcome by the occasion and optimistically reported, 'As regards the completion of the line from Laxfield to Halesworth, it may be stated confidently that the money will be forthcoming', although negotiations were at a delicate stage.

On Friday, 25th September 1908 Lieutenant Colonel P. G. Von Donop reinspected the portion of line between Haughley and Laxfield. In his subsequent report the Lieutenant Colonel noted he had originally inspected the railway in July 1905 and that the opening to passenger traffic had been declined mainly because the numerous level crossings were not equipped to the standards required by the Light Railway Order.

Von Donop found the crossings were now satisfactory and equipped with the necessary gates or cattle guards.

Notices had been erected on both railway and road approaches to the crossings. The inspector observed the company were under no obligation to provide shelters for passengers at stations, but at all stations 'shelters, nameboards and lamps have been provided'. In accordance with his previous recommendation, the MSLR had adopted Kenton as the regular crossing place for trains.

At the conclusion of the inspection Von Donop requested the company to attend to the following deficiencies: the points at Gipping siding, Mendlesham station (Haughley end), Kenton engine shed and Preston's siding at Worlingworth required to be locked by the key on the train staff. The points at Laxfield required to be properly connected to the ground frame. The inspector was advised that the line was to be worked in two staff sections, Haughley to Kenton and Kenton to Laxfield. The company also stated that only one engine in steam or two or more coupled together would be working on each section of line at any one time.

Von Donop was far from complimentary in his conclusion, 'The ballast is not very satisfactory but in other respects the line will last'. Subject to the remedial work being carried out, the inspector advised that the Mid-Suffolk Light Railway could open for passenger traffic.

Opening of the railway was planned for Tuesday, 29th September 1908 and, on receipt of confirmation from the Board of Trade, the Mid-Suffolk could open for passenger traffic, Gillingwater and some of the railway staff distributed handbills on Saturday, 26th September to villages throughout the area served by the railway. Notices were also posted at stations and the event advertised in the *East Anglia Daily Times* on Monday, 28th September.

Throughout the weekend and on the Monday all fifty staff then employed were working to prepare the line for the additional traffic. Although passengers had been carried for some time on the goods services, quite unofficially by permission of the directors and entirely at their own risk, the official opening was cause for celebrations along the line.

On the eventful Tuesday morning the first official passenger/mixed train was booked to depart Laxfield at 7.35 a.m. By 6.55 a.m. many local people had assembled at the station to watch the departure or travel on the train. J. F. R. Daniel, the official receiver and his wife had journeyed to Laxfield the previous evening in order to travel on the first train. In the bright sunshine of the fine morning they joined J. B. Chevallier and other guests on the train. So large was the crowd thronging the platform that the Laxfield station master had difficulty in deciding who wer travelling and who were mere spectators. A few minutes behind time the guard gave the driver 'right away' and the train duly departed over 30 exploding detonators on its way to Haughley, to the cheers and shouts of the considerable crowd on the platform. At each of the stations on the line passengers joined or alighted, Mrs. Chevallier and other members of her family joined the train at Aspall whilst at Brockford the local school children were given a treat and travelled to Mendlesham. Departure from each station was greeted by cheers of spectators on the platform and exploding detonators. A considerable crowd had gathered on the smart newly painted gravel platform MSLR station at Haughley to greet the arrival of the first passenger carrying train. Arrival was three minutes late when the crew and passengers were greeted by Mr. Kelly, the GER station master, dressed in his new uniform for the occasion. To commemorate the event all schoolchildren in the district were given the opportunity to travel on the line on Saturday, 3rd October. Fares were suitably reduced for the occasion and the offer proved a great success.

Winners of a local essay competition are posed in front of MSLR 0–6–0T No. 3 at Laxfield in 1909. Although the photograph is titled Stradbroke, it was certainly not taken there and possibly refers to the entrants living at Stradbroke. Part of the prize for the winners was a ride on the Light Railway to Haughley and back. In a similar competition Edgar Gladwell gained his first position as junior clerk on the 'Middy' after winning first prize. *Collection J. Watson*

MID-SUFFOLK L. RAILWAY.

The Section of the above Railway between

HAUGHLEY AND LAXFIELD

WILL BE

Opened for Passengers

ON TUESDAY, SEPTEMBER 29TH, 1908.

The Train Service, until further notice, will be as follows :—

UP TRAINS.		Week Days. a.m.	a.m.	p.m.	A p.m.	SUNDAYS. During October only a.m.	p.m.
Laxfield	depart	7.35	10. 0	3.30	8.34	7.20	5.20
Stradbroke	...	7.45	10.10	3.40	8.44	7.30	5.30
Horham	—	7.50	10.15	3.45	8.49	7.35	5.35
Worlingworth	—	7.58	10.21	3.52	8.55	7.41	5.41
Kenton	—	8. 5	10.30	4. 2	9. 4	7.50	5.50
Aspall & Thorndon (for Debenham)	—	8.11	10.44	4.11	9. 9	7.55	5.55
Brockford & Wetheringsett	—	8.19	10.52	4.21	9.17	8. 3	6. 3
Mendlesham	—	8.25	10.58	4.27	9.23	8. 8	6. 8
Haughley—M.S.L.R.	arrive	8.45	11.10	4.47	9.43	8.29	6.29
Haughley—G.E.R.	depart	8.53E	11.51	5.10	9.55	8.45	8. 5
Bury St. Edmunds	arrive	11.14	12.18	5.33	10.19	9. 9	8.29
Cambridge	..	1. 6F	4.32	6.50	...	11. 0	...
Ely	..	12.33	4.15G	6.43	...	11.31	...
March	..	1.21	5.15	7.10	...	11.57	...
Wisbech	..	1.50	5.42	7.33	...	...	...
Peterborough	..	1.46	5.52	8.48	...	...	...
Haughley—G.E.R.	depart	9.41	11.48	5.34	...	11.55	6.48
Diss	arrive	10. 4	12.13	5.57	...	12.22	7.15
Norwich (Victoria)	..	...	1. 6	...	...	1.10	8. 2
Norwich (Thorpe)	..	10.48	1. 8	6.33	...	...	...
Lowestoft (Central)	..	12.13	...	7.34	...	...	...
Yarmouth (Vauxhall)	..	12. 8	...	7.15	...	...	...
Haughley—G.E.R.	depart	8.53	11.33	5. 4	...	8.40	6.39
Stowmarket	arrive	8.58	11.40	5.12	...	8.47	6.46
Ipswich	..	9.26	12. 0	5.40	...	9.17	7.15
Felixstowe Beach	..	11. 1P	12.53	7.29	...	12. 3	8.12
Lowestoft (Central)	..	...	1.47	...	...	...	...
Yarmouth (South Town)	..	...	1.52	...	...	...	...
Colchester	..	10.50	12.38	6.45H	...	10. 3	7.59J
Liverpool Street	..	11.26	2.25	8. 5H	...	11.30	9.15J

DOWN TRAINS.		Week Days. a.m.	a.m.	B p.m.	C p.m.	D p.m.	SUNDAYS. During October only	
Liverpool Street	depart	6. 5	8.55	3.20	3.20	7.12	[illegible]	[illegible]
Colchester	..	7.55	10.30	4. 8	4. 8	8.48		[illegible]
Yarmouth (South Town)	..	7.35L	...	2.23	2.23	4.37		[illegible]
Lowestoft (Central)	..	7.40L	...	2.28	2.28	5.10		
Felixstowe Beach	..	8. 3P	9.17	3.15	3.15	7.50		
Ipswich	..	9. 8	11.17	5. 5	5. 5	9.24		[illegible]
Stowmarket	..	9.35	11.39	5.27	5.27	9.51	8.56	[illegible]
Haughley—G.E.R.	arrive	9.44	11.46	5.34	5.34	9.55	8.45	[illegible]
Yarmouth (Vauxhall)	depart	6.40N	9. 8S	—	—	—	...	
Lowestoft (Central)	..	6.25R	8.43	...	...	...	...	
Norwich (Victoria)	..	...	10. 0E	3.50	3.00 4.43	6.50	7.30	[illegible]
Norwich (Thorpe)	..	7.50N	10. 0E	...	... ...	...		
Diss	..	8.24N	10.54E	4.35	4.36 5.19	7.33	8.13	[illegible]
Haughley—G.E.R.	arrive	8.41N	11.46E	5. 4	5. 4 5.44	7.58	8.40	[illegible]
Peterborough	depart	...	7.14	12.32	12.52	4.40	...	[illegible]
Wisbech	..	...	7.40	11.40	11.40M	4. 5	...	[illegible]
March	..	...	7.57	1.26	1.25	7.11	...	[illegible]
Ely	..	—	9.12	2. 0	2. 0	6.53	...	[illegible]
Cambridge	..	7. 7	10. 0	1.40	4.12	8.41		[illegible]
Bury St. Edmunds	..	8.28	11. 6	3.10K	5.20	9.29	7.55	[illegible]
Haughley—G.E.R.	arrive	8.52	11.52	3.34	5.53	9.55	9.15	[illegible]
Haughley—M.S.L.R.	depart	10. 0	12. 0	5.39	6. 0	10. 5	9. 0	[illegible]
Mendlesham	—	10.15	12.15	5.54	6.16	10.20	[illegible]	[illegible]
Brockford & Wetheringsett	—	10.21	12.21	6. 0	6.21	10.26	[illegible]	[illegible]
Aspall and Thorndon (for Debenham)	—	10.28	12.28	6. 8	6.22	10.34	[illegible]	[illegible]
Kenton	—	10.33	12.33	6.12	6.33	10.36	[illegible]	[illegible]
Worlingworth	—	10.44	12.42	6.22	6.43	10.47	[illegible]	[illegible]
Horham	—	10.50	12.48	6.28	6.40	10.53	[illegible]	[illegible]
Stradbroke	—	10.54	12.52	6.32	6.56	10.57	[illegible]	[illegible]
Laxfield	arrive	11. 0	1. 3	6.43	7. 4	11. 0	10. 5	[illegible]

A Saturdays during October only.
B Tuesdays only.
C Not on Tuesdays.
D Saturdays during October only.
E Passengers Travel via Stowmarket.
F On Saturdays arrives at Cambridge 12.57 p.m.
G On Tuesdays and Wednesdays arrives at Ely 4.25 p.m.
H On Saturdays arrives Colchester 6.56, and Liverpool Street 8.15 p.m.
J Commencing 1st November will arrive at Colchester 8.40, and Liverpool Street 10.3 p.m.
K On Wednesdays leaves Bury at 4.15 p.m.
L Mondays only.
M On Thursdays leaves Wisbech at 12.40 p.m.
N Mondays only. Passengers travel via Stowmarket.
P Felixstowe Town Station.
R Mondays only, and will run during October only.
S Commencing 2nd November will leave Yarmouth (Vauxhall) at 6.18 a.m.

The times shown for G.E. Trains are on and from October 1st. For September times see that Company's Time Tables.

MARKET DAY TICKETS.

Third Class Market Tickets, available for return on the day of issue only, will be issued at single fare and a half to Haughley, until further notice, from all Stations on Tuesdays by the 7.35 a.m. and 10.0 a.m. from Laxfield; also on Wednesdays and Thursdays by the 10.0 a.m. from Laxfield.

CHEAP RETURN TICKETS.

Cheap Return Tickets at single fare and a quarter will be issued from Haughley to all Stations, until further notice, by the 6.0 p.m. and 10.5 p.m. on Saturdays and the 9.0 a.m. on Sundays, available for return by any Train on Sundays or Mondays; also from all Stations to Haughley by any Train on Saturdays, and on Sundays by the 7.20 a.m. from Laxfield, available for return by any Train on day of issue (Sundays or Mondays).

The 8.34 p.m. from Laxfield and the 10.5 p.m. from Haughley on Saturdays, and all Sunday Trains will be discontinued after October.

For Particulars of Rates for Parcels, Merchandise, Coal, &c., and other information, apply to the Station Agents, or to

H. R. GILLINGWATER, Superintendent.

LAXFIELD, *September, 1908.*

MID-SUFFOLK LIGHT RAILWAY.

ONLY TRIP OF THE SEASON.

On WEDNESDAY, September 30th, 1908.

Cheap Excursion Tickets will be issued to FELIXSTOWE (G.E.R.)

AS UNDER :—

FROM		AT	Fare for the double journey. THIRD CLASS.
		a.m.	
LAXFIELD		7.33	3/6
STRADBROKE		7.44	
HORHAM		7.50	3/3
WORLINGWORTH		7.56	
KENTON		8. 5	3/-
ASPALL & THORNDON (for Debenham)		8.11	
BROCKFORD & WETHERINGSETT		8.18	
MENDLESHAM		8.25	2/10
FELIXSTOWE (TOWN)	arrive	10.23	

Returning the same day from Felixstowe (Town) at 4 p.m.

Children under 3 years of age, Free; above 3 and under 12, Half-price. No Luggage allowed.

Laxfield, Sept., 1908.

H. R. GILLINGWATER, Superintendent.

During the halcyon years the 'Middy' was often used for school and Sunday School outings. Here four of the original Metropolitan coaches in close-coupled formation provide a backcloth to this group of youthful day trippers who it appears are mostly girls. *Collection G. F. Rice*

CHAPTER FOUR

Independent Years

THE successful introduction of the passenger services gave the Official Receiver and directors the impetus they required to make a further attempt to extend the line to Halesworth. Although the Commissioners had rejected their application following the enquiry, there were procedures whereby the earlier scheme could be revived and, although these had been temporarily shelved, now that passenger trains were running it was thought the time was opportune to redraft the application.

Passenger services soon settled down to provide the local populace with regular transportation to the GER network and proved especially popular on Tuesday, Ipswich market day, and Saturdays. Receipts during the first two months were encouraging, those for the few days of operation in September 1908 being:

Station	Passenger			Parcels			Sundries			Total		
	£	s.	d.	£	s.	d.	£	s.	d.	£	s.	d.
Haughley	2	7	1½	20	15	1 (R)	21	5	10	2	17	10½
Mendlesham	3	8	10½		7	6		–		3	16	4½
Aspall	2	4	10½	2	11	5			6	4	16	9½
Kenton	2	19	1½	4	0	0		6	11	7	6	0½
Stradbroke	8	11	8½	5	1	10		8	3	14	1	9½
Laxfield	26	16	5	9	3	11		13	5	36	13	9

Increased receipts reflected the first full month of passenger operation, October 1908:

	Passenger			Parcels			Sundries			Total		
	£	s.	d.	£	s.	d.	£	s.	d.	£	s.	d.
Haughley	57	15	10		7	0½ (R)	2	7	8	59	16	5½
Mendlesham	22	16	10	1	8	2		–		24	5	0
Aspall	18	17	8	7	7	8		–		26	5	4
Kenton	18	17	2	8	5	0		1	1	27	3	3
Stradbroke	34	10	7	9	4	3		12	0	44	6	10
Laxfield	79	7	8	8	5	3½	1	19	8	89	12	7½

An early photograph of Mendlesham station taken soon after passenger services commenced in 1908 and showing MSLR No. 2 pulling into the platform with a train of three close-coupled ex-Metropolitan Railway four-wheelers. The station building was painted the same Victorian brown as the locomotive and rolling stock. This view shows the staggered joints of the flat bottom track. *Collection G. F. Rice*

Hudswell Clarke 0–6–0T No. 3 drifting down the 1 in 42 bank into Haughley with a train from Laxfield on 5th August 1909. The up home signal, supplied by Mackenzie and Holland Ltd. with pitch pine post and cedar arm, was interlocked with the points on the approach to Haughley MSLR station. Note the shunt signal mounted on the post and the absence of headlamps on the locomotive.
LCGB/Ken Nunn Collection

In this second of a sequence of five photographs taken on 5th August 1909, MSLR 0–6–0T No. 3 is running round her train after arrival at Haughley. In the background and at a lower level is the GER station. The connecting line between the light railway and the GER is on the right of the picture. The spacing between the platform road and the loop is unusually wide. *LCGB/Ken Nunn Collection*

Having established relations with the loco crew, the photographer has arranged for this delightfully posed portrait of MSLR 0–6–0T No. 3 awaiting to depart from Haughley with a mixed train. The ex-Metropolitan Railway close-coupled set formed of brake third No. 8, five-compartment third No. 7, and four-compartment first No. 6, are behind the engine whilst the rear vehicle of the train is ex-GER 4-wheel passenger brake van No. 1. *LCGB/Ken Nunn Collection*

Receipts from the smaller stations at Brockford and Wetheringsett and Horham were included in the figures of the nearest adjacent station.

Wishing to enlarge the goods yard at Horham, the company purchased a small pocket of land opposite the station from A. Preston in September 1908, at a cost of £12.

For some months the receiver had been working to reduce the company's deficit. One method reluctantly adopted was to sell off stored material as well as redundant assets. In the former category, the Mid-Suffolk possessed a considerable tonnage of new rail for both the Halesworth and Westerfield line, and during October it was decided to dispose of the rails not required for the Westerfield line. The sale of rails in November to Jaego Brothers realised £3,150 which enabled the company to clear a number of minor debts. The carriage of the excess rails to Stoke was borne by the company at a cost of £19 16s. 10d.

The board meeting held on 26th November 1908 dealt with more business than had been handled for many months previous. The application by Charles Szlumper for the vacant post of manager was turned down as it was considered his general attitude was disadvantageous to the MSLR. The re-draft of the application to the Light Railway Commissioners for the Halesworth deviation, which included application to the Treasury and the local authority for monetary assistance, was discussed and finally approved. J. F. R. Daniel, who attended the meeting, reported that he had arranged to attend a site meeting at the proposed junction with representatives of the GER and the Southwold Railway.

The site meeting was duly held early in the following month and on 21st December the engineer advised the board the adoption of number two route into Halesworth. At the same time Szlumper asked if the Debenham and Westerfield route was to be totally abandoned. Ever optimistic, the directors were loathe to release the last remaining strands of their grandiose scheme and adjourned the subject for further discussion. With land at Westerfield sold and most of the rails disposed of, it was very clear that the scheme was in fact beyond redemption. It must be assumed that the directors did not wish the inevitable to be recorded for no further mention was made of the Kenton-Westerfield line at subsequent meetings.

The commencement of passenger services had brought a welcome increase in the company's revenue and the figures for the six months ending 31st December 1908 totalled £2,423 4s 6½d.

The railway suffered from its fair share of demolished level crossing gates and in one such incident early in 1909 the porter-in-charge at Brockford failed to open the gates in time for the passage of a train. Taken unawares, he had already swung one gate and was in the process of opening the second, when the train approached. Unable to stop in time, the engine partially clipped the gate, which was subsequently repaired that March by A. C. Andrews for the minimal cost of £1 10s. 0d. There is no record of the reprimand handed out to the staff involved.

The crew were obviously very obliging and the photographer managed to take this view from the footplate at Haughley. The up home signal can be seen around the curve of the track. *LCGB/Ken Nunn Collection*

Very little company business was transacted in the early months of 1909, save for the purchase of a small plot of land at Haughley to allow for the extension of facilities to the MSLR premises.

The six monthly period receipts for passenger and goods traffic continued the upward trend much to the satisfaction of the receiver and directors. Takings to the 30th June 1909 declined slightly, however, with reductions in coal and coke and other minerals, and totalled £2,261 4s 4d.

In July it was optimistically announced that the draft of the order for the extension from Cratfield to Halesworth was imminent and that a contractor would be engaged to complete the works if the necessary order was granted. The ensuing silence over the next two months resulted in the shareholders sending a letter to the board asking for the position of the company, both financially and structurally to be made public.

Soon after the opening of the line to passenger traffic the local residents of Wilby petitioned for a station to be built adjacent to the road leading to the village. In the initial planning of the line, the directors had mooted the provision of a station to serve the neighbourhood but there was a later change of heart when it was considered that the area was scattered and sparsely populated. In the spring of 1909 authority was duly given for a small station to be built with limited accommodation. The work was carried out by an unknown contractor and by July had been completed at a cost of £59 6s. 9d. The station was opened for passengers the same month. The original recommendation was only for the provision of a passenger station but during construction the superintendent advised the receiver and directors that it would be advantageous to the company to provide a siding for goods traffic. This was duly installed in the autumn with surplus rails and pointwork originally intended for the Halesworth section. Additional storage accommodation was also provided on the platform in the form of an ex-GER wagon body purchased at a cost of £21 2s. 0d. and paid by Gillingwater in December.

The importance of livestock traffic to the Mid-Suffolk company was not matched by its facilities to handle the ever increasing traffic. After several complaints by local farmers and breeders of the inadequacies of accommodation, the superintendent was requested to arrange for the provision of cattle docks where none was provided and improved cattle docks where it was considered facilities were not up to standard. The programme of work was executed throughout 1909 with £68 7s 7d being expended in the half year ending 30th June and £44 3s. 1d. in the period ending 31st December.

The paper for the Halesworth Deviation was finalised in April 1909, almost ten months later than anticipated, but before the draft was completed the application for assistance for financial backing from the Treasury and local authorities was withdrawn from the text when it was thought that the inclusion of such clauses would cause untoward problems. Following the rejection of the application after the local enquiry on 26th February 1907, the

In this final view of the sequence MSLR 0–6–0T No. 3 is seen storming up the 1 in 42 gradient out of Haughley over Haugh Lane underbridge with the same train, the 5.55 p.m. mixed to Laxfield. On numerous occasions, if rails were greasy and the train heavy, the engine would stall on the bank and have to set back for a further attempt. Behind the third coach is Haughley up home signal.

LCGB/Ken Nunn Collection

MSLR made their renewed application under Rule 977 for the revival of powers and extension of time in respect of the unconstructed portion of the authorised railway. This was necessary because the time allowed by the previous Light Railway Orders for purchase of land and completion of works had expired.

The formal application was made to the Light Railway Commissioners in May 1909 for a revival of powers authorised in the orders of 1900 and 1905. The *Halesworth Advertiser* reported great satisfaction in the district that the company at last intended to reach Halesworth. A slight hitch was discovered when it was realised that no formal agreement had been made with the GER for the protection of junctions. Full agreement was established at a meeting held in July and the order was subsequently passed to the Board of Trade on 11th August for approval. The final Light Railway Order affecting the 'Middy' was subsequently authorised on 4th December 1909 as the Mid-Suffolk Light Railway (Amendment) Order 1909. Section 5 (1) permitted the time of completion of works on the deviation between 21 miles 1 furlong and 23 miles 2 furlongs 2 chains extended to 31st December 1912. Section 5 (3) revived the powers for the construction of the railway, originally authorised in the 1905 order, beyond the 23 miles 2 furlongs 2 chains mark to Halesworth also subject to completion by 31st December 1912. The protection of the GER junction was to be cognacent with the revised agreement between the two companies made on 30th July 1909. Part of the railway authorised by the 1900 order and the whole of the railway authorised by the Mid-Suffolk (Halesworth Deviation) Order of 1905 were abandoned.

Despite the granting of the order, the monetary difficulties of the company precluded any attempt to arrange a contract to build the line. Minor works, however, continued to be carried out, A. C. Andrews supplying new crossing gates at Wilby for £3 16s. 0d. whilst a new cattle dock was installed at Brockford.

Encouraged by their recent success, the directors were brought back to reality with the publication of the six monthly receipts for the period ending 31st December 1909 showing earnings of £2,646 3s 11½d. Much of this increase was accredited to passenger and parcels traffic which more than offset reduced goods and livestock receipts.

The level crossing at Brockford came in for further attention in July 1910 when A. C. Andrews was called to supply a new gate at a cost of £2 8s. 0d., with associated ironwork costing £1 16s. 6d.

Much to the disappointment of the receiver and directors, a further reduction of traffic receipts was recorded in the first six months of 1910, a slight increase in goods traffic being more than offset by losses in passenger, coal and coke and mineral traffic, leaving a total of £2,383 2s 7½d.

To enable the company to store flammable oils and greases away from other equipment, an oil storage shed was erected near the engine shed at Laxfield in October 1910, at a cost of £8 19s. 6d.

For the six months ending 31st December 1910 receipts recovered slightly, much to the relief of the directors and receiver, with passenger takings almost doubling and leading to total earnings of £2,982 0s 9½d.

Receipts for the next half year ending June 1911 again showed a slight reduction to £2,802 8s 3½d, almost

Laxfield station, looking towards Haughley c.1912. Hudswell Clarke 0–6–0T No. 3 is shunting two ex-Metropolitan Railway 4-wheel coaches out of the platform towards the goods wagons standing on the main single line prior to rearranging the stock in the sidings. The dock road in the foreground is empty whilst coaching stock and wagons are stabled in the coal road (right) and coaching stock siding (left) beyond the coaches. The track layout at Laxfield was rather odd as the main single line weaved through parallel sidings. It was thought by former MSLR employees the S formation was laid in such form because the company intended making the station the second crossing place after Kenton. When the extension beyond Cratfield failed to materialize, lack of finances precluded rearrangement. *Collection G. F. Rice*

totally attributable to passenger traffic and coal and coke, although the fall was slightly offset by higher goods takings.

Conveyance of barley and root crops after harvesting and additional passenger traffic during the holiday period gave considerable healthier traffic receipts during the second six months of 1911 which amounted to £3,406 4s 10d.

A further accident occurred at Brockford level crossing in December 1911, when an approaching train succeeded in demolishing one of the gates before the gatekeeper had managed to open them for the passage of the train. The impact, as well as reducing the gate to matchwood, also wrenched the supporting post out of the ground. The necessary repairs were completed in February 1912 when W. R. Hewitt & Co. provided the pitch pine post for £1 15s. 0d. and Herbert Adams executed the installation of the new post for £1 0s. 9d. No charges are recorded for the replacement of the gate.

Over the years annual dinners were regularly held by the Mid-Suffolk Railway staff and the congenial atmosphere at the gatherings was enjoyed by all. At one such dinner held on 6th January 1912 at the Court House, Stradbroke, presided over by J. B. Chevallier and H. R. Gillingwater, over 80 people sat down to the meal. During the course of the evening, Mr. Privett of the superintendent's office was presented with a pipe and tobacco on the occasion of his retirement. At the conclusion of the formal business a musical programme was arranged by certain members of the staff.

When the Mid-Suffolk first opened for goods traffic not all station goods yards were equipped with the statutory loading gauge. To overcome the deficiency, the company provided a portable loading gauge which was conveyed in the brake van of the freight train. Of necessity this caused operating inconvenience if two freight trains were operating on the line and traffic was often delayed waiting for the loading gauge to be sent to site. In February 1912, to obviate such shortcomings, three loading gauges were purchased from the GER for £9 18s. 6d. and installed in goods yards of the more important of the remaining stations.

For many months the goods traffic on the Laxfield to Cratfield section had not come up to expectation, partly caused by the difficulty of traders gaining access to the railway. In February 1912 the directors and receiver decided that the section beyond Laxfield Mill to Cratfield should be abandoned, although initially the track remained *in situ*.

Traffic receipts for the first six months of 1912 were again disappointing with a reduction of £704 over the previous six months and a general decrease in all categories of traffic, leaving a balance of £2,649 15s 3½d.

Although the Laxfield Mill to Cratfield section of line had been abandoned for some months, the directors were still optimistic of the extension of the line to Halesworth. Financial shortcomings, however, precluded any attempt to negotiate with a contractor to build the section beyond Cratfield, and by August 1912 it was realised that the three years extension of time authorised in the 1909 Light Railway Order for the completion of works had almost expired. In a vain attempt to seek a further extension of time, the secretary was requested to write to the Commissioners seeking their views.

The Light Railway Commissioners duly replied to the MSLR in October 1912. Their response effectively nullified any last hopes the directors might have had of building the extension. The austere answer reiterated that a further Light Railway Order for the extension to Halesworth would only be granted if the promoters came to terms either by obtaining enough money to purchase their railway outright from the receiver or leasing their railway to another concern.

To obtain such far-reaching proposals, the MSLR board would have had to seek and subsequently receive the sanction of debenture holders, both classes of shareholders, and last but not least the many creditors of the company. The task was impossible and the board finally took the inevitable step of abandoning all hope of operating beyond Laxfield Mill. Thus after twelve long years the grandiose scheme for 50 route miles of line was finally forced into a submissive 19½ mile section from Haughley.

Receipts for the second six months of 1912 showed only a slight improvement and did little to lift the gloom of the directors. Compared with other years, passenger and goods traffic were less than expected for the period and resulted in total earnings of £2,932 12s 0d.

The winds which blew across the Suffolk landscape caused many unwelcome draughts as they penetrated the cracks and gaps in the wooden engine shed at Laxfield. By October 1912 the footplate crew was complaining that the onset of winter would make conditions worse. Perhaps surprisingly, in view of the company's financial position, repairs were duly sanctioned and carried out by B. A. Fisk for £1 18s 0d. The work involved plugging the many gaps and the manufacture of wooden shuttering which could be placed across the windows.

From 1st July 1913 there was a change in the management of the railway when W. Lindsey Badcock was appointed to the joint position of general superintendent and engineer, replacing H. R. Gillingwater and Charles Szlumper. At the same time George R. Winsor was appointed secretary. Gillingwater was found guilty of certain misdemeanours and was asked to resign his post or face legal retribution. Gillingwater, who had served the line well in his early years, chose the former and tendered his resignation to save further embarrassment.

Slight alterations in accounting procedures brought changes to the presentation of traffic receipts and the figures for the year ending 31st December 1913 revealed earnings of £6,030 9s 11½d.

J. B. Chevallier, as director of the company, made good use of the long grass growing on the banks of the Debenham branch. In the autumn of 1913 he arranged for the grass to be cut and conveyed away to his farm for animal foodstuff and silage. For the favour granted, he paid the princely sum of 10/-d. into the coffers of the Mid-Suffolk Railway in February 1914.

In contrast to the previous year, six month traffic receipts were again rendered in 1914 and the period to 30th June 1914 showed earnings of £2,691 1s 8d.

The outbreak of World War One on 4th August 1914 found the Mid-Suffolk Light Railway, with other British railway companies under government control. As the months passed, farmers were urged to increase production of vegetables and fruit to offset the deficit of imported foodstuffs caused by enemy action against shipping. Growers and cattle breeders of Mid-Suffolk, like their counterparts all over the country, rallied to the call and their results often necessitated the running of additional freight trains. Hay and straw traffic also increased as fodder and bedding were required by the many military establishments in London and East Anglia. The 'Middy' was not so strategically placed as the Suffolk coastal branches of the GER and carried few military personnel. The most active period was early in the hostilities when Scottish troops were conveyed by special train, when they were constructing the third inland defence line in the vicinity of the railway.

Because of the war effort and the need for steel, the company commenced lifting the track on the abandoned sections of the line from Laxfield Mill to Cratfield and Kenton Junction to Debenham in 1914. The project took some years to complete and appeared to be dependent on the number of staff that could be made available to carry out the task.

Beyond Laxfield Mill the line had continued as far as a temporary station at Cratfield where a siding was installed near the 21½ mile post. A small amount of freight was originally dealt with at this station which was staffed by a junior porter and later a porter-in-charge. The station, which opened in 1906, was closed in February 1912 after traffic failed to come up to expectation and on the abandonment of the extension to Halesworth. Frustratingly, no plans of the Laxfield to Cratfield extension appear to have survived, but presumably there must have been a run-round loop at Cratfield? In the absence of any photographs this short-lived section remains only in the mind's eye of those who saw it.

An amusing story regarding the station at Cratfield was often related by the older 'Middy' Railway staff. A local farmer had ordered a hen house to be delivered by the railway at Cratfield. On being notified of its delivery he drove to the railway and noted a wheeled hen-house awaiting him beside the track. As the station area appeared deserted, he hitched the hen-house to the back of his wagon and was about to rein the horse into action when a head popped out of the hen-house window and retorted 'You can't take this away. This is Cratfield station!'

From Cratfield it was then intended to continue the line via Huntingfield where a loop was planned and from there to Halesworth but little work was executed beyond Cratfield.

From Kenton the Debenham branch veered in a south-westerly direction over three occupational crossings, passing Aspall Wood on the west of the line. It then crossed the

After 1911 when some of the coaching stock was equipped with acetylene lighting, the two 3-car close-coupled sets were split up and normal working was introduced. Here MSLR 0–6–0T No. 2 is seen departing from Haughley with the 5.52 p.m. to Laxfield on 26th July 1915. The first coach is brake third No. 8 followed by a four-compartment first. The mixed train is completed by two open wagons with sheets over their loads, whilst the rear vehicle is the ex-GER 4-wheel full brake MSLR No. 1. *LCGB/Ken Nunn Collection*

B1077 Debenham to Eye road by an underbridge, 1¾ miles from the junction at Kenton, to terminate three-quarters of a mile from Debenham. Frederick J. Moore, who in 1903 was employed as a junior on the staff of Jackson & Company, recalled the engineer's office was then at Debenham. There he lodged with a carpenter and his wife at a cottage in the Aspall Road. Each morning the contractor's saddle tank locomotive *Lady Stevenson* arrived at the Aspall Road with a truck which incorporated an office which was used on pay days. The engine picked up the engineer, timekeeper and Moore to take them to site.

Unofficial goods trips were operated on this section to Kenton but in the absence of any proper goods depot or yard, wagons were propelled to the end of the line and pulled back to Kenton. Traffic was negligible and the service withdrawn in 1906. Beyond the bridge the track had continued to the banks of the River Deben just short of the projected station site. If the line had been extended the official plans allowed for stations at Framsden 5 miles (ex-Kenton), Helmingham (7), Otley (8¾), Witnesham (11), Tuddenham siding (goods only) and Westerfield.

On 4th October 1914 there was a further change to the company's officers when C. Theodore Smith was appointed secretary at a salary of £50 per annum, replacing George Winsor.

Receipts for the six months ending 31st December 1914 showed a downward trend, noticeably on the goods traffic compared with previous years and total earnings amounted to £2,873 2s 2d.

By the spring of 1915 the trackwork in the exchange sidings at Haughley was badly in need of maintenance and replacement of worn rails. The GER effected repairs in April charging the Light Railway Company £100 for their proportion of the cost.

From 1915 traffic receipts were again calculated annually and the increase in conveyance of food produced on Mid-Suffolk farms for the home markets provided increased results for the 'Middy' for the year ending 31st December 1915 to £6,388 7s 6½d.

During 1916 several tons of sleepers removed from the lifted portion of the Cratfield and Debenham sections were sold either to farmers for fencing or as firewood to local villagers.

The traffic receipts of the Mid-Suffolk Railway showed a decline in the year ending 31st December 1916 with reduced earnings from principally coal and coke and other minerals and providing a total of £6,016 1s 2d.

After several years of fairly heavy usage, the cattle pens and dock at Stradbroke were in need of repairs. The remedial work was subsequently carried out by A. W. Butcher at a cost of £4 13s 6d. in February 1917.

By the summer of the same year, lifting of the permanent way on the Laxfield Mill-Cratfield section and from Kenton to Debenham was completed. In the initial stages most of the rails were sent to assist the demand for steel armaments but in October 1917 Hadfield bought a quantity of rails for £27 9s. 1d. Later in the month rails were purchased by Glasgow Corporation for £95 17s. 7d., despatched for further use on the Glasgow Underground. In the following month Larne Harbour Trust paid £16 6s. 4d. for a small quantity whilst in December the Kettering and Irchester Construction Company completed the purchase of redundant rails for £152 12s. 4d.

Traffic receipts for the year ending 31st December 1917 showed a slight recovery with increases in passenger, merchandise and coal and coke traffic over the previous twelve months, producing a balance of £6,396 5s 5d.

The fluctuating receipts throughout the war years meant that most of the money was ploughed back on day to day maintenance, leaving none available for investment for future renewal of assets. Remedial work was kept to a minimum and in March 1918 when minor repairs were necessary to Horham station only 17s. 6d. was expended.

Major J. F. R. Daniel resigned as receiver in February 1918. As the railway was still under government control, the receivership was passed to Alexander Preston Parker of 36 Fairlop Road, Leytonstone, and assistant to the general manager of the GER. Parker also assumed the position of manager as part of his new responsibilities and it was largely in this role that he engendered a closer relationship between the light railway and the main line company.

Traffic receipts for the year ending 31st December 1918 showed that earnings were almost at a standstill and, although passenger takings were up, the increase was more than offset by reduced earnings in merchandise and livestock traffic. The full total was £6,604 13s 7½d.

The cessation of hostilities in November 1918 was greeted by all, for the strain of the war had taxed the resources of every British railway. The Mid-Suffolk was no exception for additional freight services had run to distribute the crops grown by local farmers and growers. The company's wagons, as well as those hired from the GER, ran to destinations far from their home ground in Suffolk and thus the rolling stock, which had received little maintenance, was in a poor mechanical condition.

Railwaymen, like many others, answered the call to arms in the First World War. To cover the resultant vacancies most British Railways employed women and the MSLR was no exception. Miss Eva Oakes was employed as porteress by the company at Laxfield where she is shown ably handling the 17 gallon milk churns on the platform. Tragically Eva Oakes was killed in World War Two.

Early in 1919 A. P. Parker, with the full agreement of the directors, instituted a repair and renovation programme with the GER for the MSLR locomotives, carriages and wagons, the work being carried out over a period of three years. Some MSLR wagons requiring extensive and costly repairs were scrapped as it was considered it would be cheaper to hire wagons from the GER.

In 1919 F. M. Remnant JP, although remaining on the board of the light railway, severed connections with the Mid-Suffolk district when he moved from Wenhaston Grange, Halesworth to Hutton Park, Essex.

From 26th September to 5th October 1919 there was a general railway strike when all services were suspended. This industrial action began the decline in freight train traffic for farmers and growers realised for the first time that with improved roads goods could be conveyed by lorry using second-hand army vehicles, thus motivating short haul journeys cheaper than rates charged by the 'Middy' and the GER. The door to door services were more convenient than double handling caused by the loading into and out of railway wagons. However, the primitive commercial road vehicles of the day were not capable of continuous long hauls and so the middle and long distance freight traffic remained safely in the hands of the railway company. Fortunately, the same problem was not as acute with passenger traffic, for few local people owned cars and therefore relied on the Mid-Suffolk Railway and the GER for short and long distance journeys.

For the 'Middy' the immediate post war receipts showed an up turn, with increases registered on almost all traffic categories and the figures for twelve months ending 31st December 1919 were £8,553 8s 8d.

Although nature was now reclaiming the trackbed and formation of the railway beyond Laxfield Mill, J. B. Chevallier was obviously of the opinion that the Halesworth extension could be resurrected, for in the final weeks of 1919 he made approaches to the Suffolk County Council, the Board of Trade and the Ministry of Transport for monetary and planning support. None of the parties were willing to assist and were tiring of such an ailing company which for twenty years had consistently attempted to open up such an unremunerative tract of country to rail. By January 1920 the internal combustion engine had a greater involvement in rural affairs, and within a decade was to cause the withdrawal of some rail services. The BoT and MoT had little interest in such a rural railway as the MSLR whilst the Suffolk County Council certainly had no intention of wasting public money in the recessionary times. Chevallier's pleas were refused by all parties in no uncertain terms. The MSLR was politely told to maintain as best it could the existing railway.

In the early months of 1920 a passenger, C. Warren, was injured in an accident at Haughley. After his successful claim the company paid a settlement of £30 4s. 9d. in compensation.

Much to the satisfaction of directors and shareholders, receipts for the year ending 31st December 1920 continued

MID-SUFFOLK LIGHT RAILWAY

TIME TABLE.

July 12th, 1920, and until further notice.

This Time Table is only intended to fix the time at which Passengers may obtain their tickets for any journey from the various stations, it being understood that the Trains shall not start from them before the appointed time, but notice is hereby given, that the Company do not undertake that the trains shall start or arrive at the time specified in the table, nor will they be accountable for any loss, inconvenience or injury which may arise from delays or detentions, unless upon proof that such loss, inconvenience, injury, delay, or detention arose in consequence of the wilful misconduct of the Company's Servants. The Company do not hold themselves responsible for the correctness of the times over other Company's lines, nor the arrival of this Company's own trains in time for the nominally corresponding Train of any other Company. Passengers booking at intermediate stations can only do so conditionally upon there being room in the Train.

On Bank Holidays and exceptional occasions the Train Service shewn in the Time Tables is subject to alteration. Particulars will be obtainable at the Stations.

UP TRAINS.	Week Days.			Sundays.
	a.m.	p.m.	p.m.	p.m.
Mid-Suffolk Light Railway.				
Laxfield ....dep.	8.15	1. 0	3.25	5.30
Wilby .... —	8.23	1. 8	3.33	5.38
Stradbroke .... —	8.28	1.13	3.40	5.43
Horham .... —	8.33	1.18	3.47	5.47
Worlingworth ... —	8.39	1.25	3.54	5.53
Kenton .... —	8.46	1.37	4. 3	6. 1
Aspall & Thorndon (For Debenham) —	8.53	1.44	4.15	6. 6
Brockford & Wetheringsett	9. 0	1.53	4.22	6.14
Mendlesham ...... —	9. 6	2. 0	4.28	6.19
Haughley ....arr.	9.19	2.15	4.42	6.32
Haughley—G.E.R. ... dep.	10. 2	3.10	5.12	9.14
Bury St. Edmunds ... arr.	10.25	3.33	5.35	9.37
Cambridge .... „	12.35	5.13	6.56	...
Ely .... „	12.26	6. 5	7.36 A	...
March .... „	12.54	7. 2	8.20 A	...
Peterborough .... „	1.55	7.28	8.57 A	...
Haughley—G.E.R. ... dep.	9.34	2.59	5.24	6.58
Diss .... arr.	9.58	3.24	5.50	7.23
Norwich (Thorpe) ... „	10.46	4.13	6.29	8.14
Haughley—G.E.R. ... dep.	9.52	2.40	5. 8	6.40
Stowmarket.............. arr.	9.58	2.47	5.15	6.46
Ipswich .... „	10.17	3. 3	5.43	7.11
Felixstowe (Town)... „	11. 0	4.58	7. 6	9.14
Colchester.............. „	10.58	4. 5	6.36	8.42
London (L'pool St.) „	12.39	4.58	7.52	9.10

NOTES.

A Via Cambridge.

B On Wednesdays leaves Bury at 4.10 and arrives at Haughley 4.34 p.m.

DOWN TRAINS.	Week Days.			Sundays.
	a.m.	a.m.	p.m.	p.m.
London (L'pool St.) dep.	5. 0	10.12	3.10	4.25
Colchester .... „	7.40	11.34	3.33	5.40
Felixstowe (Town) ... „	8. 0	11. 6	3.31	5. 5
Ipswich .... „	9.25	12. 7	4.50	6.22
Stowmarket .... „	9.53	12.35	5.16	6.50
Haughley—G.E.R. ... arr.	9.59	12.43	5.24	6.58
Norwich (Thorpe) ... dep.	8.51	10.22	3.44	5.54
Diss .... „	9.33	11.14	4.39	7. 3
Haughley—G.E.R. ... arr.	9.52	11.41	5. 8	7.30
Peterborough........... dep.	...	9.48	1. 5	2.33
March .... „	...	10.19	1.51	3.55
Ely .... „	...	10.52	2.30	4.32
Cambridge .... „	7.11	10.59	1.35	5. 2
Bury St. Edmunds ... „	8.30	12.25	3.32B	6.15
Haughley—G.E.R. ... arr.	8.54	12.49	3.56B	6.39
Mid-Suffolk Light Railway.				
Haughley ....dep.	10. 5	12.55	5.30	7.34
Mendlesham.........—	10.18	1. 9	5.44	7.48
Brockford & Wetheringsett	10.24	1.16	5.49	7.53
Aspall & Thorndon (For Debenham) ...—	10.32	1.25	5.57	8. 1
Kenton .... —	10.37	1.35	6. 2	8. 6
Worlingworth...... —	10.45	1.42	6.13	8.14
Horham .... —	10.55	1.48	6.19	8.20
Stradbroke .... —	11. 0	1.53	6.23	8.24
Wilby .... —	11. 5	1.58	6.28	8.29
Laxfield ....arr.	11.15	2. 5	6.35	8.36

Children under 3 years, Free; above 3 and under 12, Half-fare.

MARKET TICKETS.

On Tuesdays Third Class Market Tickets, available for return on the same day, are issued at a Single Fare and a Half to Haughley from all Stations by the first and second up trains, and

On Thursdays by the second up train only.

CONVEYANCES.

Passengers may be able to arrange with the following for conveyances to meet the trains:

MENDLESHAM—P. Clements, Back Street.

BROCKFORD & WETHERINGSETT—G. Lockwood, Brockford.

ASPALL & THORNDON (for Debenham)—J. Bull, Debenham.

KENTON—W. Everson, The Laurels.

WORLINGWORTH—Horse Vehicles—T. Whatling, Farmer.
Motors—A. J. Pipe, near The Church.

HORHAM—J. Whatling, Farmer.

STRADBROKE—W. T. Debenham & Son, Cartage Agents.

WILBY—S. Whatling, Stradbroke.

LAXFIELD—Horse Vehicles—A. Moss, Cartage Agent.
Motors—Grayston Brothers, Station Road.

For Particulars of Rates for Parcels, Merchandise, Coal, &c., and other information apply to the Station Masters, or to

W. LINDSEY-BADCOCK,
General Superintendent, LAXFIELD.

G3-2465. 100 C 400 P

J. Newby, Printer, Stowmarket.

the temporary upward trend with noticeable increases in merchandise and mineral traffic, resulting in total earnings of £12,661 15s 3d.

Despite these increased receipts, the routine running of the line was always a source of embarrassment to the company and the receiver. The combined total of running costs effectively meant the line was incurring a huge deficit. In 1920, for example, these were:

	£	s.	d.
Maintenance of way and works	7758	19	11
Maintenance of locomotives	872	14	2
Maintenance of carriages	722	18	7
Maintenance of wagons	305	4	8
Locomotive Dept. running costs	4510	6	7
Traffic costs	5685	5	6
General and administration	1962	3	9
	21817	13	2

These figures are excessively high as much urgent outstanding maintenance was completed on the track after the neglected war years. Locomotives and rolling stock were also receiving essential repairs and renovation from the GER.

Constant complaints were made after World War One regarding the lack of station identification during the hours of darkness. To rectify matters the company ordered green shades and glass nameplates for their platform oil lamps from the Lamp Manufacturing Co. Ltd. in January 1921 and the items were supplied in March at a cost of £4 6s. 9d.

In 1921 receipts reached their peak during independent operation, again with substantial increases in merchandise and mineral traffic and totalled £14,087 3s 6d.

Running costs for 1921 continued to include the costs of back maintenance whilst the locomotive entry included the charge for the hire of engines from the GER to cover

The typical Mid-Suffolk train in the period prior to takeover of the LNER, Hudswell Clarke 0–6–0T No. 2 swings over the points on the approach to Laxfield station with a mixed train from Haughley. Behind the engine are two former Metropolitan Railway four-wheel coaches, a four-compartment first and then a three-compartment brake third, followed by an MSLR cattle truck. Bringing up the rear of the train is ex-GER 4-wheel brake MSLR No. 1. To the right of the engine is MSLR cattle wagon No. 19 dating from 1905 and built by G. R. Turner of Langley Mill, Nottingham.
Collection G. F. Rice

for MSLR locomotives undergoing repairs in GER workshops.

	£	s.	d.
Maintenance of way and works	5038	13	6
Maintenance of locomotives	2324	10	7
carriages	205	8	9
wagons	151	6	0
Loco running costs	4429	9	7
Traffic costs	5297	2	9
General and administration	1891	19	10
	19338	11	0

The total capital expended on the line to 31st December 1921 was £205,894.

The stirrings of local bus services to Ipswich and the increase in use of ex-World War One army lorries by farmers saw a drastic reduction in receipts for 1922 to £11,236 18s 5½d.

By this time the routine maintenance and running costs had reduced considerably but again exceeded receipts:

	£	s.	d.
Maintenance of way and works	2825	10	1
Maintenance of locomotives	845	9	3
carriages	83	3	5
wagons	90	6	2
Loco running costs	2932	15	11
Traffic costs	4090	11	7
General and administration	1239	11	6
	12107	7	11

Under the provision of the 1921 Railways Act, the GER was amalgamated with the Great Northern, Great Central and several smaller companies on 1st January 1923 to form the London and North Eastern Railway. Included in the amalgamation scheme was the MSLR but because of its insolvency the new authority was loathe to absorb the company until the affairs of the Light Railway were investigated and terms of absorption agreed.

After meetings with the board of the local company and the receiver, the chief legal adviser of the LNER suggested to the Finance Committee that the MSLR receive £2,500 costs to help settle outstanding loans, together with £10,000 LNER preference ordinary stock and £15,000 LNER deferred ordinary stock. In return the MSLR would be requested to discharge all liabilities of the company incurred prior to 1st January 1923, and afterwards hand over the balance of all monies received in compliance with clauses under Section 11 of the Railways Act. MSLR debenture holders were expected to support the application for payment out of court of claims for £800.

During the investigation it was announced that MSLR liabilities included repayment of Lloyds bonds valued at £12,500, other debts totalling £15,541 and interest in debentures and bonds of £2,070.

The acceptance by the receiver and manager of the Mid-Suffolk Company was, however, subject to the approval of the Chancery Court.

The takeover of the MSLR was hindered by a decision made by the Railway Amalgamation Tribunal in May 1923. Quoting the case of the absorption of another company, they considered the Railway Act of 1921 to have transferred to the amalgamating company all the liabilities of the absorbed company, and the tribunal had not the jurisdiction to provide for the transfer of one company to another on the basis that all existing liabilities were nullified.

In a letter of 23rd May 1923 to the Finance Committee, the LNER chief legal adviser reported that the settlement arrived at with the debenture holders, and agreed by the committee, was based on the assumption that the payment offered would enable the LNER to take over the MSLR free from liabilities. In accordance with the tribunal's decision, this was not now possible and in order to settle the takeover it was thought three courses were open to the LNER:

1. Raise the matter with the tribunal and ascertain a ruling as to which MSLR liabilities should be paid for by the LNER.
2. Effectively settle with MSLR debenture holders and if other claims were made, dispute liability.
3. Settle with debenture holders and endeavour to buy out new claimants.

The chief legal adviser thought the last possibility impracticable whilst doubts were expressed as to what extent holders of Lloyds bonds or other creditors could claim against the MSLR. From information supplied by the MSLR, the Lloyds bonds were issued at a time when the company had created and issued debenture stock to the full extent of their borrowing powers. If that was the case, the claims of the Lloyds bond holders might be resisted on the grounds that borrowing of monies on these bonds was *ultra vires* the Mid Suffolk Company.

Other claimants against the MSLR hoping to recover their capital from the LNER were:

	£	s.	d.
Lord Stradbroke	5017	15	4
J. D. Cobbold	3590	11	6
F. M. Remnant	3666	10	9
J. B. Chevallier	95	0	10
W. H. Smith	755	12	5
McKenzie and Holland	257	18	0
Barclay & Co.	2103	10	8
C. D. Szlumper	51	2	7

It was thought that the deputy general manager (Southern area) could reopen negotiations with the debenture holders on the basis of offering a considerably lower figure than before, the justification being the amount the LNER company might have to pay by reason of the transfer and absorption of the MSLR. This was disputed and the matter was subsequently placed before the Railway Amalgamation Tribunal.

The tribunal duly met and intimated on 2nd August 1923 that the Light Railway be transferred to the LNER for a sum of £16,000 together with any liabilities that could be established against the LNE company. The main line company representative objected to the ruling as it was considered that the LNER should not pay any greater sum than the true value of the MSLR. The full liabilities of the

'Middy' amounted to £76,708 13s. 0d. on the assumption that all interest repayable on debentures was liability. Added to this were the amounts due to various small contractors for arrears of maintenance totalling £5,500 and £12,926 as deed of insurance.

The LNER objections were upheld and the terms of amalgamation finally agreed by the tribunal was the transfer of £50,000 MSLR debentures to the LNER for £13,750, in full settlement of claims by debenture holders including arrears of interest. The main line company also agreed to settle in full the loans of £2,500 raised by the receiver and manager of the MSLR.

Notices regarding the amalgamation between the two companies were subsequently posted at MSLR stations and published in the local and national press on 17th August 1923.

From 1st July 1923 the former GER station at Haughley was renamed Haughley West by the LNER whilst the MSLR station remained plain Haughley.

Whilst the legalities were being disputed away in London, the Mid-Suffolk line continued to serve the local community in its timeless way. Unfortunately for the year ending 31st December 1923 receipts were again reduced to £9,655 14s 3d.

Compared with traffic receipts, running costs continually increased to produce another overall deficit.

	£	s.	d.
Maintenance of way and works	2607	1	5
Maintenance of locomotives	264	9	2
carriages	47	1	0
wagons	34	5	0
Loco running costs	2559	5	5
Traffic costs	3836	10	9
General and administration	1213	19	6
	10562	12	3

Early in 1924 the company was shocked by the death of W. Lindsey Badcock, the general superintendent and engineer. The position of acting superintendent was taken by T. J. Dalgleish, assistant superintendent and accountant to the company from May 1905.

The legalities of the transfer of the Mid-Suffolk to the LNER were completed in March and the company was absorbed by the main line company under the LNER (MSLR) Absorption Scheme 1924 dated 3rd April 1924. The actual transfer was to date from 1st July 1924, with official transfer back-dated to 1st January 1923.

As a final get together before takeover, the 'Middy' staff gathered for a dinner at the Royal Oak, Laxfield. A. P. Parker, the official receiver and manager, and Mrs. Parker attended together with Captain, the Right Honorable Lord Huntingfield MP, Mr. Comins JP and Mr. T. J. Dalgleish. After the meal Parker as chairman reminded those present of the last occasion when he visited them, the dire straits of the company meant their accepting his suggestion for their future existence under the aegis of the LNER. He concluded on a light-hearted note by saying that on the first occasion he visited Laxfield after being appointed receiver, he had missed the last up train and returned to Haughley by platelayers trolley. A. P. Parker then presented a wallet and bank notes to T. J. Dalgleish thanking him for his loyal 19 years on the Mid-Suffolk, first in his capacity of assistant superintendent and accountant from May 1905 and then acting superintendent from early 1924.

The final receipts earned by the independent company in the six months ending June 1924 totalled £4,650 6s. 3d. subdivided as follows:

	£	s.	d.
Passenger	519	11	5
Parcels	188	10	8
Miscellaneous	141	5	4
Parcels collection and delivery	4	1	9
Goods merchandise	2127	12	11
Goods collection and delivery	91	3	11
Livestock	416	4	7
Coal and Coke	556	15	0
Other minerals	710	1	3
Warehouse rent	13	12	6
Advertising	8	2	6
Rents	31	17	1
Season tickets	24	19	0
Miscellaneous	6	19	6
	4840	17	5

Operational costs for the last six months of the independent Mid-Suffolk Light Railway still exceeded receipts to produce an operating deficit:

	£	s.	d.
Maintenance of way and works	1180	10	4
Maintenance of locomotives	121	4	9
carriages	5	19	3
wagons	4	0	7
Loco running costs	1248	9	0
Traffic costs	1836	2	5
General and administration	585	10	1
	4981	16	5

Receipts for the final month of independent operation in June 1924 for passenger and parcels traffic showed little difference from those recorded back in October 1908, confirming that the company had made little impact on the travelling habits of the inhabitants of the rural community it was supposed to serve.

	£	s.	d.
Aspall	27	3	3
Haughley	98	0	3
Kenton	49	4	3
Laxfield	98	2	7
Stradbroke	73	4	7½
	345	14	11½

'J65' class 0–6–0T No. 7253 shunting stock at Laxfield on 29th March 1937. The 6-wheel composite next to the engine is 63390 whilst the other coach is a 6-wheel three-compartment brake third. Bringing up the rear of the train is an ex-Great Central Railway 15 ton 6-wheel goods brake. Note No. 7253 has lost her tool boxes on the side tanks and has the LNER type steel cab roof.
W. A. Camwell

CHAPTER FIVE

Amalgamation and Nationalisation

THE new regime soon introduced changes to their acquisition. The three 0–6–0 tank locomotives, although classified J64 under the LNER class coding, were considered non-standard and transferred away to Ipswich and later Stratford, before being used to good effect as shunting engines at Colchester and Stratford. The old MSLR No. 3 was considered beyond economical repair and scrapped. Equally the former Metropolitan Railway passenger stock owned by the 'Middy' was considered life expired and withdrawn, whilst most of the wagons followed a similar fate. As replacement motive power the LNER allocated class J65 (ex GER E22) 0–6–0 tank engines to work the services. Ipswich shed already boasted an allocation of the class for working the Ipswich dock lines and the Eye branch and three members of the class had worked on the Mid-Suffolk line in 1920/21. For passenger services some ex-GER six-wheel coaches were allocated to the line and, although of almost the same vintage as the vehicles they replaced, the newcomers were considered to be in better condition both internally and mechanically.

The LNER to its chagrin found the amalgamation of the minor company was far from smooth, as almost each week new claims for compensation were being made against the MSLR. By 4th November 1924 when all outstanding debenture claims had been made, the main line company had expended a total of £30,231 in full settlement of liabilities for a railway it was not really interested in taking over. The costs were divided between acquisition of land, line and property £28,616 and rolling stock in accordance with the chief mechanical engineer's valuation of £1,615.

Further changes were made as the months passed as tickets, notepaper and timetables were introduced bearing the legend LNER.

The former 'Middy' was again affected by industrial action during the 1926 General Strike, although services were only curtailed for a day or so. From 31st May a substitute service of two mixed trains in each direction was introduced until matters returned to normal.

In the early 1920s the introduction of a daily bus service from Eye to Ipswich began making inroads into the branch passenger traffic and gradually over the next decade the Eastern Counties Road Car Company, later Eastern Counties Omnibus Company, extended their coverage of routes in Mid-Suffolk. Improvements in rural roads brought the

MSLR Nos. 3 and 2 stand alongside the shed offices at Stratford in August 1924 having travelled light from Ipswich on displacement from the light railway services. It appears that No. 3, running as a 2–4–0T with front coupling rods removed, has hauled No. 2 'dead'. Both engines display their polished brass domes whilst No. 3 has her portable rerailing jack mounted on the running plate by the smokebox. In the background is the water tank mounted above the shed stores. *Photomatic*

Class 'J65' 0–6–0T No. 7157 at Haughley MSLR station in 1928 waiting to depart with the branch train to Laxfield. The MSLR station was closed in November 1939 when the light railway passenger services terminated in the bay platform at the back of the up platform of the ex-GE station. *J. E. Kite*

ever increasing use and reliance on the motor vehicle. Traffic receipts during the 1920s showed little increase over receipts for 1908 and fluctuated quite considerably with most of the season tickets being issued to children attending secondary school in Stowmarket. Passenger and parcels traffic receipts for the first years of operation under the LNER regime are shown in the table opposite.

The LNER was at this period suffering traffic losses which deemed it necessary for the management at Marylebone and Liverpool Street to investigate the viability of retaining many branch line passenger services in the future East Anglian railway system. After close scrutiny the passenger train services were withdrawn from Downham to Stoke Ferry and Somersham to Ramsey East branches on and from 22nd September 1930. Less than five months later on 2nd February 1931, two further branch passenger services succumbed, those from Ely to St. Ives and Mellis to Eye. A few miles to the south of the latter and equally as vulnerable was the Mid-Suffolk Light Railway and in 1931 the authorities began to take a close interest in the line with a view to possible closure.

Dwindling passenger receipts made depressing reading for in the three years from 1925 to 1928 the number of passenger bookings from the branch stations had reduced by a third from £3,296 to £2,162. Mendlesham, handling the highest passenger traffic with an average of 51 persons booking per week in 1925, had reduced to 36 three years later. At the other end of the scale, the porter in charge at Wilby, selling an average of 14 tickets per week in 1925, was a very lonely man by 1928 when he issued barely 9 tickets per week. Of the 'important' stations on the line,

A. A. Meadows who transferred from Mellis to act as the only serving station master at Kenton in the LNER era. This photograph dated 1926 is of especial interest as it shows the second Kenton engine shed (far right) which had lost its allocation of one locomotive and associated driver and fireman in 1919. *Collection G. F. Rice*

	Passengers	Passenger Receipts £	Parcels	Parcel Receipts £	Season Tickets	Season T. Receipts £	Total £
Half year 1924							
Mendlesham	1565	125	1267	80	–	–	205
Brockford	975	69	310	36	–	–	105
Aspall	624	72	520	46	–	4	122
Kenton	655	82	120	18	–	–	100
Worlingworth	897	108	192	31	–	–	139
Horham	667	84	270	145	–	–	229
Stradbroke	1107	206	458	96	–	–	302
Wilby	405	66	69	70	–	–	136
Laxfield	1205	182	2632	180	–	–	362
1925							
Mendlesham	2666	184	2357	153	1	9	346
Brockford	1799	138	703	58	1	4	200
Aspall	1144	124	3252	231	3	16	371
Kenton	1116	125	357	48	1	13	186
Worlingworth	1404	153	413	72	–	–	225
Horham	1186	113	1915	315	–	–	428
Stradbroke	1681	278	1717	252	–	–	530
Wilby	755	119	974	208	–	–	327
Laxfield	1682	276	6338	407	–	–	683
1926							
Mendlesham	2060	164	2417	181	2	10	355
Brockford	1541	116	859	50	1	5	171
Aspall	858	124	2218	209	2	13	346
Kenton	836	94	458	59	–	–	153
Worlingworth	1096	125	618	103	–	–	228
Horham	1198	129	2640	230	–	–	359
Stradbroke	1435	257	2325	264	–	–	521
Wilby	409	75	2103	236	1	18	329
Laxfield	1405	222	10008	442	–	–	664
1927							
Mendlesham	2191	161	2186	167	2	10	338
Brockford	1670	119	843	64	1	5	188
Aspall	818	86	1589	162	1	9	257
Kenton	886	100	415	66	2	17	183
Worlingworth	1050	126	602	110	–	–	236
Horham	1190	116	2144	165	–	–	281
Stradbroke	1328	237	1953	228	1	6	471
Wilby	459	80	2019	228	–	–	308
Laxfield	1414	207	8421	340	–	–	547
1928							
Mendlesham	1883	130	1652	118	3	14	262
Brockford	1525	110	810	61	1	11	182
Aspall	971	90	509	35	1	6	131
Kenton	857	96	405	56	2	18	170
Worlingworth	1194	144	503	68	–	1	213
Horham	1195	94	1589	118	–	–	212
Stradbroke	1257	192	1493	151	1	8	351
Wilby	464	73	2002	217	–	–	290
Laxfield	1133	130	7737	221	–	–	351

After absorbing the MSLR from July 1924, the LNER quickly replaced the original Hudswell Clarke tanks with ex-GER class 'E22' 0–6–0Ts (LNER class 'J65') and three were then outbased at Laxfield shed, two working the services with one spare. LNER 'J65' No. 7247, fitted with original stovepipe chimney, was one of the class regularly working the line and is shown at Laxfield in March 1931. As GER No. 247 she had been loaned to the MSLR in September 1920.
Dr. I. C. Allen

the average number of passengers joining trains was also on the decline.

	1925	1928
Kenton	21	16
Stradbroke	32	24
Laxfield	32	22

All stations showed reduced receipts on the passenger and parcels side during the same period, the biggest reductions being Aspall £7 2s. 8d. per week in 1925 to £2 10s. 2d. in 1928 and Laxfield where receipts almost halved from £13 2s. 7d. in 1925 to £6 15s. 10d. in 1928.

The investigation into the Mid-Suffolk Light Railway by the LNER authorities was to take a far different course to those adopted with other East Anglian branch railways, for amongst the proposals was the scheme to convert the track bed into a self-contained motor road. To this end, a committee, formed of H. Gardner, assistant superintendent (Eastern) as chairman, W. J. Pepper, F. C. C. Stanley, R. J. M. Inglis and James Hilton, was requested to investigate such possibilities.

From enquiries made, the total passenger revenue for the year 1930 showed a similar deficit to previous years:

	Total Receipts £	Branch Proportion £
Ordinary and excursion	831	434
Season tickets	159	129
Parcels and miscellaneous	2002	437
Parcel post	238	80
	3230	1034

The initial investigation revealed the obvious fact that passenger traffic on the branch was light and most of the bookings from stations were to Stowmarket, Ipswich or London with very little passing between individual stations on the line.

It was established that the branch stations served a catchment area with a population of 12,464 but here the committee were somewhat optimistic as to their understanding of the word 'catchment' for many of the villages or hamlets listed were over 3 miles distance from the railway and the days of prospective passengers walking such distances to join the train were past.

Station	Village	Population	Distance from station miles
Mendlesham	Mendlesham	934	–
	Mendlesham Green	–	1½
	Thwaite	105	2
Brockford	Wetheringsett	812	½
Aspall	Aspall	129	¾
	Debenham	1085	2¼
	Helmingham	303	6½
	Pettaugh	171	5
	Rishangles	135	1¼
	Thorndon	553	3¼
	Winston	200	3½
Kenton	Ashfield	202	3½
	Bedingfield	220	1¾
	East Soham	543	4
	Kenton	227	–
Worlingworth	Bedfield	267	2
	Monk Soham	233	3
	Redlingfield	147	2
	Southolt	101	½
	Tannington	158	2½
	Worlingworth	504	1½
Horham	Athelington	54	½
	Denham	178	3
	Horham	292	–
Stradbroke	Stradbroke	927	½
	Wingfield	458	3
Wilby	Wilby	332	1
	Fressingfield	986	3¼
Laxfield	Laxfield	787	–
	Badingham	597	3
	Cratfield	424	3
	Heveningham	208	3½
	Linstead Magna	67	4
	Ubbeston	125	3
		12464	

On the freight side, tonnages and receipts were also in decline. Farmers and growers on much of the agricultural land served by the branch were increasing their average output of sugar beet so that by the late 1920s and 1930 the considerable portion of traffic was seasonal, with a peak between October and January. Empty wagons were worked to the branch stations either on mixed trains or daily goods and when occasions warranted by special working. The wagons were then loaded daily in the station yards and forwarded via Haughley to the sugar beet processing factories at Ipswich and Bury St. Edmunds. Imports to the line consisted mainly of domestic coal, foodstuffs, fertilizers and, ironically, road-making materials. Gross tonnages and receipts for the year 1930 were:

	Tons	Total Receipts	Branch Proportion
Merchandise	14336	£11873	£2967
Coal and coke	9983	5649	550
Other minerals	36529	10493	3946
Livestock	577 head	2308	306
Miscellaneous receipts		344	344
		£30667	£8113

the branch proportion equating to £156 per week.

Investigations proved that as the area served by the railway was entirely agricultural with no evident industry, there was little likelihood of an increase in population and conversely the population was in decline. Unlike other areas where passenger train services had been withdrawn, there was no replacement bus service available to follow the route of the railway.

From their findings the committee initially thought the case for the road replacement of the railway proven on grounds of dwindling receipts. They then ascertained that the available land occupied by the branch consisted of 22 miles 25 chains of track, formed of 19 miles 35 chains of main single line, 13 chains of loop line and 2 miles 57 chains of sidings. After various site meetings and inspections, the civil engineer was requested to provide estimates for the replacement of the permanent way by a tarmacadam road following the same course as the railway. Originally it was proposed to have a road 12 feet wide, suitable for light road vehicles only, and opened to the public as a toll road. The overbridge carrying the Ipswich-Norwich road across the railway near Brockford was considered to have adequate clearance with 16 feet span across the railway and 15 feet above the track. Conversely the underbridge at Haugh Lane was found to be in poor condition and if the road were constructed the structure would require rebuilding.

One major problem, however, had been initially overlooked. The Ministry of Transport stipulated any road built for two-way traffic was to have a minimum width of 20 feet. When this was realised not only had both bridges, together with a stream bridge near Horham, to be completely demolished and rebuilt, but also the railway company would be required to purchase an additional 8 feet of land where the formation was only 12 feet wide. At Brockford further land would also be required as the main road bridge would have to be replaced by crossroads.

At the conclusion of the study the committee estimated the cost of converting the Mid-Suffolk trackbed to a roadway at £227,823 whilst the £7,994 10s. 3d. estimated cost of recoverable and re-usable railway material, left a net cost of £219,828 9s. 9d. The annual maintenance and renewal costs when compared showed a favourable figure for the retention of the railway. Permanent way and works costs were £3,699 whilst the road renewal programme of £400 per mile showed a total of £7,600 per annum.

The cost of converting the railway to road became even less inviting when the expense of running a replacement bus service along the new road was estimated. The Eastern Counties Omnibus Co. Ltd., as a subsidiary of the LNER, when asked to quote for the traffic as per any agreement with the railway company, quoted the price for such service at an exorbitant 9½d per mile. Compared with the internal branch passenger and season ticket receipts of £563 the passenger train mileage totalled 35,568, hardly a prosperous proposal, if buses were to be introduced. To offset this cost, it was estimated that the annual toll collection for traffic using the road would accrue £4,900, but again the income hardly justified the full expenditure and the scheme was subsequently abandoned, the committee advising the LNER authorities of the making good necessary of any deficiencies in the light railway.

On 29th September 1932 approval was given to the abolition of the station signal box at Haughley, leaving the control of all signals and points including access to and from the Mid-Suffolk line concentrated on the junction signal box. The plan included the provision of the electrical working of the main line crossover and the installation of an electrically released ground frame to work the back platform connection. The level crossing gates were also to be locked from the signal box. Although the cost was estimated at £2,185 it was thought that the recoverable material valued at £2,054 would offset the high cost of the scheme. Haughley station signal box was subsequently abolished in May 1933.

The decline in passenger traffic receipts on the light railway was halted momentarily in the mid-1930s when holidays and rambles in the country were fashionable. Often groups of ramblers would descend on to the branch train at Haughley, alight at one of the stations and walk to another, before returning on the last up train of the day. On at least two occasions the LNER arranged for special services to run. A fair number of passengers used the branch trains at weekends and bank holidays, taking advantage of their days off, either returning the same day or if travelling outward on Saturday returning on the Monday.

Local bus services based at Ipswich or Stowmarket made further inroads into the area served by the light railway and as the decade reached its declining years so did passenger receipts again decline. Goods receipts, however, remained steady with losses on livestock traffic being offset by the regular conveyance of sugar beet between October and January.

In 1939 the question of the Halesworth extension was resurrected when Edgar Granville, MP for Eye, asked the Minister of Transport in the Commons on 3rd August if representations could be made to the LNER to complete the unfinished portion of the MSLR, in order to provide increased direct transport facilities in the area where road transport did not achieve that purpose. In reply the Minister, Captain Ewan Wallace, said the powers authorised

Approaching Mendlesham in May 1934, class 'J65' 0–6–0T No. 7157 trundles along a straight section of line with a Haughley to Laxfield passenger working formed of two 6-wheel composites and two 6-wheel brake thirds. Before transfer to the light railway services, No. 7157 (ex-GER No. 157) was regularly outbased at Eye for working the branch to Mellis. In this photograph No. 7157 still carries tool boxes on the side tanks and has the GER style shallow curved wooden roof. There is also a wooden door fitted to the lower part of the to the MSLR had lapsed 27 years ago and if the portion was to be completed, fresh powers would have to be obtained.

With the impending outbreak of World War Two, the LNER merged with other major railway companies under the Railway Executive Committee from 1st September 1939. Following the commencement of hostilities two days later evacuees were conveyed by the branch train, some from the inner London area viewed the countryside for the first time in their lives. Numbers were small compared with other areas of East Anglia.

To safeguard against air raids, especially at night, the oil lamps at stations remained dimmed and staff utilized shielded hand lamps to attend to train and shunting duties. As a further precaution, some of the station nameboards were removed and stored in the station buildings.

The agricultural nature of the freight handled by the Mid-Suffolk Light Railway was again of the utmost importance as the vital provisions of home grown food, vegetables, grain and fruit were despatched to markets. In addition to the outward flow of produce, the war years brought an influx of tinned food for distribution to the Ministry of Food storage depots in the area. Because of fuel rationing and the reduction of lorries on the roads, the branch freight often ran with maximum loads.

After initially announcing in the war emergency timetable the abandonment of all services, the LNER later rescinded such drastic action and from October 1939 a passenger service of two trains in each direction was introduced — a feature which persisted until closure of the line. Nevertheless, the light railway carried its fair share of traffic as petrol rationing and the reduction of local bus services forced additional passengers to use the line. Rationing of petrol also brought the withdrawal of many vans and lorries from local roads and the urgency of foodstuffs meant an increase in freight traffic leaving the branch stations for destinations in London, the Midlands and North of England. Many cheap day facilities were withdrawn and all excursion traffic curtailed. As late as 1941 occasional evacuees were still being sent down to Suffolk destinations on the branch. From August 1939 a large petrol dump was opened at Haughley and tanker trains were regularly consigned to the station in the five years to June 1944.

During the war years the branch assumed some strategic importance as a supply route to the United States Airforce airfields at Mendlesham and Horham. Initially roadstone, cement and tarmacadam were conveyed by special freight services to the local station yards, where the material was transported to site and used in the construction of roadways and runways. Thereafter supplies for men stationed at the two airfields were conveyed by train whilst bombs and ammunition were also conveyed by special goods trains. To cater for these heavier loads and also the petrol traffic, the first half mile of the Mid-Suffolk branch from the junction at Haughley was relaid with heavier rails to enable larger locomotives including LNER 'J39' 0—6—0s and USA 'Austerity' 2—8—0 tender locomotives to bank trains up the 1 in 42 gradient. The 'J15' 0—6—0 allocated to the branch for these heavy goods then hauled the train on to either Mendlesham or Horham as necessary. Most of the ammunition trains ran at night under cover of darkness and on arrival at the destination station the bombs and other items were quickly offloaded and conveyed to ammunition dumps near to or on the airfield. For obvious reasons of infrequent passenger services, few military personnel travelled by the branch train and most were conveyed to Stowmarket, Diss or Ipswich and thence to the airfields by road vehicles.

From November 1939 the former Mid-Suffolk Haughley station was closed with branch passenger and mixed trains being diverted to the up side bay platform of Haughley West LNER station. The track in the former station area was then utilized as sidings for the petrol dump and also for the sorting and storage of wagons.

The period after the war found the railways resuming peacetime services with run-down rolling stock and equipment, with stations and buildings sadly in need of repair. Quite frequently the branch 'J65' class 0—6—0T failed in traffic and services were delayed until the other branch engine could be summoned to assist. On one occasion, a lady, who was the sole passenger on the train, had to hitch a ride on a milk lorry to her destination. The severe weather early in February 1947 brought problems, initially with falling snow which effectively blocked the line for over 24 hours, and later by thawing snow which caused a local stream to rise and flood the line at about six places. Fortunately, it was possible to maintain the services with trains proceeding at severe caution through the trouble spots.

In the final year of independence, the LNER completed the replacement of flat bottom track with heavier bullhead rails and this improvement enabled the 'J15' class 0—6—0 tender engines, previously only permitted to work engineers' trains or special freights at reduced speeds, to take over officially all services from the 'J65' class tank engines. 'J15s' unofficially had often worked passenger services in the war years.

The nationalisation of the railways from 1st January 1948 brought few changes to the Laxfield branch which retained a GER/LNER atmosphere until the withdrawal of passenger services. Most stocks of LNER tickets remained until the branch closed, although a few in constant demand were replaced by tickets bearing the legend 'Railway Executive'. Locomotives working the Mid-Suffolk line soon lost the NE or LNER identity in lieu of the rather austere BRITISH RAILWAYS identity of the side tanks or tender. However, varnished teak or brown paint remained on the branch coaching stock until closure to passenger traffic.

Freight traffic showed a further decline in the post nationalisation years as fuel rationing ended and farmers preferred to send or take their produce to market by motor lorry. Livestock traffic was now almost non existent and only sugar beet and coal was conveyed in any quantity as exports and imports respectively. From 1949 the goods train only ran on Mondays, Wednesdays and Fridays. Passenger traffic, never very heavy, declined further and except during schooldays when the branch train was extended to Stowmarket in the morning and from there in the evening, for the convenience of schoolchildren, few passengers were carried. On many occasions no passengers were carried at all and a feature writer for the *Suffolk Mercury* reported in 1949 that for the majority of the journey he travelled in 'splendid isolation' before being invited to ride with the guard and then with the engine crew.

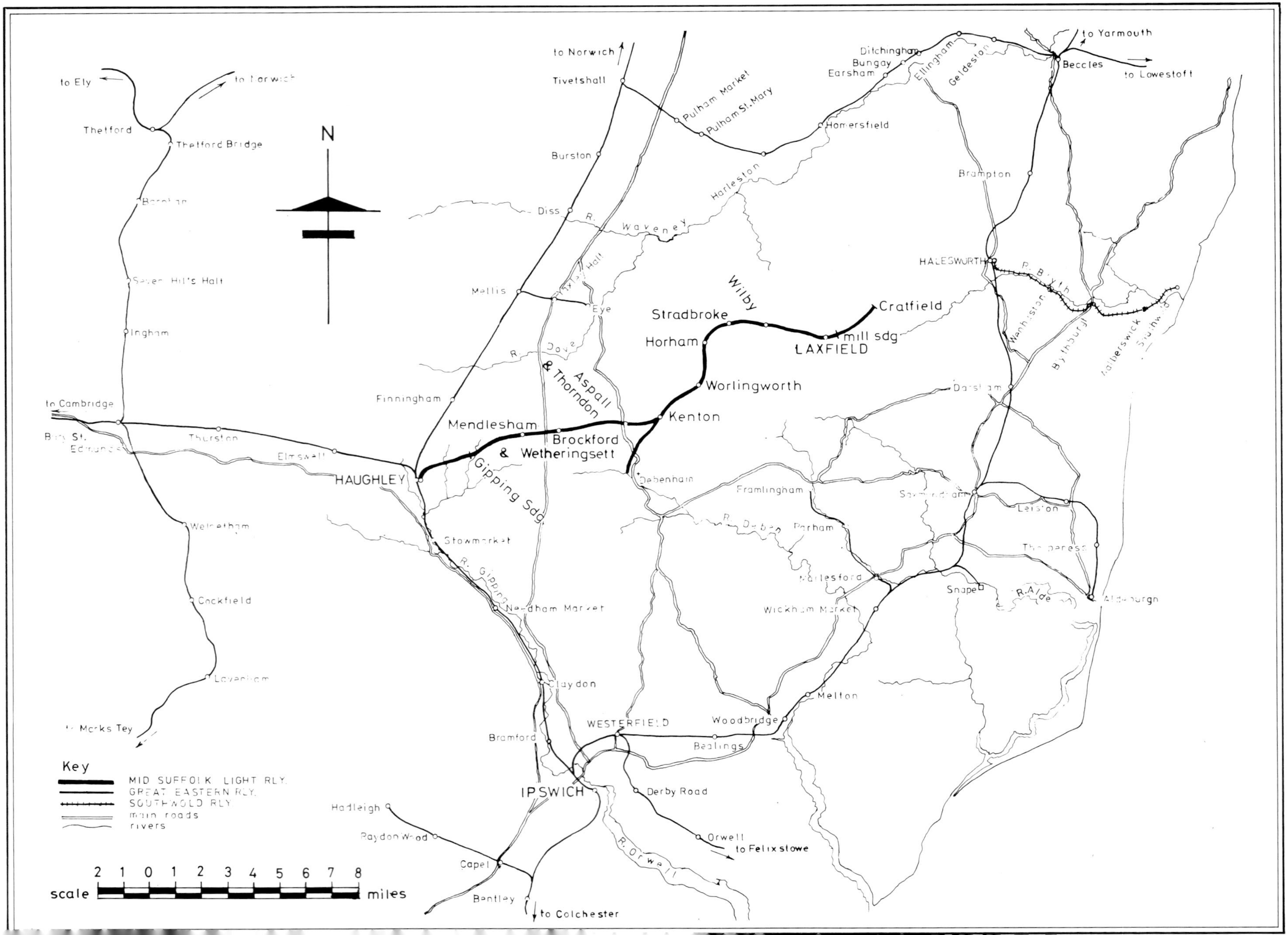

to Ely
Thetford
Thetford Bridge
N
Seven Hill's Halt
Ingham
to Cambridge
Bury St. Edmunds
Thurston
Elmswell
HAUGHLEY
Welnetham
Cockfield
Lavenham
to Marks Tey
to Norwich
Tivetshall
Burston
Diss
R. Waveney
Mellis
Finningham
Eye
R. Dove
Aspall & Thorndon
Mendlesham
Brockford & Wetheringsett
Gipping Sdg.
Stowmarket
R. Gipping
Needham Market
Claydon
Bramford
IPSWICH
Hadleigh
Raydon Wood
Capel
Bentley
to Colchester
Pulham Market
Pulham St. Mary
Harleston
Homersfield
Earsham
Bungay
Ditchingham
Ellingham
Geldeston
Beccles
to Yarmouth
to Lowestoft
Brampton
HALESWORTH
R. Blyth
Wenhaston
Blythburgh
Walberswick
Southwold
Wilby
Stradbroke
Horham
Cratfield
mill sdg
LAXFIELD
Worlingworth
Kenton
Debenham
Darsham
Framlingham
Saxmundham
Leiston
Thorpeness
R. Deben
Parham
Marlesford
Snape
R. Alde
Aldeburgh
Wickham Market
Melton
Woodbridge
WESTERFIELD
Bealings
Derby Road
Orwell
to Felixstowe
R. Orwell
Key
MID SUFFOLK LIGHT RLY.
GREAT EASTERN RLY.
SOUTHWOLD RLY.
main roads
rivers
scale
2 1 0 1 2 3 4 5 6 7 8
miles

CHAPTER SIX

The Line Described

HAUGHLEY station (82 miles 75 chains from Liverpool Street) on the GER main line to Norwich, was the junction for the line to Bury St. Edmunds, Cambridge and Ely and also the Mid-Suffolk Light Railway. Known originally as Haughley Junction, it was opened on 7th July 1849 as a replacement for the original station built one mile away to the west in 1846. This new station was renamed Haughley Road in 1866 and further renamed Haughley in 1890. The main line platforms, located north of Station Road level crossing, were slightly staggered and connected by footbridge No. 288 at 82 miles 73 chains. This was rebuilt in 1910 by E. C. Keay Ltd. of Birmingham for £344 2s. 6d. The main buildings on the up platform, 420 ft. long, were of impressive Eastern Counties Railway design with an ornate entrance and included booking and parcels office, waiting room, gentlemen's toilet, ladies waiting room, porters room and station master's house. The down side platform, 430 ft in length, was an island with a small waiting shelter and a 240 ft long canopy offering waiting passengers protection from the elements. The up and down main lines served the respective platforms whilst the back platform road, serving the western face of the island platform, was utilised by Bury line services which could gain access via facing and trailing crossovers in the up direction and normal facing and trailing points in the down direction. On the west side of the back platform road was a loop 560 feet long which enabled engines to run round their train. This line also served the 200 ft long tank road and the 350 ft long turntable road, the latter leading to the 42 ft diameter turntable (lengthening irons extended this to 44 ft 3 ins). Also at the south end of the back platform road, a short 100 ft siding served the goods shed, whilst to the east of this siding was a 40 ft long headshunt.

Signals and points at the south end of the station, together with the level crossing gates, were controlled from Haughley station signal box located south of Station Road crossing on the down or western side of the line. The points and signals at the north end of the station and the junction of the Norwich and Bury lines came under the control of Haughley Junction signal box, set back into the cutting on the down side of the down back platform line opposite the junction points.

The track layout for the Mid-Suffolk Light Railway at Haughley evolved over a period of time and commenced with Jackson, the contractor, laying a simple straight line and single siding with a loop to enable the engine to run round its train of spoil and materials wagons. Much of the initial permanent way appears to have been conveyed to Haughley by the GER and then transhipped by horse and wagon to the MSLR site east of Haughley station. After due negotiation a simple connection with points in a trailing connection for up trains was provided from the GER up main line, 180 ft north of the end of the up platform to a short reception siding. At the south end of this siding points led through a gate in the MSLR boundary fence to join up with the run round loop. It was through this connection that the coaching stock used for Lord Kitchener's special train in September 1902 gained access to the Light Railway. In the final months of the same year the MSLR and GER reached agreement as to interchange sidings for

Class 'D16/3' 4–4–0 No. 62566 piloting a class 'B17' 4–6–0 on a Cambridge/Ely to Ipswich train into Haughley up platform on 18th April 1949. On the right is the station nameboard which advised intending passengers of the junction for the Mid-Suffolk Light Railway. The wagons in the background are standing on the 800 ft long siding on the site of the former light railway terminal. *W. A. Camwell*

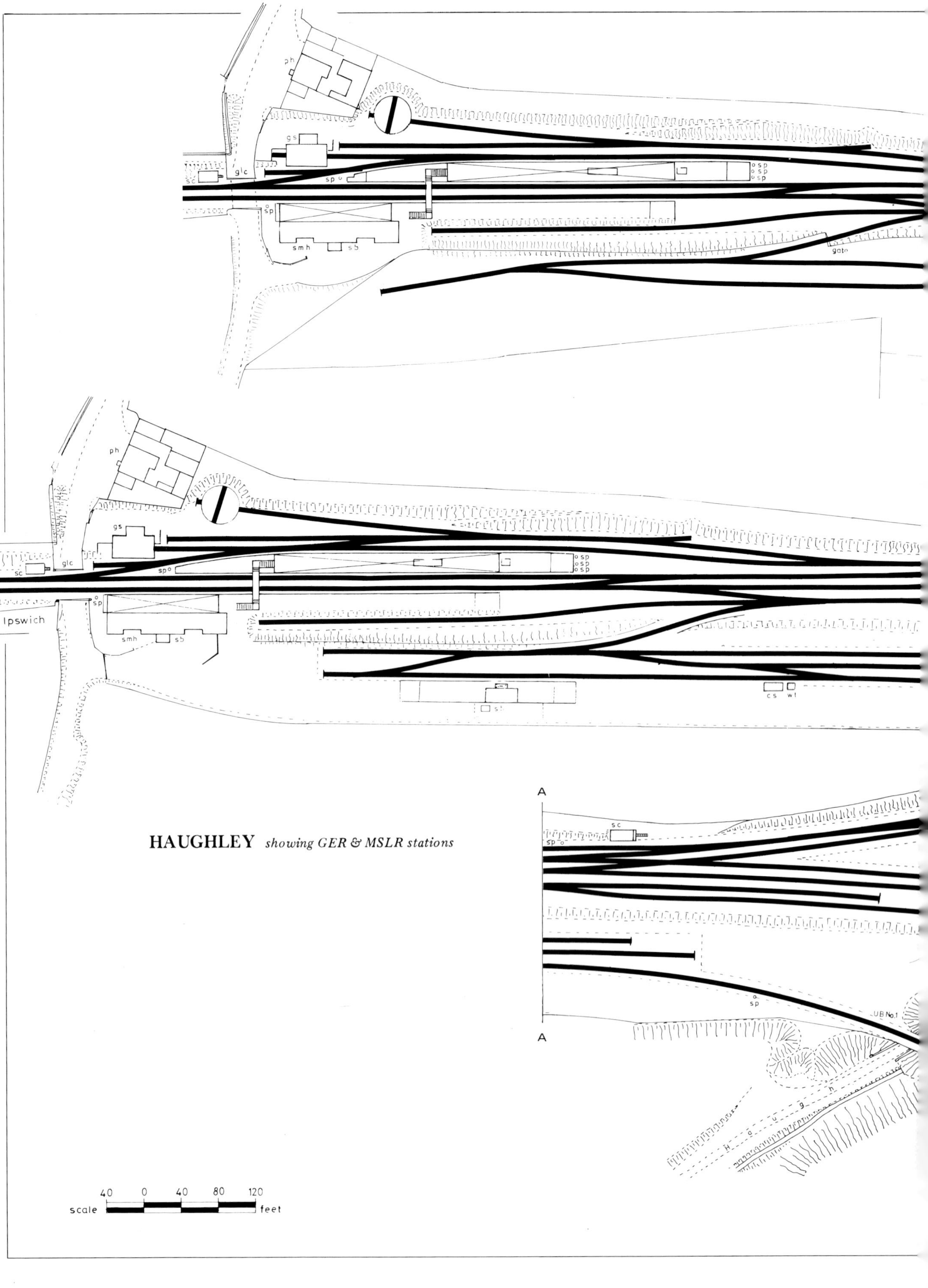

HAUGHLEY *showing GER & MSLR stations*

CHAPTER SIX

The Line Described

HAUGHLEY station (82 miles 75 chains from Liverpool Street) on the GER main line to Norwich, was the junction for the line to Bury St. Edmunds, Cambridge and Ely and also the Mid-Suffolk Light Railway. Known originally as Haughley Junction, it was opened on 7th July 1849 as a replacement for the original station built one mile away to the west in 1846. This new station was renamed Haughley Road in 1866 and further renamed Haughley in 1890. The main line platforms, located north of Station Road level crossing, were slightly staggered and connected by footbridge No. 288 at 82 miles 73 chains. This was rebuilt in 1910 by E. C. Keay Ltd. of Birmingham for £344 2s. 6d. The main buildings on the up platform, 420 ft. long, were of impressive Eastern Counties Railway design with an ornate entrance and included booking and parcels office, waiting room, gentlemen's toilet, ladies waiting room, porters room and station master's house. The down side platform, 430 ft in length, was an island with a small waiting shelter and a 240 ft long canopy offering waiting passengers protection from the elements. The up and down main lines served the respective platforms whilst the back platform road, serving the western face of the island platform, was utilised by Bury line services which could gain access via facing and trailing crossovers in the up direction and normal facing and trailing points in the down direction. On the west side of the back platform road was a loop 560 feet long which enabled engines to run round their train. This line also served the 200 ft long tank road and the 350 ft long turntable road, the latter leading to the 42 ft diameter turntable (lengthening irons extended this to 44 ft 3 ins). Also at the south end of the back platform road, a short 100 ft siding served the goods shed, whilst to the east of this siding was a 40 ft long headshunt.

Signals and points at the south end of the station, together with the level crossing gates, were controlled from Haughley station signal box located south of Station Road crossing on the down or western side of the line. The points and signals at the north end of the station and the junction of the Norwich and Bury lines came under the control of Haughley Junction signal box, set back into the cutting on the down side of the down back platform line opposite the junction points.

The track layout for the Mid-Suffolk Light Railway at Haughley evolved over a period of time and commenced with Jackson, the contractor, laying a simple straight line and single siding with a loop to enable the engine to run round its train of spoil and materials wagons. Much of the initial permanent way appears to have been conveyed to Haughley by the GER and then transhipped by horse and wagon to the MSLR site east of Haughley station. After due negotiation a simple connection with points in a trailing connection for up trains was provided from the GER up main line, 180 ft north of the end of the up platform to a short reception siding. At the south end of this siding points led through a gate in the MSLR boundary fence to join up with the run round loop. It was through this connection that the coaching stock used for Lord Kitchener's special train in September 1902 gained access to the Light Railway. In the final months of the same year the MSLR and GER reached agreement as to interchange sidings for

Class 'D16/3' 4–4–0 No. 62566 piloting a class 'B17' 4–6–0 on a Cambridge/Ely to Ipswich train into Haughley up platform on 18th April 1949. On the right is the station nameboard which advised intending passengers of the junction for the Mid-Suffolk Light Railway. The wagons in the background are standing on the 800 ft long siding on the site of the former light railway terminal. *W. A. Camwell*

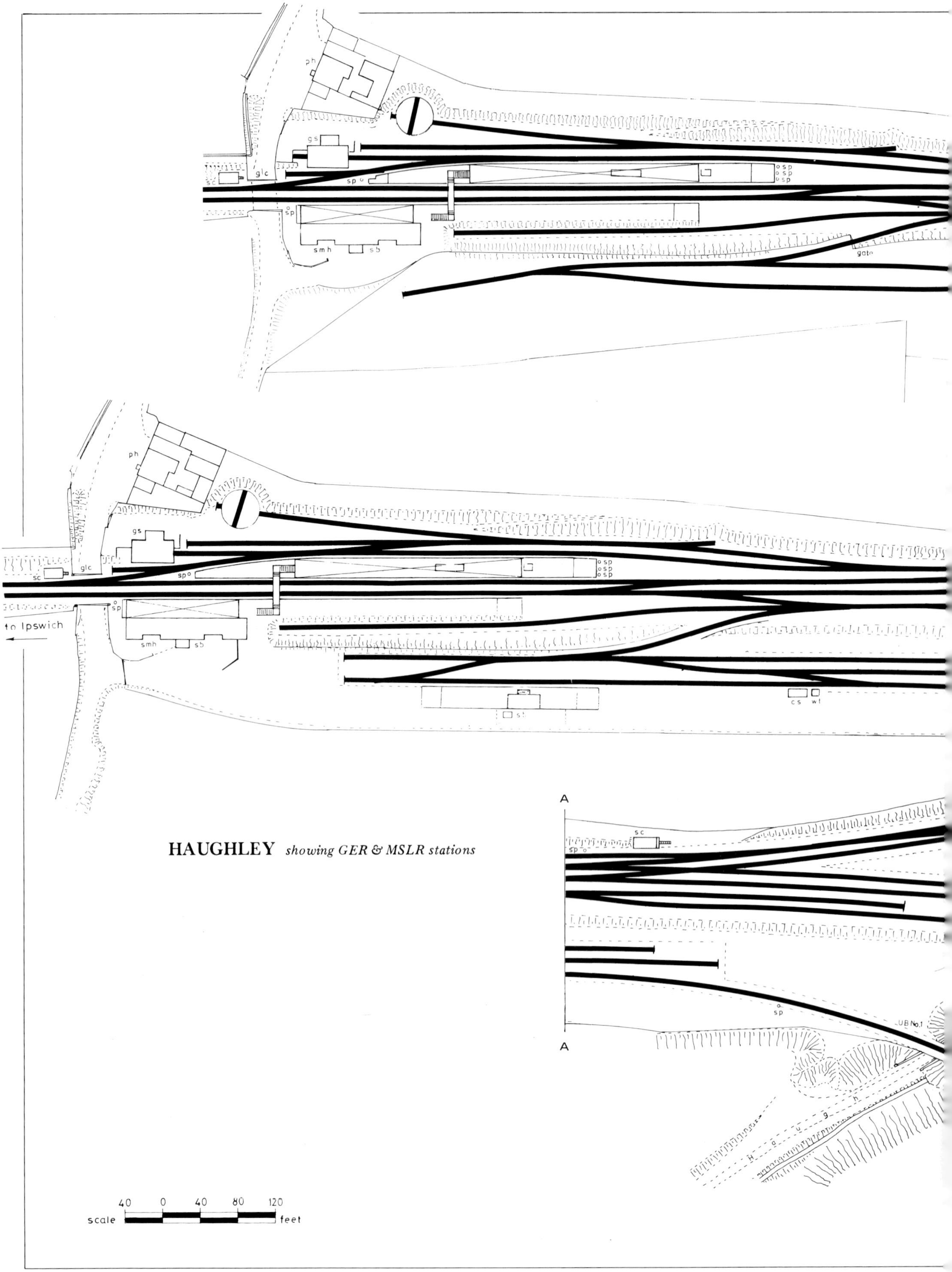

HAUGHLEY *showing GER & MSLR stations*

HAUGHLEY *showing original MSLR track layout*

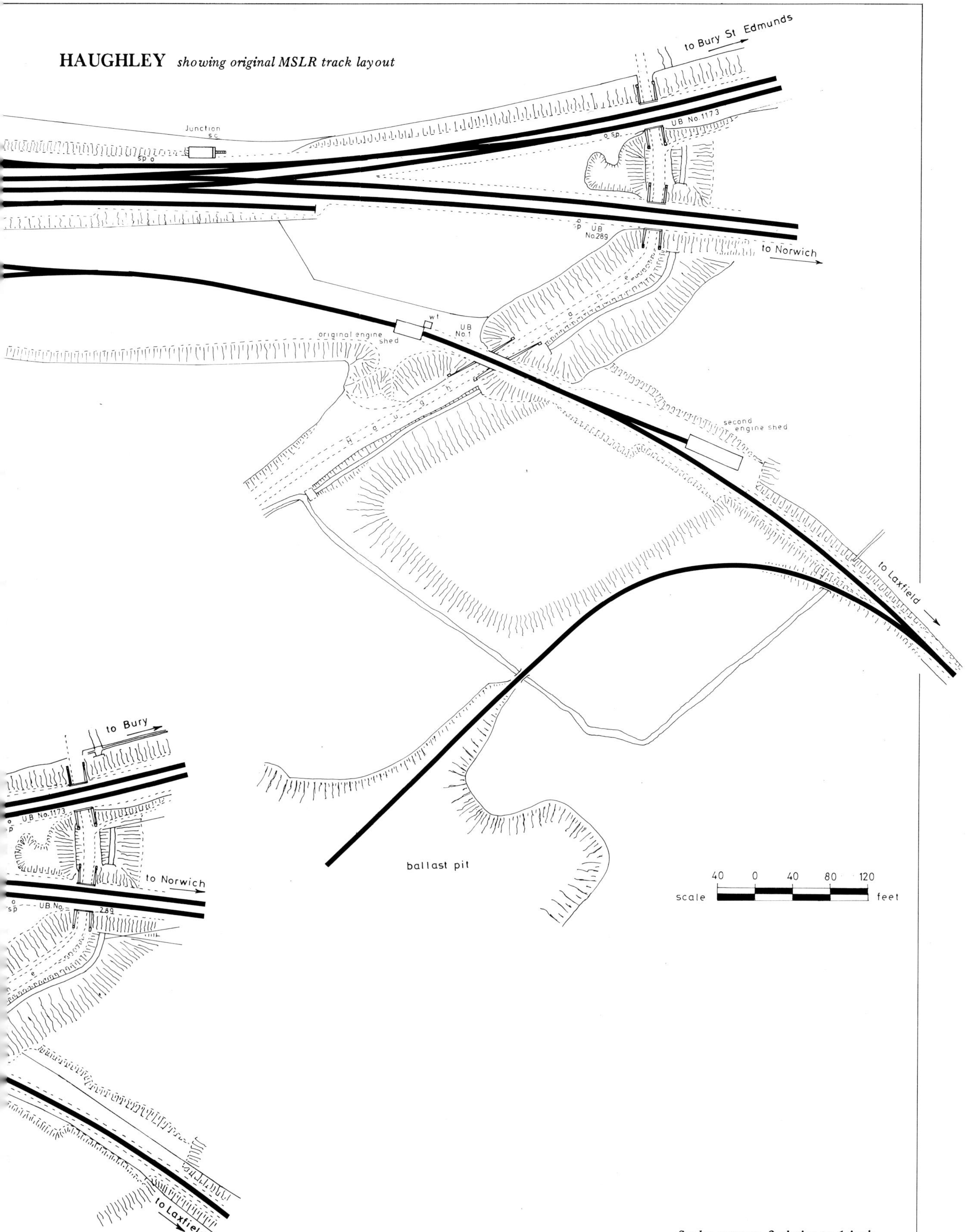

Scale: approx. 2 chains to 1 inch

The imposing station building of Haughley GER station with railway offices and rooms on the ground floor and station master's accommodation above. View from the approach road.
L & GRP

the delivery of construction materials and exchange of traffic. To this end the main line company substantiated the original temporary layout by extending the reception siding further north, parallel to the up main line, a total length of 320 feet to terminate at buffer stops almost opposite the junction of the Norwich and Bury lines. A further siding, 560 ft in length, was laid, curving slightly to run at the back of the up main line platform to terminate at buffer stops situated a few yards short of the main buildings of the GER station. The third siding penetrated the boundary fence between the Light Railway and the main line company and made a south facing

Haughley station (82 miles 75 chains from Liverpool Street) on the GER main line to Norwich was the junction for the line to Bury St. Edmunds, Cambridge and Ely and also the Mid-Suffolk Light Railway. The view from the up main line platform 420 ft long facing north shows the down side island platform 430 ft long and the footbridge connecting the platforms. In this photograph dating from 1949 the main line crossover used by the through trains from Stowmarket to Laxfield can be seen at the north end of the platforms. Mid-Suffolk services departed from the bay on the extreme right.
Lens of Sutton

The 4.00 p.m. SX empty stock train from Haughley to Stowmarket departing from Haughley behind 'J15' No. 65447. The engine and coaches then worked back from Stowmarket at 4.25 p.m. as the school train, arriving at Haughley at 4.29 p.m. After negotiating the crossover between the down and up main lines, the train continued its journey on to the branch departing the junction at 4.35 p.m. SX. As there were no school children to convey, the train departed Haughley at 3.44 p.m. on Saturdays. *Dr. I. C. Allen*

connection into the Mid-Suffolk run round loop. The work was completed early in 1903 at a cost of £840 12s. 4d. which included the necessary interlocking of points and signals operated by Haughley Junction GER signal box.

The Mid-Suffolk terminal layout by early 1904 consisted of a single line which terminated on curving track to avoid the entrance drive to the GER station. A run round loop 460 ft in length ran to the west of the main single line and was penetrated by the points leading to and from the GER interchange sidings. 1100 ft from the buffer stops and 360 ft from the north end of the loop, Jackson constructed a small engine shed, 30 ft by 12 ft, straddling the main single line as it curved away to the north east from the GER Norwich-Ipswich main line.

By September 1904 the layout had grown considerably. The existing trailing connection from the up GER main line was retained but to the north the main line company had excavated into the cutting and embankment to lay in an additional 330 ft siding to handle the exchange of traffic. To the south of these points the single siding, serving as a 560 ft long headshunt, ran to the back of the up platform of Haughley GER station.

The layout was further developed after additional land was purchased and by 1908 the main single line followed a straight course serving the single platform Mid-Suffolk, Haughley station on the east side of the formation. The south end ramp of the 185 ft long platform was 80 ft from the buffer stops. The platform was host to a double-ended, timber-framed, station building clad in zinc-coated sheets of iron in a brickwork pattern which was then painted to look like a brick building! The structure contained booking office, parcels office and staff accommodation. Other buildings on the platform included a parcels store at the north end and a gents toilet at the south end. A station nameboard and creosoted wood paling fence formed a backing to the platform. Two post type oil lamps and a

Haughley station GER signal box, located on the down side of the Ipswich-Norwich main line, controlled signals and points at the south end of the station together with the adjacent level crossing gates which were hand operated. After rationalisation of the track layout in the early 1930s the signal box was closed in May 1933 when control of points and signals was concentrated on Haughley Junction signal box. *Collection G. F. Rice*

The 11.08 a.m. mixed train to Laxfield waits to depart from the bay platform at Haughley on 18th May 1948. Apparently branch line malpractice was in operation for the class 'J15' 0—6—0 at the head of the train, No. 65407, was only fitted with a steam brake and was thus incapable of providing the Westinghouse brake to the coaching stock. In the background is the curved roof of the canopy of the waiting shelter on the down main line platform, whilst the run-round loop is in the foreground. *W. A. Camwell*

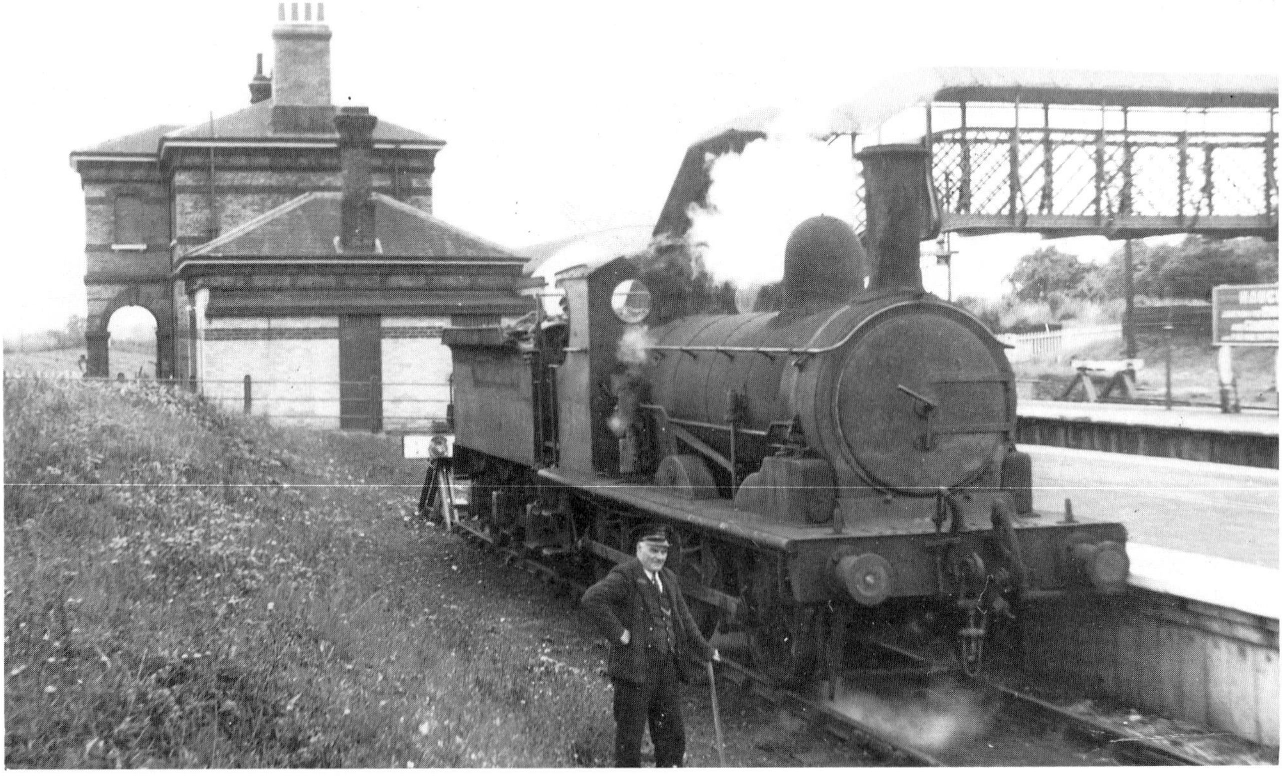

In the bay platform road at Haughley there was just enough space to accommodate a 'J15' class locomotive between the buffer stops and the hand-operated points to the run round loop. No. 65459 has acquired a BR shed plate on the smokebox door but has not been equipped with a smokebox number plate.

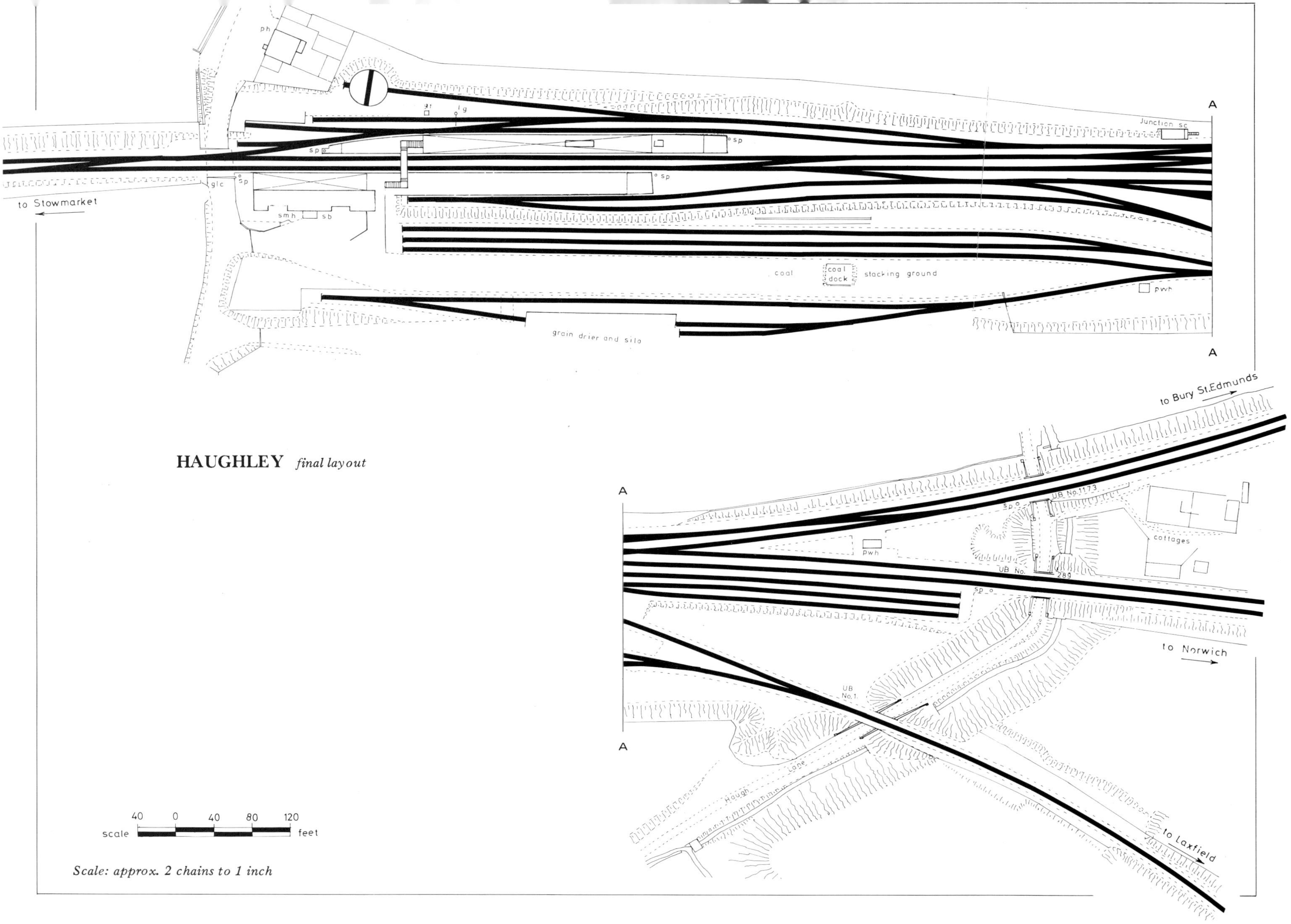

HAUGHLEY *final layout*

Scale: approx. 2 chains to 1 inch

View facing north from the up platform at Haughley on 14th September 1949 showing the crossover between the down and up main lines and the trailing connection from the up main line to the Laxfield branch. 'J15' class 0–6–0 No. 65467 departs from the down bay platform with the 11.08 a.m. to Laxfield. *B. D. J. Walsh*

Soon to go their separate ways, fireman Jack Law on 'J15' class 0–6–0 No. 65447 departing Haughley with the 11.15 a.m. to Laxfield watches 'K3' class 2–6–0 No. 61889 leave for Bury St. Edmunds. In the background beyond Haughley Junction signal box a 'B17' class 4–6–0 is held at the junction signals for an up Norwich express, 5th July 1952. *G. R. Mortimer*

A bird's eye view of the junction at Haughley taken from the top of the grain silo. The route to Bury St. Edmunds, Ely and Cambridge curves away to the west out of the left of the picture whilst a 'B1' class 4–6–0 tackles the climb away from the station with a Norwich train. In the foreground is the site of the former Mid-Suffolk station and the later connection to the main line platform. The light railway can be seen curving away to the right over Haugh Lane underbridge and up the 1 in 42 gradient. The open land on the down side of the line beyond the underbridge was the site of the second MSLR shed at Haughley. *Dr. I. C. Allen*

hanging lamp provided illumination during the hours of darkness whilst a solitary platform seat was provided for the comfort of intending passengers.

Originally the buildings at Haughley, as at other stations, were painted in the MSLR maroon/brown livery. After grouping the LNER gradually introduced their dark brown and cream style which after World War Two reverted to a drab grey livery at certain stations. Fifty feet from the buffer stops, points led to the 525 ft run-round loop which followed the same wide looping path of the original. At the north end of the loop facing points led to two sidings known as outside road, 480 ft and inside road, 390 ft. A further 250 ft siding paralleled the main single line at the south end of the run-round loop. Facing points in the run-round loop also led through the gate in the boundary fence between the MSLR and GER to the main line company's interchange sidings. By 1907 the GER were experiencing problems transferring vehicles to and from the light railway and in 1908 two north end GER exchange sidings were established, the original having been extended to a length of 470 ft whilst a second siding 450 ft long was provided. The headshunt behind the up side platform of the GER station remained at 560 ft.

The track formation of the Mid-Suffolk station remained unaltered until after amalgamation with the LNER. On 1st July 1923 the new regime, however, renamed the former GER station Haughley West to differentiate the establishment from the MSLR Haughley station. No further improvements were made until the early 1930s, possibly because the LNER management were awaiting the outcome of the enquiry of the rail to road conversion programme. Certainly passengers requiring the interchange to or from the light railway were required to walk the short distance between the ex-MSLR and West stations. In 1932/3 considerable rationalisation of signalling and track layout at Haughley was achieved. These alterations, authorised in September,

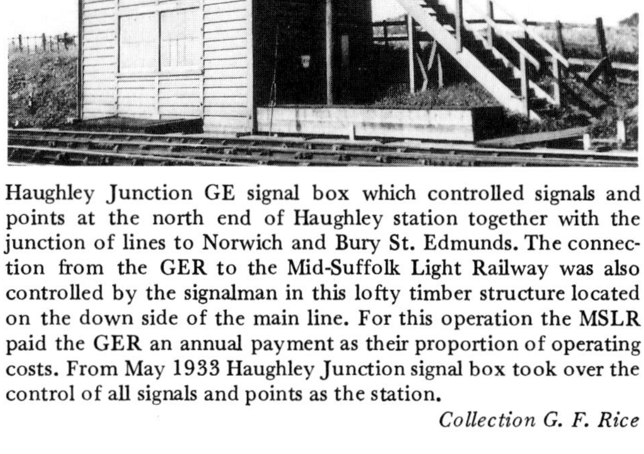

Haughley Junction GE signal box which controlled signals and points at the north end of Haughley station together with the junction of lines to Norwich and Bury St. Edmunds. The connection from the GER to the Mid-Suffolk Light Railway was also controlled by the signalman in this lofty timber structure located on the down side of the main line. For this operation the MSLR paid the GER an annual payment as their proportion of operating costs. From May 1933 Haughley Junction signal box took over the control of all signals and points as the station.

Collection G. F. Rice

'J15' No. 65447 shunting coaching stock on the Mid-Suffolk as 'D16/3' class 4—4—0 No. 62607 trundles past Haughley Junction signal box with a Cambridge-Ipswich train in 1951. In the foreground is the down loop starting signal. *Dr. I. C. Allen*

involved the abolition of the station signal box and the transfer of the control of all signals and points, including access to the Mid-Suffolk line to the junction signal box. The work was completed by the spring of 1933 and the station signal box was closed in May.

From September 1932 the station and yard, together with the MSL station, reverted to the combined name of Haughley.

The next major alterations came about as a result of the siting of a petrol dump at Haughley and the increased traffic brought about by the Second World War. The necessity to provide through access to the MSLR for military traffic and much needed fuel brought with it the relaying of the connection to the MSLR and the strengthening of the track for a quarter of a mile beyond the station limits. From November 1939 Mid-Suffolk trains were re-routed

Climbing away from the main line at Haughley, 'J15' No. 65459 makes for Laxfield with the 11.08 a.m. mixed train. The grain silo on the site of the former MSLR is under construction in the background. *Dr. I. C. Allen*

Climbing away from Haughley, 'J15' class 0–6–0 No. 65459 makes heavy work with a relatively light mixed train bound for Laxfield in January 1950. The LNER and later BR designated the former MSLR route availability 1 (RA1) but the 'J15' class were only given unrestricted clearance to work the line after all the flat bottom track had been replaced by bullhead rails in 1947. The area to the right of the engine was the site of the second engine shed built for the MSLR at Haughley. *Dr. I. C. Allen*

into the newly constructed bay platform at the back of the up main line platforms using the alignment of the former GER headshunt siding. Alongside this a loop road was provided to enable the engine to run round its train. The new alignment swung to the right beyond the platform to join up with the original MSLR main single line near Haugh Lane underbridge. The former light railway run-round loop and main single line were replaced by three long sidings whilst the old platform and station buildings were demolished. Equally at the north end of the layout an additional siding was added to the two originally installed by the GER. The points connecting the light railway with the up main line and also the run-round loop and associated signalling came under the control of Haughley Junction signal box.

In the new layout the main single line of the light railway terminated at buffer stops and served the 280 ft up bay platform. A run-round loop, 800 ft in length, was installed to the east of the main single line to enable the engine to run round its train. At the north end of the main single line, 330 ft beyond the end of the platform, a trailing connection for down trains led to the up main line. Beyond these points a facing connection led to the three interchange sidings 480, 430 and 430 ft respectively. As the main single line swung to the right to join up with the original alignment of the Mid-Suffolk route, the north end points of the run-round loop trailed in on the up side. Where the main line joined its former alignment, a single trailing connection controlled by ground frame, released from the junction signal box led to three sidings, the easterly one following the alignment of the former Mid-Suffolk main single line. Two further connections led to the two sidings installed on the former track layout and these, 940 ft and 800 ft respectively, ran parallel with the run-round loop and new main single line but on an embankment and at a higher level than the bay platform road. In the final years of the line a large grain silo was erected adjacent to and served by an additional siding with loop partly on land once occupied by the MSLR station.

After the withdrawal of light railway train services, the layout remained intact and was used for storage of permanent way and recovery trains. In 1960 further rationalisation took place when the bay platform road and run-round loop were removed. Next to go were the north end

Cab view of 'J15' No. 65447 pounding up the 1 in 42 out of Haughley with the 11.15 a.m. to Laxfield on 5th July 1952. Around the curve to the top right of the photograph is Silver Street crossing cottage. Fireman Law is driving and talking to an enthusiast invited along for the ride while driver Skinner is busy firing. *G. R. Mortimer*

interchange sidings. Goods facilities were finally withdrawn on and from 28th December 1964 whilst Haughley station closed for passenger traffic on and from 2nd July 1967. Today very little remains of the station buildings and what is left is utilized as a signal box to control the level crossing gates and immediate protecting signals. The junction for Bury St. Edmunds has been altered to single line connection in the down direction from the down main line. Up trains now gain the up main line via a crossover. Signals and point movements at the junction were under the control of Haughley signal box situated in the old station building but since electrification have been controlled from Colchester power signal box.

Leaving Haughley, the Mid-Suffolk Light Railway negotiated a 20 chain right-hand curve, climbing away from the main line to Norwich on a 1 in 42 gradient over Haugh Lane underbridge No. 1 at 0 miles 18 chains. Just south of the bridge was the site of the first engine shed at Haughley, 30 ft long, which actually straddled the main single line. It originally provided accommodation for the locomotive hired by Jackson, the contractor, and the 0–6–0 tank engine *Lady Stevenson.* This shed was totally inconvenient once construction of the line commenced, and it was later removed. A few yards beyond Haugh Lane underbridge on the down side of the line was the site of the second Haughley engine shed, located at the end of a 150 ft long siding entered by facing points from the main single line. This 60 ft long shed was initially used as a replacement for the inconveniently situated shed astride the main single line and housed Jackson's *Lady Stevenson.* When the Mid-Suffolk commenced the working of goods trains, one of the Mid-Suffolk engines was outbased at the shed with the other at Kenton but after March 1905 the second engine was shedded at Laxfield and in July 1905 the Board of Trade inspector requested the removal of the connection.

Beyond the site of the former engine shed siding, the main single line continued climbing at 1 in 42 before straightening out for a short section at the commencement of which the site of the former ballast siding had trailed in on the up side. The siding, some 750 ft in length, curved away to the east to serve ballast pits which supplied the initial ballast for the permanent way when the track was laid. The pits were exhausted by the end of 1903 and when Lieutenant Colonel Von Donop made his inspection in 1905 he requested the removal of the temporary connection leading from the main single line.

The 1.45 p.m. Laxfield to Haughley train, hauled again by 'J15' No. 65447, descending the 1 in 42 gradient past Haughley branch outer home signal on 8th June 1952. In the background, just to the right of the Locomotive cab, can be seen the MSLR crossing keeper's cottage at Silver Street. The section of track over which the train is travelling was strengthened during World War Two to enable heavier engines to shunt Haughley yard and assist ammunition trains away from Haughley. *G. R. Mortimer*

No. 65447 again, this time pounding up the 1 in 42 out of Haughley past the up outer home signal with the two-coach 3.55 p.m. SO Haughley-Laxfield train on 28th June 1952.

The climb continued past the up outer home signal installed by the LNER to a minor summit at Silver Street level crossing, protected by gates, for many years under the control of Mrs. Bloom, the resident gatekeeper who lived in the cottage adjacent to the line. A run of half a mile on undulating gradients, initially falling at 1 in 50 first curving slightly to the right and then left, brought the line to High Road, Old Newton level crossing where the B1113 Finningham to Stowmarket Road crossed the railway and was protected by gates. These were also opened and closed by a resident gatekeeper who resided in the adjacent gate-house provided by the company. Beyond High Road crossing the line fell at 1 in 100 to cross the valley of the infant River Gipping. The stream was bridged by a culvert as the railway climbed again at 1 in 50 before levelling out on the approach to the open level crossing at Brown Street. During the early construction of the railway, a 200 ft long siding was located on the up side of the line, 680 ft west of Brown Street crossing. It was used for the contractor's locomotive and equipped with a water tank at the Laxfield end, on the south side of the main single line so that the engine could be topped up with water whilst standing on the main line or siding. Brown Street crossing, where the back road from Ford's Green to Old Newton crossed the railway, was protected by cattle guards and, as at other open crossings on the light railway, notices bearing the figure 10 were erected 300 yards on both rail approaches, to advise the drivers of trains to restrict their speed to 10 miles per hour within 200 yards of and over the ungated crossing. The figures on the notices were of the same ornate style as those used on station nameboards. From Brown Street the railway followed a straight course climbing at 1 in 50 to clear the 200 ft contour. After breasting a minor summit, the railway swung to the right on a 40 chain radius curve to cross open fields and an occupational foot-path crossing. Following another short straight section the line descended at 1 in 400/100/50 curving sharply to the left on a 20 chain radius curve to cross the bridle track known as Gipping Lane by an ungated crossing. Beside Gipping Lane crossing was the remote Gipping siding, 2 miles 44 chains ex-Haughley, located on the up or south side of the main single line. The siding was in the form of a loop, 480 ft in length from the facing to trailing points, with points released by Annett's key attached to the train staff. It was used mainly for agricultural traffic and had a 102 ft long spur at the west end and 40 ft spur at the east end of the loop, with a 200 ft headshunt between the points.

Gipping siding saw little use after World War Two although during the early years of hostilities it was occasionally utilized for the storage of loaded ammunition wagons *en route* to Mendlesham or Horham. If the weight of the train was too heavy for the 'J15' class 0–6–0 tender engines, the second portion of the train was left in the siding whilst the first portion was delivered. The engine then returned for the remainder of the trucks. Empties were also stored occasionally if Haughley yard was congested with wagons. The flat bottom track in the siding was in a bad state of repair and overgrown with weeds in the final years.

Beyond Gipping siding the light railway followed a straight undulating course bisecting initially a bridle track

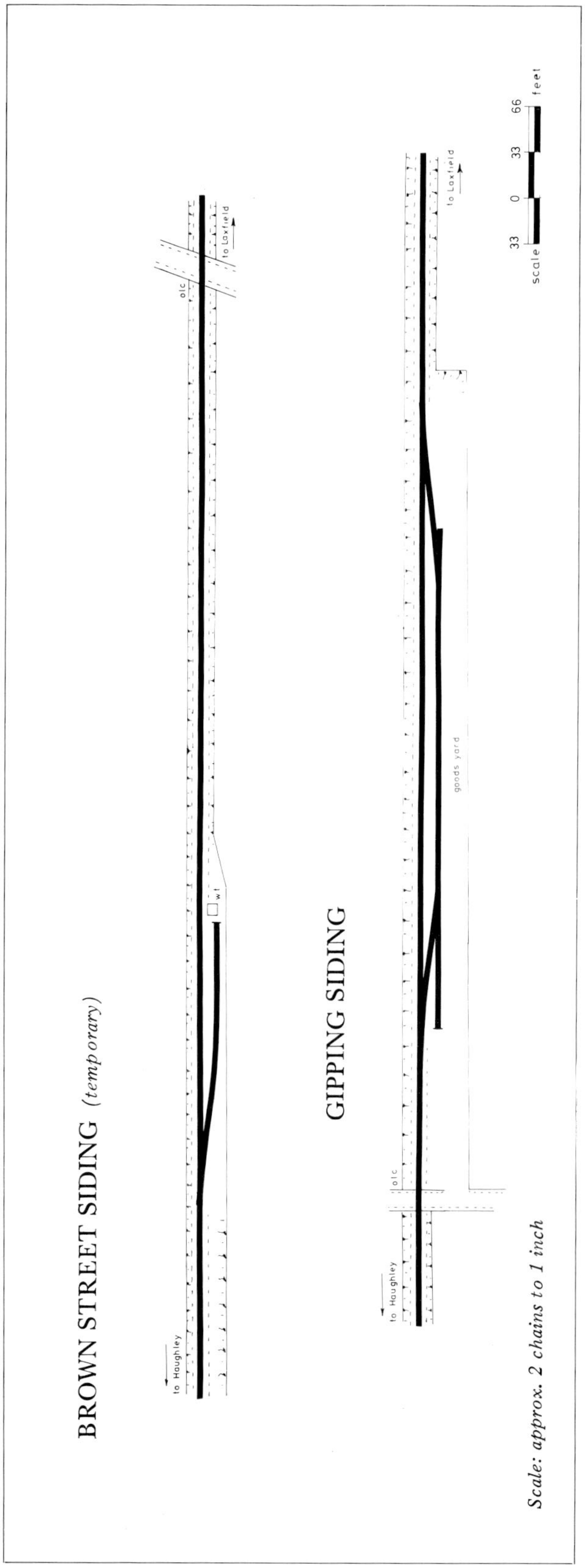

Mendlesham station facing Haughley with a down train hauled by 'J15' class 0–6–0 No. 65467 approaching. The 550 ft long loop siding serving the goods yard is beyond the platform. In the absence of the gate, laying against the bank on the left, the level crossing was partly protected by a rope strung across the roadway, to which a red flag was attached. *D. Thompson*

'J15' class 0–6–0 No. 65447 again, approaching Mendlesham with the 11.15 a.m. Haughley to Laxfield mixed train on 26th June 1952. To the right is the dock siding serving the loading/cattle dock. Although the main single line is laid with bullhead rails, the siding retains the original 56 lbs per yard flat bottom track. The single lever ground frame was released by Annetts Key on the train staff, used to operate the points to the siding. *R. F. Roberts*

Mendlesham station, 4 miles 37 chains from Haughley. This view, taken facing Laxfield, shows the 130 ft long platform on the down side of the main single line and level crossing gates protecting the Mendlesham to Stowmarket road beyond. The buffer stops to the left are at the end of the spur siding serving the loading dock. *Lens of Sutton*

connecting Grange Farm and Redhouse Farm and then half a mile further on the Cotton to Mendlesham Green road at Wimble open level crossing. The railway then swung to the right before entering a short straight stretch of track on a falling gradient of 1 in 100 over the Mendlesham to Mendlesham Green road by another ungated level crossing. Views of the moated Mendlesham Hall were to be seen on the down side of the line before the railway negotiated a 20 chain radius left-hand curve over yet another occupational open crossing, which carried a bridle track from Mendlesham to Hawkins from across the line.

The light railway then swung to the right on a 20 chain radius right-hand curve past a goods yard, to enter Mendlesham station (4 miles 37 chains from Haughley). The straight platform, 130 ft long and 2 ft 9 ins above rail level, with brick facing walls on the down side, was host to the standard timber-framed, corrugated iron-clad, standard double-ended station building provided by the MSLR.

A close-up of the timber-framed, corrugated iron-clad, double-ended station building at Mendlesham complete with its decorative finials and end boarding. As already mentioned, buildings were originally painted Victorian brown, the same colour as the rolling stock, but the LNER later introduced a cream yellow up and brown lower section, and in the latter years they were painted grey. *Lens of Sutton*

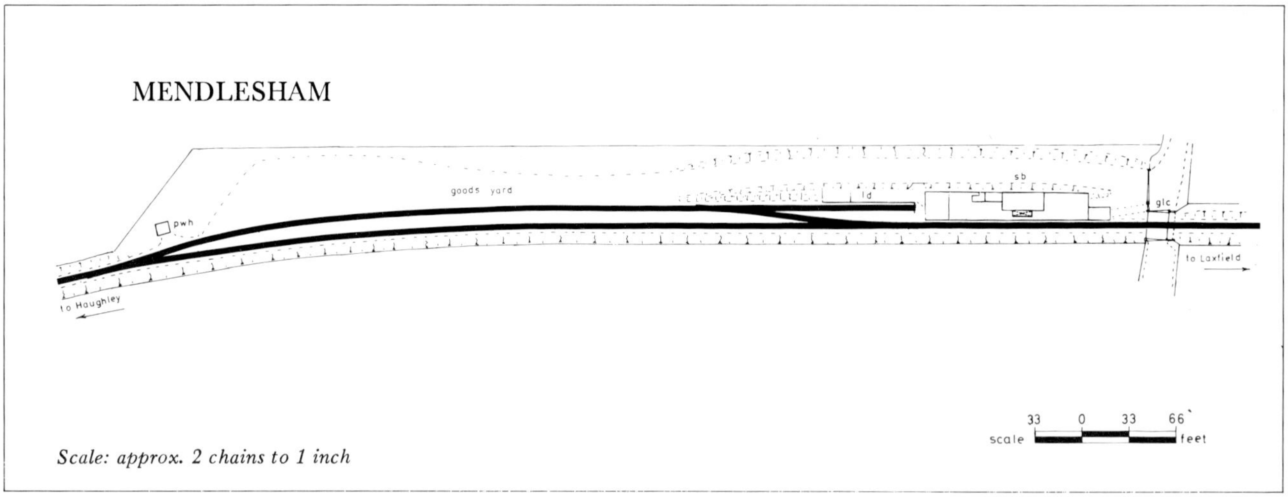

The double-ended, timber-framed, corrugated iron-clad station building at Mendlesham, looking towards Haughley on 14th July 1952.
B. D. J. Walsh

No. 65447 leaving Mendlesham with the 11.15 a.m. Haughley to Laxfield train formed of ex-GE bogie two-set in June 1952. The impending closure of the line is evident as the PW staff have allowed the grass to grow on the banks each side of the track. *R. F. Roberts*

The ornate station nameboard and creosoted wooden fencing at Mendlesham, typical of all stations on the MSLR. The roadway in the background led to the goods yard. *C. S. Bayes*

The structure included a small booking office at one end and a store room at the other end, separated by an open waiting shed which had a small ornate canopy fronting the building over the platform. To the west of the main building was a corrugated iron store shed and gentlemen's toilet. An ornate station nameboard and two posts and one wall-mounted oil lamp completed the amenities on the tarmac-covered platform. Immediately west of the station, on the down side and curving parallel with the main single line, was the 550 long loop siding serving the goods yard, entered by facing and trailing points from the main single line. A 140 ft long spur was provided at the east end of the siding terminating at buffer stops immediately at the west end of the station platform. This spur served the loading dock at the east end of the goods yard whilst at the west end of the yard were the coal grounds of local coal merchants. Road access to and from the yard was via a gate and roadway leading behind the station. The siding was devoid of a loading gauge.

Leaving Mendlesham station, the main single line immediately crossed the road leading from Mendlesham to Stowmarket, the level crossing protected by gates being opened and closed by station staff. Beyond the level crossing the line followed a short straight course before curving to the left and then straightening out for a quarter of a mile before bisecting another road leading from Mendle-

The 11.15 a.m. Haughley to Laxfield mixed train negotiating the cutting beyond the A140 Norwich road overbridge No. 2 at 5 miles 42 chains between Mendlesham and Brockford on Saturday, 28th June 1952. With a life of only four weeks, the branch was attracting the attention of railway enthusiasts, one of whom has secured a ride on the footplate of 'J15' No. 65447. This view makes an interesting comparison to the photograph taken when the bridge and cutting were under construction.
G. R. Mortimer

View from the tender of 'J15' class 0–6–0 No. 65447 hauling the 11.15 a.m. Haughley to Laxfield mixed train on 5th July 1952, approaching the A140 Norwich-Ipswich road bridge. The structure had brick abutments and wing walls supporting cast iron girders with a 16 ft skew span across the railway. It was located in a cutting approached on both sides by a falling gradient to obviate the provision of a level crossing. The temporary line of rails ran along the top of the embankment to the left of the picture when the railway first opened. *G. R. Mortimer*

sham to Hill Farm by an ungated level crossing protected by cattle guards. Beyond the crossing the line crossed a small stream by a culvert and swung slightly to the right across arable country. Bucks occupational crossing heralded the approach of a cutting as the line swung to the left before following a straight course, falling initially at 1 in 50 to pass under overbridge No. 2 at 5 miles 42 chains from Haughley, which carried the Ipswich to Norwich A140 road across the railway. The structure had brick abutments and wing walls supporting cast iron girders with a 16 ft skew span across the railway. The distance between the corrugated iron parapets was 22 ft and the bridge span was 15 ft above the top of the rails.

Climbing out of the cutting at 1 in 50, the line curved slightly to the right with views of the hamlet of Brockford Green on the up side of the railway. The road from Brockford Green to Wetheringsett approached from the south before crossing the railway at Stulphs Road gated level crossing near Knaves Green. Here the gates were opened and closed by a resident gatekeeper and later by train men. A hundred or so yards further on, the line crossed the Wetheringsett to Mickfield road, protected by a gated level crossing, where the gates were opened and closed by station staff, to enter Brockford and Wetheringsett station (6 miles 4 chains ex-Haughley). The straight platform on the down or north side of the main single line was the statutory 130 ft in length and 2 ft 9 ins above rail level. Despite the rather grandiose title, the station was open to the elements with only a small timber-framed, corrugated iron-clad hut at the Laxfield end of the platform, serving as a booking office-cum-staff room and store. A smaller shed at the back of and midway along the platform served as a waiting shelter for intending passengers. The amenities were completed by three post-mounted platform oil lamps later reduced to one adjacent to the ornate nameboard which proclaimed BROCKFORD only. The ornate cast iron lettering used at all stations and peculiar to the Mid-Suffolk Light Railway, was supplied by Walter Macfarlane Ltd. in 1908. At the west end of the platform was a large noticeboard whilst an old waiting room bench provided seating

'J15' No. 65459 rouses the echoes as she departs from Brockford and Wetheringsett with the morning mixed train from Laxfield to Haughley in February 1952. The leading vehicle is bogie brake third E62181E. Note the dilapidated condition of the level crossing gate with bars missing and the wicket gate wedged in the open position. *Lens of Sutton*

The simple wayside Brockford and Wetheringsett station viewed from the road facing Laxfield. Beyond the 130 ft long platform located on the down side of the main single line is the small goods yard with its 455 ft long siding. Although the gradient in the yard was level, the main line descended at 1 in 50 beyond the points leading to the siding and this made shunting rather difficult. *Lens of Sutton*

Typical of the smaller MSLR stations, the remote Brockford and Wetheringsett view across the field from the Wetheringsett to Mickfield road in 1951. The gate to the right led to the goods yard with the corrugated iron-clad booking office/staff room at the end of the platform and waiting shed to the centre. The whole of the platform was backed by creosoted paling fencing. *Lens of Sutton*

The simple wayside station at Brockford viewed from the train, facing Haughley, on 14th September 1949. The PW ganger on his bicycle obviously has no care for customer relations with his boot on the platform seat. *B. D. J. Walsh*

Sylvan scene with the morning service from Laxfield to Haughley entering Brockford station behind 'J15' class 0–6–0 No. 65459 in February 1952. As the 'J15s' working the line operated tender first in one direction, the tender attached to 65459 is fitted with a timber built back plate. Despite the remote siting of this wayside station, a number of passengers are waiting to join the train. *Lens of Sutton*

for those awaiting the infrequent service of trains. The whole of the platform was backed by creosoted paling fencing whilst public access to the station was via a gate adjacent to the level crossing at the west end of the platform.

Brockford goods yard, also located on the down side of the line, was served by a single siding with access via a trailing connection operated from a ground frame, released by Annett's key and located 265 ft east of the end of the platform ramp. The single siding, 455 ft in length, split into two sections, 165 ft west of and 290 ft east of the points leading from the main single line, the latter serving a loading dock. Road access to the goods yard was via a gate at the west end of the yard leading from a small side road which ran parallel to the railway.

Away from Brockford and Wetheringsett, the line descended at 1 in 50, veering to the right on a 25 chain curve to cross the valley of a small stream, passing on the

Brockford station, facing Haughley, on 17th July 1952, with a brake van and open wagon standing on the main single line by the level crossing gates while the engine shunts the station siding. The height of the brick-fronted platform, 2 ft 9 ins, was common to all MSLR stations. The GER waiting room seat to the right was in use as a platform bench. *R. F. Roberts*

BROCKFORD & WETHERINGSETT

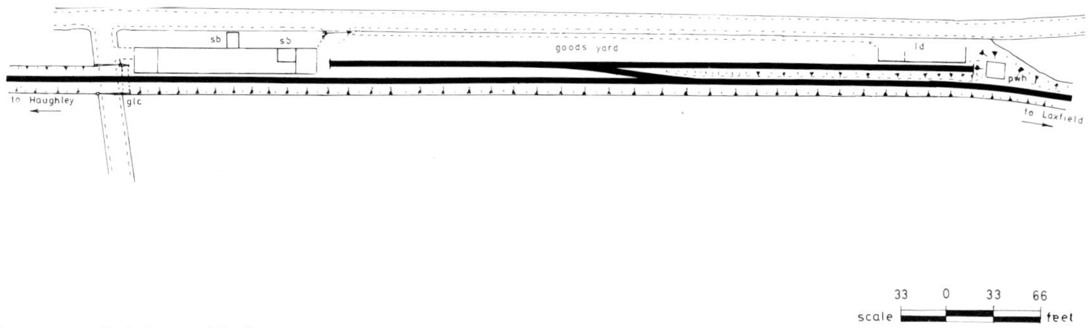

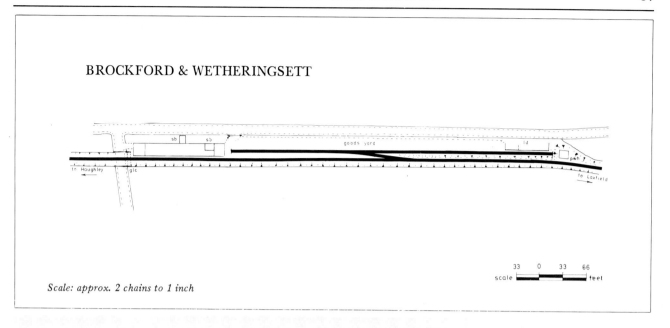

Scale: approx. 2 chains to 1 inch

Brockford and Wetheringsett station, facing Haughley, with the 130 ft long platform located on the down or north side of the main single line. Both buildings were timber-framed, corrugated iron-clad structures. The level crossing gates of MSLR style located at the west end of the platform protected the Wetheringsett to Mickfield road and were opened and closed for the passage of each train by station staff.

D. Thompson

Aspall and Thorndon station, facing Haughley. At the west end of the platform is the level crossing protecting the B1077 Debenham to Eye Road. Aspall station, as well as serving the district of that name to the south of the line, also served the village of Thorndon 3½ miles to the north-east and was advertised as the station for Debenham 2½ miles to the south. Of course, had the Kenton to Westerfield line been completed, Debenham would have had its own station. *D. Thompson*

Aspall and Thorndon station, 8 miles 41 chains ex-Haughley, facing Laxfield, with the 130 ft long platform on the down side of the main single line. The timber-framed corrugated iron-clad main building at Aspall, formerly a contractor's hut, differed from the other structures in having only a central door leading to the booking office and waiting room, and at the west end of the platform was a lock-up store. *Lens of Sutton*

down side another of the many moated houses common to the district. The gradient changed dramatically as the line swung to the right on a 20 chain radius curve to cross the Blacksmith's Green to Brockford station lane by another ungated level crossing protected by cattle guards. A fairly straight course followed as the railway passed the hamlet of Blacksmith's Green, a quarter of a mile to the south of the line, before negotiating Roses Road gated level crossing, originally opened and closed by a resident gate-keeper and later by train men.

The road crossing the railway connected Blacksmith's Green and Thorndon. After negotiating a slight left-hand curve beyond the level crossing, the light railway ran for nearly three-quarters of a mile in a straight but undulating course with fluctuating changes of gradient. Beyond Hestley Green occupational crossing, the line negotiated a short 25 chain radius right-hand curve, climbing once again above the 200 ft contour at 1 in 100. A further left-hand curve brought the line across open arable country to Aspall station level crossing, the seventh gated crossing on the line, which was opened and closed by station staff at Aspall. Immediately beyond the crossing the line entered Aspall and Thorndon station (8 miles 41 chains ex-Haughley), serving the district of Aspall to the south of the line, the village of Thorndon 3½ miles to the north-east, and was also advertised by the railway company as the station for Debenham 2½ miles to the south. The brick-faced 130 ft long platform, 2 ft 9 ins high, on the down side of the line had another of the ubiquitous station buildings of timber framing with corrugated iron cladding similar to the standard two-end office type provided by the light railway company. The building at Aspall, however, only had a central door leading to the booking office and waiting rooms and was formerly a contractor's hut. The structure was devoid of the central waiting shed and ornate awning fronting on to the platform. A small timber frame corrugated building serving as a lock-up store stood alongside the main building at the west end of the platform. Public access to the station was by a gate at the west end of the platform adjacent to the B1077 Debenham-Eye road level crossing. Illumination during the hours of darkness was provided by two post-mounted oil lamps, one each side of the buildings and a wall-mounted oil lamp by the booking office door. A single nameboard denoting ASPALL was mounted on posts constructed of old rails whilst a platform seat was also provided against the main building. Neat gardens with rambler roses enhanced the scene and during the summer months effectively concealed most of the creosoted timber paling fencing backing the platform.

Four hundred and fifty feet beyond the platform end, trailing points for trains in the down direction, controlled by key on the train staff, provided access from the main single line to Aspall and Thorndon goods yard siding located on the up side. As at Brockford, Aspall goods yard could only be shunted effectively by down mixed or goods services, although special traffic was shunted using pinch-bars and the tow rope attached to the engine, standing on the main single line. The single siding was 660 ft in length, split into two sections, 475 ft west of the points and 185 ft east of the points from the main line. The loading dock was located at the centre of the yard siding. Public access to the

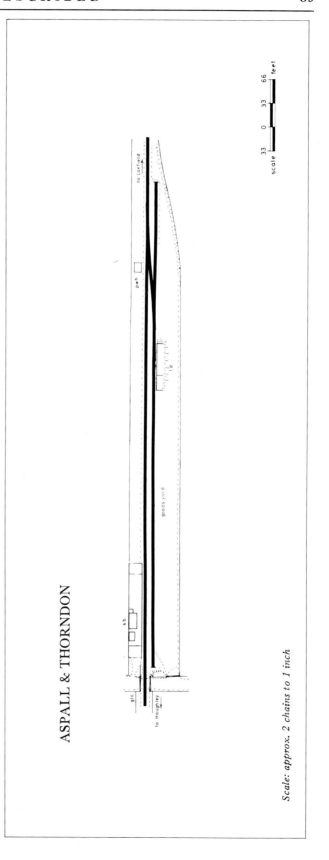

ASPALL & THORNDON

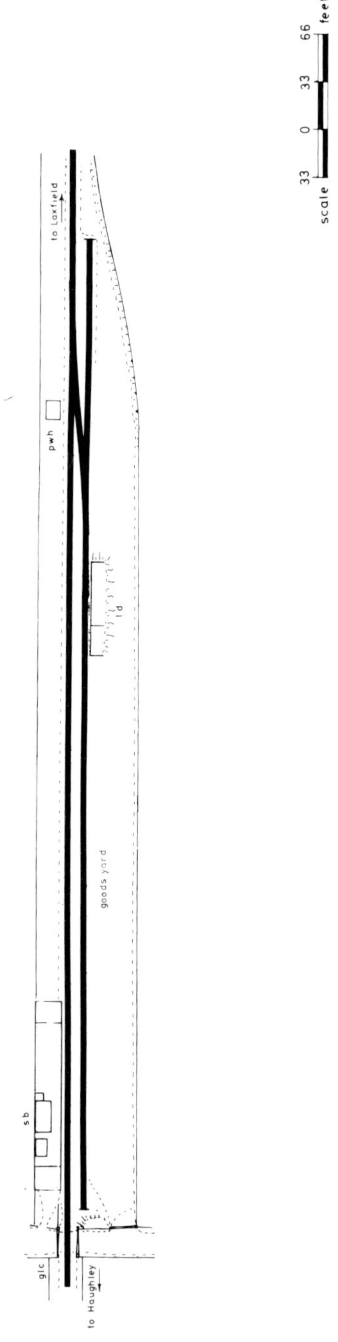

Scale: approx. 2 chains to 1 inch

KENTON *1903 track layout and site of first engine shed*

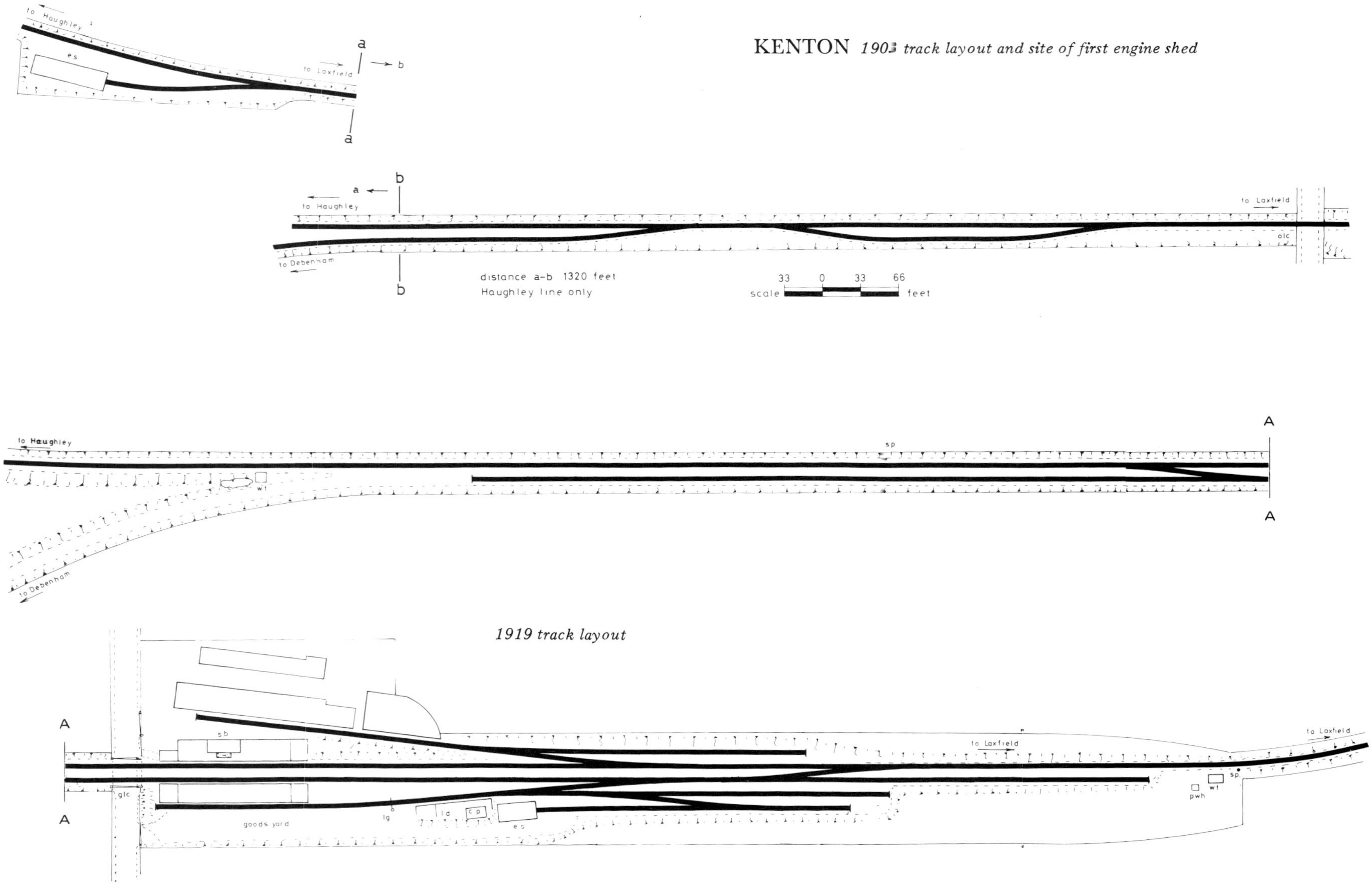

Scale: approx. 2 chains to 1 inch

The approach to Kenton station viewed from the cab of 'J15' class 0–6–0 No. 65447 standing at the down home signal. This lower quadrant signal was supplied by Mackenzie and Holland. *Dr. I. C. Allen*

goods yard was via a gate from the Debenham-Eye road. Aspall yard was chiefly noted for handling coal and sugar beet traffic.

Away from Aspall and Thorndon, the single track railway continued a straight course for two hundred yards, climbing slightly before curving to the right to follow an east-south-easterly course across remote countryside before passing the trees of Low Plantation on the south side of the line. Beyond the copse the railway turned sharply to the north-east on a 20 chain radius curve, passing over an occupational crossing. A short straight section took the railway past the site of the original Kenton engine shed, 60 ft by 12 ft, and its single 170 ft siding, with access from the main single line by trailing points for down trains. The light railway then negotiated a 40 chain radius left-hand curve before following a straight course past the locomotive water tank, on the up side of the line and the adjacent pond which supplied the necessary water. Immediately beyond the tank the trackbed of the former Debenham branch curved in from the right. The main single line then ran parallel to a long siding which was all that remained in the latter years of the intended line to Westerfield. A lower quadrant down home signal on the north side of the line heralded the approach to Kenton before trailing points from the up loop led to the gated level crossing where the railway bisected the Kenton to Rishangles road. Immediately beyond the gates the line entered Kenton station (10 miles 1 chain ex-Haughley) with the crossing loop 858 ft between points. The down loop line and up side loop line served the down and up side platforms respectively, each 130 ft in length. The up side platform was an island although the track at the back of the platform had no connection with the up loop line at the west end and terminated at buffer stops. This platform was mostly grass covered in later years and, being devoid of buildings, had only an ornate station nameboard and solitary post type oil lamp.

The down side platform in contrast possessed the standard Mid-Suffolk double-ended station building with offices at each end separated by an open-fronted waiting shed with canopy over the platform. As at the other stations, the timber-framed corrugated iron-clad structure was adorned with ornate bargeboards and end finials. The structure contained the booking office, staff room and parcels store. The usual creosoted paling fencing backed the platform whilst a solitary station nameboard was placed west of the building. Illumination during the hours of darkness was by two post-mounted oil lamps, one at each end of the platform and a wall-mounted lamp under the open-fronted waiting shelter. Kenton station served the hamlet of Kenton, a mile to the south of the railway.

In addition to the crossing loop, the track layout here consisted of the single 430 ft Mill Siding on the down side

The thrice-weekly goods 1.30 p.m. Haughley to Laxfield enters Kenton Junction behind 'J15' class No. 65407. The line to the left was part of the proposed line to Westerfield which was laid for almost two miles to the outskirts of Debenham before lack of finance forced the scheme to be aborted. Beyond the buffer stops is the water tank fed from a pond by an ancient petrol engine. Driver G. Rouse, who had previously driven the Beyer-Garratt class 'U1' 2–8–8–2 on the Wath incline before transferring to Laxfield, is in charge of the much smaller 'J15'. *Dr. I. C. Allen*

Kenton station (10 miles 1 chain ex Haughley) facing Laxfield with 'J15' 0–6–0 No. 65447 standing at the up platform with the 1.45 p.m. Laxfield to Haughley train on 17th July 1952. The 858 ft long crossing loop served up and down platforms both 130 ft in length. The double track level crossing (the only one on the light railway) carried the Kenton to Rishangles road across the railway. Protection was afforded by GER style gates. The hamlet of Kenton was a mile south of the railway. *R. F. Roberts*

A view across the level crossing gates as 'J15' class 0–6–0 No. 65447 departs Kenton with a Laxfield to Haughley train on 16th April 1952. The level crossing gates, unlike others on the line, are of Great Eastern manufacture. *R. M. Casserley*

of the line, with access via trailing points from the down crossing loop line, 310 ft east of the platform ramp. At the western end, this siding initially served the premises of Harry Capon. In later years the siding was extended 290 ft at the east end and later served East Anglian Farmers Co-operative Ltd. On the up side of the line was the western reception siding, 705 ft long, occupying the former course of the Debenham branch which terminated at buffer stops. Another reception siding, 350 ft long, ran parallel to the main single line as a continuation of the up loop line at the Laxfield end of the station. Branching from the up loop line was the 480 ft dock siding serving the cattle dock which terminated at the back of the up platform. Two other sidings were located at the eastern end of the station. One, 340 ft long, formed a headshunt for the dock road siding whilst points from this led to the former engine shed

'J15' class 0–6–0 No. 5459 pauses at Kenton with the 1.50 p.m. Laxfield to Haughley train on 18th April 1949. The station buildings on the down side platform are painted in grey livery. *W. A. Camwell*

Kenton station, 10 miles 1 chain from Haughley, looking towards Laxfield, showing the 858 ft long crossing loop serving the down platform (left) and up platform, both 130 ft in length. At the back of the up platform is the 480 ft long dock siding serving the cattle dock and equipped with a loading gauge. Apparently it was the MSL Company's intention to use the outer face of the up platform for Westerfield trains to connect with Halesworth to Haughley trains, the Westerfield train departing from the back platform after the departure of the Haughley train. This idea was shelved and the intended line at the back of the up platform assumed the role of a dead end siding.

Lens of Sutton

siding, 305 ft long, split into two sections, the eastern end forming a 65 ft headshunt and the western end 240 ft serving the small 30 ft second engine shed at Kenton. Dock road siding was equipped with a fixed loading gauge, one of those supplied by the GER.

During the building of the railway, the Mid-Suffolk Company originally laid a 350 ft passing loop to the west of the level crossing at Kenton. This was essentially to allow the engine handling the contractor's train to run round wagons if travelling from Debenham to Haughley or vice-versa. This was removed when the station was sited east of the level crossing. It is thought that the original intention of the company was to provide an island platform only between the loop lines east of the level crossing and this was in fact built. The plan was later abandoned in favour of the crossing loop with platforms on the outer faces of

Kenton down side platform viewed from the train facing towards Haughley on 14th September 1949. At the back of the platform terminating at buffer stops is the 430 ft long Mill siding.

B. D. J. Walsh

View from the train of the up platform at Kenton, looking towards Haughley on 1st September 1951. *H. C. Casserley*

A busy time at Kenton as 'J15' class 0–6–0 No. 65447 working the 11.08 a.m. Haughley to Laxfield mixed train enters the down platform while sister locomotive No. 65361 waits in the up loop line with the Laxfield to Haughley goods in 1951. *Dr. I. C. Allen*

A break during shunting operations at Kenton as guard Peachey Betts poses for the camera. 'J15' class 0–6–0 No. 65388 working the Laxfield to Haughley goods stands on the up loop line with a train which includes a horse-box. In the far distance can be seen the up home signal and east end water tank. *Dr. I. C. Allen*

After shunting at Kenton, the driver of 'J15' No. 65447 collects the Kenton-Laxfield split staff from the porter-in-charge on 5th July 1952. As wagons were deposited in the up side yard, the train, the 11.15 a.m. Haughley to Laxfield, is departing from the up loop line and the engine is negotiating the crossover to the main single line. In the background is the premises of the East Anglian Farmers Co-operative Ltd. *G. R. Mortimer*

A 'regular' performer on the light railway, 'J65' class 0–6–0 No. 8212 darkens the landscape departing from Kenton with a down mixed train in the summer of 1947. No. 8212 was withdrawn in the following November without receiving her BR number. As GER No. 157 and later LNER 7157 she had first deputised on the light railway in June 1919 and after the closure of the Eye branch in 1931 was often outbased at Laxfield. *Dr. I. C. Allen*

the loop. The down platform was built complete with station building before the original island platform was demolished. Once this platform was removed the up loop line was laid parallel with the down loop and a new platform built on the south side of the up loop. Apparently it was intended to use the outer face of the island platform for Westerfield trains to connect with Halesworth to Haughley trains, the Westerfield train departing from the back platform after the departure of the Haughley train.

Just prior to the withdrawal of the six-wheel ex-GE coaches 'J15' class 0–6–0 No. 65459 works a down mixed train beyond Kenton with a main line bogie composite substituting for a 6-wheel composite, a 6-wheel brake third and an LNER Toad E goods brake. The bogie vehicle had been worked from Ipswich to Haughley earlier that morning. *Dr. I. C. Allen*

This idea was shelved and the intended line at the back of the platform later assumed the role of a dead end siding.

An interesting working at Kenton was operated when brake vans were exchanged. The crossing loops then became effectively bi-directional, the down train using the up loop and platform and the up train using the down loop and platform. It is known that officialdom frowned upon such practice but turned a blind eye to the operation unless inspections were being made. Normal left-hand running persisted at all other times.

Leaving Kenton, the main single line continued on a straight course, passing both the up home signal and engine water tank (served by a well) located on the south side of the line, and bisecting occupational crossing No. 61 before curving slightly to the left and then right, to follow a fairly straight section over an open level crossing, protected by cattle guards, where a narrow byway from Monk Soham Green to Bedingfield Street crossed the railway. Climbing at 1 in 100, within a quarter of a mile the line crossed Flemings Hall open level crossing, where the moated hall could be viewed on the down side of the railway. Curving slightly to the right beyond the crossing, the light railway continued its north-easterly course over undulating gradients, with the moated Bedingfield Hall on the up side of the line. A minor summit was approached on gradients of 1 in 100/50 as the line negotiated two occupational crossings in quick succession where footpaths bisected the line. With the village of Southolt away to the north, the railway then curved to the right on a 40 chain radius curve to cross Shop Street gated level crossing with its adjacent gate-

Passenger's view of a scene so typical of the rural Mid-Suffolk Railway. The train, hauled by a 'J15' class 0–6–0, is halted at Shop Street level crossing for the fireman to open the gates for the train to cross the road. After the train had passed through, the guard closed the gates again across the railway, 1st September 1951. *H. C. Casserley*

Much of the extensive running time between Haughley and Laxfield was in later years occupied by train crews opening and shutting the gated level crossings on the light railway after resident crossing keepers were withdrawn. On 5th July 1952 'J15' No. 65447, working the 11.15 a.m. Haughley to Laxfield mixed train, has halted short of Shop Street crossing near Worlingworth while fireman Jack Law opens the gates.
G. R. Mortimer

At gated level crossings away from stations, the MSLR provided small timber-framed corrugated iron-clad cottages for the resident crossing keepers. Typical of the single storey structures is the cottage at Shop Street crossing near Worlingworth. For many years Mrs. Hambling was employed as resident crossing keeper.
G. F. Rice

keeper's cottage. In the latter years trainmen were required to open and close the gates, although this was not mentioned in the working timetables. The crossing carried the minor road from Shop Street to Southolt across the line.

Beyond the crossing a sharp 20 chain radius left-hand curve was followed by a short straight section, before the railway crossed the minor road leading from Worlingworth to Athelington by a gated level crossing to enter Worlingworth station 12 miles 9 chains from Haughley. The platform on the down side of the line, of similar length and height to others on the light railway, was host to the standard timber-framed corrugated iron-clad, standard Mid-Suffolk station building, but with the office at the Laxfield end of the structure only. One half of the building was formed by an open-fronted waiting shelter with a canopy fronting onto the platform. At the east end of the station, adjacent to the main building, was a corrugated iron-clad, lock-up shed, whilst at the Laxfield end of the main structure was a gentlemen's toilet. Illumination during the hours of darkness was given by two post oil lamps, one

Worlingworth station, 12 miles 9 chains from Haughley, looking towards Laxfield, showing the single 130 ft long platform on the down side of the line and the 580 ft long siding serving the goods yard on the up side. The station served Worlingworth 1½ miles to the east, Shop Street ¾ mile to the east, and Southolt 1¼ miles away to the west. Note the sleeper-built PW hut beyond the platform and the complete lack of housing in the area.

A closer view of the timber-framed corrugated iron-clad standard MSLR single-ended building at Worlingworth. The office was at the Laxfield end of the structure whilst the open-fronted waiting shelter, with canopy fronting on to the platform, occupied the remaining section, and a lock-up shed with end door abutted the main building. The platform, in common with others on the line, was 2 ft 9 ins in height. *Lens of Sutton*

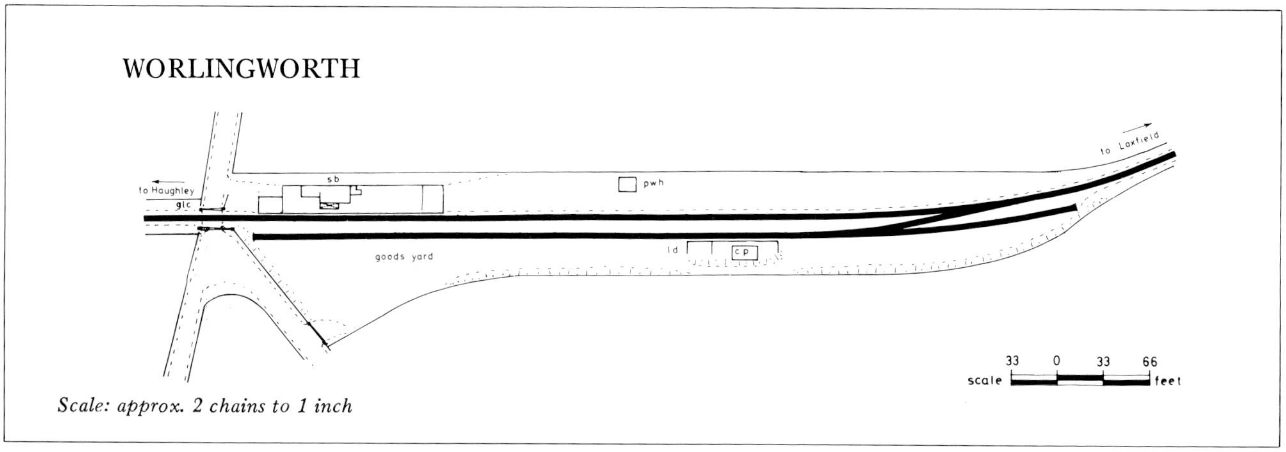

Scale: approx. 2 chains to 1 inch

each end of the station and a wall-mounted oil lamp in the open-fronted waiting shed. The single nameboard mounted on rail type posts was located at the east end of the platform, whilst the ubiquitous creosoted paling fence formed a backing to the platform. Public access to the station was by a gate leading from the adjacent road. The station served Worlingworth, 1½ miles to the east, Shop Street, ¾ mile east, and Southolt 1¼ miles to the west.

The goods yard at Worlingworth on the up side of the line was almost identical to that at Aspall with access to the single siding, 580 ft in length, being afforded by points leaving the single line and forming a trailing connection for down trains 400 ft east of the end of the platform. The siding was split into a short 185 ft eastern section and a longer 395 ft western siding by the access points from the main line. Buffer stops were provided at each end of the siding. A gravel road served the yard with access from the Worlingworth-Athelington road by a gate at the Haughley end of the layout. The loading dock at Worlingworth was at the centre of the yard. Part of the yard and a portion

A glimpse of a typical Mid-Suffolk Light Railway station at Worlingworth, viewed from the adjacent Worlingworth to Athelington road. The goods yard, served by the siding in the foreground, dealt mainly with coal imports and sugar beet exports. *D. Thompson*

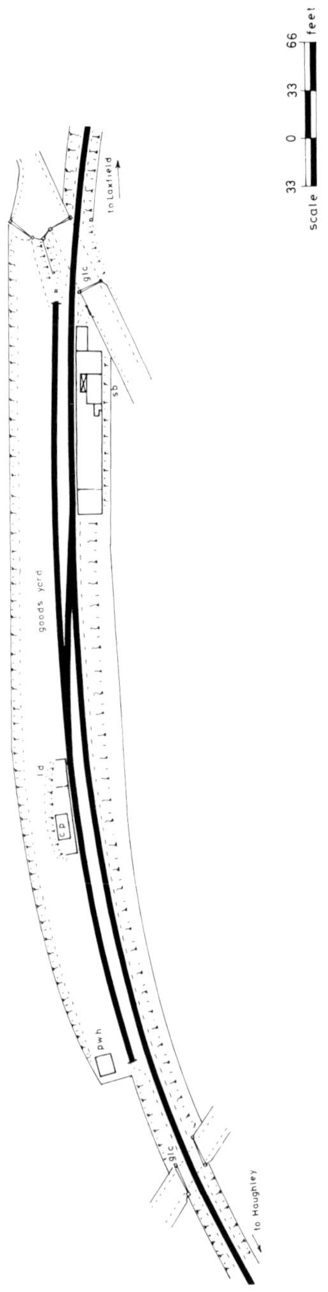

HORHAM

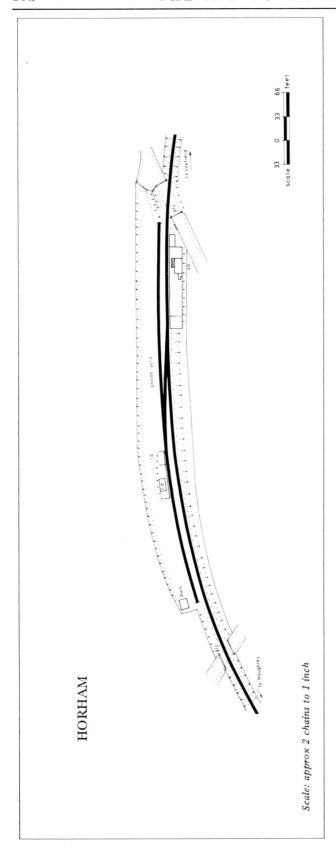

Scale: approx 2 chains to 1 inch

Driver Skinner keeps a sharp lookout on the road ahead as fireman Law builds up the fire on 'J15' No. 65447 hauling the 11.15 a.m. Haughley to Laxfield mixed train on a straight section of line between Worlingworth and Horham on 5th July 1952.

G. R. Mortimer

of the siding was initially hired by a Mr. Preston but the tenancy was surrendered after a few years.

Away from Worlingworth the main single line swung slightly on a 20 chain radius left-hand curve to follow a northerly course across agricultural fields, passing two occupational crossings before following a straight undulating section to Athelington ungated level crossing where the minor road leading from Redlingfield to Wilby bisected the line. The railway continued its almost straight course for almost a mile, falling initially at 1 in 160 and then rising at 1 in 300. Another moated farm was passed on the down side of the railway as the line climbed Athelington bank on a rising 1 in 44 gradient over an occupational footpath crossing. A slight left-hand curve brought the railway to the eleventh gated level crossing on the branch known as Horham Top Gates protecting the Athelington to Horham minor road. Beyond the crossing the line negotiated a 25 chains radius right-hand curve to enter Horham station (13 miles 74 chains from Haughley), with its 130 ft long platform located on the up or east side of the line. The platform was host to the standard timber-framed, corrugated iron-clad building which was identical to that at Worlingworth with an open-fronted waiting shed with canopy, adjoined at the Haughley end by a booking office cum staff room. Also at the west end of this building was a smaller corrugated structure containing the gentlemen's toilet. Horham for some reason was never provided with a lock-up store for parcels and perishables and these had, therefore, to be stored in the booking office, which at times caused considerable inconvenience.

In the months prior to closure Horham, like other stations on the line, was provided with a chemical toilet housed in a concrete hut located at the south end of the platform ramp. Two post-mounted oil lamps provided platform illumination during the hours of darkness, being located at the back of the platform, each side of the main building. A third oil lamp was provided in the open-fronted waiting shelter. The nameboard mounted on rail posts at the Haughley end of the platform, stood in a small garden which backed the tarmac and gravel surface of the

Horham station, 13 miles 74 chains from Haughley, located on the up side of the main single line, was unique to the MSLR in that it was sited on a curve. This view, looking towards Laxfield, shows the 525 ft goods yard siding on the left and Horham station level crossing beyond the platform. *Lens of Sutton*

'J15' class 0–6–0 No. 65467 eases the 11.15 a.m. Haughley to Laxfield mixed train round the curve and into Horham station on 14th July 1952. The connecting points to the siding can be seen beyond the wagon. *B. D. J. Walsh*

Another footplate view of 'J15' class 0–6–0 No. 65447 at Horham station level crossing with the railway descending around the curve at 1 in 50 in the distance. Fireman Law is building up the fire again while the driver is looking back for the 'right away' signal on 5th July 1952. The train is the 11.15 a.m. Haughley to Laxfield mixed. *G. R. Mortimer*

Horham station level crossing where the Worlingworth to Horham road bisected the light railway. This view c.1925 shows the station building and fencing painted a light grey whilst on the right is the entrance to the goods yard. The siding is occupied by three private owner coal wagons, the nearest of which is a Coote and Warren vehicle. The LNER notice on the telegraph pole advises the public 'Beware of trains and look both up and down the line before you cross'. *Collection G. F. Rice*

platform. The gardens were backed at each end of the platform by the creosoted paling fencing. The station served Horham village, half a mile away to the north-east.

Horham goods yard was located on the down side of the railway opposite the platform with access from the main single line by points forming a trailing connection for down trains. The single siding curving parallel to the main line was 525 ft long with buffer stops at each end. The siding was divided into two sections by the points, that at the north being 290 ft long whilst the south end serving the small loading dock was 235 ft long. Public access to the goods yard was via gates leading from the Worlingworth to Horham road at the Laxfield end of the yard.

Immediately on leaving Horham, the light railway passed over the Worlingworth to Horham road by a gated level crossing opened and closed by station staff and then descended around a right-hand curve on a 1 in 50/44 falling gradient to follow a straight level course across the valley of a small stream. After negotiating a short embankment 15 ft in height, the railway crossed the rivulet by underbridge No. 3 at 14 miles 36½ chains, before negotiating a 22 chain right-hand curve through a minor cutting and climbing at 1 in 50 over a footpath crossing to continue on a straight section in a north-easterly direction.

A short downhill straight section then brought the line to Stradbroke station (15 miles 8 chains from Haughley) with its adjacent goods yard. The 130 ft long platform on the up or south side of the line was host to the standard Mid-Suffolk double-ended station building constructed of timber frame and corrugated iron cladding. Separating the booking office at one end and the station master's and clerk's office in later years, was the open-fronted waiting shelter with canopy over the platform. The usual decorative bargeboards at the end of the building were surmounted by the customary finials. At the Haughley end of the

By the spring of 1951 the roofs of the six-wheel coaches were no longer watertight and on wet days a bogie coach was often sent from Ipswich to Haughley on a passing local train so that Mid-Suffolk passengers could enjoy a relatively dry journey. In October 1951 the old six-wheelers were replaced by four ex-GER bogie suburban coaches recently displaced by electrification, and formed into two sets. In June 1952 'J15' class 0–6–0 No. 65447 enters Stradbroke with one set of these coaches on a down mixed train. *Dr. I. C. Allen*

With steam shut off and blower on, 'J15' class 0–6–0 No. 5471 approaches Stradbroke with the 11.08 a.m. Haughley to Laxfield mixed train in the summer of 1948. The train is formed of two 6-wheel composites with a 6-wheel brake third in the centre of the formation. Bringing up the rear is an ex-LNER Toad B 20-ton goods brake. The yard connection is in the foreground and the 145 ft dock siding on the left.

Dr. I. C. Allen

On 6th August 1952 'J15' 65388 was sent down the branch to collect empty wagons left behind or not cleared by traders when the line closed on 26th July. Here the 'J15' has cleared Stradbroke yard and propels her wagons toward the brake van before setting off for Laxfield.
Dr. I. C. Allen

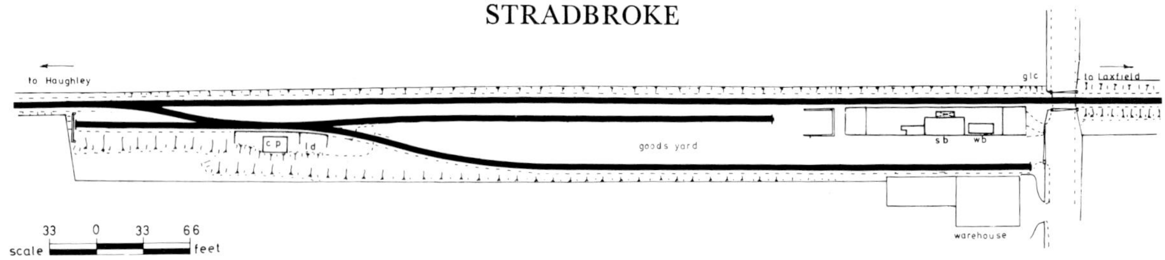

Scale: approx. 2 chains to 1 inch

Stradbroke station, looking towards Laxfield. The 130 ft long platform was host to the standard Mid-Suffolk double-ended station building constructed of timber frame with corrugated iron cladding. Separating the booking office at one end and the station master's office at the other was the open-fronted waiting shelter with canopy over the platform.
Lens of Sutton

Stradbroke station (15 miles 8 chains from Haughley) looking towards Haughley with the 130 ft long platform on the up side of the main single line. Beyond the platform open wagons stand in the 260 ft long coal road. In LNER days Stradbroke was the administrative centre for the Mid-Suffolk line, under the control of a station master. *D. Thompson*

main building was a corrugated iron toilet, whilst at the opposite end was a lock-up shed formed of a covered van body. Two post type oil lamps at each end of the platform and a wall oil lamp in the open-fronted waiting shed provided illumination during the hours of darkness. The platform was backed by the usual creosoted fencing whilst the station nameboard was located at the west end of the platform. Stradbroke was the only station equipped with a public telephone. The station served Stradbroke village located a mile to the north of the railway.

Stradbroke goods yard was sited at the Haughley end of the station on the up side of the single main line. Entrance to the yard was via points from the main line, forming a facing connection for down trains some 515 ft west of the platform. The points led to two sidings: the 'back road', 422 ft long, in later years served a corn warehouse, whilst the shorter coal road, 260 ft long, served the coal grounds of local fuel merchants. At the west end of the yard was the short 145 ft siding serving the cattle dock and loading dock.

Immediately at the Laxfield end of the platform the single main line, bisected the Wilby to Stradbroke road by

Stradbroke station facing Laxfield. The level crossing gates protecting the Wilby to Stradbroke road were opened and closed by station staff. The standard MSLR ornate station nameboard was illuminated by the unpretentious post-mounted oil lamp. The platform seat was of GER origin. *Lens of Sutton*

On a sunny summer day in 1948 'J15' 0–6–0 No. 5471, complete with stovepipe chimney, departs from Stradbroke with the 11.08 a.m. Haughley to Laxfield mixed train. *Dr. I. C. Allen*

The remotely situated Wilby station viewed from a train facing Laxfield on 1st September 1951. Passenger traffic was never very remunerative as the hamlet of Wilby was over 1½ miles away across the fields. *H. C. Casserley*

a gated level crossing, opened and closed by station staff, and beyond ran along a straight section, passing over an occupational crossing and Wootten Green ungated level crossing in quick succession, the latter carrying a minor road from Stradbroke across the railway. A long raking 60 chain radius right-hand curve swung the line in an easterly direction across plateau farmland and Barley Green where a bridle path crossed the line. A straight section of half a mile on undulating gradient brought the light railway to Wilby station, remotely situated over a mile and a half north of the hamlet and a quarter of a mile south of the Stradbroke to Laxfield B1117 road.

Although initially planned for the system, Wilby station (16 miles 33 chains ex-Haughley) was not opened for traffic until July 1909. In consequence of this later opening, facilities on the 130 ft platform, located on the down side of the line, were sparse. Originally only a timber-framed corrugated iron hut was located on the platform serving as a booking office and staff room, but lack of storage space for perishables and parcels necessitated the provision of a lock-up store. This was duly provided in the form of an old GER wagon body. The platform was tarmacadamed nearest to the track edge but the backing was of earth and gravel. Illumination was provided by two post oil lamps whilst the Wilby nameboard, with the MSLR ornate cast lettering on wooden backing and mounted on wooden posts, was at the Haughley end of the platform. A row of fire-buckets attached to the corrugated station hut completed the equipment. The station, being the least used on the line, was not even provided with a platform seat for intending passengers.

The goods yard at Wilby was on the up side of the line with similar track layout to that at Horham except in reverse. The points leading to the siding from the main single line formed a facing connection to down trains and were located 215 ft west of the station. The siding, 545 ft long, was divided into two, the east end being 225 ft long and the west end 320 ft. Buffer stops were provided at each end of the siding but no loading gauge. As at other stations, the yard siding was later laid with bullhead rails. There was, however, no loading dock provided here.

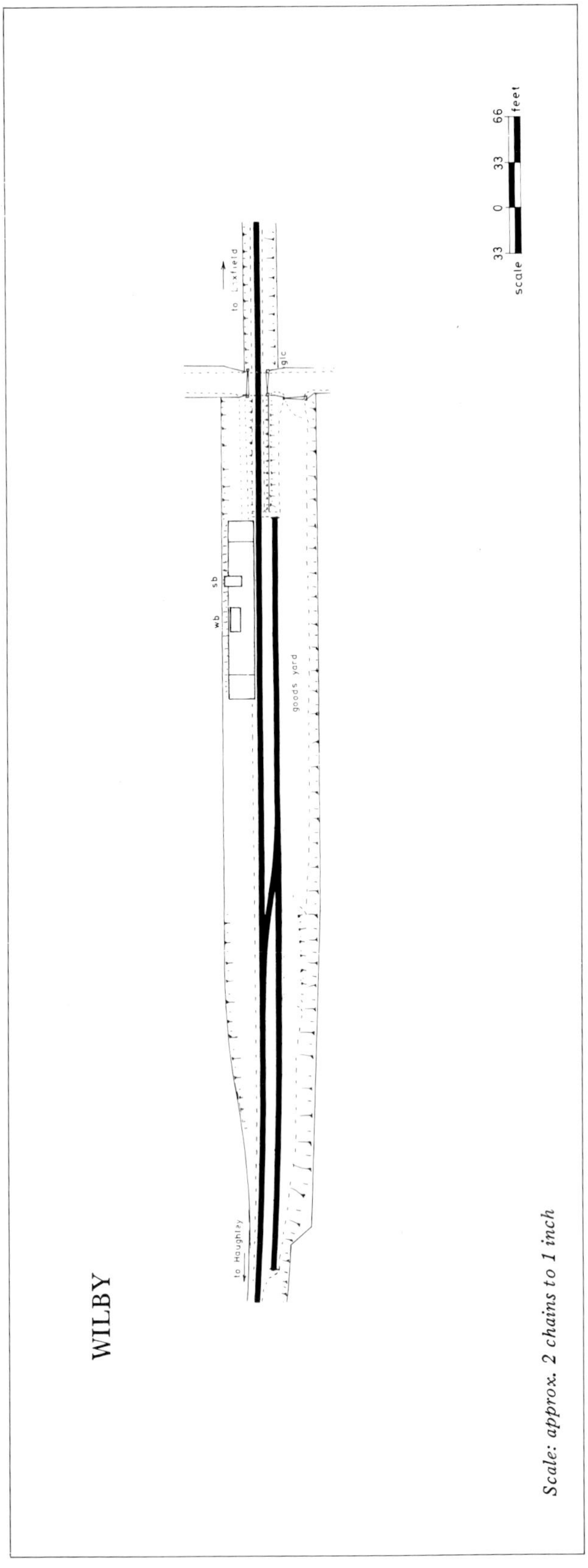

At Wilby station, 16 miles 33 chains from Haughley, the platform was on the down side of the main single line. The goods yard to the left was served by a 545 ft long siding, here occupied by three open wagons. This view was taken looking towards Haughley in 1952.

D. Thompson

Wilby station viewed from the platform facing Haughley on 14th September 1949. Traffic at this station was sparse and the only item on the 11.08 a.m. ex-Haughley is a returned empty milk churn. The mixed train of 6-wheel coaches has a tail load of one open wagon and goods brake.

B. D. J. Walsh

Wilby station, 16 miles 33 chains from Haughley, facing Laxfield. Although initially planned for the system, the remote wayside station was not opened for passenger traffic until July 1909. In consequence of the later opening, only a small timber-framed corrugated iron-clad hut, serving as a booking office and staff hut, was originally provided. Lack of storage space for parcels and perishables later necessitated the provision of the old GER wagon body as a lock-up store. The goods yard siding is on the right whilst the MSLR style level crossing gates, opened and closed by station staff, protected the B1117 road. *Lens of Sutton*

Beyond Wilby the Mid-Suffolk line continued its straight course, bisecting another gated level crossing where the connecting road from the B1117 to Wilby crossed the railway. The level crossing gates were opened and closed by the porter-in-charge. The single track railway continued on a straight course for a further quarter of a mile, crossing a small stream by a culvert. A slight right-hand curve then took the railway in a straight east-south-easterly direction for half a mile where the line bisected a bridle road leading from Ashfield Green to Wells Corner. A 40 chain radius left-hand curve carried the light railway on a rising 1 in 100 gradient over another bridle path crossing and the B1116 road leading from Framlingham and Dennington to Fressingfield by White Horse Road gated level crossing, with its adjacent gate house. The Mid-Suffolk Company, and later the LNER, employed a gatekeeper to open and close the gates for passing trains but after the Second World War economies were effected and the gatekeeper was with-

With safety valves lifting, 'J15' class 0–6–0 No. 65447 stands at Wilby with a Haughley to Laxfield mixed train formed of a two-coach Ilford bogie GER set with open wagon and goods brake. To the left is the goods yard served by a 545 ft siding, here occupied by two coal wagons. *Dr. I. C. Allen*

'J15' class 0–6–0 No. 65459 near White Horse Road gated level crossing with a down train formed of 6-wheel composite, 6-wheel brake third, 6-wheel composite and a goods brake. It was near this crossing that the branch train once halted to reverse and pick up guard Willis Keeble who had been left behind on the platform at Wilby. *Dr. I. C. Allen*

View of the curve and falling gradient on the approach to Laxfield from the cab of a 'J15' class 0–6–0. Laxfield's upper quadrant home signal, just to the left of the telegraph pole, is in the 'off' position. To the far left is Laxfield engine shed. This lightweight simple wire fencing was located alongside the light railway for most of its length. *Dr. I. C. Allen*

drawn. From then on trainmen were responsible for the opening and closing of the gates for the passage of each train.

From White Horse Road level crossing the line continued on a straight section before curving to the right to cross another bridle road. Passing through open arable fields, a long raking 30 chains radius left-hand curve on a falling gradient heralded the approach to Laxfield, the administrative and operating headquarters of the light railway in independent days. The main single line continued curving past the down home signal to follow a straight course for a short distance before crossing a stream by a wooden culvert bridge. Immediately beyond the bridge on the up side of the line was the locomotive water storage tank with water supplied from the adjacent stream, except during the summer months, by a petrol pumping engine. Backing on to the water tank was Laxfield engine shed, 60 ft long, with space to accommodate two of the Mid-Suffolk 0–6–0 tank engines or their 'J65' replacements. The building was constructed of timber with two windows each side and four smoke vents on the ridge of the roof. The wall of the structure at the west end backing on to the stream was timber-clad with no windows, whilst the double opening doors were at the east end of the structure.

The track layout at Laxfield was rather odd for the main single line swung to the right over points past the engine shed whilst the apparent continuation of the straight running line was in fact a coal siding, 610 ft long from the toe of the points. The main single line ran parallel to the coal siding for 256 ft before being diverted to the right again, over a second pair of points, to enter the straight platform road and Laxfield station (18 miles 71 chains ex-Haughley). The second relinquished straight, continuing 293 ft from the toe of the points, paralleled with the platform road to terminate at buffer stops beside a loading dock located on the down side of the line. The coal and dock roads were united by a crossover which paralleled another connecting the main line and the dock road. The stub ends of the dock road and coal road were thus reduced to 148 and 108 feet by these connections. A 445 ft siding running back (west) from the platform road parallel to the main single line served to stable coaching stock, trap points initially protecting any runaway from the main line.

The 60 ft long raised platform on the up side of this siding hosted the former MSLR superintendent's office which after 1924 was used as an enginemen's mess room. This building, like others on the line, was timber-framed

Laxfield engine shed, the largest on the erstwhile MSLR and indeed the only shed in use after 1919, had accommodation for two of the Hudswell Clarke 0–6–0Ts. When Kenton shed was closed all three engines were stabled there, a practice which continued after the LNER took over the working of the line in 1924. It was then usual for two locomotives to handle the diagrams, leaving the third spare or receiving maintenance. On 5th July 1936 class 'J65' No. 7253 is pictured here outside the shed awaiting her next working. In the foreground is the main single line and to the right the coal siding. The points by the shed were operated by a ground frame and interlocked with the down home signal seen in the background. The ground frame was released by Annetts key attached to the train staff. *H. C. Casserley*

Laxfield engine shed from the west in 1923. Note the solid boarding of the end wall and the small corrugated iron hut used in the early years as the enginemen's messroom. The adjacent water tank was one of two used to replenish locomotives at Laxfield when water supplies were obtained by damming up a small stream which passed under the railway near the shed. The scheme involved the use of a petrol engine to pump the water from the stream into the tank. Note the condemned MSLR wagon sheet on the right. *G. F. Rice Collection*

Saturday afternoon at Laxfield. The coaching stock is stabled on the coal siding whilst two goods wagons and a brake stand by the former superintendent's office with steam-braked 'J15' 0–6–0 No. 65388. An early arrival has ensured the early disposal of 'J15' No. 65467 standing by the coaling stage after its fire had been thrown out. This engine, required for the Monday service, is conveniently stabled alongside the coal stage so that the tender can be replenished on Sunday night by the shedman. Once the driver (seen in centre of the picture) has left the premises, the railway at Laxfield remained dormant and deserted for nearly thirty-six hours. *Dr. I. C. Allen*

The remains of the gale-gutted engine shed at Laxfield in 1952 with front doors and end wall missing and the east end of the timber structure shored up with baulks of timber. *D. Thompson*

'J15' 0–6–0 No. 65447 on the points from the main single line to the engine shed at Laxfield on 17th July 1952.
R. F. Roberts

with zinc iron sheets, the cladding being painted in the form of brickwork. Visiting engine cleaners or relief train crews from Ipswich also lodged in this building when out-based at Laxfield. At its west end the carriage road curved slightly as it continued through yet another trailing crossover which provided access from the main single line. The locomotive coaling stage and the adjacent oil store were also on the south side of this line as it continued to form the 115 ft long shed road to terminate in the engine shed. An inspection pit was located between the rails inside the shed. It was thought by former MSLR employees that the S formation of the main single line at Laxfield was laid out in such form because the company intended making the station the second crossing place on the line after Kenton. When the extension beyond Cratfield failed to materialise no rearrangement was possible because of the shortage of finances and the peculiar layout persisted to the end.

On the 130 ft long platform on the up side of the main single line was the standard timber-framed, corrugated iron clad, single-ended building housing the booking office and parcels store. Adorned by a small canopy, the remaining section was simply an open-fronted waiting shelter. On the west end of this building was a gentlemen's toilet whilst at the Haughley end of the platform was a corrugated iron, timber-framed lock-up store which bore the station name-board. A post-mounted platform oil lamp stood alongside. A second post oil lamp was located east of the station buildings fronting onto the creosoted paling fence. This separated the platform from the access road to the goods yard which ran at the back of the station. Access to both goods yard and station was via separate gates leading from the Laxfield to Stradbroke road at the east end of the station. A separate gated access led to the loading dock on the down side of the line. In 1926 Thomas Moy gained access to the coal road by purchasing land north of the railway and later in 1928 opened up a gap in the boundary fence to offload coal from wagons onto carts and later motor lorries. The station served the village of Laxfield located a quarter of a mile east of the railway.

As at Haughley and Kenton, points and signals at Laxfield were operated from a ground frame located on the down side of the main single line opposite the engine shed. The master point and home signal were interlocked. To operate the subsidiary points, during shunting or when the

The MSLR superintendent's office at Laxfield c.1920. Located on a 60 ft long platform alongside the carriage stock siding, west of Laxfield station, the building was similar in design to other structures on the light railway with timber framing. Instead of corrugated iron cladding, zinc-coated sheets of iron in a brick pattern similar to that at Haughley MSL station protected the structure. This was then painted to resemble bricks. On amalgamation with the LNER the building became a locomen's messroom.
Collection G. F. Rice

The Mid-Suffolk terminal at Laxfield, looking east on 14th June 1952. The station, with its 130 ft long platform, stands on the up side of the line adjacent to the level crossing. The building in the foreground on the 60 ft long platform was the former superintendent's office. The odd track layout at Laxfield shows the main single line centre foreground swinging over points to run past the station platform and over the crossing. The track on the right is the 445 ft coaching stock siding whilst the goods brake is standing on the 610 ft long coal siding. The continuation of the straight section from the main single line points led to the cattle dock. *R. E. Vincent*

Another view of the peculiar track layout at Laxfield viewed from the west end on 9th July 1952. 'J15' class 0–6–0 No. 65447, running tender first, is shown departing with the two-coach train for Haughley. On the left alongside the coal road a Moy's coal lorry is being loaded with coal from an open wagon. The gap in the fence was authorised by the LNER in the 1920s.

On 18th May 1948 'J15' class 0–6–0 No. 5470, still adorned with LNER on the tender, eases over the points of the main single line during shunting operations at Laxfield. The three 6-wheel coaches on the left are standing against a wagon on the dock siding whilst the other 6-wheel stock is occupying the platform.

Laxfield station from the west in 1923. The vehicle beside the cattle and loading dock, a GER cattle wagon, is standing on the 148 ft long dock road. The siding on the left is the coal road. The points operated by weighted levers were released by a subsidiary point key which in turn was retained in a master point container which was released by Annetts key on the train staff. *Collection G. F. Rice*

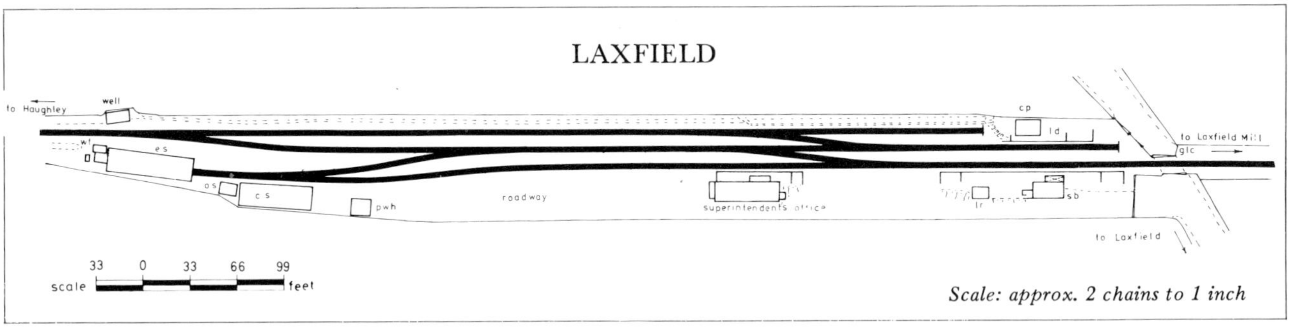

Left: The standard timber-framed corrugated iron-clad station building at Laxfield, shown c.1920, housed the booking office and parcels store at the west end whilst the open-fronted waiting shelter, adorned by a small ornate canopy, offered waiting passengers protection from the elements. To the right of the building is the primitive gentlemen's toilet. Note the flagpole alongside the finial. *Right:* The corrugated iron timber-framed lock-up store at the Haughley end of Laxfield station platform, again c.1920. At this time the ornate nameboard was painted with light backing and dark letters. The oil lamp mounted on a post was of similar design to GER wall-mounted oil lamps.

Collection G. F. Rice

Laxfield station, 18 miles 71 chains from Haughley, with its 130 ft long platform on the up side of the single running line. This view facing east in 1951 shows the station building still painted in LNER cream (upper) and brown (lower) livery. *Lens of Sutton*

locomotive was required to run round the train, necessitated the foreman in charge obtaining the split train staff for the Kenton-Laxfield section from the driver before returning the home signal to danger. The key on the staff was then inserted in the ground frame so that the points could be changed and a key for the subsidiary points released. The subsidiary points were then locked and unlocked as required and the point lever pulled over to allow the necessary movements. Before a train was permitted to depart in the up direction it had to be formed up on the main single line so that the subsidiary points could be locked and the key returned to the ground frame. The road was then set for the main single line and the ground frame relocked by the key on the train staff. The home signal, initially lower quadrant but in later years replaced by an upper quadrant arm, was only cleared when the main single line was clear

Another close up view of the timber-framed corrugated iron-clad lock-up store at the Haughley end of Laxfield platform, this time painted in LNER cream and brown. *R. F. Roberts*

The 1.50 p.m. Laxfield to Haughley formed of 'J15' class 0–6–0 No. 5459 in LNER livery, 6-wheel composite E63404 and 6-wheel brake third E62338 awaiting departure at Laxfield on 18th April 1949. *W. A. Camwell*

The rural railway scene that has gone forever, 'J15' 0–6–0 No. 65447 awaiting to depart from Laxfield with the 1.45 p.m. mixed train to Haughley on 5th July 1952. In the background a Toad E goods brake languishes in the coal siding as sulphurous smoke is blown by the summer breeze across the yard. The bars fitted across the droplights and short door handles of the ex-GE bogie suburban coach show clearly here. No. 65447 was formerly GER 'Y14' class No. 647, renumbered by the LNER in 1924 to 7647, before becoming 5447 in the 1947 renumbering. She was withdrawn in April 1959. *G. R. Mortimer*

Laxfield station on 1st September 1951. *H. C. Casserley*

The muddy station approach and roadway at Laxfield in 1923. A GER cattle wagon stands by the cattle dock.
J. Langford, courtesy G. F. Rice

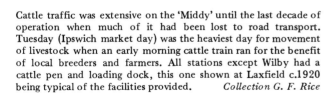

Cattle traffic was extensive on the 'Middy' until the last decade of operation when much of it had been lost to road transport. Tuesday (Ipswich market day) was the heaviest day for movement of livestock when an early morning cattle train ran for the benefit of local breeders and farmers. All stations except Wilby had a cattle pen and loading dock, this one shown at Laxfield c.1920 being typical of the facilities provided. *Collection G. F. Rice*

Laxfield station approach from the road on 1st September 1951. The open landscape almost devoid of habitation was typical of the Mid-Suffolk area served by the light railway. *H. C. Casserley*

The road entrance to Laxfield station on 2nd August 1933 with class 'J65' 0–6–0T No. 7157 shortly after arrival with a train from Haughley. The locomotive is carrying the single white disc on the lamp bracket denoting a stopping passenger service. These discs, used by the GER, were introduced on the light railway after the LNER took over the line in 1924. The LNER advertisements on the hoarding by the gate offer summer tickets at a penny per mile and return journeys at single fares for passengers and cyclists. *Collection M. Brooks*

to the platform. If two trains were running with the split token working in operation, the second train was allowed into the section once the first train had arrived, but was held at the home signal until the first train had completed full shunting duties and the subsidiary points and main points set to normal and the first section of the staff withdrawn from the ground frame.

Immediately on leaving Laxfield station, the main single line bisected the Laxfield to Stradbroke B1117 road by a level crossing, protected by gates and opened and closed by station staff. Beyond the crossing the Mid-Suffolk company placed a single tongue catch point to the main single line to protect the line from runaway vehicles in the down direction. This was later removed by the LNER.

From Laxfield the line curved slightly to the right on a falling gradient, passing the 19 mile post and the engine water tank located on the down side of the line. This supply, fed from a pond, was used during the summer months when the supply from the stream by Laxfield engine shed often dried up. The frequently obstinate petrol pumping engine was transferred to the pond and pumped water into the storage tank. The local cemetery was on the up side of the line as the railway curved to the left. Twenty-seven chains beyond the single line catch points was a trailing connection for down trains which led to the 185 ft Gorham's siding, located on the down side of the line serving Laxfield Mill. Beyond these points the single line continued a further five chains and 5 links to the end of

High level view of the 130 ft long platform and corrugated iron station buildings at Laxfield from the west in April 1949. Beyond the gated level crossing the line followed a straight course before curving to the left to terminate near Laxfield Mill just visible in the left background. *W. A. Camwell*

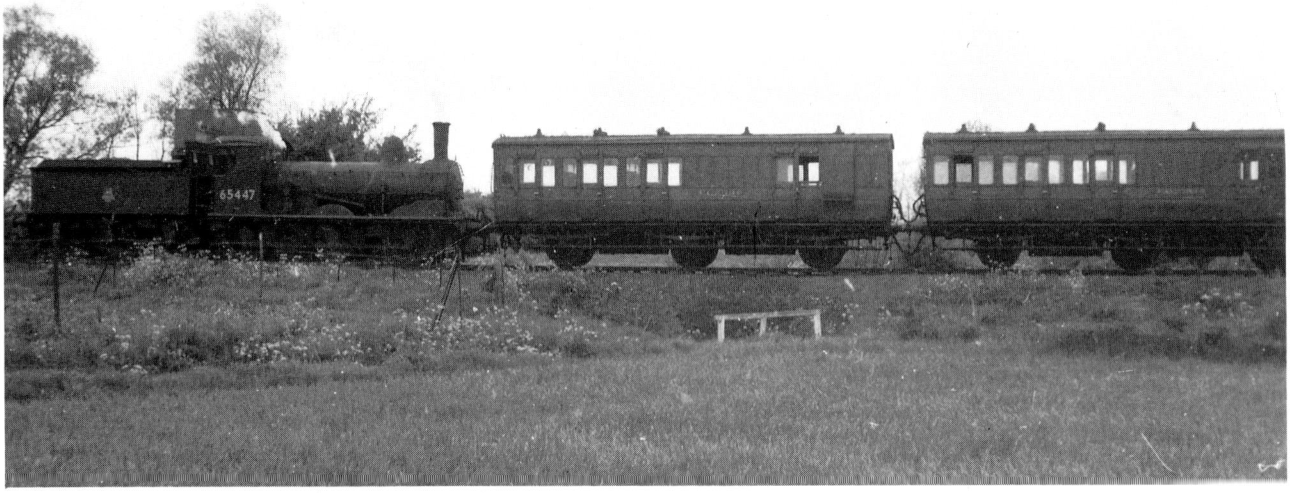

On several occasions when the tender tank required replenishing with water from the static tank by the pond, in order to save time after shunting, the engine propelled the coaching stock beyond Laxfield station towards the Mill siding. In this view, having pushed 6-wheel brake thirds E62331 and E62334 down the line, 'J15' 0–6–0 No. 65447 slows by the trackside tank prior to topping up in May 1950.

Dr. I. C. Allen

Class 'J15' 0–6–0 No. 65388 standing beside the pond which supplied water to the storage tank near Laxfield Mill, east of Laxfield station. The water supply was used during the summer as a standby when the stream supplying the tank by Laxfield engine shed dried up. The ancient petrol engine was then transferred to pump water from the pond into the tank. This photograph, taken on the afternoon of 7th August 1952, shows the locomotive about to have its tank replenished. The engine had entered the branch at 6.30 a.m. with an engineers train. By this time the driver was concerned but his worries were nullified when the tank was topped, enabling the locomotive to work on before leaving the branch in the late evening.

Dr. I. C. Allen

LAXFIELD MILL *(Gorham's siding)*

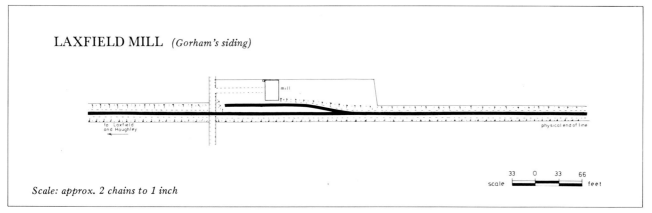

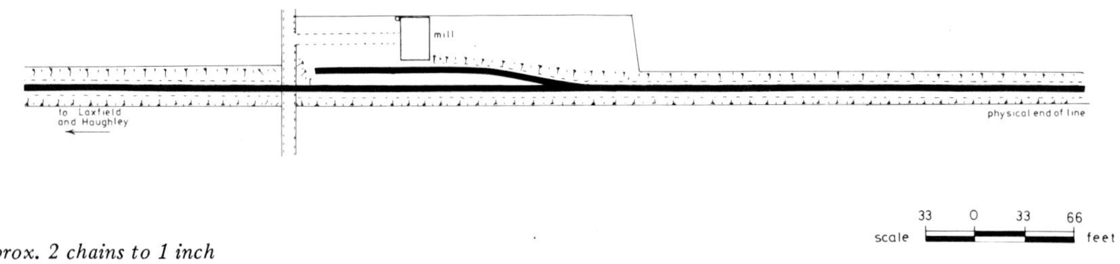

Scale: approx. 2 chains to 1 inch

the line 19 miles 32 chains from Haughley, although no buffer stops were erected and the track finished in plain rails. The last few chains of track were never relaid with bullhead rails and Vignoles 56 lbs per yard rails remained in use until closure.

With a view to extending beyond Laxfield, the MSLR entered into an agreement with the Gorham family on 21st January 1904 for the purchase of land, provided that within one year the railway company laid out the formation of permanent way across the estate and kept it in good order. In addition the company was required to install a siding at least 300 ft long. The railway company subsequently arranged for the provision of the siding but, because of engineering difficulties, the contractor constructed the shorter siding on a different site than originally stipulated. The siding soon became a 'white elephant' and the Gorham

Laxfield Mill and siding facing towards Haughley showing the flat bottom track and staggered joints beyond the lead. The siding was provided for the use of the Gorham family as part of an agreement made when the railway company purchased land from the family to extend the railway beyond Laxfield. The 185 ft siding provided was shorter than stipulated and located on a different site than originally proposed. View taken on 24th September 1949. *J. H. Meredith*

family never received or despatched goods from the siding neither would they allow other possible users to cross their private land to gain access to it. The railway company and the owners later rectified differences of opinion and the siding was used infrequently by farmers and growers until the service was withdrawn in 1952.

The speed limit on the Middy was fixed, by virtue of Light Railway standard, to 25 mph with the speed limit reduced to 10 mph when approaching the warning boards situated 300 yards on the approach to all ungated level crossings protected by cattle guards. A board with the figure '10' painted thereon was erected at such points to call the driver's attention to the limit. The operational line was noted for its excessive number of crossings. In MSLR days, apart from the eleven level crossings at or near stations, there were seven gated level crossings away from stations under the charge of a gatekeeper, twelve open level crossings protected by cattle guards and warning boards and no fewer than 86 occupational or bridle crossings, a full total of 116 on 19 miles of line. By 1930 the LNER had reduced the number of public level crossings by two when there were seventeen protected by gates and eleven by cattle guards.

'J15' class 0–6–0 No. 5471 drifting past Gorham's Mill siding at Laxfield in the summer of 1948. The exact reason for the visit is difficult to understand as the siding is devoid of wagons.
Dr. I. C. Allen

In the latter years Laxfield Mill was used for the storage of potatoes. On a hot sunny day 'J15' 0–6–0 No. 65459 stands in Gorham's siding beside the mill with an open wagon loaded with the vegetables. The falling gradient of the main single line as it curves towards the water tank by the pond is evident in this view.
Dr. I. C. Allen

Laxfield Mill and siding, looking east towards the physical end of the line. The track was actually laid a further two miles on to Cratfield where a goods station was maintained from 1906 to 1912. After this section was lifted, the trackwork ended without buffer stops 19 miles 32 chains from Haughley. The 56 lbs per yard track survived to the end on this section. *C. S. Bayes*

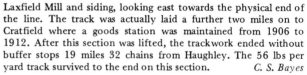

No. 65447 at the farm crossing almost at the end of the rails beyond Laxfield Mill in 1951. *Dr. I. C. Allen*

This final view of the Cratfield line shows old sleepers placed across the physical end of the track beyond Laxfield Mill. In the foreground is one of the many occupational crossings. *C. Bayes*

MID-SUFFOLK LIGHT RAILWAY.

Refnce. to other Tables.	DOWN TRAINS.	Week Days morn (Mondays only)	Week Days morn (Not on Mondays)	Week Days morn	Week Days morn	Week Days even	Sundays morn	Sundays even
106 to 112	**LONDON (Liverpool Street)** dep.	5 5	6 38	11 45		3 20	—	4 20
	Colchester "	6 30	8 19	1 8		4 5	...	5 35
129	Felixstowe (Town) dep.	—	8 3	11 48		4 0	—	5 29
106 to 112	Ipswich dep.	7 1	9 8	1 48		5 0	7 45	6 17
	Stowmarket "	7 35	9 35	2 15		5 22	8 38	6 46
	Haughley arr.	7 40	9 41	2 25		5 29	8 45	6 53
113 to 119	**Norwich** Thorpe dep.	—	—	12 23		—	—	—
	Norwich Victoria "	6 45	9 2	—		3 50	7 30	6 5
	Diss "	7 30	9 30	1 5		4 34	8 13	7 3
	Haughley arr.	7 57	9 46	1 28		5 4	8 40	7 30
89	**Peterborough** dep.	—	—	9 30	—	12 52	—	3 8
	March "	...	...	10 28	...	1 26	...	3 40
	Ely "	—	—	10 52	—	2 10	—	4 32
	Cambridge "	...	7 7	...	12 25	4 12	...	5 3
	Bury St. Edmunds "	6A42	8 28	—	1 54	5 29	7 45	6 14
	Haughley arr.	7A40	8 52	12 46	2 18	5 53	8 9	6 38
Mid-Suffolk Light Railway.	**Haughley** dep.	8 10	9 52	3 0		5 55	8 50	7 35
	Mendlesham	8 23	10 5	3 18		6 8	9 3	7 48
	Brockford and Wetheringsett	8 28	10 10	3 25		6 13	9 8	7 53
	Aspall & Thorndon (*for Debenham*)	8 36	10 18	3 40		6 21	9 16	8 1
	Kenton	8 41	10 23	3 55		6 26	9 21	8 6
	Worlingworth	8 49	10 31	4 3		6 34	9 29	8 14
	Horham	8 55	10 37	4 12		6 43	9 35	8 20
	Stradbroke	8 59	10 41	4 16		6 47	9 39	8 24
	Wilby	9 4	10 46	4 21		6 52	9 44	8 29
	Laxfield arr.	9 12	10 54	4 29		7 0	9 52	8 37

Refnce. to other Tables.	UP TRAINS.	Week Days morn (Mondays only)	Week Days morn (Not on Mondays)	Week Days morn (Wednesdays only)	Week Days morn (Not on Wednesdays)	Week Days even	Sundays morn	Sundays even
Mid-Suffolk Light Railway	**Laxfield** dep.	6 40	8 20	11 35	11 55	3 20	7 0	5 17
	Wilby	6 47	8 27	11 42	12 2	3 27	7 7	5 24
	Stradbroke	6 52	8 32	11 47	12 7	3 32	7 12	5 29
	Horham	6 57	8 37	11 52	12 12	3 37	7 17	5 34
	Worlingworth	7 3	8 43	11 58	12 18	3 44	7 23	5 40
	Kenton	7 10	8 50	12 5	12 25	3 54	7 30	5 47
	Aspall & Thorndon (*for Debenham*)	7 17	8 57	12 14	12 34	4 2	7 37	5 54
	Brockford and Wetheringsett	7 25	9 5	12 22	12 42	4 11	7 45	6 2
	Mendlesham	7 30	9 10	12 29	12 49	4 19	7 50	6 7
	Haughley arr.	7 47	9 27	12 49	1 9	4 37	8 7	6 27
90	**Haughley** dep.	8 4	9D16	2G34	2 34	5 10	8 45	9 0
	Bury St. Edmunds arr.	8 27	11 5	1G24	2 58	5 33	9 9	9 24
	Cambridge "	9 31	1B5	4 39	4 30	6 50	11 0	...
	Ely "	10 8	12 35	4 19	4 19	6 43	11 31	—
	March "	10 50	1 21	5 15	5 15	7 23	12 0	...
	Peterborough "	11 22	1 45	5 52	5 52	8 48	—	—
106 to 112	**Haughley** dep.	9 41	9 41	2 25	2 25	5 29	8 19	6 53
	Diss arr.	10 4	10 4	2 48	2 48	5 51	8 43	7 20
	Norwich Victoria "	...	...	3 33	3 33	...	...	8 7
	Norwich Thorpe "	10 50	10 50	—	—	6 33	9 35	—
113 to 119	**Haughley** dep.	7 57	9 46	1 28	1 28	5F1	8 39	6 39
	Stowmarket arr.	8 4	9 52	1 35	1 35	5F6	8 47	6 47
	Ipswich "	8 38	10 10	1 53	1 53	5F37	9 17	7 13
129	Felixstowe (Town) arr.	10 21	11 1	4 11	4 11	7 17	10 4	9 4
113 to 119	Colchester arr.	9 11	10 51	4 4	4 4	6 55	10 3	9 11
	LONDON (Liverpool Street) "	10 33	12 27	3 43	3 43	7F8	11 30	9H15

On Bank Holidays several Trains will not run, and others will run at altered times. For particulars see special announcements and page vi.

A Passengers travel via Stowmarket. **B** On Saturdays arrives Cambridge 12.37 p.m. **D** Except on Wednesdays Passengers travel via Stowmarket. On Wednesdays Passengers leave at 10.39 a.m.

F From September 12th to 30th inclusive will leave Haughley at 5.1, and arrive Stowmarket 5.20, Ipswich 5.51, and Liverpool Street 8.14 p.m.

G Passengers for Bury leave Haughley at 1.0 p.m.
H On July 31st will arrive Liverpool Street at 10.5 p.m.

GER Passenger Timetable July 1910

See page		Week Days morn	Week Days even	Sundays morn (October only)	Sundays even
30 to 32	**LONDON (Liverpool St.)** dep.	5 9	3 22	...	4 25
	Colchester "	7 40	4 36	—	5 40
	Ipswich "	9 25	5 3	...	6 22
	Stowmarket "	9 53	5 25	8 38	6 51
	Haughley arr.	9 59	5 33	8 45	6 58
33 to 35	Norwich (Thorpe) dep.	8 54	3C42	7V30	6 11
	Diss "	9 34	4C37	8 13	7 8
	Haughley arr.	9 51	5C6	8 39	7 36
68	Ely dep.	—	4 39	—	4A32
	Cambridge "	7 11	...	...	5 3
	Bury St. Edmund's "	8 30	5 26	7 55	6 15
	Haughley arr.	8 54	5 50	8 19	6 39
	HAUGHLEY dep.	10 5	B 5 55	8 50	7 40
	Mendlesham	10 19	6 9	9 4	7 54
	Brockford and Wetheringsett	10 25	6 14	9 9	7 59
	Aspall and Thorndon (*for Debenham*)	10 32	6 22	9 17	8 7
	Kenton	10 37	6 27	9 22	8 12
	Worlingworth	10 48	6 35	9 30	8 20
	Horham	10 56	6 41	9 36	8 26
	Stradbroke	11 3	6 45	9 40	8 30
	Wilby	11 8	6 50	9 45	8 35
	LAXFIELD arr.	11 15	6 57	9 52	8 42

See page		Week Days morn	Week Days even (Tuesdays and Thursdays only)	Week Days even	Sundays morn (October only)	Sundays even	Sundays even
	LAXFIELD dep.	8 15	12 55	3 25	7 30	5 30	...
	Wilby	8 23	1 3	3 33	7 38	5 38	—
	Stradbroke	8 28	1 8	3 40	7 43	5 43	...
	Horham	8 33	1 13	3 47	7 47	5 47	—
	Worlingworth	8 39	1 20	3 54	7 53	5 53	...
	Kenton	8 46	1 33	4 3	8 1	6 1	—
	Aspall and Thorndon (*for Debenham*)	8 53	1 40	4 15	8 6	6 6	...
	Brockford and Wetheringsett	9 1	1 48	4 22	8 11	6 11	—
	Mendlesham	9 6	1 55	4 28	8 19	6 19	...
	HAUGHLEY arr.	9 23	2 10	4 42	8 32	6 32	—
69	**Haughley** dep.	10 2	3 5	5 11	8 45	9 15	...
	Bury St. Edmund's arr.	10 25	3 28	5 34	9 9	9 39	—
	Cambridge "	11 55	5 13	6 48	11 1	...	...
	Ely "	12 6	5A39	7A36	11A44	—	—
30 to 32	**Haughley** dep.	9 34	2 58	5 33	—	6 58	—
	Diss arr.	9 58	3 23	5 59	...	7 25	...
	Norwich (Thorpe) "	10 46	4 15	6 35	—	8V12	—
33 to 35	**Haughley** dep.	9 51	2 22	5 6	8 39	6 40	7 36
	Stowmarket arr.	9 57	2 29	5 13	8 49	6 46	—
	Ipswich "	10 16	2 53	5 37	9 17	7 13	...
	Colchester "	10 57	3 38	6 29	10 3		8 42
	LONDON (Liverpool St.) "	12 39	4 47	7 42	11 30	...	10 6

A Via Cambridge. **B** On Saturdays will await arrival of 4.55 p.m. ex Norwich Victoria due Haughley 5.57 p.m., and run correspondingly later throughout.
C On Saturdays leaves Victoria Station Norwich at 4.55, Diss 5.30 and arrives Haughley at 5.57 p.m.

From GER Passenger Timetable October 1915

CHAPTER SEVEN

Timetables and Traffic

THE Mid-Suffolk Light Railway was built essentially to provide cheap and speedy transport for agricultural products, from an area of 190,000 acres previously devoid of rail transport. Unfortunately, the trunkated section finally constructed restricted the catchment area from which traffic was originally envisaged and freight receipts were not as lucrative as forecast. Despite the failure to reach their intended goal, the directors were gratified in the knowledge that their labours to open up new tracts of country were not in vain, and receipts from goods traffic always formed the higher percentage of total takings.

Most of the land served by the Light Railway formed part of large agricultural estates and consequently the majority of the populace were employed on the land with no commuting to or from work. The company in their prospectus advised that the population to be served exclusively by the railway numbered some 40,000 but as the figures quoted below show, the actual totals were in fact much less, around the 6,000 mark. The line carried most of its passengers on Ipswich market day and the majority of other traffic was long distance and spasmodic. With most trains running as mixed, a service of between two and five trains available to passengers did little to attract trade and the population of the area declined by almost 12 per cent during the period the line was open.

	1901	*1911*	*1921*	*1931*	*1951*
Haughley	789	828	814	921	929
Mendlesham	961	927	934	862	862
Wetheringsett-cum-Brockford	812	822	812	801	665
Aspall	116	133	129	113	95
Thorndon	550	572	553	442	460
Kenton	242	209	227	181	136
Worlingworth	552	575	504	495	506
Horham	287	290	292	246	234
Stradbroke	1016	1012	927	903	832
Wilby	331	343	332	340	317
Laxfield	827	813	787	763	673
Total including Haughley	6483	6524	6311	6067	5709
Total excluding Haughley	5694	5696	5497	5146	4780

The initial service offered when the line opened to goods traffic on Tuesday, 20th September 1904 consisted of one train in each direction. The down service departed Haughley at 8.00 a.m. and took 3¼ hours to reach Laxfield with 20 minutes allowed for shunting at Mendlesham, Aspall and Horham, 18 minutes at Stradbroke and 15 minutes at Kenton. The return up working departed Laxfield at 1.00 p.m. and with stops of 20 minutes for shunting at Stradbroke, Horham and Aspall, 19 minutes at Mendlesham and 15 minutes at Kenton, arrived at Haughley at 4.15 p.m. From January 1905 a cattle train commenced running on Tuesdays only, departing Laxfield at 4.30 a.m. An unadvertised 'as and when required' trip from Kenton ran on the Debenham line although the working soon proved unremunerative and ceased by 1906.

Once two locomotives were in operation, the company instituted a service of two goods trains in each direction initially working the line with engines based at Haughley and Kenton, later Kenton and Laxfield. One goods train ran during the morning and the other in the afternoon/early evening. When required a special goods train also ran at short notice.

As early as 1905, in response to enquiries, the company was forecasting a service of two passenger trains each way daily. Although no definite times could be quoted, it was expected that trains would depart Laxfield at 7.00 a.m. and 3.30 p.m., returning from Haughley at 8.15 a.m. and 5.35 p.m. This basic service was to be augmented on Tuesday, Ipswich market day by an additional special leaving Laxfield at 10.15 a.m.

The initial passenger service offered by the Mid-Suffolk Light Railway from 29th September 1908 was: Laxfield dep. 7.35 a.m, 10.00 a.m., 3.30 p.m., 8.34 p.m. SO, the latter running during the month of October only. In the down direction trains departed Haughley at 10.00 a.m., 12 noon, 5.30 p.m. Tuesday only, 6.00 p.m. Tuesdays excepted, and 10.05 p.m. SO, the latter during October only. A Sunday service of two trains in each direction was also offered during October only, departing Laxfield at 7.20 a.m. and 5.20 p.m. and returning from Haughley at 9.00 a.m. and 7.35 p.m. The following year the Sunday services were only operated during the summer months and were withdrawn after the first Sunday in October.

The timetable for July 1910 showed a basic service on the Mid-Suffolk of three passenger carrying services in each direction on weekdays and two each way on Sundays. On Mondays the first up working departed Laxfield at 6.40 a.m. with a 67 minute timing to Haughley whilst on Tuesdays to Saturdays the train departed at 8.20 a.m. The late morning departure left Laxfield at 11.55 a.m. except on Wednesday when it ran 20 minutes earlier at 11.35 a.m. The final up train of the day departed Laxfield at 3.20 p.m. with a 77 minute timing to the junction. On Sundays the first up working at 7.00 a.m. ran as a passenger service arriving at Haughley at 8.07 a.m. whilst the 5.17 p.m. ex Laxfield ran as a mixed train with a 70 minute timing. In the down direction the first departure ex Haughley was 8.10 a.m. MO and 9.52 a.m. MX with afternoon departures at 3.00 p.m. mixed, with a 1 hour 29 minutes booked timing to Laxfield and the 5.55 p.m. which ran as a passenger train on a 65 minutes timing between Haughley and Laxfield. On Sundays the two down services, 8.50 a.m. and 7.35 p.m. ex Haughley, ran as passenger trains with 63 and 62 minute timings for the 19 miles journey.

The fastest down journey from London was available on the 3.20 p.m. GER train ex Liverpool Street which connected with the 5.55 p.m. ex Haughley and provided a 3 hour 40 minute timing to Laxfield whilst the slowest was 4 hours 17 minutes by the 4.20 p.m. ex Liverpool Street on Sundays which connected with the 7.35 p.m. ex Haughley. In the up direction passengers leaving Laxfield by the 5.17 p.m. on Sundays were afforded the fastest journey to the capital in 3 hours 58 minutes whilst the slowest timing was by the 7.00 a.m. on Sundays which

Stradbroke station, looking towards Haughley in the winter of 1908/9 with No. 2 entering the platform with a down train bound for Laxfield. *Collection J. Watson*

connected with a GER service giving arrival at Liverpool Street 4 hours 30 minutes later.

In October of the same year the service was reduced to two passenger trains each way and a short working between Kenton and Haughley and return, whilst Sunday trains were withdrawn. In the up direction trains departed Laxfield at 8.20 a.m. and 3.20 p.m. with a 12 noon Kenton to Haughley. In the down direction balancing services departed Haughley for Laxfield at 10.00 a.m., 5.45 p.m. SO and 5.55 p.m. SX, whilst the short Kenton working departed Haughley at 2.37 p.m. In the up direction the best timings to London were pathetically slow with 4 hours 37 minutes for passengers joining the 8.20 a.m. at Laxfield and an inferior 4 hours 45 minutes by the afternoon departure. Travellers fared better on the down road with a timing of 3 hours 16 minutes by catching the 3.30 p.m. ex Liverpool Street which connected with the 5.45 p.m. SO ex Haughley. Compared to this those hardy individuals joining the 5.05 a.m. ex Liverpool Street finally arrived at Laxfield at 11.02 a.m., 5 hours 57 minutes for the 102 mile journey!

The passenger timetable for 1911 showed departures from Laxfield at 6.40 a.m. MO, 8.20 a.m. MX, 12.10 p.m. MSO, 3.20 p.m. also from Kenton to Haughley at 12.10 p.m. TThO. Trains returned from Haughley at 10.00 a.m., 2.37 p.m. SX to Kenton only, 3.00 p.m. and 5.55 p.m. On Sundays trains departed Laxfield at 7.00 a.m. and 5.17 p.m., returning from Haughley at 8.50 a.m. and 7.35 p.m., these only running June to October.

No improvements had been made to passenger services by April 1914 when the basic service consisted of two trains in each direction weekdays only with three trains on Tuesdays and Thursdays. Up departures left Laxfield at 8.15 a.m., 11.39 a.m. TThO (mixed) and 3.20 p.m. (mixed) with timings ranging from 68 minutes to 77 minutes. In the down direction trains departed Haughley at 10.00 a.m. and 5.40 p.m. TO, 5.55 p.m. TX, with an unbalanced 12.15 p.m. Kenton to Laxfield mixed on Tuesdays and Thursdays only. The timings of the down passenger services varied between 62 and 65 minutes for the 19 mile journey. In July 1914 summer Sunday services were resumed. The basic weekday up services consisted of departures from Laxfield at 8.15 a.m., 12 noon TThO, and 3.20 p.m., whilst the down service from Haughley departed at 10.00 a.m., 12.40 p.m. Kenton to Laxfield calling at Horham and Wilby by request only, 2.39 p.m. Haughley to Kenton mixed and 5.55 p.m. On Sundays two trains ran in each direction – 7.00 a.m. and 5.17 p.m. ex Laxfield, returning at 8.50 a.m. and 7.35 p.m. from Haughley. Journey times on the branch ranged from 62 minutes for passenger services to 77 minutes for mixed trains, whilst the fastest up journey between Laxfield and Liverpool Street was achieved in 3 hours 40 minutes by passengers catching the 12 noon TThO and the GER connection thence from Haughley. In the down direction a time of 3 hours 37 minutes was possible by catching the 3.20 p.m. ex Liverpool Street which connected with the 5.55 p.m. Mid-Suffolk train.

The passenger service from July 1915 showed a slight reduction with only two trains in each direction on weekdays and Sundays with an additional up working on Tuesdays and Thursdays only. Up services departed Laxfield at 8.15 a.m. mixed, 12.55 p.m. TThO mixed and 3.25 p.m. mixed on weekdays, and 7.10 a.m. and 5.30 p.m. on Sundays. Down departures from Haughley were 10.05 a.m. mixed and 5.52 p.m. on weekdays and 8.50 a.m. and 7.40 p.m. on Sundays. The winter timetable for the same year showed only one morning train each way on Sundays during the month of October, departing Laxfield at 7.30 a.m. and returning from Haughley at 8.50 a.m. The only alteration to weekday services was the later departure of the last down working at 5.55 p.m. On Saturdays this train awaited the arrival of the 4.55 p.m. GER train ex Norwich Victoria due at Haughley at 5.57 p.m. The Mid-Suffolk train then ran later throughout.

The timetable from May 1916 was basically unaltered on weekdays whilst the Sunday service of two trains in each direction was reintroduced between June and September. From October the Sunday service was retained but with the one working each way transferred from morning to evening. By January 1917 the up services from Laxfield departed at 8.15 a.m. mixed, 12.55 p.m. TThO mixed and 3.25 p.m. mixed on weekdays, and at 5.30 p.m. on Sundays. Down trains departed Haughley at 10.05 a.m., 5.40 p.m. SX, and 6.00 p.m. SO on weekdays, and 7.40 p.m. on Sundays.

The working timetable for 1919 showed a service of two mixed trains in the up direction departing Laxfield at 8.15 a.m. and 3.25 p.m., supplemented on Tuesdays and Thursdays by an additional mixed train departing the terminus at 12.55 p.m. Timings for the journey varied between 1 hour 8 minutes and 1 hour 17 minutes. The 8.15 a.m. up was barred from working trucks, except livestock in cattle wagons from Laxfield. On Thursday excepted, trucks could be attached at Kenton, provided they were shunted ready on the down main line and were double or screw coupled. On Thursday the train was not permitted to attach vehicles at Kenton or stations beyond. The 3.25 p.m. ex Laxfield, being the last up train of the day, was permitted to work any traffic from Laxfield, all classes of tranships from Wilby, but only tranships for London from other stations. On Monday, cattle wagons containing livestock for foreign company stations could be conveyed from intermediate stations between Laxfield and Kenton provided the guard had been previously advised. Head Office permission was required for similar traffic to be attached at Kenton and stations to Haughley. On Tuesday and Thursday the 3.25 p.m. ex Laxfield could attach at Kenton loaded and empty trucks off the 9.35 a.m. as required, ex Wilby or 9.45 a.m. ex Stradbroke goods, provided they were ready in the middle road and double or screw coupled. On Wednesday the train conveyed livestock in cattle wagons from intermediate stations for Stowmarket only provided the guard had received previous notification. The additional Tuesday and Thursday 12.55 p.m. ex Laxfield mixed was worked by the Laxfield based engine to Kenton and the Kenton-based engine thence to Haughley. The train was permitted to attach livestock in cattle wagons at Kenton together with traffic off the previous up goods if it terminated at Kenton. Livestock in cattle wagons could be attached at all other stations provided the guard received prior notification, whilst loaded and empty trucks fitted with double or screw coupling could be attached at Mendlesham if they were ready at the top points.

Up goods services departed weekdays only from Wilby at 9.35 a.m. when required or 9.45 a.m. ex Stradbroke. On Mondays the train called as required at Horham and Worlingworth and terminated at Kenton at 10.25 a.m. This train worked all traffic except tranships for London and livestock as well as empty vehicles. Loaded vehicles were then shunted at Kenton ready for attaching to the 4.00 a.m. cattle train ex Laxfield on Tuesdays. The Kenton engine and brake then shunted into Mill Siding before attaching to the 10.00 a.m. down mixed train ex Haughley. This was double headed to Laxfield to enable the Kenton engine to work the 4.00 a.m. cattle train ex Laxfield the following morning. On Tuesdays and Thursdays the up goods was extended beyond Kenton as and when required, departing at 10.40 a.m., calling at Aspall and Brockford as required, arriving at Haughley at 11.25 a.m. This train worked all descriptions of traffic except tranships for London as well as empty vehicles. If the train terminated at Kenton, livestock and important traffic were attached to the 12.55 p.m. ex Laxfield mixed, whilst surplus wagons were attached to the 3.25 p.m. mixed ex Laxfield provided they were double or screw coupled and ready in the middle road. On Wednesdays, Fridays and Saturdays the 9.35 a.m. ex Wilby (9.45 a.m. ex Stradbroke) ran through to Haughley calling at Kenton from 10.25 a.m. to 10.55 a.m. and other stations as required, arriving at Haughley at 11.55 a.m. On these days the train worked all descriptions of traffic except tranships for London as well as empty vehicles. Aspall, Brockford, Mendlesham and Gipping siding were also cleared of wagons provided the staff advised Kenton of the number of wagons for the train by sending a message on the 10.00 a.m. down mixed train ex Haughley.

Additional up goods trains ran on Mondays and Thursdays, departing Kenton at 5.45 a.m. and arriving at Haughley an hour later. The train called at all intermediate stations but not Gipping siding, and conveyed livestock in cattle wagons and passenger train vehicles as well as loaded and empty goods wagons, the number of vehicles requiring conveyance being notified by station staff to Kenton by the 5.40 p.m. down mixed ex Haughley on the previous Saturday or Wednesday, separate details being given for ordinary goods and livestock. On Thursdays livestock in passenger train vehicles for Stowmarket and other foreign line stations was conveyed by this train and not the 8.15 a.m. mixed train ex Laxfield. To cater for the large transfer of livestock to Ipswich market, a Tuesdays only cattle train departed Laxfield at 4.00 a.m., stopping to attach cattle traffic only at all intermediate stations to Kenton where the train was booked to stand for ten minutes from 4.45 a.m. to 4.55 a.m. The train then stopped at Aspall and Brockford when required and at Mendlesham for cattle traffic before arrival at Haughley at 5.45 a.m. where the trucks were attached to the waiting GER goods. This train conveyed from any station livestock in cattle wagons and passenger train vehicles for Ipswich only and was worked by the Kenton based engine which was stabled overnight at Laxfield with its crew lodging. Station staff were required to have all traffic ready for collection to ensure the minimum delay to the train and thus ensure punctual arrival at Haughley to avoid any delay to the forwarding GER train. This train also worked from Kenton all traffic except tranships left by the previous day's 9.35 a.m. ex Wilby as required (9.45 a.m. ex Stradbroke goods). If the train was running in good time and the tail load was not too heavy, empty goods trucks could be attached at Aspall and Brockford provided the staff had advised Kenton the previous day of the number of vehicles to go forward, separating ordinary goods and cattle trucks. Similar arrangements persisted at Mendlesham.

In the down direction the 1919 working timetable showed only two mixed trains running on weekdays, departing Haughley at 10.00 a.m. and 5.40 p.m., the former taking 1 hour 10 minutes and the latter 1 hour 2 minutes for the journey to Laxfield. The morning train conveyed livestock in cattle wagons to Worlingworth and beyond, other loaded and empty vehicles to Worlingworth and Laxfield, and tranships for Worlingworth, Wilby and Laxfield. Outstanding livestock traffic for stations Mendlesham to Kenton was also conveyed by this train, if movement was unavoidable by any other train. On Mondays the train was double-headed from Kenton to Laxfield to enable the Kenton engine and brake to run to the terminus ready for the up cattle train on Tuesdays. The 5.40 p.m. mixed train ex Haughley, conveyed livestock in cattle wagons to any station but other truck loads only to Laxfield. On Saturdays during March this train connected with the GER train ex Norwich Thorpe due at Haughley at 6.00 p.m. and departed at 6.03 p.m., running 23 minutes later throughout to Laxfield.

Down goods trains commenced with the 7.00 a.m. ex Haughley which ran on Tuesdays only to Stradbroke although the train was extended to Wilby as required. The train called at Mendlesham, Brockford, Aspall and Horham as required and Worlingworth to pick up cattle traffic only, and shunted at Kenton between 8.00 a.m. and 8.46 a.m. Loaded and empty vehicles, except those for Worlingworth, were also conveyed whilst livestock in cattle wagons were conveyed to any station. If shunting took place at Mendlesham, vehicles with double or screw couplings were to be placed at the top points ready for the 12.55 p.m. Tuesday and Thursdays only up mixed train. If the train was extended to Wilby, the Stradbroke station master was to make the necessary arrangements. On Mondays and Thursdays only, the goods departed Haughley half an hour later at 7.30 a.m. making the same stops as the Tuesday train. Only 31 minutes were spent at Kenton, ensuring the same arrival time, 9.10 a.m. at Stradbroke or 9.30 a.m. at Wilby. On these days the train conveyed livestock to any station and other loaded and empty vehicles only to Mendlesham, Kenton and stations beyond except Worlingworth. Double or screw coupled vehicles left at Mendlesham for the 12.55 p.m. Tuesdays and Thursdays only up mixed train ex Laxfield, had to be placed at the top points. The train also worked forward from Kenton any traffic left by the 1.10 p.m. goods ex Haughley on Wednesday, Friday and Saturday. On Wednesday, Friday and Saturday, the morning goods started at 8.46 a.m., running in the same path as other days to Stradbroke or Wilby if required although on these days no call was made at Worlingworth. This train conveyed traffic left at Kenton by the 1.10 p.m. ex Haughley Wednesday, Friday and Saturday and 2.55 p.m. ex Haughley Tuesday and Thursday only goods to Kenton. The company also ran afternoon goods trains from Haughley to Kenton. On Tuesday and Thursday the train departed the junction at 12.15 p.m., running only if required, arriving at Kenton at 12.50 p.m. Instructions were given for the train to be given a clear run and when operated it conveyed loaded trucks only for Kenton and beyond, the latter being worked forward by the 10.00 a.m. mixed train ex Haughley the following day. A further mandatory goods train ran on Tuesdays and Thursdays only, departing Haughley at 2.55 p.m., stopping at intermediate stations when required and terminating at Kenton at 3.55 p.m. On Wednesdays, Fridays and Saturdays the train departed Haughley at 1.10 p.m. Both these trains were rostered to convey tranships except those for Worlingworth, Wilby and Laxfield and all truck load traffic and empty vehicles except for Worlingworth and Laxfield to any station. Traffic for Horham and beyond was to be worked forward from Kenton by the 8.46 a.m. goods ex Kenton. Livestock traffic for stations beyond Kenton was not permitted to be worked by this train. On Fridays if necessary a special goods was to be arranged by the station master at Haughley at short notice, running as far as Brockford and calling at Mendlesham and Gipping on the return run, to arrive in time again to leave Haughley not later than 2.55 p.m., with arrival at Kenton an hour later.

On Sundays the timetable only made provision for one passenger train in each direction, departing Laxfield at 6.15 p.m. and returning from Haughley at 7.40 p.m. with 1 hour 2 minutes timing in each direction. Both trains were specifically noted to run as passenger trains unless otherwise instructed.

Even these post-First World War timings between Laxfield and Liverpool Street or return were barely encouraging for the intrepid traveller. The fastest down journey on the 3.10 p.m. ex Liverpool Street, which connected at Haughley with the 5.40 p.m. MSL train to give a 3 hours 32 minutes timing to Laxfield, was express compared with the exhausting 6 hours 5 minutes by travellers on the 5.10 a.m. ex Liverpool Street which connected with the 10.05 a.m. ex Haughley. In the up direction no passenger could travel from Laxfield to London in under 4 hours and the fastest timing of 4 hours 5 minute was possible by catching the 12.55 p.m. TThO MSL train which connected with the GER train at Haughley due in Liverpool Street at 5.00 p.m.

From the autumn of 1919 after the transfer of the Kenton-based engine and men, the train services were worked entirely from Laxfield. By July 1920 the service had been increased to three trains in each direction on weekdays but only one each way on Sundays. Up trains departed Laxfield at 8.15 a.m., 1.00 p.m. and 3.25 p.m., returning from Haughley at 10.05 a.m., 12.55 p.m. and 5.30 p.m. Timings varied between the almost express 61 minutes of the 8.15 a.m. ex Laxfield to 77 minutes of the 3.25 p.m. ex Laxfield. On Sundays the solitary train of the day departed Laxfield at 5.30 p.m., arriving at Haughey 62 minutes later. The train returned from the junction at 7.34 p.m. again with a 62 minute timing to Laxfield.

The timetable for 1921 showed three mixed trains in the up direction, departing Laxfield at 7.35 a.m. TuX, 8.10

In the early months of 1924 MSLR 0–6–0T No. 1 waits to depart Haughley with a mixed train for Kenton. Passenger accommodation consists of the two 4-wheel 5-compartment thirds Nos. 4 and 7 with the end doors locked off and handles removed. Although the engine and coaching stock could provide a fitted head to the train, the guard had no control over the Westinghouse brake as he obviously rode in the brake van at the rear of the wagons. The driver on No. 1 is Charlie Brunning. *Real Photographs*

a.m. TuO, 11.05 a.m. and 3.25 p.m., supplemented by the Tuesdays only livestock train which departed at 4.00 a.m. calling at Kenton from 4.40 a.m. to 4.45 a.m. and other stations as required before arrival at Haughley at 5.40 a.m. The daily goods service departed the terminus at 12 noon, calling all stations as required to pick up wagons, to obviate calls being made by the following mixed trains and terminated at Kenton at 1.00 p.m. After shunting as necessary, the train was extended to Aspall, departing Kenton at 1.30 p.m. If sufficient traffic required to be forwarded to Haughley, the 12 noon goods was cancelled and a freight departed at 11.35 a.m., calling at Worlingworth, Stradbroke and Kenton only, and specially if required at other stations. The mixed trains were permitted 1 hour 5 minutes for the run from Laxfield to Haughley except the 3.25 p.m. which was allowed an additional ten minutes to work London and via London tranships and trucks from Laxfield and Mendlesham, also Kenton if ready marshalled. Stradbroke was also permitted to attach a truck destined for London if it could be simply picked up without any extra shunting. In all cases the superintendent at Laxfield was to be advised of the tail loading especially where livestock was involved. Of the other mixed trains the 7.35 a.m. TuX and 8.10 a.m. Tu Only ex Laxfield worked the through GER van containing milk traffic for Ilford, Stratford or Liverpool Street whilst the former also worked livestock and any wagons from Kenton ready marshalled from the previous day. On Tuesdays the 4.00 a.m. ex Laxfield train worked livestock for Ipswich as well as other traffic as required by the traffic inspector.

In the down direction a service of three mixed trains was provided, departing Haughley at 9.40 a.m., 12.55 p.m. and 5.40 p.m. with timings of 1 hour 5 minutes to 1 hour 7 minutes for the journey to Laxfield. The 9.40 a.m. except on Tuesdays was required to work livestock traffic for any station as well as trucks for Aspall and Laxfield and tranships for Aspall. The 12.55 p.m. called additionally at Gipping siding if required and worked the GER van conveying empty milk churns. This train also worked tranships for Wilby, Laxfield and other stations except Aspall as well as livestock traffic for any station. Traffic, except for Worlingworth and Laxfield, for stations beyond Kenton, were detached or left at Kenton for forwarding by the afternoon goods. The last mixed train of the day, 5.40 p.m. ex Haughley was permitted to work livestock to any station and wagons for Kenton and beyond. Beyond Kenton the train only worked Laxfield wagon traffic, and vehicles for intermediate destinations remained at Kenton for forwarding by the goods train the following day. Freight traffic was handled by a 7.00 a.m. Tuesday only goods ex Haughley, the return working of the up livestock train. This worked livestock traffic and trucks for all stations and tranships for Aspall. A daily goods ran from Aspall, departing at 1.50 p.m. to Laxfield with ten minutes allowed at Kenton for shunting or picking up traffic. With other stations served as required, the train arrived at Laxfield at 2.55 p.m. If the up goods was extended to Haughley the return working departed the junction at 1.30 p.m., calling at Kenton from 2.20 p.m. to 2.25 p.m. and other stations as required, before arriving at the later time of 3.15 p.m. at Laxfield. If the 1.50 p.m. ex Aspall ran, it worked vehicles to Kenton for forwarding by up services whilst the as required 1.30 p.m. ex Haughley worked livestock and wagons for any station except Laxfield, picking up wagons left at Kenton by the down mixed services. Sunday services were abandoned after 1921.

The following year adjustments were made to the timetable, commencing on 10th July. In the up direction the Tuesdays only livestock train departed Laxfield at the earlier time of 3.55 a.m. with a correspondingly earlier arrival at Haughley of 5.30 a.m. The up goods now departed at 12 noon, running as far as Aspall but not on Tuesdays and Saturdays, or if required through to Haughley, Saturdays excepted. On Saturdays freight traffic was handled by an additional goods train departing Laxfield at 7.00 p.m., calling all stations as required to arrive at Haughley at 8.15 p.m. allowing for a 5 minute stop at Kenton.

In the down direction the Tuesdays only goods departed Haughley at the earlier time of 6.15 a.m., calling all stations as required to Laxfield, where arrival was booked at 7.50 a.m. The afternoon down mixed train was slightly adjusted to depart the junction at 1.00 p.m. whilst the return goods departed Aspall at 1.50 p.m., not Tuesdays and Saturdays, or when required from Haughley at 2.55 p.m. Saturdays excepted. On Saturdays the return working of the up goods was an additional mandatory mixed train, departing Haughley at 8.55 p.m. with arrival at Laxfield at 10.00 p.m.

The initial service operated after the LNER take-over in July 1924 showed few alterations. The SO goods ex Laxfield at 7.00 p.m. and return 8.55 p.m. mixed ex Haughley no longer ran whilst the last down mixed train now departed the junction at 5.40 p.m. SX and 6.05 p.m. SO.

Because of the coal strike in 1926 it was necessary for the LNER to make economies and passenger train services were reduced in number. On the Mid-Suffolk only the following trains ran from 31st May.

Laxfield to Haughley West	*Haughley West to Laxfield*
7.35 a.m. TX	9.40 a.m. TX
8.05 a.m. TO	9.45 a.m. TO
3.25 p.m.	5.40 p.m. SX
	6.05 p.m. SO

By 1928 the Tuesdays only early morning livestock train from Laxfield and return goods workings had been withdrawn, and the service settled down to a pattern which was retained until the outbreak of the Second World War. In the up direction the service consisted of three mixed trains Tuesdays excepted, one passenger and two mixed trains Tuesdays only, supplemented by a 12 noon goods train ex Laxfield which ran as far as Aspall. This train was extended through to Haughley when required to lessen the tail load on the last up mixed train 3.25 p.m. ex Laxfield. The solitary passenger train was timed to depart Laxfield at 8.05 a.m., half an hour later than the first mixed up train departure the rest of the week, and was permitted three minutes extra between Mendlesham and Haughley West for recovery of time lost by exceptional circumstances. The 11.05 a.m. and 3.25 p.m. mixed train ex Laxfield and the 'when required' 2.05 p.m. Aspall to Haughley goods were allowed two minutes for the same purpose.

In the down direction the service consisted of three mixed trains from Haughley West to Laxfield supplemented by the return goods departing Aspall at 2.05 p.m. If this train was extended through to Haughley on the up working, the goods departed the junction for Laxfield at 3.15 p.m. Of the mixed trains the Tuesday only working departed Haughley at 9.45 a.m. five minutes later than other weekdays whilst the last train departed Haughley at 5.40 p.m. SX and 6.05 p.m. SO.

Two years later only minor alterations had been made. The first up train on Tuesdays and Thursdays only ran as mixed, departing Laxfield at 7.25 a.m. with a booking of 1 hour 17 minutes to Haughley. On Tuesdays and Thursdays excepted the mixed train departed ten minutes later with a timing of 1 hour 10 minutes for the 18 miles 71 chains journey. The former was allowed ten minutes and the

MID SUFFOLK LIGHT RAILWAY COMPANY'S TRAINS ARRIVING AT AND DEPARTING FROM HAUGHLEY.

WEEK DAYS.	1	2	3	4	5	6	7	8	9	10	11	12	SUNDAYS.	13	14	15
	Live Stk.	Mxd.	Mxd.		Mxd.	Gds.		Mxd.								
From	Laxfield.	Laxfield.	Laxfield.		Laxfield.	Laxfield.		Laxfield.								
	TO	NT	TO			WR										
Haughley ... ... arr.	a.m. *5 30*	a.m. 8 40	a.m. 9 15	.....	p.m. 12 10	p.m. *2 15*	.....	p.m. 4 40	.....	.....	.....	.....		.....	.....	.....

WEEK DAYS.	1	2	3	4	5	6	7	8	9	10	11	12	SUNDAYS.	13	14	15
	Gds.		Mxd.		Mxd.	Gds.		Mxd.		Mxd.						
	TO					WR		NS		SO						
Haughley ... ... dep.	a.m. *6 15*	.....	a.m. 9 40	.....	p.m. 1 0	p.m. *2 55*	.....	p.m. 5 40	.....	p.m. 6 5	.....	.....		.....	.....	.....
To	Laxfield.		Laxfield.		Laxfield.	Laxfield.		Laxfield.		Laxfield.						

From LNER Working Timetable 1924

HAUGHLEY WEST AND LAXFIELD LIGHT RAILWAY (For regulations for working see Appendix.)

Single line worked by train staff, or ticket with ticket staff.

Miles from Han'ly W.	DOWN WEEK DAYS.		1	2	3	4	5	6	7	8	9	10	11
				Mxd.		Mxd.	Gds.	Gds.	Mxd.	Mxd.			
								WR	NS	SO			
				a.m.		p.m.	p.m.	p.m.	p.m.	p.m.			
M. C.	Haughley West ...... Ⓢ	dep.		9 40		1 0		3 15	5 40	6 5			
2 44	Gipping Siding	"	—	—	—	—	—	—	—	—	—	—	—
4 37	Mendlesham	arr.		9 52		1 12			5 52	6 17			
		dep.	—	9 53	—	1 20	—	3 35	5 53	6 18	—	—	—
6 4	Brockford	arr.		9 57		1 24			5 57	6 22			
		dep.	—	9 58	—	1 28	—	3 40	5 58	6 23	—	—	—
8 41	Aspall and Thorndon	arr.		10 5		1 35		3 47	6 5	6 30			
		dep.	—	10 10	—	1 36	2 5	3 52	6 6	6 31	—	—	—
10 1	Kenton ...... Ⓢ	arr.		10 14		1 40	2 10	3 57	6 10	6 35			
		dep.	—	10 20	—	1 45	2 25	4 13	6 15	6 40	—	—	—
12 9	Worlingworth	arr.		10 26		1 51	2 32	4 20	6 21	6 46			
		dep.	—	10 27	—	1 52	2 37	4 25	6 22	6 47	—	—	—
13 74	Horham	arr.		10 32		1 57	2 43	4 31	6 27	6 52			
		dep.	—	10 33	—	1 58	2 48	4 36	6 28	6 53	—	—	—
15 8	Stradbroke	arr.		10 37		2 2	2 53	4 41	6 32	6 57			
		dep.	—	10 38	—	2 3	3 3	4 44	6 33	6 58	—	—	—
16 33	Wilby	arr.		10 42		2 7	3 8	4 51	6 37	7 2			
		dep.	—	10 43	—	2 8	3 13	4 56	6 38	7 3	—	—	—
18 71	Laxfield ...... Ⓢ	arr.		10 50		2 15	3 20	5 3	6 45	7 10			

5 Does not run when 6 runs. 6 Does not run when 5 runs.

UP WEEK DAYS.		1	2	3	4	5	6	7	8	9	10
		Mxd.	Mxd.		Mxd.	Gds.	Gds.	Mxd.			
		TThO	NTTh				WR				
		a.m.	a.m.		a.m.	a.m.	p.m.	p.m.			
Laxfield ...... Ⓢ	dep.	7 25	7 35		11 . 5	11 50		3 25			
Wilby	arr.	7 32	7 42	—	11 12	11 57	—	3 32	—	—	—
	dep.	7 33	7 43		11 13	12 5		3 33			
Stradbroke	arr.	7 37	7 47	—	11 17	12 9	—	3 37	—	—	—
	dep.	7 41	7 48		11 18	12 35		3 42			
Horham	arr.	7 45	7 52	—	11 22	12 40	—	3 46	—	—	—
	dep.	7 46	7 53		11 23	12 45		3 47			
Worlingworth	arr.	7 51	7 58	—	11 28	12 50	—	3 52	—	—	—
	dep.	7 52	7 59		11 29	12 58		3 53			
Kenton ...... Ⓢ	arr.	7 58	8 5	—	11 35	1 5	—	3 59	—	—	—
	dep.	8 1	8 8		11 40	1 45		4 6			
Aspall and Thorndon	arr.	8 6	8 13	—	11 45	1 50	—	4 11	—	—	—
	dep.	8 7	8 14		11 46		2 5	4 13			
Brockford	arr.	8 14	8 21	—	11 53	—	—	4 20	—	—	—
	dep.	8 15	8 22		12 0		2 12	4 21			
Mendlesham	arr.	8 19	8 26	—	12 4	—	—	4 25	—	—	—
	dep.	8 20	8 27		12 5		2 16	4 31			
Gipping Siding	"	—	—	—	—	—	—	—	—	—	—
Haughley West ...... Ⓢ	arr.	8 42	8 42		12 20		2 30	4 43			

=1, 2 & 4 Allowed 10, 3 & 2 mins. extra respectively between Mendlesham & Haughley W. for recovery of time lost by exceptional circumstances. =2 May attach at Stradbroke and Kenton, but not at both stations on any one day. Stradbroke and Kenton to arrange

LNER Working Timetable 1930

HAUGHLEY AND LAXFIELD LIGHT RAILWAY (For regulations for working see Appendix.)

Single line worked by split train staff, for each of the two sections but without tickets.

Miles from Haughley	DOWN WEEK DAYS.		1	2	3	4	5	6	7	8	9	10	11
			Mxd.		Mxd.		Gds.		Gds.		Mxd.		Mxd.
									Q		SX		SO
			a.m.		p.m.		p.m.		p.m.		p.m.		p.m.
M. C.	Haughley ...... Ⓢ	dep.	9 40		1 0				3 15		5 30		6 5
2 44	Gipping Siding	"	—	—	—	—	—	—	—	—	—	—	—
4 37	Mendlesham	arr.	9 52		1 12						5 42		6 17
		dep	9 55	—	1 20	—	—	—	3 35	—	5 43	—	6 18
6 4	Brockford	arr.	10 3		1 28						5 51		6 26
		dep	10 4	—	1 32	—	—	—	3 45	—	5 52	—	6 27
8 41	Aspall and Thorndon	arr	10 11		1 39				3 52		5 59		6 34
		dep	10 16	—	1 40	—	2 5	—	3 57	—	6 0	—	6 35
10 1	Kenton ...... Ⓢ	arr.	10 20		1 44		2 10		4 2		6 4		6 39
		dep.	10 26	—	1 49	—	2 25	—	4 13	—	6 9	—	6 44
12 9	Worlingworth	arr.	10 32		1 55		2 32		4 20		6 15		6 50
		dep.	10 33	—	1 56	—	2 37	—	4 25	—	6 16	—	6 51
13 74	Horham	arr.	10 38		2 1		2 43		4 31		6 21		6 56
		dep.	10 39	—	2 2	—	2 48	—	4 36	—	6 22	—	6 57
15 8	Stradbroke	arr.	10 43		2 6		2 53		4 41		6 26		7 1
		dep.	10 44	—	2 7	—	3 3	—	4 44	—	6 27	—	7 2
16 33	Wilby	arr.	10 48		2 11		3 8		4 51		6 31		7 6
		dep	10 49	—	2 12	—	3 13	—	4 56	—	6 32	—	7 7
18 71	Laxfield ...... Ⓢ	arr.	10 56		2 19		3 20		5 3		6 39		7 14

UP WEEK DAYS.		12	13	14	15	16	17	18	19	20	21
		Mxd.				Mxd.		Gds.	Gds.	Mxd.	
									Q		
		a.m.				a.m.		a.m.	p.m.	p.m.	
Laxfield ...... Ⓢ	dep.	7 25				11 5		11 50		3 25	
Wilby	arr.	7 32	—	—	—	11 12	—	11 57	—	3 32	—
	dep	7 33				11 13		12 5		3 33	
Stradbroke	arr.	7 37	—	—	—	11 17	—	12 9	—	3 37	—
	dep.	7 38				11 18		12 35		3 40	
Horham	arr.	7 42	—	—	—	11 22	—	12 40	—	3 44	—
	dep.	7 43				11 23		12 45		3 45	
Worlingworth	arr.	7 48	—	—	—	11 28	—	12 50	—	3 50	—
	dep.	7 49				11 29		12 58		3 51	
Kenton ...... Ⓢ	arr.	7 55	—	—	—	11 35	—	1 5	—	3 57	—
	dep.	7 58				11 40		1 45		4 4	
Aspall and Thorndon	arr.	8 3	—	—	—	11 45	—	1 50	—	4 9	—
	dep.	8 4				11 46			2 5	4 11	
Brockford	arr.	8 11	—	—	—	11 53	—	—	—	4 18	—
	dep	8 12				12 0			2 12	4 19	
Mendlesham	arr.	8 22	—	—	—	12 10	—	—	—	4 29	—
	dep.	8 23				12 11			2 22	4 35	
Gipping Siding	"	B	—	—	—	B	—	—	—	B	—
Haughley ...... Ⓢ	arr	8 42				12 24			2 34	4 54	

5 Does not run when 7 runs.
Trainmen to open and close Stulphs Rd. crossing gates between Mendlesham and Brockford. Trains are allowed 4 mins. extra on the down and 6 mins. on the up journey for this purpose.

D 35 JLY.

LNER Working Timetable 1939

latter three minutes extra between Mendlesham and Haughley for recovery of time lost by exceptional circumstances. The 7.35 a.m. TuThO was also permitted to attach wagons at Stradbroke and Kenton but not from both on the same day. The only other alteration in the up direction was the goods which departed Laxfield at 11.50 a.m. instead of 12 noon. In the down direction the first train ex Haughley departed at the common time of 9.40 a.m. each weekday.

Little had changed by 1935 when the up timetable showed three mixed trains departing Laxfield at 7.25 a.m., 11.03 a.m. and 3.25 p.m. supplemented by the 11.50 a.m. goods from Laxfield to Aspall, arriving at 1.50 p.m. If required the train was extended to Haughley, departing Aspall at 2.05 p.m. All mixed trains called at Gipping siding as required and were allowed between 1 hour 17 minutes and 1 hour 29 minutes for the 18 mile 71 chain journey. In the down direction the same number of trains were provided, the mixed workings departing Haughley at 9.38 a.m., 1.00 p.m., 5.30 p.m. SX and 6.05 p.m. SO. The down goods continued to depart from Aspall at 2.05 p.m. although if it was extended to Haughley on the up run the train departed the junction at 3.15 p.m., arriving at Laxfield at 5.03 p.m. and crossing the 3.25 p.m. mixed train ex Laxfield at Kenton. In the down direction the mixed trains were slightly faster, covering the journey between 1 hour 9 minutes and 1 hour 19 minutes. All trains were allowed 4 minutes extra on the down journey and 6 minutes extra on the up journey for the train men to open and close Stulphs Road crossing between Mendlesham and Brockford. By 1939 the only alterations were that the 9.38 a.m. down departed at 9.40 a.m. and the 11.03 a.m. up ex Laxfield departed two minutes later at 11.05 a.m.

The initial emergency timetable issued after the outbreak of war in September 1939 showed a complete suspension of all services on the light railway. This instruction was rescinded and services operated on a reduced basis for about three weeks. In October 1939 the emergency timetable introduced established the pattern for the last thirteen years of operation with only two mixed trains in each direction departing Laxfield at 7.25 a.m. and 2.30 p.m., returning from Haughley at 11.00 a.m. and 4.50 p.m., the 11.00 a.m. taking 2 hours on the 19 mile journey.

By April 1940 the train service on the branch consisted of two mixed and one goods train in each direction. The mixed trains departed Laxfield at 7.45 a.m. and 2.30 p.m.

'J15' class 0–6–0 No. 5470 at Laxfield waiting to depart for Haughley with a train formed of two 6-wheel compos, a 6-wheel brake third and goods brake in 1947. *Collection G. F. Rice*

with the return workings from Haughley departing at 11.08 a.m. and 4.50 p.m. The goods departed Laxfield at 10.15 a.m., returning from the junction at 1.30 p.m. Additional trains ran, as and when required, to Mendlesham and Horham with traffic for the airfield. The strengthening of permanent way beyond the junction enabled heavy armament traffic to be banked up the 1 in 42 so that the branch engine could haul the train thence to Mendlesham. The timetable remained in operation until 1943 when timings were adjusted. Up mixed trains departed Laxfield at 7.45 a.m. and 1.50 p.m., in timings of 1 hour 15 minutes and 1 hour 20 minutes respectively for the 18 miles 71 chains journey. In the down direction the return workings departed Haughley at 11.08 a.m. and 3.54 p.m. in timings of 1 hour 32 minutes and 1 hour 15 minutes. By now the engine working these services also worked a short goods trip from Haughley, departing 9.30 a.m. to Mendlesham, returning from there at 10.15 a.m., with a fifteen minutes timing in each direction. The up goods departed Laxfield at 10.15 a.m., calling at Kenton from 11.30 a.m. to 12 noon and other stations as required before terminating at Haughley at 12.45 p.m. The return goods departed the junction at 1.30 p.m. with a 1 hour 55 minutes timing to Laxfield including a 35 minutes stop at Kenton from 2.10 p.m. to 2.45 p.m. and calling at all other stations if required.

These timings remained in operation until 1946.

Unlike other East Anglian branches, the Mid-Suffolk line train services were not restored to pre-war levels by 1947 and two mixed trains continued to suffice in each direction, departing Laxfield at 7.35 a.m. and 1.50 p.m., returning from Haughley at 11.08 a.m. and 3.54 p.m. Between the arrival at the junction of the first up working at 8.50 a.m. and departure at 11.08 a.m. down mixed train, the engine worked a short goods trip as required from Haughley to Mendlesham and back to cater for the lingering military traffic to Mendlesham airfield. The down trip left Haughley at 9.30 a.m. and returned from Mendlesham at 10.15 a.m., both trains being allowed 15 minutes for the 4 miles 37 chains journey. The second engine on the branch worked the one goods train each way, weekdays only, departing Laxfield at 10.15 a.m. with a stop over at Kenton from 11.30 a.m. to 12 noon, arriving at Haughley at 12.45 p.m. The return trip departed the junction at 1.30 p.m. and with a 35 minute stop over at Kenton from 2.10 p.m. to 2.45 p.m., arrived back at Laxfield at 3.25 p.m. Both up and down goods trains only called at the other intermediate stations as and when required. All trains continue to be allowed the additional 4 and 6 minutes on down and up journeys respectively for the trainmen to open Stulphs Road crossing gates between Mendlesham and Brockford.

The timetable for 1949 showed little alteration to that of previous years. All passenger carrying trains running under Class B headcode were deemed mixed trains. The first up train departed Laxfield slightly earlier at 7.21 a.m. whilst the 1.45 p.m. train, after arrival at Haughley at 3.18 p.m., formed the 4.00 p.m. empty cars to Stowmarket SX to form the return school train. In the down direction

HAUGHLEY AND LAXFIELD LIGHT RAILWAY

For regulations for working see Appendix.

Single line worked by split train staff (for each of the two sections) without tickets.

DOWN — WEEKDAYS

Miles from Haughley M. C.	No.	1	2	3	4	5	6	7	8	9	10	11	12	13	14	15
	Description					Mxd								Mxd		
	Class															
			Q am			am				PM				PM		
— —	**Haughley** (S)		9 [illegible]			11 8				1 30				3 54		
4 37	Mendlesham		9 45			11 20				*				4 6		
— —	Mendlesham					11 25								4 8		
6 4	Brockford					11 33				*				4 16		
— —	Brockford					11 35								4 17		
8 41	Aspall and Thorndon					11 42				*				4 24		
— —	Aspall and Thorndon					11 46								4 25		
10 1	**Kenton** (S)					11 50				2 10				4 29		
— —	**Kenton**					11 58				2 45				4 37		
12 9	Worlingworth					12 4				..				4 43		
— —	Worlingworth					12 8				*				4 44		
13 74	Horham					12 13				..				4 49		
— —	Horham					12 17				*				4 51		
15 8	Stradbroke					12 21				..				4 55		
— —	Stradbroke					12 25				*				4 57		
16 33	Wilby					12 29				..				5 1		
— —	Wilby					12 33				*				5 2		
18 71	**Laxfield** (S)					12 40				3 25				5 9		

UP — WEEKDAYS

Miles from Laxfield M. C.	No.	1	2	3	4	5	6	7	8	9	10	11	12	13	14	15
	Description			Mxd									Mxd			
	Class															
				am		Q am			am				PM			
— —	**Laxfield** (S)			7 35					10 15				1 50			
2 38	Wilby			7 42					..				1 57			
— —	Wilby			7 43					*				2 0			
3 63	Stradbroke			7 47					..				2 4			
— —	Stradbroke			7 48					*				2 8			
4 77	Horham			7 52					..				2 12			
— —	Horham			7 53					*				2 15			
6 62	Worlingworth			7 58					..				2 20			
— —	Worlingworth			7 59					*				2 21			
8 70	**Kenton** (S)			8 5					11 30				2 28			
— —	**Kenton**			8 10					12 0				2 40			
10 30	Aspall and Thorndon			8 15					..				2 45			
— —	Aspall and Thorndon			8 16					*				2 46			
12 67	Brockford			8 23					..				2 53			
— —	Brockford			8 24					*				2 54			
14 34	Mendelsham			8 34					..				3 4			
— —	Mendelsham			8 35		10 15			*				3 6			
18 71	**Haughley** (S)			8B50		10 30			12 45				3 20			

Trainmen to open and close Stulph's Road crossing gates between Mendlesham and Brockford, and trains are allowed 4 minutes extra on the Down and 6 minutes on the Up journey for this purpose.

LNER Working Timetable for 6th October 1947

HAUGHLEY AND LAXFIELD LIGHT RAILWAY

(NO SUNDAY SERVICE)

For regulations for working see Appendix.

Single line worked by split train staff (for each of the two sections) without tickets.

DOWN — WEEKDAYS

Miles from Haughley	No.	1	2	3	4	5	6	7	8	9	10	11	12	13	14	15
	Class		K			B			K			B			B	
	Description					Mxd						Mxd			Mxd	
			Q						MWF			SO			SX	
M. C.			am			am			PM			PM			PM	
— —	**Haughley** (S)		9 30			11 8			1 30			3 44			4 35	
4 37	Mendlesham		9 45			11 20			*			3 56			4 47	
— —	Mendlesham					11 21						3 57			4 48	
6 4	Brockford					11 29			*			4 5			4 56	
— —	Brockford					11 30						4 6			4 57	
8 41	Aspall and Thorndon					11 41			*			4 17			5 8	
— —	Aspall and Thorndon					11 45						4 18			5 9	
10 1	**Kenton** (S)					11 49			2 10			4 22			5 13	
— —	**Kenton**					11 57			2 45			4 30			5 21	
12 9	Worlingworth					12 7						4 40			5 31	
— —	Worlingworth					12 9			*			4 41			5 32	
13 74	Horham					12 14						4 46			5 37	
— —	Horham					12 15			*			4 47			5 38	
15 8	Stradbroke					12 19						4 51			5 42	
— —	Stradbroke					12 21			*			4 52			5 43	
16 33	Wilby					12 25						4 56			5 47	
— —	Wilby					12 26			*			4 57			5 48	
18 71	**Laxfield** (S)					12 37			3 25			5 8			5 59	

14 Formed by 4.25 p.m. ex Stowmarket. Haughley arr. 4.29 p.m.

UP — WEEKDAYS

Miles from Laxfield	No.	1	2	3	4	5	6	7	8	9	10	11	12	13	14	15
	Class		B			K			K				B			
	Description		Mxd										Mxd			
						Q			MWF							
M. C.			am			am			am				PM			
— —	**Laxfield** (S)		7 21						10 15				1 45			
2 38	Wilby		7 32										1 56			
— —	Wilby		7 33						*				1 58			
3 63	Stradbroke		7 37										2 2			
— —	Stradbroke		7 38						*				2 4			
4 77	Horham		7 42										2 8			
— —	Horham		7 43						*				2 10			
6 62	Worlingworth		7 48										2 15			
— —	Worlingworth		7 49						*				2 16			
8 70	**Kenton** (S)		7 59						11 30				2 27			
— —	**Kenton**		8 4						12 0				2 35			
10 30	Aspall and Thorndon		8 9										2 40			
— —	Aspall and Thorndon		8 10						*				2 41			
12 67	Brockford		8 21										2 52			
— —	Brockford		8 22						*				2 53			
14 34	Mendelsham		8 32										3 3			
— —	Mendelsham		8 33			10 15			*				3 4			
18 71	**Haughley** (S)		8 48			10 30			12 45				3 18			

12 SX Forms 4.0 p.m. ECS to Stowmarket.

Trainmen to open and close crossing gates at Stulph's Road (between Mendlesham and Brockford), Roses Road (between Brockford and Aspall & Thorndon), Kenton Road (between Kenton and Worlingworth), White Horse Road (between Wilby and Laxfield), and trains are allowed 16 minutes extra on the Down and 18 minutes on the Up journey for the purpose.

BR (ER) Working Timetable for 5th June 1950

the last train from Haughley departed at 3.44 p.m. SO and 4.35 p.m. SX. The latter started back as the school train from Stowmarket at 4.25 p.m., arriving at Haughley at 4.29 p.m. The path for the short trip working between Haughley and Mendlesham and return continued to be shown between the first up arrival and down departure but was by now rarely used. The greatest change brought about by the continued loss of freight traffic to road competitors was the running of the goods train 10.15 a.m. ex Laxfield and 1.30 p.m. ex Haughley return on Mondays, Wednesdays and Fridays only. Because of further staff cuts, all trains were now allowed 16 minutes extra on the down and 18 minutes extra on the up journey for trainmen to open and close crossing gates at Stulphs Road between Mendlesham and Brockford, Roses Road between Brockford and Aspall & Thorndon, Kenton Road between Kenton and Worlingworth, and White Horse Road between Wilby and Laxfield.

The final working timetable for 1952 showed the weekdays only service of two mixed trains in each direction, departing Laxfield at 7.21 a.m. and 1.45 p.m., arriving at Haughley at 8.45 a.m. and 3.18 p.m. respectively. The down trains departed Haughley at 11.15 a.m. and 4.42 p.m. SX, 3.55 p.m. SO, arriving at Laxfield at 12.44 p.m., 6.06 p.m. SX and 5.19 p.m. SO respectively. The 7.21 a.m. up and 4.42 p.m. down working continued to work to and from Stowmarket to convey schoolchildren. On Mondays, Wednesdays and Fridays the goods ran from Laxfield at 10.15 a.m., reaching Haughley at 12.45 p.m. before returning from the junction at 1.30 p.m.

During independent years the running time allowed from start to stop between stations for moderately loaded passenger and mixed trains (details for goods trains are given on page 146) in each direction was:

Laxfield and Wilby	7 minutes
Wilby and Stradbroke	4 "
Stradbroke and Horham	4 "
Horham and Worlingworth	5 "
Worlingworth and Kenton	6 "
Kenton and Aspall	4 "
Aspall and Brockford	7 "
Brockford and Mendlesham	4 "
Mendlesham and Haughley	12 "

Originally not more than 15 wagons were permitted to be attached to mixed trains, with the last vehicle being a brake van with a guard in charge. In cases where no wagons were attached, the under guard was required to ride in the rear van. The maximum load for one engine working an up train was 15 vehicles, with down trains loaded to 10 vehicles from Haughley to Mendlesham and 15 vehicles from Mendlesham to Laxfield.

From 1921 these instructions were slightly amended when the number of wagons permitted to be attached to mixed trains was:

With passenger brake in the rear	up to 10 wagons
With No. 1 goods brake in the rear	up to 10 wagons
With No. 2 goods brake in the rear	up to 14 wagons
With No. 1 and No. 2 goods brakes in the rear	up to 28 wagons

provided each brake was in charge of a guard.

The maximum number of vehicles permitted to be worked by mixed trains on the MSLR from 1921 was: up trains with one engine, 18 vehicles; down trains with one engine Haughley to Mendlesham, 12 vehicles; and from Mendlesham and beyond, 18 vehicles.

Staff were requested to make every effort to avoid delaying GE connecting trains at Haughley and an allowance of at least 7 minutes was required to re-book passengers and transfer luggage. The attaching and detaching of vehicles from mixed trains at intermediate stations was also to be carried out promptly with station staff providing every assistance to the guard. Passenger train vehicles loaded or empty could be attached or detached at any station to or from a passenger or mixed train except on restricted workings advised from time to time. Wherever possible empty passenger train vehicles were to be worked by goods train and station staff were required to promptly advise the guard if coaching stock was to be attached.

FARES

The initial ordinary fares charged were 1d per mile third class and 2d per mile first class. Examples were Haughley to Mendlesham third class single 4½d and period first class return Haughley to Laxfield 5/3d. For children three years to under 12 years old half fares were issued.

In addition to ordinary fares, the Mid-Suffolk company initially offered third class market tickets at a single fare plus a half available for return on the day of issue only by the following trains: 7.35 a.m. and 10.00 a.m. ex Laxfield Tuesdays only, and 10.00 a.m. ex Laxfield on Wednesdays and Thursdays. To encourage weekend travel, the company also issued cheap day return tickets at a single fare plus half from Haughley to all stations on the light railway. These were available for use on the 6.00 p.m. and 10.05 p.m. ex Haughley on Saturdays, and 9.00 a.m. ex Haughley on Sunday, with availability for return by any train on Sunday or Monday. The facility was also available from all stations to Haughley by any train Saturday and by the 7.20 a.m. ex Laxfield on Sunday with availability for return by any train on Sunday or Monday. The fare charged was to a minimum of 6d. In the early years tickets were printed and supplied by Bemrose and Company but from 1914 Edmunson tickets were in use.

By 1920 when the passenger services were contracting many of the concessions were withdrawn. The market day ticket was only available to third class passengers and was restricted to the second up train of the day to Haughley only. Two years later this was superseded by the introduction of a cheap day one and a quarter single rate return to Ipswich on Tuesdays and Stowmarket on Thursdays. These were quickly followed by weekend returns between Mid-Suffolk and GER stations at a minimum rate of 5/-d third class, fractions of 3d being charged as 3d. On Saturdays cheap day and half day tickets were available from all the light railway stations to Haughley. In the latter years of independence through bookings were available to Stowmarket, Ipswich and Liverpool Street.

The fares between Liverpool Street and the branch stations in 1936 were:

		Single		Monthly Return	
Miles		*First*	*Third*	*First*	*Third*
83	Haughley	17/6	10/6	21/-	14/-
87	Mendlesham	18/6	11/1	22/6	15/-
89	Brockford and Wetheringsett	18/9	11/3	22/6	15/-
92	Aspall and Thorndon	19/4	11/7	23/3	15/6
93	Kenton	19/7	11/9	23/9	15/9
96	Worlingworth	20/-	12/-	24/-	16/-
97	Horham	20/5	12/3	24/9	16/6
98	Stradbroke	20/8	12/5	25/3	16/9
99	Wilby	21/-	12/7	25/8	17/-
102	Laxfield	21/6	12/11	26/-	17/3

whilst local fares between Haughley and the stations were:

Mendlesham	1/-	7d	1/6	1/-
Brockford and Wetheringsett	1/3	9d	1/9	1/3
Aspall and Thorndon	1/10	1/1	2/3	1/6
Kenton	2/1	1/3	2/9	1/9
Worlingworth	2/6	1/6	3/-	2/-
Horham	2/11	1/9	3/9	2/6
Stradbroke	3/2	1/11	4/3	2/9
Wilby	3/6	2/1	4/8	3/-
Laxfield	4/-	2/5	5/-	3/3

The final fare structure on the light railway before closure in July 1952 was:

Liverpool Street to	*Ordinary Singles*	
	First	*Third*
Haughley	18/3	12/2
Mendlesham	19/3	12/10
Brockford and Wetheringsett	19/9	13/2
Aspall and Thorndon	20/2	13/5
Kenton	20/5	13/7
Worlingworth	21/-	14/-
Horham	21/3	14/2
Stradbroke	21/9	14/6
Wilby	21/11	14/7
Laxfield	22/5	14/11

whilst single fares from Haughley were:

Mendlesham	9d	6d
Brockford and Wetheringsett	1/6	1/-
Aspall and Thorndon	1/11	1/3
Kenton	2/2	1/5
Worlingworth	2/9	1/10
Horham	3/-	2/-
Stradbroke	3/6	2/4
Wilby	3/8	2/5
Laxfield	4/2	2/9

Through tickets continued to be issued from the branch stations to Stowmarket, Ipswich and Liverpool Street.

EXCURSIONS

The first excursion offered by the Mid-Suffolk in conjunction with the GER was to Felixstowe on Wednesday, 30th September 1908. Fares charged were from Laxfield and Stradbroke 3/6d; Horham and Worlingworth 3/3d; Kenton, Aspall and Thorndon for Debenham and Brockford 3/-d, and Mendlesham 2/-d. This excursion, the only one offered by the MSLR in the 1908 season, was fairly well patronised.

The excursion and special traffic programme offered by the Mid-Suffolk company could not be compared with the facilities offered on GER branch lines. The company was entirely reliant on the main line company for affording facilities beyond Haughley and thus any excursion offered on the Light Railway had to be run and arranged in conjunction with excursions from GER stations. Although agricultural workers' wages were low, the fares offered were attractive enough to permit manual workers to visit the coastal resorts, some travelling to the sea for the first time in their life.

In the early years excursions ran once a year from the light railway stations to East Anglia resorts served by the GER. Destinations varied; in 1909 the train ran in connection with Yarmouth races, whilst Clacton was the venue in 1912. Local events were also catered for and in May 1914 cheap return tickets were issued from all stations to Kenton to enable local people to attend the sports day at Debenham. The offering of such excursion fares usually involved the company running an additional up service in the morning and down service in the evening to connect with the GER trains.

Between the two world wars the excursion programme available to residents served by the Mid-Suffolk line were gradually extended. This was especially relevant once the LNER had taken over the line for as well as including the usual East Anglian destinations, fares were offered for a short time to Lincoln and York. During the First World War the excursion programme was abandoned and after hostilities the number of trips and variety of destinations was cut back severely. Until closure of the line, Felixstowe and Yarmouth were the destinations most regularly offered.

GOODS TRAFFIC

Before the advent of the railway in Mid-Suffolk the inhabitants of the villages and towns of the area were reliant on the carrier's cart or wagon for the conveyance of their produce to and from local markets. The carriers also conveyed commodities to and from the various GER railheads serving the locality. The unmade roads in the area meant that the carriers' wagons were slow and ponderous on their journey especially in wet weather when they sank axle deep in the mud and ruts, perishable produce was often not of the best quality by the time destinations were reached when journeys were sometimes made in the outward direction one day with the return the following day.

In 1896 from Laxfield, Henry Chandler was journeying to Framlingham on Mondays, Thursdays and Saturdays whilst John Newman served Halesworth on Tuesdays and Fridays. Walter Meene had far longer distances to cover going to Woodbridge, Wickham Market and Ipswich on Mondays and Thursdays, and Norwich on Tuesdays and Fridays. From Stradbroke his brother William Meene was carrier to the Bull Inn, Ipswich on Mondays and Fridays and the Lamb Inn, Norwich on Fridays only. He also worked a service to Diss on Tuesdays and Fridays along with E. Rose who journeyed to Diss on Mondays, Wednesdays and Saturdays. The village of Horham had only one carrier service, that operated by Charles Larter, who went daily to Eye connecting with the GER branch to Mellis. Wilby was a pick-up point for William Meene on his Monday and Friday Ipswich runs although the services did not return to the village until the following day. Mr. Capon was local carrier at Brockford, serving Stowmarket on Thursdays and the GER station and village at Finningham on

Tuesdays and Saturdays. Ipswich was served by Mr. Stannard whose wagon travelled to the county town on Tuesdays and Saturdays. The neighbouring village of Wetheringsett enjoyed the carrier service of Charles Rose to Ipswich on Tuesdays and Saturdays. Mendlesham was fortunate in having the most frequent number of carrier services with Jolly serving Ipswich on Tuesdays, Thursdays and Saturdays, whilst F. Reason served the same town on Tuesdays only. The same carrier served Stowmarket on Thursdays as did Lockwood and E. Abbott. Stowmarket was also served on Mondays, Tuesdays, Thursdays and Saturdays by Mr. Arbourn.

By 1904 just before the opening of the line to traffic, few changes had been made. Alfred Freeman was carrier from Laxfield to Framlingham daily, whilst Sidney Rose had joined his brother Charles as carrier from Wetheringsett to Ipswich on Tuesdays and Saturdays. At Stradbroke, Spencer Watling had taken over the Monday, Wednesday and Friday runs to the Lamb Inn at Norwich.

Unfortunately, the transfer of goods traffic from carrier's cart to railway wagon when the line first opened was not as heavy as forecast. This was most noticeable on Ipswich and Stowmarket market days when local farmers and growers as well as a cross-section of the community continued to travel by wagon or horse-drawn cart conveying their wares to market. As in many rural communities, the market gave opportunity for a day out or break from routine away from village and farm, for a leisurely drink and conversation with fellow travellers and traders from other villages. The ride by road made for an early start and other travellers were met or overtaken on the journey and pleasantries passed. Equally the return from market could be made as the individual required.

None of these leisurely timeless arrangements were possible by rail, for the Mid-Suffolk dictated when commodities should be loaded or unloaded; a deadline was also given when no further items could be accepted for transhipment. Items had to be loaded or offloaded into and out of railway wagons in the station yards where there were no fellow travellers to converse with and catch up with the latest gossip. Many of the older farm workers resisted the railway, for it meant no day away from the farm or trip to market with the incentive of a pint or two of ale *en route.* Once delivered, the farmer or labourer returned to his work to await the return wagons from Ipswich or Stowmarket. Routines of a Suffolk lifetime were slow to change and only after a few years' usage, combined with poor weather which made roads and track almost impassable, did the Mid-Suffolk Light Railway overcome former prejudices and habits to provide the rapid transit of goods to and from local markets, as well as destinations all over Britain.

As predicted at the early exploratory meetings to form the railway, barley, wheat, straw, hay and vegetables formed the basic commodities conveyed by rail. These items were responsible for the highest receipts in the early years when the Ipswich Corn Company established distribution points in Horham, Worlingworth and Laxfield station yards. Barley was initially conveyed to the maltings at Needham Market, Stowmarket, Ipswich and Bury St. Edmunds, but after rationalisation of these establishments and breweries, the barley was sent further afield to Kings Lynn, Godmanchester and destinations in Scotland. Much of the agricultural traffic in later years was handled by the Eastern Counties Farmers Co-operative Ltd. who established a mill adjacent to the railway at Kenton.

Fruit traffic, noticeably apples, plums and soft fruit, was another important commodity. The produce was loaded at Wilby, Laxfield and Cratfield, for local markets as well as Spitalfields market, London, Leeds and Bradford. The apples were loaded into baskets or skips into vans hired from the GER whilst soft fruits and plums contained in punnets were conveyed in the passenger brake van and transferred into the GE train at Haughley. Often the partitions were taken out of the MSLR horse-boxes so that fruit could be conveyed. After 1923 a through van was introduced by the LNER. As an extension of the apple growing, Chevalliers produced cider at Aspall and despatched supplies regularly by rail from the station. The firm was later taken over by the Aspall Cider Company.

From the late 1920s much of the agricultural land served by the Mid-Suffolk line was turned over to the growth of sugar beet. By the early 1930s a considerable proportion of goods receipts were being earned by the seasonal conveyance of sugar beet from the branch stations to the sugar processing factories at Bury St. Edmunds and Ipswich, and to a lesser extent Cantley. Between October and January empty wagons were worked to the branch stations, either on mixed trains or daily goods and during peak lifting periods by special workings. The wagons were then loaded daily and forwarded via Haughley to Bury or Ipswich. The continuation of flow so vital to the production at the factories often necessitated the opening of the line on Sundays to clear the beet traffic and place empties for the following Monday. This practice ceased, however, after the Second World War. The peak year for conveyance of beet was 1934 when 21,000 tons were loaded at Laxfield alone. Approximately 500 wagons were regularly despatched whilst the maximum number handled in the three month season was 672. This, however, was exceeded at Worlingworth where Tom Hambling as porter-in-charge labelled over 1,000 wagons of sugar beet in one season destined for Ipswich and Bury St. Edmunds.

Milk was regularly sent from all branch stations to Stowmarket, Ipswich and Bury St. Edmunds in the familiar 17 gallon churns; later the milk was sent further afield to London. Two loads were despatched daily in summer and one in winter months, the first by the early morning mixed train, usually loaded in MSLR van No. 1 attached next to the engine to facilitate the transfer of churns between the MSLR and GER stations at Haughley. In summer months a smaller number of churns were loaded in the same van on the afternoon up mixed train. If passenger van No. 1 was not available, a van was hired from the GER. Van No. 1 or the GER van was then worked back to Laxfield at the rear of the last down train of the day when empty churns were offloaded at each station. From 1912 the GER, and later LNER, provided a milk van for the churn traffic. The van was worked through from Laxfield to London, offloading at Stowmarket and Ipswich *en route.* The van was worked up on the first mixed train of the day before being attached to the rear of the main line train at Haughley. Similarly a van with empty churns was worked back from London to connect with the last down train from Haughley to Laxfield. This traffic ceased after the Second World War.

The largest commodity by far received in the goods yards on the light railway was coal. Even before the opening of the line to goods traffic, various merchants were requesting sites for coal storage at station yards. By February 1905 Thomas Moy and Fred Reason had secured coal allotments at Mendlesham with Mr. Cole at Stradbroke. A large coal store served by a private siding was provided by Harry Capon at Kenton. Within six months the number of fuel merchants receiving supplies of coal had increased to eight with Coote and Warren based at Kenton, Thomas Moy at Kenton, Aspall, Stradbroke and Mendlesham, R. Chambers at Kenton and Laxfield, F. H. Fosdick at Kenton, Stradbroke and Horham, H. Manby at Kenton and Laxfield, Beaumont and Company at Aspall and Laxfield, W. King at Stradbroke, R. Collier and Son at Laxfield, and Cole at Stradbroke. Within a few years many of the smaller merchants were bought out by the larger combines and in the latter years Coote and Warren and Thomas Moy were the chief recipients of rail-borne fuel in the station yards. Both possessed their own private owner wagons and before the Second World War most coal came in these wagons. Moys established a fuel yard at Laxfield in 1926 when they purchased a plot of land on the down side of the railway, removed part of the fencing and built an access road to serve the coal plots enlarged in 1928. Coal and coke supplies came chiefly from the Midlands collieries in private owner wagons but later imported coal was transhipped the short distant from Ipswich and Felixstowe Docks. Private owner wagons regularly used included Fosdick, Moys and Coote and Warren's.

Other imports received in the goods yards on the light railway included seed potatoes from Scotland, animal foodstuffs and fertilizers for local farms, agricultural machinery and 'smalls' traffic for local shops and warehouses. Ironically, the railway also helped to serve its own death warrant as early as the 1930s by transporting road-making materials from ballast pits at Wymondham and Holwell Sidings between Welwyn Garden City and Hertford to the various station yards where it was then carted to site to improve local roads. Altogether goods traffic conveyed locally reached 700 to 1,000 tons per week before takeover by the LNER.

Livestock handled by the freight services was two-way traffic. In the early years horse traffic was conveyed in the MSLR horse-boxes and those hired from the GER attached to both mixed and goods trains and destinations included Ipswich, Colchester, Norwich and Bury St. Edmunds. Very often if there were insufficient horse-boxes available, horses were overcrowded and in one instance a horse was found to be dead on arrival. On at least one occasion a horse-box special was run in connection with a meet of the local fox-hounds. With improvements in roads and increased number of motor vehicles, horse traffic declined and by the late 1930s horse-box traffic was rarely conveyed.

From September 1904 cattle traffic provided a considerable percentage of total goods traffic receipts and cattle pens were established at all stations except Haughley, Gipping and Wilby. At the outset cattle wagons were hired from the GER, pending delivery of the six new cattle wagons purchased by the MSLR. Even after the delivery of these wagons in 1905 vehicles continued to be hired from the GER initially at a cost of 3/-d per day. Cattle traffic was even heavy at the smaller stations and Tom Hambling remembers that six trucks of cattle were regularly despatched in a day from Worlingworth *en route* to Ipswich, Stowmarket, Bury St. Edmunds, Norwich or Colchester markets. On a few occasions cattle were sent to Tufnell Park for Smithfield Market and Chelmsford. Until the late 1920s a special cattle train departed Laxfield as early as 3.55 a.m. on Tuesdays conveying beasts for Ipswich market. In order to get traffic to market, the cattle vans were often overloaded or loaded without the due licence being available authorising the movement of cattle. In the halcyon days a combined total of up to 600 head of livestock was forwarded and received each week from Stradbroke, Kenton, Aspall and Laxfield, with other stations providing smaller amounts. Incoming livestock included sheep from Lockerbie. By the late 1930s much of the cattle traffic was transferred to road transport for conveyance to local markets although during the war years petrol rationing and the withdrawal of non essential vehicles from the roads brought a steady return of cattle wagons to the branch. After the hostilities and the easing of petrol supplies, the traffic quickly returned to road haulage and very little movement of livestock was made by rail in the last few years.

Reference has been made to the part played by the light railway in the two World Wars when additional vegetable, fruit, hay and straw traffic was conveyed to local and London markets to ease the shortages caused by losses resulting from enemy action on shipping. Early in the First World War Scottish troops arrived to assist in the building of earthworks and trenches of the third defence line, whilst throughout this conflict additional horse traffic was conveyed to military establishments. During the Second World War two airfield were established near the light railway and initially materials for constructing the runways were conveyed by special freight trains to Horham and Mendlesham stations. While operational, food, stores, armaments and bombs were transported by rail across the branch to be offloaded at Mendlesham or Horham, before conveyance by road, usually in the hours of darkness, to the airfields or the nearby ammunition storage areas concealed in local woodland. To ease the loading for the branch engines on the ascent of Haughley bank, the first half mile of line from the junction was relaid with heavier 90 lb per yard bullhead track to enable class 'J39' 0–6–0 or USA 2–8–0 and 'Austerity' 2–8–0 tender engines to bank the heavy train up the incline. Usually the 'J15' class engine then took the train through to Mendlesham or Horham stations or, if the load was beyond its capabilities, the first section of the train was taken to Gipping siding and left there while the second section was taken through to its destination station. The engine and brake van then returned to Gipping siding for the first portion, the engine and van running through to Haughley initially so that the locomotive could run round the brake van. During these periods it was the unwritten rule that Gipping siding traffic, then very sparse, was to be cleared by the earliest available train so that the siding was available for stowage of wagons. During the war Haughley also had a large petrol depot, receiving 681 trains from

Class 'J39' 0–6–0 No. 64829 shunting near Haugh Lane Bridge. *Dr. I. C. Allen*

August 1939 to June 1944, 445 of them in the last six months.

PARCELS TRAFFIC

After the line opened for goods traffic, all receipts for parcels were accountable to Haughley and takings during the initial months were:

	£ s. d.
September 1904	13 7
October	3 0 10
November	3 13 1
December	4 9 10
January 1905	3 11 4
February	4 6 2
March	6 7 4

From April 1905 Stradbroke and Kenton became accountable for parcels and sundries traffic when the initial receipts were:

	Parcel	*Sundries*
	£ s. d.	£ s. d.
Haughley	4 8 9	6 8 10
Kenton	1 16 8	2 13 8
Stradbroke	2 0 8	4 13 8

The following month Laxfield was added to the receiving stations and takings for May 1905 were:

	Parcel	*Sundries*
	£ s. d.	£ s. d.
Haughley	5 13 7	9 4 11
Kenton	2 10 9	2 8 1
Stradbroke	4 19 0	2 0 8
Laxfield	3 15 6	1 17 2

Later in the year Mendlesham was added to the list of stations accounting for their own traffic. The initial entry for August 1905 showed total parcels and sundries receipts as:

	£ s. d.
Haughley	2 2 0
Mendlesham	2 5 4
Kenton	3 19 0
Stradbroke	6 9 0
Laxfield	6 5 10

The minor stations of Horham and Worlingworth whilst handling traffic were included for receipts with the neighbouring station. In April 1906 Aspall became accountable but the total figure for parcels and sundries for the month showed an alarming reduction.

	£ s. d.
Haughley	16 4
Mendlesham	9 7
Aspall	1 7 6
Kenton	2 1 2
Stradbroke	4 13 10
Laxfield	4 3 6

Later parcels receipts were included with the passenger and goods statistics and are shown in Chapters 3 and 4.

There were no mechanical aids available to staff for goods or parcels traffic although weighing machines were provided at each station for the latter. In the absence of wagon weighbridges, the loads were required to be weighed at the point of destination or at intermediate points, and all Railway Clearing House charges and tolls applicable to the MSLR were dealt with by the GER. Lock-up stores were provided at each station for parcels and sundries.

An interesting item of equipment used on the 'Middy' was the portable loading gauge already referred to in Chapter 4. This could be conveyed to site alongside a wagon and assembled to form the necessary gauge for loading. It was often conveyed by freight train across the line and used at the intermediate stations, but after the purchase of three loading gauges from the GER in February 1912 for installation at Kenton, Stradbroke and Mendlesham, the portable loading gauge was mostly utilized at Laxfield only. The gauges at Mendleham and Stradbroke were removed in later years.

To ease shunting operation, the use of a tow rope was unofficially utilized by staff during the independent years at most stations to enable the engine to shunt or pull wagons in the adjacent siding. The LNER evidently frowned upon such practice but the tow ropes, normally kept in the goods brake vans, Nos. 1 and 2 and their later LNER replacements, were used up until closure of the line.

Cartage of goods received at railway stations was always entrusted to outside carriers during independent days providing some recompense to them for the loss of traffic to the railway. No specific carrier gained full monopoly and amongst those employed were E. Mayhew, F. Reason, A. Freeman, J. Foulston and E. W. Lister.

The Mid-Suffolk Light Railway Company stipulated the following maximum loads for their locomotives:

	Locomotives Nos. 1 and 3	*Locomotive No. 2*
Up trains	21 vehicles	18 vehicles
Down trains		
Haughley – Gipping	14 goods (or equivalent)	11 goods (or equivalent)
Gipping – Cratfield	21 vehicles	18 vehicles

based on the proportion of mineral wagons to goods wagons for computing the loads of engines from Haughley –

1 mineral equals 1 goods	2 minerals equal 3 goods
3 " " 4 "	4 " " 6 "
5 " " 7 "	6 " " 8 "
7 " " 10 "	8 " " 11 "
9 " " 13 "	10 " " 14 "

3 empties equal 2 loaded goods

The LNER wagon load limit on the Laxfield branch was 25 vehicles and the full list of authorised loads permitted for Class 'J15' locomotives was:

	Minerals	*Goods*	*Empties*
Haughley to Laxfield	14	22	25
Laxfield to Haughley	14	22	25

Under British Railways the limit remained at 25 wagons but loads authorised were slightly amended to 13 heavy, 23 goods and 25 empties. The 'J65' class tank engines and the 'E4' 2–4–0 conveyed seven heavy wagons or equivalent less than the above loads.

Quite often the loads of up trains exceeded the load limit, to ensure traffic reached its destination promptly. If the load was of thirty wagons or over, the train was split at the top of Haughley bank, after which the engine took the first section down to Haughley yard before returning for the second section.

The running time allowance (start to stop) between stations for moderately loaded goods trains as permitted by the MSLR was:

Laxfield and Wilby	11 minutes	
Wilby and Stradbroke	6 "	
Stradbroke and Horham	6 "	
Horham and Worlingworth	8 "	
Worlingworth and Kenton	9 "	
Kenton and Aspall	6 "	*
Aspall and Brockford	11 "	
Brockford and Mendlesham	6 "	
Mendlesham and Haughley	18 "	

*one minute additional outside Kenton for picking up the train staff.

CHAPTER EIGHT

Signalling and Civil Engineering

IN the initial years from 1904, the line was worked by train staff only, divided into two sections Haughley-Kenton and Kenton-Laxfield, with only one engine in steam or two or more coupled together being permitted in each section at any one time. Lieutenant Colonel P. G. Von Donop visited the railway for the official inspection in July 1905 and expressed dissatisfaction with the arrangements at Kenton which was the accepted staff station but not built as a crossing place between Haughley and Laxfield. In the absence of signalling and interlocking of points it was possible for two trains to approach the station simultaneously without proper protection. Von Donop advised the adoption of Kenton as the permanent crossing place and the provision of signalling and interlocking of points operated from a ground frame. Similar arrangements were required on the approaches to Haughley and Laxfield stations. At other stations and sidings, points leading to or from the main single line were required to be locked and unlocked by a key attached to the train staff. The company acceded to most of the inspector's requests but when he returned in September 1908 to reinspect the line prior to the introduction of passenger services, he found the points at Gipping Siding, Mendlesham station (Haughley end), Kenton engine shed and Preston's siding at Worlingworth were not locked by key on the train staff. In addition, the points at Laxfield were required to be properly connected to the ground frame.

By 1919 the train staff only working was proving an operational inconvenience to the company, for increasing traffic often required the running of two trains in the same direction, and, under the existing method of working, delays to traffic were experienced awaiting another train to return the staff. To obviate the problem and save expenditure in installing block signalling, the company decided to introduce the split or divided staff system of working for each section of line. Although common on the continent, the split staff method of working the single line was relatively unknown on railways in Britain. Split staffs were supplied for each of the existing sections Haughley to Kenton and Kenton to Laxfield. Only one engine in steam or two or more coupled together carrying the train staff or a ticket with the ticket staff were permitted to enter the Haughley-Kenton or Kenton-Laxfield sections. If two light engines or trains, or a light engine or train, required to run through the section in the same direction, the driver of the first light engine or train was given the ticket and the ticket staff, at the same time being shown the train staff by the person in charge of the starting station. After proceeding through the section, the driver of the light engine or train was required to hand the ticket and ticket staff to the person in charge of the station at the end of the section. The ticket was withdrawn and cancelled before being sent to the company's head office at Laxfield. The person-in-charge of the station at the end of the section then telephoned the station at the other end of the section to advise the arrival of the first light engine or train, thus giving permission for the second light engine or train to enter the section. On receipt of this information, the person-in-charge at the starting point then handed the driver of the second train the train staff. On the arrival of the second light engine or train in the same direction the person-in-charge at the station at the end of the section, after receiving the train staff from the driver, screwed this ticket staff into the train staff and locked both together with the special key provided.

When the LNER took over the working of the line, the train staff tickets were abolished and the two sections worked by split train staff for each of the sections. The train conveying the ticket staff was, however, still subject to the same instruction applicable to a train conveying a ticket.

Thus when a train was ready to start from either Haughley, Kenton or Laxfield and no second train was intended to follow before the staff was required for a train in the opposite direction, the person in charge of the staff working handed the complete train staff to the driver of the train before it proceeded through the single line section concerned. If another train was to follow the first train before the staff was returned, the train staff was to be divided and the driver of the first train given the ticket half of the staff and the driver of the second train given the other half of the staff. On the arrival of both trains at the other end of the section, the person in charge of the staff working was required to screw the ticket staff into the train staff and lock it with the key provided.

The train carrying the train staff only was not permitted to follow a train conveying the ticket staff for the same section, until the person in charge had ascertained by telephone that the preceding train had passed out of the single line section.

Points at intermediate stations were operated by a small ground lever released and locked by Annett's Key attached to both the train staff and ticket staff portions of the split staff. At Haughley, Kenton and Laxfield the main points on the approach to the station protected by home signal were designated the master points. When a train required to shunt at these stations by using points other than those set for the main line, the Annett's Key unlocked the master points releasing another key which was used to operate the subsidiary points at the station. When shunting was completed, the subsidiary points were locked and the road set for the main single line, after which the subsidiary points key was reinserted in the master point container on the ground frame. This was then locked by the Annett's Key attached to the train staff. The home signals could only be cleared when the road was set for the main single line or the appropriate loop line at Kenton.

Signalling on the Mid-Suffolk Light Railway was kept to the absolute minimum stipulated by Board of Trade requirements. Only the terminal stations at Haughley and Laxfield and the crossing station at Kenton were provided with protecting signals. Home signals were supplied and installed early in 1906 by McKenzie and Holland at a cost of £257 18s 0d. The up home signal at Haughley, up and down homes at Kenton, and the down home signal at Laxfield, were considered adequate for all train movements and were of the usual pattern supplied by McKenzie and Holland to the GER. These were lower quadrant with cedar arms, wrought and cast iron fittings on pitch pine posts, topped off with attractive finials. All signals were interlocked with the immediate points they protected and were operated by a lever from a ground frame. No signal boxes were provided. At Haughley a shunt signal was provided on the same post as the home signal to allow forward movements into the run round loop or sidings.

From June 1911 the Mid-Suffolk Company was required to pay a proportion of the maintenance and manning costs for the physical junction between the light railway and the GER at Haughley. The initial six months payment included £10 as the MSLR proportion of the working of Haughley Junction signal box, whilst the maintenance costs for points and permanent way were also £10. At the same time charges of £306 12s 10d were raised as back payment for the period November 1904 to December 1910 inclusive.

Thereafter six monthly payments were made and these included in February 1912 £10 10s 0d for the rent of a GER siding at Haughley, £3 10s 7d for the working of the junction signal box and £8 16s 9d for the maintenance of the junction. Similar charges remained until after the First World War when for the six months ending December 1919 the only charge raised was £8 16s 10d for the working of Haughley Junction signal box.

Maintenance costs of signalling on the 'Middy' were minimal and if any work was required it was usually carried out by GER signal fitters. In the spring of 1913 repairs to buffer stops and minor attention to the signalling by the GER cost the MSLR £9 19s 5d. In the summer of 1914 one of the train staffs must have been damaged or mislaid for the light railway obtained a replacement from McKenzie and Holland Ltd. for £1.

Minor signalling alterations were made after the LNER closed the former Mid-Suffolk station at Haughley and re-routed trains into the ex-GER Haughley station. An upper quadrant outer home signal led to two upper quadrant up home signals provided on the same post on the branch just south of Haugh Lane bridge, the upper arm when clear authorised the driver to proceed with his train into the up bay platform whilst the lower arm authorised movement into the up main line platform. A down starting signal was provided for branch trains starting from the up bay platform whilst calling on arms only were provided for trains wishing to proceed to the branch from the up main line. In 1936 the signal post at Laxfield and up home post at Kenton were found to be rotting and were replaced by a tubular iron post. At the same time, the old wooden lower quadrant arms were replaced by upper quadrant metal arms. Another innovation of the LNER was the notice erected on the down side of the line, some 100 yards east of the home signal at Laxfield advising 'Drivers not to pass this board without permission of the train staff or ticket' when departing in the up direction.

On several occasions over the years the semaphore signals failed and with typical light railway or branch line malpractice, until repairs could be effected, trains were permitted to pass signals at danger without any hand signal being displayed. In the years prior to closure Kenton down home signal was inoperative for months and, as no repairs had been carried out, drivers of trains blandly passed the signal at danger if the level crossing gates were open. On one occasion the porter in charge at Kenton, having opened the gates for a down service, returned to the booking office to issue a ticket to a prospective passenger with whom he passed the time of day. Soon afterwards he heard the sound of the engine whistle and on returning to the platform was mystified to discover the train had halted at the down home signal. Realising officialdom might be aboard, he quickly dashed back to his office to re-emerge with what must have been an original MSLR handsignalman's flag. The porter in charge then displayed the fading green cloth to the driver authorising him to proceed with the train into the platform. When the train arrived the VIP on the footplate was announced as R. H. N. Hardy, the newly appointed shed master at Ipswich, making his first trip on the line.

The maintenance of signalling equipment on the light railway after the grouping was the responsibility of the signal fitters based at Stowmarket.

CIVIL ENGINEERING

The initial permanent way of the Mid-Suffolk Light Railway was formed of 56 lbs per yard, Vignoles flat-bottom flanged rails in 30 ft lengths. The rails were secured to the sleepers by dog spikes and fang bolts. The rectangular and half round sleepers measured 9 ft by 9 inches by 4½ inches laid on ballast which was a mixture of gravel, sand and burnt clay, said to be laid to a depth of 10½ inches below the sleepers. The rails were laid in staggered formation and were joined by fishplates. Drainage of the permanent way through the sub-soil was considered adequate and provided no difficulties. The width of the formation was on average 14 feet but where there were stations or sidings, the width was 25 feet or more. Fencing of the railway was seven (later six) strands of wire stretched between 4 ft high wooden posts set 6 ft apart. In later years many of the wooden posts were replaced by light iron standards.

Once the ballast pits at Haughley were exhausted in 1903 the company resorted to using ashes and clinker, material much favoured by the GER for ballasting permanent way on their branch lines. Wagon loads were readily available from the many motive power depots on the GER as well as a small amount from the MSLR, and later LNER and BR continued to use the material for ballasting of the permanent way. After the 1920s supplies of ashes and clinker were also available from the British Sugar Corporation factories at Bury St. Edmunds and Ipswich.

The original permanent way was not particularly well laid; in 1903 the rolling stock was reported to be rolling badly and as early as June 1905 the company were involved in paying demurrage charges of £22 9s 0d to the GER for main line wagons detained in MSLR sidings after consignees had refused to pay, saying that the delay to the trucks was caused by the bad state of the goods yard sidings and adjacent roadways.

Most of the original Vignoles 56 lbs per yard rail remained in use during the independent years, the only removals being from Laxfield Mill to Cratfield and the Debenham

The 56 lbs per yard rail was not fully replaced on the line until 1947. The tethered goat is said to have been owned by a member of the permanent way staff and was occasionally allowed to feed on the grass verges alongside the track.
R. G. Pratt, courtesy G. F. Rice

branch which, as mentioned previously, were lifted in the First World War and sold off in 1917. After the war the MSLR intended to replace defective sections of line and purchased a large quantity of second-hand sleepers from the GER in September 1920 at a cost of £224 16s 6d. Most of these, however, were used to replace rotting sleepers under the existing rails and it was reported just prior to the takeover by the LNER in July 1924 that only a short section of the main single line, near Haughley, had been relaid with second-hand 80 lbs per yard bullhead rails.

The new regime carried out few improvements to the permanent way, initially concentrating on the replacement of defective rails or sleepers with excess rails or second-hand sleepers already in stock. By 1930, however, a start had been made on the improvement programme and two miles of the Mid-Suffolk line had been relaid with 80 lbs per yard bullhead track. Pending the enquiry into closure and possible conversion to a road, the LNER considered the light railway to be of the lowest priority. When, however, it was decreed the line should stay open, a ten year relaying programme was announced. The outbreak of the Second World War interrupted the programme and it was early 1947 before the whole branch had been relaid with the 80 lbs per yard bullhead track, enabling the displacement of the 'J65' class 0–6–0 tank engines and the full introduction of 'J15' class 0–6–0 tender engines on all services. As previously mentioned, during the early years of hostilities the first half mile of the main single line out of Haughley was relaid with 90 lbs per yard rails to enable heavier locomotives to shunt trains into the petrol dump and also bank the ammunition trains, destined for Mendlesham and Horham, up the 1 in 42 gradient away from the junction. Flat-bottom track remained, however, on the last 18 chains of the line near Laxfield Mill and the sidings at Mendlesham. Some of the original flat-bottom track was believed to have found further use in Ipswich Docks after removal by the LNER.

As the Mid-Suffolk Light Railway followed for most of its length the contours of the land, civil engineering was negligible. There were numerous culverts but only three bridges on the 19 miles of line between Haughley and Laxfield. Underbridge No. 1 at 0 miles 18 chains spanning Haugh Lane and the stream bridge No. 3 at 14 miles 36½ chains both had semi-circular brick arches with 15 ft span. They also had brick abutments and wing walls but Haugh Lane was later rebuilt with wrought iron parapets. Overbridge No. 2 at 5 miles 42 chains carried the Ipswich to Norwich main road A140 across the railway. The bridge had a steel girder span supported by brick abutments and wing walls. The width between brick parapets was 22 ft with 16 ft skew span across the railway and a height of 15 ft from the top of the rails. During the course of construction the railway was laid on temporary track along the top of the embankment and across a level crossing, until the bridge was completed. Because of the insecure nature of the surrounding embankment, 34 wagons of brickbats were purchased from the Woolpit Brick Company at £1 per

A more conventional method of transportation on the 'Middy'. Two of the permanent way staff standing on the hand trolley at Laxfield. *Collection G. F. Rice*

The MSLR ash and clinker ballast was notorious for sustaining weed growth and this often required the services of the GER weed-killing train. Here 'E22' class 0—6—0T No. 247 has paused while the operator checks the former locomotive tender containing the chemical. On top of the tender is George Bloom, the MSLR P.W. inspector. *Collection G. F. Rice*

wagon to infill the structure. This bridge often caused problems and these were not finally overcome until the summer of 1920 when the GER District Engineer carried out repairs at a cost of £97 9s 8d. The bridge over the Aspall Road at Debenham was also a skew bridge and F. J. Moore reported that it was a puzzle to local bricklayers who could not understand why the arches should slightly overlap at each end with a tooth edge. The resultant odd patch in the construction was still visible years after the line was closed.

The initial maintenance of permanent way and structures was divided into three gangs with ganger, later permanent way inspector, George Alfred Bloom, who resided at Silver Street crossing in charge of the maintenance of the whole line. For these supervisory duties he earned the four-weekly salary of £5 10s 0d in 1906 but later received an increase to two guineas per week. Bloom's sons were employed in the motive power section of the light railway whilst Mrs. Bloom was resident crossing keeper at Silver Street. Altogether about twenty men were on permanent way duties, the platelayers initially earning 18/- per week, 3/- above the rate for a farm labourer.

When the LNER took over the line Robert Pleasance, a ganger, lived in the cottage at Roses Road crossing, whilst sub ganger Allan Pleasance resided at Worlingworth. The rent for the cottage accommodation initially charged by the LNER was £5 4s 0d per annum.

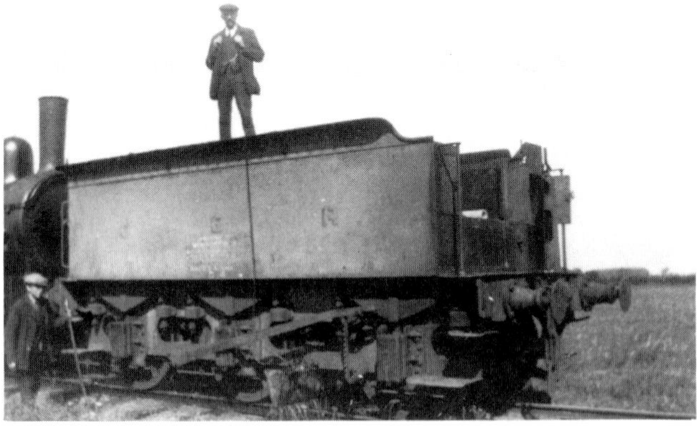

P.W. inspector George Bloom was responsible for permanent way matters during the independent years, earning 2 guineas per week. *Collection G. F. Rice*

In later years, under the LNER and BR regimes, two sets of permanent way staff were responsible for the maintenance and repair of track and buildings. The gang based at Laxfield consisted of a ganger and two lengthmen covering the section from Laxfield Mill to Stradbroke inclusive, whilst the nine man gang based at Brockford covered the remainder of the line to Haughley exclusive. For this extensive length they had the use of a petrol-driven trolley which, when not in use was stabled at Brockford.

If the men were using the trolley when out on repairs or maintenance during the times a train was required to use the line, the trolley was removed at any of the short sections of track laid at right angles to the main single line near each station. At each of these places a plug point was located to enable the ganger in charge to advise the nearest staff stations that the line was clear for the train to pass. The provision of the trolley was not new as the MSLR permanent way staff had the use of a pedal velocipede for some years.

Despite having their own staff before grouping, the MSLR often requested the GER district engineer to carry out minor repairs or maintenance work when local expertise was inadequate. On one such occasion in July 1913 staff from Ipswich executed maintenance on a number of sidings and repaired a set of buffer stops, the main line company charging £9 19s 5d for the services. The GER also on occasions ran their weed-killing train over the Mid-Suffolk line at the request of the local superintendent and receiver.

In addition to attending to day-to-day track maintenance, the permanent way staff were responsible for cleaning toilets where no mains drainage existed as well as repairing occupational crossing gates, fencing and cattle guards. On hot dry summer days, especially during harvest time, they patrolled the line, acting as beaters to extinguish small fires caused by stray sparks emitted from passing locomotives.

The maintenance of way and works in the final years of independent operation were:

Year ending / **Half-year ending*	*1920*	*1921*	*1922*	*1923*	*June 1924**
	£ *s.* *d.*	£ *s.* *d.*	£ *s.* *d.*	£ *s.* *d.*	£ *s.* *d.*
Bridges	255 16 6	30 11 9	15 5 5	30 6 1	4 13 3
Roads	750 14 6	1093 5 4	238 1 4	165 18 7	64 1 3
Signalling	7 17 4	15 6 5	4 1 5	6 5	1 13 5
Stations	143 11 0	72 16 7	29 11 10	4 7 5	2 8 11
Engine Shed	3 2 11	3 4 4	4 0 9		16 11
Permanent Way –					
Works	2965 6 5	2538 11 1	1757 10 0	1679 18 4	816 4 6
Maintenance	2362 17 7	638 2 7	286 8 11	350 7 5	179 11 3
Engine Power	368 2 1	77 5 2			
	6857 8 4	4469 3 3	2334 19 8	2231 4 3	1069 9 6

End view of the GER weed-killing spray tender with MSLR P.W. inspector G. Bloom standing on the left. *Collection G. F. Rice*

Unloading at Kenton down side platform in the 1920s with goods guard W. Thorndyke standing next to the van. Note the two P.O. coal wagons of Messrs. Coote and Warren standing in Mill siding. *Collection C. Scholey*

CHAPTER NINE

Directors and Staff

THE original Board of Directors of the Mid-Suffolk Light Railway consisted of Francis Seymour Stevenson of Playford Mount, Woodbridge, Suffolk, and Member of Parliament for Eye; Bernard Mancha Kilby of London; the Earl of Stradbroke of Henham Hall, Wangford, Suffolk; Mr. J. B. Chevallier of Aspal Hall, Stonham Aspal, Suffolk; F. M. Remnant, Wenhaston Grange, Halesworth, Suffolk; and J. D. Cobbold, banker and brewer of Holy Wells, Ipswich.

Francis Stevenson, largely instrumental in promoting the railway, severed his links with the company on being declared bankrupt in May 1906. The chairmanship of the company was then taken over by the former vice-chairman, the Earl of Stradbroke. After the appointment of a receiver in October 1906, only three directors remained on the board, the Earl of Stradbroke and Messrs. Chevallier and Remnant, the last two named serving in that capacity until the line was completely absorbed by the LNER from 1st July 1924.

On the opening of the railway to goods traffic in 1904, one of the engineers of the company, H. L. Godden, was appointed general manager to oversee the smooth commencement of services, assisted by H. J. Rednal as traffic manager. The efforts of these two were not as effective as desired. From September 1904 H. R. Gillingwater, the son of the GER station master at Diss and a former employee of the GER and Lancashire, Derbyshire and East Coast Railway, was appointed assistant manager and then superintendent to take full charge of the day-to-day operation of the line.

With the sacking of Jeyes and Godden as engineers to the company, C. D. Szlumper was appointed engineer from 1905. Szlumper also attempted to take over as general manager but this position was reduced by the directors to traffic manager and offered to Gillingwater. In his capacity as traffic manager, and later the reinstated general manager, Gillingwater was initially a tower of strength to the company and its employees, guiding them through the difficult days of receivership. Both Gillingwater, who later blackened his character and was asked to resign, and Szlumper were replaced in July 1913 when W. Lindsey Badcock, AIME, AI Loco E, MIT, was appointed to the combined role of general superintendent and engineer.

Lindsey Badcock, born in 1871 and educated at Tavistock Grammar School, was a qualified civil engineer who spent the early part of his career in Plymouth Docks. In 1899 he joined the Chief Engineer's Office of the Great Western Railway and then resigned from Paddington to join the Mid-Suffolk Light Railway. Lindsey Badcock continued to establish good working relationships and was well respected by the staff. He occasionally tried to introduce Great Western practices into the MSLR working and staff conditions of service, but on the appointment of A. P. Parker, a GER man, as receiver from February 1918, Great Eastern practices prevailed. Lindsey Badcock died whilst still in office early in 1924 and was replaced by T. J. Dalgleish who was created acting superintendent pending the satisfactory take-over of the company by the LNER.

Dalgleish, a tall Scotsman, had served the Mid-Suffolk faithfully for many years. On the promotion of Gillingwater to acting manager in May 1905, Dalgleish was appointed assistant superintendent and accountant, serving both Gillingwater and Lindsey Badcock in that capacity. As acting superintendent from early 1924 to 1st July 1924, the Scotsman had the difficult task of ensuring a high staff morale during the protracted negotiations, when it was known that rationalisation would prove safe jobs for some and redundancy and displacement for others.

The first secretary of the company was Norman P. Jeffrey, employed in a temporary capacity from June 1900 to January 1902. T. H. Bryant, the Laxfield schoolmaster, was later appointed as local secretary. It is said that Bryant, who had served the promoters of the railway since 1898, spent so much time on railway affairs that the education of the local children suffered. He was subsequently given an ultimatum by the local education authorities to mend his ways. Despite this edict he was appointed as local auditor for station accounts in February 1905 on a part time basis. In 1902 one of the clerks employed by W. H. Smith, Ernest H. Messeder, was appointed secretary and served in that

T. J. Dalgleish, a Scotsman who served the Mid-Suffolk faithfully. In 1905 he was appointed assistant superintendent and accountant and continued in that capacity until early 1924 when he was appointed acting superintendent until takeover of the line by the LNER in July 1924. *Collection G. F. Rice*

capacity until 1904 when he handed in his resignation. This was refused but later the position of secretary, initially in an acting capacity, was taken by W. Warren. In October 1906 Warren was appointed the first receiver of the Mid-Suffolk Light Railway but the position was only of a temporary nature, and in February 1907 Major J. F. R. Daniel, a qualified engineer, took over the post. In the meantime Warren remained secretary until 1913 when his place was taken by George R. Winsor. From 4th October 1914 Winsor was in turn replaced by C. T. Smith as secretary.

Daniel continued as receiver and guided the 'Middy' through the difficult war years before relinquishing the position in February 1918. As all British Railways were then under the Government control, with possible grouping under discussion, it was thought advisable to appoint an officer of the GER to the position of both receiver and manager. A. P. Parker of 36 Fairlop Road, Leytonstone, assistant to the general manager of the GER, was duly appointed as receiver and manager until the completion of the amalgamation. It was to Parker's credit that all rolling stock received post war maintenance attention by the main line company and it was largely on his recommendation that the MSLR was absorbed into the LNER to provide a further 28 years service to the community instead of remaining independent with the threat of immediate closure.

TRAFFIC STAFF

Civil engineering and motive power staff have been mentioned in their respective sections but brief reference must be made to the traffic staff employed on the railway and the important contribution they made to the smooth running of the line.

As early as 1905 the staff employed on the railway totalled 16 and in addition to the superintendent, H. R. Gillingwater and secretary W. Warren, the following were on the payroll: H. J. Rednal, station agent, Haughley, who was formerly employed by the GER at Halesworth, T. H. Bryant, auditor of station accounts, together with one canvasser, four clerks, one engine driver, one fireman, one engine cleaner, one guard, two porters and one pump man.

As traffic increased so additional staff were employed. Haughley, Mendlesham, Aspall, Kenton, Stradbroke and Laxfield had station masters and other stations employed a porter-in-charge dealing with all parcels and goods work as well as shunting and loading and offloading van traffic. As the stations were adjacent to level crossings, the staff were also responsible for opening and shutting the gates for the trains. After the Board of Trade inspection and in time for the introduction of the passenger train services, the company employed seven crossing keepers where gated level crossings were away from stations. Usually the crossing keepers were wives of permanent way staff who resided in the small crossing keepers' cottages located adjacent to the crossings.

By 1908 the number of staff employed reached a total of about 60 which included officers, superintendent's office staff, motive power and permanent way personnel. Of these the superintendent's personnel included a traffic foreman, later inspector, and three clerks. Station personnel totalled about 19, located as follows:

Haughley	Station master, 2 porters
Gipping Siding	Nil
Mendlesham	Station master
Brockford & Wetheringsett	Porter-in-charge
Aspall & Thorndon	Station master
Kenton	Station master, 2 porters
Worlingworth	Porter-in-charge
Horham	Porter-in-charge
Stradbroke	Station master, porter
Wilby	Porter-in-charge
Laxfield	Station master, 2 porters, junior Porter
Cratfield	Porter-in-charge

together with seven crossing keepers employed at the following gated level crossings away from stations: Silver Street, High Road (Old Newton), Stulphs Road, Roses Road, Kenton Road, Shop Street and White Horse Road.

For many years the gates at Silver Street were under the control of Mrs. Bloom, the wife of George Bloom, the MSLR permanent way inspector, whilst the gates at High Road (Old Newton) were opened and closed by Mrs. Borley. Mrs. Hambling opened and shut the gates at Shop Street crossing and Mrs. Bloom, the wife of Cliff Bloom, the driver, was crossing keeper at White Horse Road for a number of years.

In the independent years four guards were employed, one based at Kenton and three at Laxfield. The Kenton guard worked with his own brake van on the same trains as the Kenton-based engine and men which included the combined working Mondays only with the 10.00 a.m. mixed train ex-Haughley between Kenton and Laxfield. This enabled the Kenton guard to lodge and then work with his own brake van the 4.00 a.m. cattle train ex-Laxfield on Tuesdays. The Laxfield guards worked the weekdays passenger or mixed trains as well as the Sunday passenger trains. In the event of the full brake No. 1 or goods brake vans being attached at the rear of the wagons of a mixed train, the senior guard acted as passenger train guard and rode in the coaching stock brake/third whilst the junior guard rode in the rear brake, acting as assistant guard/travelling shunter.

After 1919 the Kenton guard was transferred to Laxfield with his brake van and worked turn and turn about with his colleagues.

In the working instructions issued to Mid-Suffolk Railway staff, the station master or porters-in-charge were instructed to take care that on the arrival of a passenger or mixed train the name of the station was to be called out in a distinct and audible manner. Guards were also required to carry out this instruction. The general instructions issued by the MSLR also advised that no persons including the company's servants, were to travel without a ticket or pass either by goods or passenger train. Any person violating the rule was to be charged full fare. Locomotive men, guards and porters, when travelling to or from duty, were exempted.

Guards or other servants of the company were also forbidden to carry any description of package either for themselves, their friends or the public without proper authority for the free transit of the package, or unless the package was properly stamped, ticketed or entered on a

MSLR Headquarters staff at Laxfield. *From left to right:* E. Cann, Edgar Gladwell, E. Norman and S. Francis. *Collection G. F. Rice*

way bill. Servants of the company, whether on or off duty, were not permitted to smoke in the non-smoking compartments of passenger coaches.

During the independent years staff numbers fluctuated very little and it was only after the takeover of the Mid-Suffolk Light Railway by the LNER from 1st July 1924 that changes took place.

The new regime very quickly found the line to be drastically overstaffed and within months rationalisation began. The former superintendent's office at Laxfield was disbanded and later the station masters replaced by a porter-in-charge. The accounts and paybills for the line were then centred at Stradbroke where a station master was appointed in charge of the branch stations, exclusive of Haughley, with a clerk to assist in the day-to-day administrative duties. Initially crossing keepers were retained but later they were withdrawn from four of the crossings where trainmen were required to open and close the gates for the passage of a train. Traffic staff then totalled 16 including crossing keepers, being distributed as follows:

Haughley	Trains attended by main line station staff
Silver Street	Crossing keeper
High Road (Old Newton)	Crossing keeper
Gipping Siding	Nil
Mendlesham	Porter-in-charge
Brockford	Porter-in-charge
Aspall	Porter-in-charge
Kenton	Porter-in-charge
Shop Street	Crossing keeper
Worlingworth	Porter-in-charge
Horham	Porter-in-charge
Stradbroke	Station master, clerk, porter-in-charge
Wilby	Porter-in-charge
Laxfield	Foreman, 2 porters

The number of guards at Laxfield was reduced from four to three when A. W. Bryant was forced to retire through ill health on 17th March 1928. Bryant, who subsequently died on 22nd July 1928, had originally joined the MSLR as a guard on 29th September 1908. Later the total was further reduced to two.

Mention must specifically be made of the following staff, most of whom were characters in their own right, relating tales of the 'Middy' in the years before and after grouping and nationalisation.

At Haughley F. R. Samuel was station master at the time of the takeover by the LNER, but, when that station was placed under the control of the station master at Haughley West in 1931 Samuel was transferred to a similar post at Stradbroke where he took charge of the day-to-day running of the light railway, assisted by a clerk who dealt with administrative duties and accounts for all stations.

Along the line at Mendlesham, Donald Goose was station master for a number of years, but in the last months of independent operation he transferred to take charge at Aspall and Thorndon. He retained his position under the LNER until May 1929 when the position was downgraded to porter-in-charge and Goose transferred to Trimley on the Felixstowe branch as station master. In the final years of the line Mr. Roberts was porter-in-charge at Mendlesham and, being the only member of staff on duty, worked a split shift arrangement, the early and late turn being divided by a short break during the middle of the day. On the last day of the service Fred Keeble was in attendance.

Brockford station was noted for its cleanliness and spick and span appearance in the years after the war when Mrs. 'Dot' Seaman was porter-in-charge. She had taken over the role at the station after the previous occupant volunteered for war service. Whilst in charge she regularly earned Third Class 'Best Kept Station' awards both from the LNER and British Railways. At the next station, Aspall, Claude Eade was in sole command as porter-in-charge during the last years of the line, dealing not only with passengers from Thorndon but also Debenham. In Mid-Suffolk days Kenton was an important crossing point and, as stated earlier, boasted a staff of three. Initially, after absorption, the LNER decided to retain a station master at the station and G. A. Avery, who had entered the service of the MSLR as a clerk at Kenton in 1906, was promoted to take charge together with Worlingworth and Horham. On Avery's promotion to Eccles Road in 1925 A. A. Meadows was transferred from Mellis to take up the post. In 1929 the post was downgraded to porter-in-charge to bring it in line with all other stations except Stradbroke, and Meadows was transferred to Forncett as station master. In the last years of the service, Walter Thorndyke was at Kenton with the responsibility of working signals, the level crossing, and exchanging the single line tokens, in addition to his normal duties.

The picturesque station at Worlingworth was under the command of porter-in-charge Tom Hambling. Hambling was employed on the Mid-Suffolk Light Railway all his railway career, commencing as junior porter at Cratfield. After the closure of the goods station he was transferred to Laxfield before taking up duties at Worlingworth. Tom and his wife lived in the nearby crossing cottage and before the abolition of crossing keepers' posts, Mrs. Hambling was employed to open and shut the gates.

In LNER days from 1929 Stradbroke was the administrative centre for the Mid-Suffolk line and staff totalled three, station master, clerk and porter-in-charge. The station master employed in the last years of independence was a Mr. A. Kingsbury. In 1931 he was promoted to North

Superintendent's office staff at Laxfield. *Left to right:* E. Norman, Charlie H. Nicholls (chief clerk), Edgar Gladwell and W. Brown. Gladwell, an organist at Laxfield Parish Church, gained his first position as clerk with the company after winning a writing competition for local schoolchildren. After 1924 he moved to Stradbroke as clerk and later station master. When the light railway closed he finished his career as goods clerk at Framlingham.

Collection G. F. Rice

Elmham and his place taken by F. R. Samuel who transferred from Haughley. Samuel was later replaced by Bob Wilson whilst the last occupant of the post before the closure in 1952 was Edgar Gladwell. Gladwell had an interesting career on the Mid-Suffolk, gaining his first position with the company as junior clerk at Laxfield after winning a writing competition for local schoolchildren. He later became chief clerk in the superintendent's office and after amalgamation moved to Stradbroke, initially as clerk and then promoted to station master before the Second World War. For many years Gladwell was organist at Laxfield Parish Church. When the line closed Edgar Gladwell was transferred to Framlingham where he was rather reluctantly employed as goods clerk until his retirement. Gladwell's colleague in the last years at Stradbroke was Ollie Botwright, who as clerk was responsible for the day-to-day accounts of the branch. After the withdrawal of the services, Botwright was transferred to the district manager's office at Ipswich. The porter-in-charge at closure was Harry Smith who had served 23 years at various stations on the 'Middy'.

Initially, Laxfield was the administrative centre for the Mid-Suffolk Light Railway and in the halcyon days traffic staff totalled three, station master, foreman and porter. The station master for a number of years before take-over by the LNER was Jim Moss but when the post was abolished in 1929 and the line administration taken over by Stradbroke, Moss was transferred to take over as station master at Homersfield on the Tivetshall-Beccles (Waveney Valley line). Charlie H. Nicholls was clerk at Laxfield from 1906 and at the time of the closure of the line in 1952 was the oldest surviving employee of the former light railway company. On his retirement his place was taken by Edgar Gladwell.

In the final years of operation the three station staff employed were Frank Bloomfield as foreman, Tom Hambling, porter, and Frank Hubbard, porter. Bloomfield, who moved from Norwich to join the branch staff in 1927, had worked as porter-in-charge at every station on the line before being promoted to foreman at Laxfield.

The two Keeble brothers also served many years at Laxfield, Fred Keeble as odd job man and then carriage cleaner, before transferring to the position of porter-in-charge at Mendlesham. On the closure of the line he was transferred as ticket collector to Stowmarket. Fred's brother, Willis Keeble, was for some time goods guard at Laxfield before being promoted to the position of passenger guard. Willis Keeble as a boy travelled on the first Mid-Suffolk passenger train and began working for the company in 1915, initially as junior porter. He was promoted to guard in 1917 and was responsible for working the last passenger trains on the Mid-Suffolk and on closure of the branch was transferred to Ipswich as a summer season relief guard. In complete contrast to deepest rural Suffolk, Keeble finished his career as guard in the London area of the Eastern Region.

Charles H. Nicholls, chief clerk in the MSLR superintendent's office at Laxfield. He commenced his career with the railway in 1906 and on retirement was succeeded by Edgar Gladwell.

Collection G. F. Rice

The MSLR Permanent Way Department velocipede at Laxfield. At the controls is goods guard A. Snowling, hitching a lift is driver C. Brunning whilst Dick Tacon looks on. *Collection G. F. Rice*

Whilst on the 'Middy' Willis Keeble suffered the ignominy of being left behind on the platform when his train departed from Wilby. Keeble, whilst chatting to the porter-in-charge, was stressing a point and inadvertently raised his hand. As the green flag or whistle was rarely used to give 'right away' on the Mid-Suffolk in the latter years, the fireman thought Willis had given the signal for the train to depart. The fireman failed to glance back after the driver opened the regulator and Keeble and the porter-in-charge were left standing aghast as the train departed in the direction of Laxfield. Willis thought better of giving chase but immediately decided to set out on the 2½ mile walk to the terminus. Fortunately a local passenger had noted Keeble's plight and pulled the communication cord, halting the train half a mile from Wilby. Walking back along the train to investigate, the driver was advised of the circumstances. He quickly reset the tabs at the end of the coach and returned to the cab to release the brakes. The driver then reversed the engine and propelled the train back along the line towards Wilby. Within a couple of minutes the delighted Willis Keeble noted the train approaching. The itinerant guard then rejoined his train for the rest of the run to Laxfield with officialdom none the wiser of the escapade.

Willis Keeble's counterpart on the alternative shift was guard Peachey Betts who started on the Mid-Suffolk Light Railway in 1913 as porter with a weekly wage of 8/6d. In comparison, a guard then earned 11/-d and an engine driver 13/-d per week.

Peachey Betts remembered a particular embarrassing incident which hung like a cloud over his career as guard on the 'Middy'. It was customary for Mrs. Betts to travel from Laxfield to Kenton once a week to visit some of her relatives. A quite lengthy visit was accomplished by catching the first up train out of Laxfield in the morning and returning on the last down train in the evening. On the eventful occasion Peachey was working the last down train. It was a known fact to the footplate crews and the porter-in-charge at Kenton that Mrs. Betts was expected and all went well to Kenton where arrival was on time. Shunting was quickly carried out but on completion there was no sign of Mrs. Betts. The porter-in-charge kept a watchful eye on the road leading to the station but after ten minutes there was still no sign of the good lady. Being reassured, she had not caught the earlier train Peachey decided enough was enough, the railway was not running for the sole benefit of his wife. The 'right away' signal was given to the driver and off towards Laxfield steamed the final train of the day. Just as the rear vehicle disappeared round the bend in the line, Mrs. Betts arrived puffing and panting on the platform. At first upset at being stranded in the wilds of Mid-Suffolk for the night, Mrs. Betts then prepared to return and stop the night with her relatives. Fortunately, soon after setting off along the road, a passing motorist, stopping to ask directions, heard of her plight and offered the good lady a lift to her home. This kind invitation was readily accepted and thus Mrs. Betts arrived home well before Peachey 'signed off' duty for the night. We are left to ponder what happened behind the four walls of the Betts' cottage, but there is no doubt that Peachey had his 'ears bent' for he remained strangely silent when subsequently questioned on the outcome of the incident.

Although the workforce of the Mid-Suffolk Light Railway were proud of their independence and formed a close-knit community, most welcomed the LNER take-over. As well as providing job security for the majority, it meant the receipt of a regular pay packet each week. In the ailing years of independence, the Mid-Suffolk company were quite often unable to make regular payments to their staff and it was not unknown for personnel to wait up to three weeks before receiving their wage packet.

Dick Tacon, the Laxfield 'odd job man', standing by the entrance to the cattle dock and coal siding in 1923. *Collection G. F. Rice*

MSLR 0–6–0T No. 2 alongside the water tank at Haughley on 28th July 1915. The trio of tank engines showed affinity to the GER by being fitted with Westinghouse brake equipment only. Driver Alec Boag and fireman Bloom are on the footplate. *LCGB/Ken Nunn Collection*

CHAPTER TEN

The Locomotive Department

THE light construction of the Mid-Suffolk Light Railway, with its steep gradients and numerous curves, severely restricted the choice of motive power. The 56 lbs per yard flat-bottom track dictated a maximum axle loading of 12 tons on any pair of wheels and the railway company wisely bought new from a major private locomotive construction company, instead of purchasing second-hand from a main line railway. Fortunately, the GER was also endowed with suitable traction for such a lightly laid line, when called upon to provide assistance in times of shortage.

The LNER Engine Route Availability book permitted only the following classes to use the branch: tender – 'J15' for working ballast and breakdown trains at reduced speed, tank – 'J62', 'J65' and 'J70'. Later the LNER and British Railways designated the line to route availability group 1 (RA1) with class 'J70' of RA2 also permitted. Double heading was prohibited. The initial restriction on the use of the 'J15s' was officially lifted from 1947 when all the flat-bottom track had been replaced by bullhead track, although the working timetables continued to show the restriction.

Unfortunately, there is no definitive record of the first steam locomotive to run over the line, save that it was employed by Jackson, the contractor, soon after he commenced construction work. During this time it was used to haul a GER saloon and brake forming the special train conveying Lord Kitchener from Mendlesham to Haughley on 23rd September 1902. Jackson hired a steam locomotive to assist on construction after this date, but whether on a continuing basis or an 'as and when required' is not known. Neither is it certain whether he hired the same locomotive each time or different engines.

By the end of 1902 construction of the railway was advancing so rapidly that Jackson considered it prudent to have a locomotive available at all times and duly placed an order with Manning Wardle for an 0–6–0 saddle tank locomotive. The engine, a standard Manning Wardle 'L' class, makers No. 1570, was ex works on 16th March 1903, delivered as new to Stowmarket and then worked to Haughley. Ironically, the MSLR paid the £9 4s 9d delivery charges although the bill was not settled until October 1904. The principle dimensions were:

Cylinders	12 in x 18 in
Driving wheels	3 ft 0 in diameter
Wheelbase	5 ft 5 in + 5 ft 4 in = 10 ft 9 in
Boiler diameter	3 ft 1 in
Boiler length	7 ft 9 in
Heating surface tubes	402 sq ft
Firebox	46 sq ft
Total	448 sq ft
Firebox diameter	7 sq ft
Water	450 galls
Weight in working order	19 tons 18 cwt

The engine was immediately put to work on construction trains and removing wagons of spoil. When not in use it was stabled in the small locomotive shed at Haughley and later at Kenton. Soon after delivery the locomotive was named *Lady Stevenson* in honour of the mother of the chairman of the Mid-Suffolk Light Railway. The diminutive machine was popular with its crew and worked the first official goods train between Haughley and Laxfield on 20th September 1904. It was then used daily until the arrival of the Hudswell Clarke tank engines when it was demoted to a secondary role as standby engine. After the Mid-Suffolk directors severed links with Jackson, he went into receivership. Most of the equipment used to build the line remained on the light railway pending a decision as to its disposal. During this period *Lady Stevenson,* with some of the contractor's wagons, was placed in store at Haughley. When Jackson's affairs were resolved, *Lady Stevenson* was sold to the Bettisfield Colliery Company Limited, Bagillt, near Flint, on the London and North Western Railway Chester to Holyhead line.

The Mid-Suffolk Light Railway Company owned three tank locomotives. All were built by Hudswell Clarke and Company at their Leeds Works and were typical of that firm's 'Philadelphia' or 'Canal' class of tank locomotive supplied to the Manchester Ship Canal Company and other private owners during the early years of the twentieth century.

Initially two locomotives were ordered from the firm on 5th October 1904 and the first, an 0–6–0T, maker's No. 711, must have been under construction for she was released from the works on 28th November 1904. During the course of construction, the MSLR requested a representative of the National Boiler and General Insurance Company to test the boiler and inspect the engine. For these professional services the insurance company charged the light railway £5 5s 0d for each inspection and £5 7s 9d for the boiler insurance. Before leaving the works, the engine posed in its official Works Grey livery for a photograph with the name *Haughley* painted on the side tanks, but the same picture showed no evidence of the spark arrester on the chimney and siren whistle with which the engine was, according to the official Hudswell Clarke register, supposedly fitted.

Either just before departure from Leeds or soon after arrival on the light railway, the name was obliterated from the side tanks, to be replaced by 'MSLR'. The number '1' was carried on brass plates on the bunker sides and painted on the front and rear buffer beams. The leading dimensions of No. 1 as released from works were:

Cylinders (inside)	14 in x 20 in
Motion	Stephenson with slide valve
Boiler max dia. outside	3 ft 8 ins
Barrel length	8 ft 10 ins
Firebox length outside	3 ft 6 ins
Pitch	6 ft 3 ins
Heating surface firebox	51.28 sq ft
Tubes	496.0 sq ft
Total	547.28 sq ft

Hudswell Clarke works photograph of MSLR No. 2 (works No. 723). Smaller than No. 1, the engine, supposedly ordered as a 2—4—0T and intended as a passenger engine, was built as an 0—6—0T and was reputedly to have been named *Kenton* but there is no evidence that the name was actually carried. *Collection G. F. Rice*

Grate area	9 sq ft
Boiler pressure	150 lbs psi
Coupled wheels	3 ft 4 ins
Length over buffers	25 ft 6 ins
Wheelbase	11 ft 6 ins
Weight (full)	30 tons
(empty)	24 tons 5 cwt
Water capacity	650 galls
Coal capacity	1 ton 6 cwt

The locomotive was hauled 'dead' to Haughley, the GER charging the MSLR £16 7s 6d for combined carriage of the engine over the various main line railways. On delivery the locomotive and its boiler were inspected by GER staff before entering service. According to the Hudswell Clarke official register, the price of No. 1 was around £1,400 but the light railway company must have negotiated a lower price for they only paid a total of £1,034 14s 2d in two instalments on the locomotive, £507 14s 6d in August and £526 19s 8d in September 1905. Within days of delivery the new locomotive had taken over the more important work from *Lady Stevenson* and proved a tremendous asset to the company as freight traffic increased. One minor shortcoming with the engine when delivered was the three link couplings but these were quickly replaced with standard screw couplings.

On 24th March 1905 the second tank locomotive No. 2 (works No. 723) was released by Hudswell Clarke. Smaller than No. 1, the engine was reputedly to have been named *Kenton* but there is no evidence that the name was actually carried. No. 2 was supposedly built as a 2—4—0T and intended as a passenger engine. In addition to the steam brake, she was fitted with Westinghouse brake equipment for the train, the pump being mounted on the right-hand side of the smokebox. Before release from works, however, the light railway company decided it could not afford the luxury of separate goods and passenger engines and No. 2 reverted to an 0—6—0 wheel arrangement. As before, the National Boiler and General Insurance Company were requested to inspect the new engine, charging £13 13s 0d for professional services and £3 15s 0d for the boiler insurance. Like her sister engine, No. 2 carried the numbers on brass plates attached to the bunker sides. Principal dimensions of No. 2 as built were:

Cylinders (inside)			13 in x 20 in
Motion			Stephenson with slide valves
Boiler	Max dia. outside		3 ft 8 ins
	Barrel length		8 ft 4 ins
	Firebox length		3 ft 6 ins
	Pitch		6 ft 3 ins
Heating surface		Firebox	49 sq ft
		Tubes	465 sq ft
		Total	514 sq ft
Grate area			8.8 sq ft
Boiler pressure			150 lbs psi
Coupled wheels			3 ft 4 ins
Length over buffers			25 ft 0 ins
Wheelbase			11 ft 6 ins
Weight (full)			27 tons 15 cwt
(empty)			22 tons 15 cwt
Water capacity			600 galls
Coal capacity			1 ton 3 cwt

Being a smaller engine with shorter wheelbase and boiler barrel, No. 2 had various detailed differences to No. 1. The leading sandboxes on No. 2 were located above the running plate, whereas on her sister locomotive they were located below and in front of the leading coupled wheels. The maker's plates on No. 2 were located on the sandboxes whilst on No. 1 they were carried on the front footstep above the top step. Both locomotives had curved edge profile to the footstep backing plate and were fitted with copper-capped chimneys and brass domes.

The quoted price for No. 2 was £1,375 but the actual price appeared much less. As before, the Mid-Suffolk company took a considerable time in settling their account with an initial payment of £525 on 8th December 1905 and a balancing £550 13s 4d due in May 1906. Because of insolvency the final amount was paid by the courts, leaving the company to arrange a hiring agreement for the locomotive until the sum could be paid. The locomotive was finally purchased in 1907 when the company made two payments, £300 in May and £250 13s 4d in June.

The engine was delivered via the GER to Haughley at the end of March 1905 together with new wagons from the Lincoln Carriage and Wagon Company, the MSLR paying the main line company £29 17s 6d carriage charges. As locomotive and wagon arrived together, in all probability the train was routed via the GN and GE Joint line. Before entering traffic, Hudswell Clarke fitters attended to the locomotive at Haughley, charging the company £10 4s 0d.

Unfortunately, once the locomotives entered regular service, their availability was erratic and they suffered regular mechanical failures. As early as July 1905 Hudswell Clarke sent a fitter to repair a blower on one of the engines, at a cost of £6 14s 11d. Three months later the company effected further repairs and replacements after sending for a drawbar spring, Westinghouse brake pipes and another blower, at a cost of £37 16s 0d. Perhaps the lack of driving technique and the overloading of engines contributed to these early failures.

These problems escalated after the break of contract with Jackson, when repair work was being effected to one of the engines, leaving the other to handle all traffic. To minimise delays this often meant the operating engine was being worked harder on trains that were far heavier than the stipulated loadings. Another and more crucial factor which affected availability was that the Mid-Suffolk Light Railway never employed a qualified fitter, and the maintenance of rolling stock was left to the inexperienced hands of an odd job man who was also employed at times as a locomotive fireman. Thus, if anything other than routine work was required, the services of outside firms or the GER were summoned and this often meant delays until the necessary repairs could be effected.

By February 1906 Hudswell Clarke had repaired axleboxes and supplied replacement boiler tubes at a cost of £17 0s 11d but when the company handyman was unable to effect repairs, the firm sent one of their fitters to advise on the correct procedures, charging the MSLR £1 5s 0d for the service. In the following month and again in June 1906 the GER repaired locomotive axleboxes, charging 16/-d on each occasion. During July and August both locomotives were repaired by Woods and Company, the firm charging £2 7s 4d. Three months later Cobbold Brothers of Ipswich were called to Laxfield to effect further repairs, charging £14 15s 4d, although there are no details of the repairs required or work performed.

Early in 1907 No. 1 required a new drawbar and spring which Hudswell Clarke supplied at a cost of £20 3s 11d. The same engine was further troubled in May when Cobbold Brothers effected repairs totalling £35 13s 2d. No. 2 suffered leaking tubes for some time, which restricted her availability, and in June 1907 Hudswell Clarke supplied replacements for 11s 8d. Cobbold Brothers again carried out the repairs and fitted new brake blocks to both engines in October 1907 at a cost of £12 1s 2d whilst E. Young and Company were called to effect further repairs in December, charging the MSLR £5 13s 3d.

After a period of working with one locomotive, the company motive power position improved and for over a year both engines appeared to have operated a trouble free service. In July 1908, however, No. 2 suffered further problems with the boiler and injectors, which necessitated the procurement of new injector steam cock spindles and again replacement blower pipes from Hudswell Clarke at a cost of £2 16s 9d. Once repairs were effected, the Mid-Suffolk was back to one hundred per cent availability of their locomotive fleet. At the end of October 1908, however, the motion and wheels of No. 1 were showing signs of extreme wear, necessitating withdrawal from traffic. Once again the services of a fitter from Hudswell Clarke were obtained and his inspection confirmed the need for the replacement of defective material. In November the light railway company ordered two slide blocks, trailing axlebox brasses, trailing side-rod brasses and three slide bars at a cost of £8 9s 2d. After effecting repairs at a cost of £6 6s 1d, the Hudswell Clarke fitter suggested that the GER inspect the wheels of the locomotive. The examination was carried out by staff from Ipswich Motive Power Depot and the main line company charged 12/6d. As a result of the inspection, new springs were fitted to the driving and leading wheels, Hudswell Clarke charging £3 2s 4d for the driving and £3 4s 6d for the leading springs, and £5 5s 0d for the fitter's wages. The repairs were carried out at Laxfield.

The failure of No. 1 at such a crucial time in the company's affairs, soon after the commencement of passenger train working, meant No. 2 was effectively overworked, with every train running as mixed to enable the locomotive to shunt the goods traffic in sidings. In November 1908 an order for another locomotive similar to No. 1 was placed with Hudswell Clarke with a request for urgent delivery. Unfortunately, the company had full order books and could not promise an early delivery, so prior to the return of No. 1 to service early in 1909, the company decided to hire a locomotive to handle the freight diagram. Initially, an approach was made to C. D. Phillips of Emlyn Works, Newport, Monmouthshire, and locomotive *Emlyn* and a number of wagons were hired for a short period from the end of November until a long term hire contract could be arranged. The Mid-Suffolk paid a hire charge of £30 for the locomotive and £8 13s 2d for the wagons to C. D. Phillips on 2nd December 1908. After further enquiries, a long term hire was secured when a Manning Wardle 0–6–0T locomotive *Chamberlain* was hired from Holme and King Ltd., contractors of Garston, the first monthly payment of £80 being handed over in January 1909. Other payments included £100 in December 1909 and £143 1s 4d in April 1910. *Chamberlain* remained on the light railway until June 1910. On the arrival of the Manning Wardle locomotive, *Emlyn* was returned to Phillips. *Chamberlain* was built in 1905 (works No. 1663) and was released to traffic on 31st August. Her principal dimensions being:

Cylinders (outside)	14 in x 20 ins
Boiler diameter	3 ft 6 ins
length	8 ft 8 ins
Tubes heating area	600 sq ft
Firebox " "	60 sq ft
Total	660 sq ft
Firebox	8.8 sq ft
Water	600 gallons
Driving wheels	3 ft 6 ins
Wheelbase	5 ft 11 in + 6 ft 1 in = 12 ft 0 ins
Weight in working order	29 tons

After completion of work on the Mid-Suffolk line, *Chamberlain* was transferred to Grassmoor Ltd., Grassmoor Colliery, near Chesterfield, and was finally scrapped in 1935.

Mid-Suffolk locomotive No. 3 (Hudswell Clarke works No. 867) was released from works on 2nd April 1909 and delivered to the light railway soon after. Similar in all dimensions to No. 1, except for the fitting of cast iron wheel centres and mild steel boiler, she was to have been named *Laxfield* but again never carried the title. The engine was inspected by J. Benton on arrival at Laxfield, the Mid-Suffolk paying a fee of two guineas for his services. The cost of the engine was quoted as £1,440 but as the railway was in the hands of a receiver, payment was made by Jellicoe and Hammond, the railway company subsequently hiring the engine until full settlement was made to the financiers. The process was to take nearly three years and was made as follows:

30 June 1910	£742 14s 11d
September 1910	£ 59 6s 5d

The partnership subsequently changed hands and future payments were made to Hammond and Richards:

21st December 1910	£ 59 5s 5d
4th January 1911	£ 58 12s 8d
30th June 1911	£117 10s 7d
30th December 1911	£116 13s 4d
30th June 1912	£116 16s 2d
31st December 1912	£116 10s 1d

The Mid-Suffolk motive power position remained fairly stable with three locomotives and *Chamberlain* available for traffic for almost eight months. No. 1 was then withdrawn from service with a worn big end. The GER fitter removed the brasses at Laxfield and they were remetalled at Ipswich in January 1910 for 4/8d. To cover traffic requirements another *Emlyn* was on loan from C. D. Phillips during December, the MSLR paying £35 10s 11d hire charges.

After introduction in service, each of the three Suffolk engines were equipped with a re-railing jack mounted on their left-hand running board just to the rear of the smokebox. These were utilized in the event of minor derailment to engines, carriages or wagons to save the line being blocked for longer periods than necessary. In all probability a failure of one of the jacks occurred, for in January 1910 the Mid-Suffolk requested the GER to repair and renovate the jacks on a systematic basis, starting with that on locomotive No. 1. All were completed the following month at a cost of £3 2s 3d. In May 1910 the big end brasses for No. 2 were remetalled at Ipswich by the GER at a cost of 4/8d whilst in August No. 2 was again out of service for a few days when a boilersmith repaired a pressure gauge, the GER charging the light railway company 11/5d.

Although the latest addition to the fleet, No. 3 was taken to Ipswich GER shed in January 1911 for extensive maintenance and unknown repairs costing £52 5s 4d. An additional £1 10s 0d was also charged for hauling the engine from Haughley to Ipswich and return. Two months later No. 2 received attention from the main line company at a cost of £29 19s 7d, probably at Laxfield, as no haulage charges were raised. By this time the Mid-Suffolk directors and receiver must have regretted the decision not to appoint a skilled man for maintenance as the 'odd job man' was only performing very minor repairs. During the summer of 1911 the GER boilersmith and mate from Ipswich visited Laxfield to renew defective and leaking tubes on all three locomotives, Nos. 1 and 3 costing £29 14s 7d. At the same period the GE Ipswich breakdown train was called to attend a derailment which was beyond the capabilities of the lifting jacks on the engines. A combined bill for the retubing of No. 2 and the rerailing exercise totalled £25 17s 8d. The three engines subsequently received little attention for nearly a year. A problem which then presented itself was the uneven tyre and flange wear of the engine caused by the locomotive working on the undulating and curving road without being able to turn to even the wear. In July 1912 No. 2's tyres were so hollow and worn that Hudswell Clarke retyred the wheels for £39 15s 0d.

The trio of Mid-Suffolk tank engines then enjoyed a trouble free period of working for 20 months before further modifications were made. Despite repair work on the boilers of Nos. 1 and 2, the locomotives were not renowned for their free steaming and, in order to try and rectify the matter, the blast pipe on No. 1 was renewed in March 1914 at a cost of £2 11s 3d. No. 2 also received a new blast pipe that July when she became the first of the trio to receive heavy repairs and overhaul at the GE Stratford works. Whilst at Stratford she received a new set of cylinders and firebox. The cylinders and blast pipe were obtained from Hudswell Clarke for £67 19s 11d, whilst the GER charged a total of £110 12s 10d for the shopping (Stratford account D & P 3334). At the same time sundry brasses were obtained from Hudswell Clarke to save the MSLR or GER manufacturing their own. No. 2 was outshopped in September and immediately returned to Suffolk. The repairs received by No. 2 when in the hands of the GER were evidently a credit to the works staff at Stratford for she received little attention, other than routine maintenance, over the next four years.

Having established a works repair programme with the main line company, the receiver and railway management arranged for No. 1 to be shopped by the GER the following

The ornate yellow and vermilion lining and lettering applied to MSLR tank engines is evident in this photograph of No. 2 standing at the platform at Haughley on 28th July 1915. The polished dome, copper-capped chimney and brass safety valves, together with brass number plate and builders plates complemented the attractive Victorian brown (red/brown) livery. No. 2 later had her copper-capped chimney removed but in this picture has already acquired ordinary handles on the smokebox door.
LCGB/Ken Nunn Collection

year. During the period in the works the engine received a new set of cylinders, originally ordered by the MSLR from Hudswell Clarke in February at a cost of £71 17s 3d, together with new slide valves. While other remedial work was being carried out, the main line company forwarded the wheels to Hudswell Clarke, who charged the MSLR £82 8s 6d for repairs. No. 1 remained in Stratford works for some considerable period before being outshopped in May 1915, the GER ultimately charging £215 7s 3d for the repairs (Stratford account D & P 3846).

In October 1915 No. 3 required new slide valves and these were obtained from Hudswell Clarke at a cost of £1 11s 0d. They were fitted when GER fitters attended to other repairs on the same engine the following month, the main line company raising charges of £43 17s 8d for services rendered. No. 3 was the next locomotive scheduled for shopping and, prior to her visit to Stratford, a new set of cylinders was obtained from Hudswell Clarke in January 1916 for £79 10s 0d. The next month the engine worked under its own steam from Haughley to Stratford, a much more expensive way to travel than being hauled 'dead', as the MSLR authorities were shocked to find that instead of the 13/7d previously charged for a rider on No. 1's journey to Stratford, the bill from the GER totalled £9 17s 9d for the journey, together with £3 6s 0d for coal supplies.

The repairs executed whilst the engine was at Stratford included the provision of the new cylinders bored to 14 ins x 20 ins, together with a new firebox. The engine was released from works in March when an initial payment of £187 12s 6d was made to the GER (Stratford account D & P 4425). The repairs carried out were quite extensive, but, because of the company's insolvency, the full account was not settled until December 1919 when a further £331 was paid to the main line company. The engine returned 'dead' to Haughley with the GER charging £1 1s 4d for a rider.

No. 1 was the next locomotive to encounter problems and in February 1917 she was withdrawn from traffic and sent to Stratford works again, this time for the fitting of a new firebox and other unknown remedial work. The locomotive was hauled to Stratford with side rods removed, the GE charging 14/11d for the provision of a rider on the 'dead' engine. The shopping took some time to complete and No. 1 was not released from works until July 1917, the cost being £384 11s 3d (Stratford works account No. D & P 5711) although, because of the insolvency of the company, the account was not settled until January 1919. On release to traffic, the locomotive was hauled 'dead' to Haughley.

After their visit to works the three locomotives ran trouble free for almost a year, receiving only the barest of routine maintenance. Early in 1918 No. 3 ran 'hot' and required the trailing axleboxes remetalling. The work was of a fairly minor nature and was carried out by a visiting GER fitter at Laxfield in February at a cost of £1 7s 8d. The continuing movement of heavy traffic and minimal maintenance over the ensuing months, however, soon combined to cause a deterioration in the mechanical condition of the trio. By May 1919 No. 1 was again suffering cylinder defects, whilst No. 2 wheel flanges and tyres were worn and hollow through lack of tyre turning. As with all MSLR stock, the absence of turntables meant vehicles suffered uneven tyre and flange wear. No. 2 was immediately withdrawn from traffic and sent to Ipswich for new tyres to be fitted. Arrangements were duly made to hire a GER tank engine as a replacement and one of Holden's 'E22' class, 0–6–0T No. 254, was sent to assist on the line from 24th May until 20th June 1919. Almost immediately No. 1 was considered to be in such poor mechanical condition that withdrawal from traffic was inevitable. Thus on 10th June, 'E22' class 0–6–0T No. 157 joined her sister engine on the 'Middy', the GER charging a combined £102 7s 6d for the hire of both locomotives to 20th June. The use of the class of engine was not new to the Mid-Suffolk for members of the class had regularly hauled the GER weed-killing train across the line as well as the occasional ballast or breakdown working.

The Mid-Suffolk was now in the unenviable position of having two-thirds of its motive power hired, with only No. 3 to soldier on with the GE locomotives. No. 157 and No. 254 remained at Laxfield until August, the GER charging £152 5s 0d for hire from June. Midway through August No. 2 returned complete with new tyres to the light railway, the GE charging £62 16s 2d for the work. On return to traffic, one of the 'E22s' was returned to her parent company, leaving the second engine on hire, the GER charging £95 13s 5d for its services to the end of September.

In the meantime the Mid-Suffolk was requested to order a new set of cylinders from Hudswell Clarke for No. 1, at a cost of £157, to be delivered direct to Stratford, and on receipt the engine was despatched to Stratford for the works' attention. Whilst *en route* this engine also received attention at Ipswich where the tyres were turned. A combined charge of £107 6s 3d was raised for this work and the continued hire of a 'E22' class 0–6–0 locomotive. No. 1 was subsequently shopped at Stratford works in November

The sun glistens on the boiler and smokebox of 0–6–0T No. 1 as she stands on the run-round loop at Haughley in 1921. The re-railing jack mounted on the left-hand running board just to the rear of the smokebox, was carried to provide assistance in the event of minor derailments. Note the leading sandboxes below the running board in front of the leading coupled wheels and the brass builder's plate on the leading curved profile footstep.

GER 'E22' class 0–6–0 tank locomotives were regularly sent to work the Mid-Suffolk services when the Hudswell Clarke tanks were under repair. The arrangement continued after the grouping and before takeover of the line by the LNER from July 1924. In late 1923 'E22' No. 250, now designated class 'J65', stands at Laxfield with driver Charlie Brunning on the footplate.

Collection G. F. Rice

1919 where the new cylinders, bored to 13¾ x 20 ins diameter, were fitted at a cost of £123 (Stratford works account D & P 6944), the account being settled in December.

No 1 returned to Laxfield before Christmas and the 'Middy' was back to full strength with its own locomotive fleet for the first time for over a year. This high availability only endured for five months before No. 3 required firebox repairs. The GE boilersmiths were again called upon to carry out the remedial work and, together with repairs to parcels van No. 1, the main line company charged the light railway company £188 14s 8d for its services. By August 1920 both No. 2 and No. 3 were in poor condition, necessitating the hire of GER 'E22' class 0–6–0T No. 247 from September, at a cost of £98 per month. This engine remained on the Mid-Suffolk, except for maintenance and boiler washout, until February 1921. She then alternated with another of the class until June 1921. Various minor repairs were carried out to the Mid-Suffolk engines during the autumn of 1920 to keep them running until shopping could be arranged, the GE charging £71 15s 8d.

In the new year No. 2 was deemed to be in the worst condition and arrangements were made to obtain a new set of cylinders from Hudswell Clarke. These were delivered direct to Stratford works in February at a cost of £207 15s 9d. The following month No. 2 was hauled to Stratford and entered works in April. During her period of shopping, extensive repairs were carried out including the fitting of the new cylinders and a replacement firebox; the boiler pressure was also reduced to 140 lbs psi. When originally delivered, the Hudswell Clarke locomotives were each fitted with small copper-capped chimneys but during this overhaul No. 2's chimney was replaced with a taller cast version.

The MSLR settled the costs in two payments, the May instalment being £294 4s 1d including carriage and wagon repairs, followed by settlement of £469 0s 4d in July 1921 (Stratford account No. D & P 8125).

On the return of No. 2 from works attention in June, the locomotive hired from the GER was returned. In the

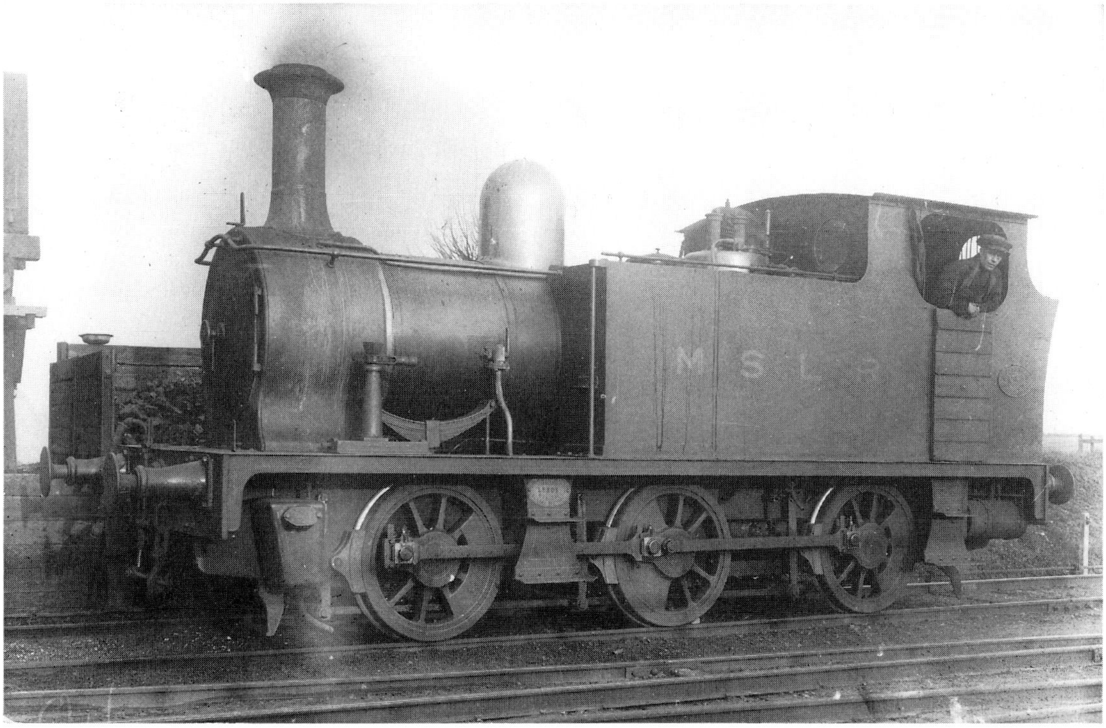

MSLR 0–6–0T No. 1, fitted with a longer cast chimney in place of the original copper-capped chimney, standing by the coal stage at Haughley in early 1924. Charlie Brunning is the driver leaning out of the cab over the wooden plank door added to stop the draught through the side sheets. Brunning was the driver involved with the burst tube on the engine working a return Sunday excursion. *Real Photographs*

same month No. 3, by now mechanically unsound, made the journey to Stratford again, where, after a few weeks standage, she entered works in August. As with the sister engine, No. 3 was given a thorough overhaul, at the same time receiving a new firebox. The boiler was somewhat younger than that on No. 2 so No. 3 retained a working pressure of 150 lbs psi. Repairs were completed in September 1921 at a cost of £556 12s 9d (Stratford works account D & P 8923) and she returned to Laxfield the same month.

During the subsequent months the newly shopped engines received little maintenance other than routine inspection, and No. 1, having now run the highest mileage, received minor repairs from GER fitters. By the late spring of 1922 No. 1 was ailing with a leaking firebox and tubes. Arrangements were made for her to enter Stratford works in August for general repairs including the fitting of a copper firebox and steel tubes. The work was costed at £372 13s 2d and £33 8s 6d respectively (Stratford works account D & P 594), although the former amount also included repairs to a Mid-Suffolk wagon. At the same time the boiler pressure of No. 1 was reduced to 140 lbs psi, again probably because of the age of the boiler and, as with No. 2, a taller cast chimney replaced the original copper-capped variety.

With the trio of engines in almost ex works condition, the LNER before take-over found that few repairs were required. By June 1923, however, minor attention was given to No. 2 by the LNER, the bill for the repairs being included in the total for a supply of locomotive coal of £94 8s 4d. The new regime originally intended to renumber the engines 1315 (No. 3), 1316 (No. 1) and 1317 (No. 2), but these numbers were never carried.

After official absorption by the LNER from 1st July 1924, the three Mid-Suffolk engines were thoroughly inspected pending a decision as to their future use with the new owners. No. 3, found to be in poor mechanical condition, was initially hauled to Ipswich. She then hauled No. 2 to Stratford shed from where she was withdrawn in August 1924. No. 1 continued working the Mid-Suffolk trains for about two weeks before being replaced by the ex GER Holden 'E22' class 0–6–0 tank locomotives by now reclassified 'J65'. All three MSLR tanks were at Stratford by the first week of August.

The surviving pair of Mid-Suffolk tanks were classed 'J64' by the LNER and, being in fair condition, were considered for further service. No. 2 spent some time at Ipswich shed, shunting the yard sidings before again venturing to Stratford minus leading coupling rods. She underwent general repairs, emerging on 5th March 1925 repainted in smart LNER unlined black livery renumbered 8317. During the works visit the travelling jack was removed from the footplate.

Two months later No. 1 entered works for an intermediate repair when her cylinders were rebored to 13 7/8 ins x 20 ins. She was also renumbered to 8316 but retained the MSLR red livery. As with 8317, the travelling jack was removed.

Principal dimensions of the engines in their final condition as registered by the LNER were:

	No. 8316	*No. 8317*
Cylinders (inside)	13 7/8 ins x 20 ins	13 ins x 20 ins
Motion	Stephenson with slide valve	
Boiler		
Max dia. outside	3 ft 8 ins	3 ft 8 ins
Barrel length	8 ft 10 ins	8 ft 4 ins
Firebox length outside	3 ft 6 ins	3 ft 6 ins
Pitch	6 ft 3 ins	6 ft 3 ins
Heating surface		
Firebox	52.41 sq ft	52.41 sq ft
Tubes (104 x 1¾ ins)	434.75 sq ft	410.95 sq ft
Total	487.16 sq ft	463.36 sq ft
Grate area	8.86 sq ft	8.86 sq ft
Boiler pressure	140 lbs psi	140 lbs psi
Coupled wheels	3 ft 4½ ins	3 ft 4½ ins
Tractive effort	11,110 lbs	9,931 lbs
Length over buffers	25 ft 6 ins	25 ft 0 ins
Wheelbase	12 ft 0 ins	11 ft 6 ins
Weight (full)	29 tons 3 cwt	28 tons
Max axle load	11 tons 2 cwt	12 tons 7 cwt
Water capacity	570 galls	600 galls
Coal capacity	1 ton 6 cwt	1 ton 3 cwt

The engines never returned to the Mid-Suffolk Railway as the 'J65s' were considered well suited to the task. Both were used as yard shunting engines on similar duties to the 'J65s'; in 1926 No. 8316 was at Ipswich and No. 8317 at Parkeston. In January 1928 No. 8316 was withdrawn for scrapping, leaving No. 8317 to continue in service, initially at Parkeston and then for a short time in 1929 as a replacement for 0–4–0T No. 7230 as carriage shunting pilot at Stratford works. No. 8317 was finally withdrawn in December 1929 after a service of only 24½ years.

GER ENGINES

In 1889 James Holden introduced ten six-coupled passenger tanks for light branch line duties and classified the locomotives 'E22'. The first six, Nos. 150-156, were sent to work on the Fenchurch Street to Blackwall line, with the result that they quickly received the nickname of the 'Blackwall' tanks. A further ten were built with detailed differences in 1893. In addition to their use on the East London services, the engines were allocated for use on the Buntingford, Stoke Ferry, Saffron Walden and Eye branches, whilst others were shedded at Ipswich, Norwich, Parkeston and Cambridge for shunting duties. The Ipswich

LNER class 'J64. 0–6–0T No. 8316 (ex-MSLR No. 1)

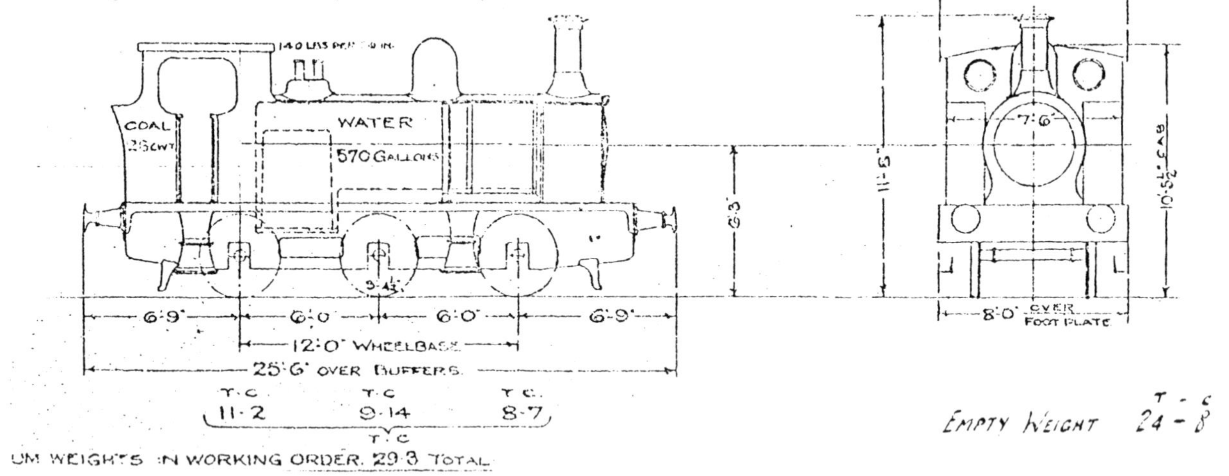

LNER class 'J64' 0–6–0T No. 8317 (MSLR No. 2)

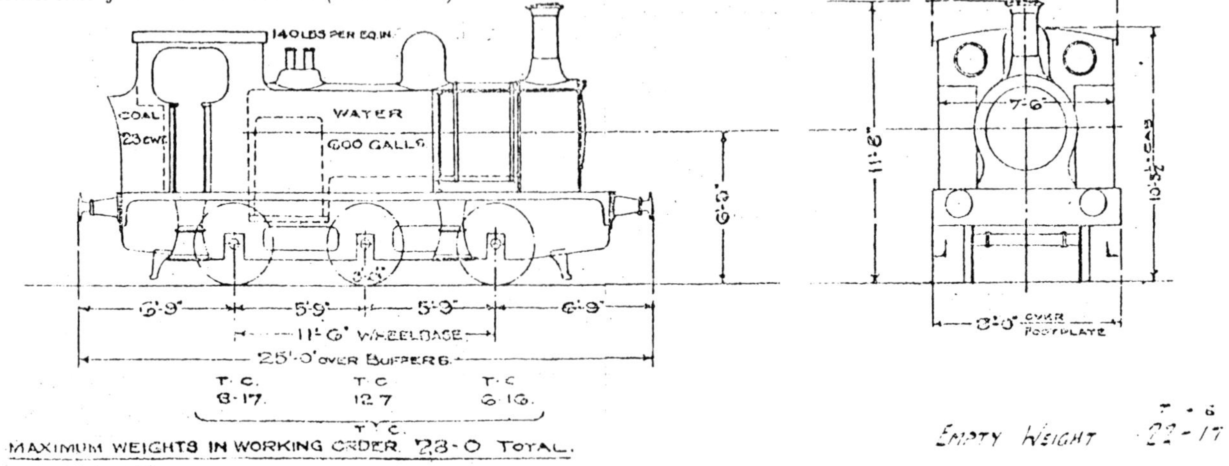

MSLR 0–6–0T No. 3 (Hudswell Clarke No. 867) awaiting shopping at Stratford in company with a GER class 'T26' 2–4–0 and 'S69' class 4–6–0 No. 1548. No. 3 was identical to MSLR No. 1 except for the fitting of cast iron wheel centres and a mild steel boiler. She was to have been named *Laxfield* but never carried the title.
Real Photographs

0–6–0T No. 1 at Stratford Works on 3rd April 1925, retaining her MSLR livery and brass number plate on the bunker. This view of the right-hand side of the engine shows to good effect the compactness of the Hudswell Clarke tank with the Westinghouse brake pump mounted alongside the smokebox, the curved profile of the side steps and flush sided coupling rods. In May 1925 No. 1 entered works for an intermediate repair when her cylinders were rebored to 13 7/8 in by 20 in. She was renumbered 8316 but retained the MSLR red livery.
LCGB/Ken Nunn Collection

Immediately on takeover of the MSLR in July 1924 the LNER withdrew the Hudswell Clarke tank engines from the light railway and sent them to Ipswich to await disposal. By August, No. 3, running as a 2–4–0T, had hauled No. 2 minus coupling rods to Stratford. Here, on 6th August 1924, No. 2 awaits a decision as to its future, standing bunker to bunker with No. 3. The engine carries its rather dented longer chimney fitted in 1921 and has shaded lettering on the side tanks. Also evident is the rerailing jack behind the sandbox on the running board.
LCGB/Ken Nunn Collection

Only one of the trio of ex-Mid-Suffolk tank engines was painted in full LNER unlined black livery. No. 2, after spending some time at Ipswich shed, entered Stratford Works for general repairs early in 1925 and emerged in pristine condition on 5th March as No. 8317. She was allocated to Parkeston for shunting duties previously performed by the GER 'E22'/LNER 'J65' 0–6–0Ts. By 1929 No. 8317 returned to Stratford as a replacement for 0–4–0T No. 7230 as carriage shunting pilot at the works. No. 8317 was finally withdrawn as the last of the trio in December 1929. *LCGB/Ken Nunn Collection*

based engines also worked the Eye branch and soon after the opening of the Mid-Suffolk Light Railway, the low axle loading enabled members of the class to work the GER weed-killing train or the Ipswich breakdown train between Haughley and Laxfield.

So suited were the locomotives to the line that when the Mid-Suffolk Company were forced to seek assistance for locomotive power from the GER because of engine failure in May 1919, the main line company allocated No. 254 to Laxfield. The engine remained on the MSLR services from 24th May to 20th June 1919. On 10th June she was joined by sister engine No. 157 and both worked the 'Middy' services until August. From then on 'E22' class engines were drafted to the line when the Mid-Suffolk motive power position required assistance, and in September 1920 No. 247 was recorded on loan.

At grouping the Mid-Suffolk engines were all at work but, as recorded earlier, when the light railway was finally taken over by the LNER in July 1924, No. 3 was almost immediately withdrawn from traffic. Under the LNER the 'E22s' became class 'J65' and within weeks members of the class had taken over the full working of the Mid-Suffolk Light Railway, with three of the Ipswich allocated locomotives regularly outbased at Laxfield. The engines were renumbered in 1924 by having 7000 added to their former numbers. Compared with the Hudswell Clarke tanks, the local crews initially thought the 'E22s' were inferior machines and underpowered, being unable to handle the tail loads normally hauled. After a few months' usage their attitude changed and the 'J65s' proved popular and reliable in service.

Standard dimensions of the 'J65' class were:

Cylinders (2 inside)	14 ins x 20 ins
Motion	Stephenson with slide valve
Boiler Max dia. outside	4 ft 2 ins
Barrel length	9 ft 1 in
Firebox length outside	4 ft 6 ins
Pitch	6 ft 9 ins
Heating surface	
Firebox	78.0 sq ft
Tubes (227 x 1 5/8 in)	909.4 sq ft
Total	987.4 sq ft
Grate area	12.4 sq ft
Boiler pressure	160 lbs psi
Coupled wheels	4 ft 0 in
Tractive effort	11106 lbs
Length over buffers	27 ft 2 ins
Wheelbase	13 ft 4 ins
Weight (full)	36 tons 11 cwt
Max axle load	13 tons 3 cwt
Water capacity	650 galls
Coal capacity	2 tons 10 cwt

Initially, at grouping in 1923, only 157 and 247 were allocated to Ipswich for use on the Eye branch and local shunting as well as cover for the Mid-Suffolk line, but after take-over the allocation was increased to reflect the increased number of 'J65s' required to cover the Mid-Suffolk diagrams. Following the discontinuation of the Millwall, Stoke Ferry and Eye branch passenger services, many of the 'J65s' were withdrawn and scrapped. By March 1937 Laxfield shed was host to three of the class, Nos. 7156, 7157 and 7253, but by the end of the year only five remained in service, Nos. 7155, 7157, 7247 and 7253 at Ipswich and 7250 at Parkeston. Of the four at Ipswich three were outbased at Laxfield but in 1939 this was reduced to two as traffic reductions brought about a rationalisation in engine workings.

During the Second World War Nos. 7155, 7157 and 7247 continued to work the branch services to be joined for a short period in 1946 by 7250 and 7253. In 1947 the 'J65s' were finally ousted from the Mid-Suffolk line by the 'J15' class 0–6–0 tender engines and the remaining survivors worked out their final days on shunting duties at Ipswich and Yarmouth Beach. No. 8211, however, returned to the line to work the Laxfield passenger diagram for two weeks in May 1948 and was the last of the class to work on the 'Middy', where their association was equal in years to the original tanks.

The full list of 'E22' ('J65') class known to have worked on the Mid-Suffolk line and their withdrawal dates are given below:

GER No.	*LNER 1924 No.*	*LNER 1946 No.*	*BR No.*	*Withdrawn*
153	7153	–	–	September 1931
155	7155	8211	68211	November 1953
156	7156	–	–	August 1937
157	7157	8212	–	November 1947
247	7247	8213	–	February 1948
250	7250	8214	68214	October 1956
253	7253	8215	–	May 1949
254	7254	–	–	June 1937

From 1947 the gradual demise of the 'J65' class meant the LNER had to find alternative motive power to work the Mid-Suffolk branch services. Fortunately, suitable traction with light axle loading was readily available in the 'J15' class 0–6–0 tender locomotives. The engines, originally introduced in 1883, to the design of T. W. Worsdell, were designated class 'Y14' by the GER. Such was the success of the design that building continued until 1913. All except 19 of the class of 289 locomotives were built at Stratford and the others by Sharp Stewart and Co.

As already mentioned, initially the 'J15s' were only permitted on the light railway hauling ballast or breakdown trains at reduced speed, and it was only after all the old flat-bottom track had been replaced from 1947 that they were allowed regularly to work the passenger services. However, during the war years the 'J15s' worked services in exceptional circumstances and on 5th May 1943 No. 7569 was noted in charge of a train composed of two six-wheel coaches and nine wagons. Once the 'J15s' took over the full workings of the branch it was usual for Ipswich to outbase at Laxfield a Westinghouse/vacuum braked engine for the passenger diagram and a steam brake only engine for the freight diagram. The Laxfield footplate staff took a great pride in keeping their passenger diagram 'J15' in immaculate condition, as indeed they had done with the 'J65s'.

Principal dimensions of the 'J15' class were:

Cylinders (2 inside)	17½ ins x 24 ins
Motion	Stephenson with slide valves
Boiler: Max dia. outside	4 ft 4 ins
Barrel length	10 ft 0 ins
Firebox length outside	6 ft 0 ins
Heating surface:	
Firebox	105.5 sq ft
Tubes 242 x 1 5/8 ins	1063.8 sq ft
Total	1169.3 sq ft
Grate area	17.9 sq ft
Boiler pressure	160 lbs psi
Coupled wheels	4 ft 11 ins
Tender wheels	4 ft 1 in
Tractive effort	16942 lbs
Length over buffers*	47 ft 3 ins
Wheelbase Engine	16 ft 1 in
Tender	12 ft 0 in
Weight Engine	37 tons 2 cwt
Tender	30 tons 13 cwt
Max axle load	13 tons 10 cwt
Water capacity	2640 gallons
Coal capacity	5 tons

*engine and tender

'J15s' known to have worked on the Mid-Suffolk Light Railway and their withdrawal dates are:

	LNER 1924 No.	*LNER 1946 No.*	*BR No.*	*Withdrawn*
S	7509	5429	–	November 1950
S	7510	5430	65430	January 1956
	7542	5470	65470	December 1959
	7543	5471	65471	June 1960
	7561	5459	65459	February 1960
	7569	5467	65467	February 1959
	7647	5447	65447	April 1959
S	7836	5361	65361	September 1962
S	7883	5388	65388	May 1959
S	7910	5404	65404	October 1956
S	7914	5407	65407	April 1951
S	7915	5408	65408	December 1951
S	7937	5422	65422	July 1955

S – Steam brake only used on freight diagram

The Westinghouse and vacuum brake fitted 'J15s' also found use on the Framlingham and Aldeburgh branches, hauling passenger and mixed trains when a class 'F6' tank locomotive was not available. In the latter months of the Mid-Suffolk Railway, No. 65447 was regularly used on the passenger diagram and received considerable attention from the engine crews, with polished brass fittings and cab interior painted a sandy buff colour, akin to former GER practice. No. 65447 worked the passenger services on the last day of service, 26th July 1952.

In the autumn of 1946 a drastic shortage at Ipswich of suitable motive power to work the Mid-Suffolk services forced the motive power foreman to outbase an 'E4' class 2–4–0 tender locomotive No. 7466, later renumbered 2782, at Laxfield. Although officially restricted by nature of its RA2 availability, the engine was utilized for some weeks with no serious problems being incurred on the permanent way and she last saw use at Laxfield in January 1947, being replaced by the ubiquitous class 'J15' 0–6–0s.

The engine diagrams employed during the independent years were remarkably diverse for such a small railway and involved the working of two locomotives, one based at Laxfield and the other at Kenton. The Laxfield engine on Mondays, Wednesdays, Fridays and Saturdays worked two round trips to Haughley and back, hauling mixed trains on each occasion, commencing with the 8.15 a.m. ex Laxfield and finishing with the 5.40 p.m. ex Haughley. This locomotive was also responsible for hauling the one or two Sunday services in each direction. On Tuesdays and Thursdays the diagram was not so straightforward and the enginemen worked longer hours. As on other weekdays, the engine worked the 8.15 a.m. up mixed train to Haughley, returning with the 10.00 a.m. from the junction. Here the alteration from other weekdays occurred, for instead of laying over until 3.25 p.m., the engine worked the 12.55 p.m. mixed train from Laxfield as far as Kenton where it was relieved by the Kenton engine which worked the train forward to Haughley. The Laxfield engine then worked back light to Laxfield, departing Kenton at 1.30 p.m., although this ran as a goods if traffic required. The engine then took up its booked working at 3.25 p.m. ex Laxfield, mixed train to Haughley and 5.40 p.m. return from the junction.

In complete contrast the Kenton engine and men were involved almost totally on goods workings and the day to day alterations in the diagrams reflected the fluctuating nature of the traffic on the line and was a good example of flexible rostering. On Mondays the engine and crew worked a relatively short day, departing Kenton at 5.45 a.m. with the goods for Haughley. The return goods working departed the junction at 7.30 a.m. and ran through to Stradbroke or, if required, Wilby. The final part of the diagram involved working the 9.35 a.m. ex Wilby or 9.45 a.m. ex Stradbroke to Kenton.

The Kenton engine and men then worked down to Laxfield, coupled to the front of, and double heading from Kenton, the 10.00 a.m. mixed ex Haughley. At Laxfield the men lodged for the Monday night before working the 4.00 a.m. Laxfield to Haughley cattle train on Tuesday. The return goods working, 7.00 a.m. ex Haughley ran to Stradbroke or, if required, Wilby. The diagram then involved the working of a goods train 9.35 a.m. ex Wilby (9.45 a.m. ex Stradbroke) to Kenton or, if traffic required, through to Haughley. If the latter occurred, a goods ran from Haughley to Kenton, departing the junction at 12.10 p.m. On arrival at Kenton, engine and men then relieved the Laxfield engine on the 12.55 p.m. mixed ex Laxfield and worked the train to Haughley, arriving at 2.10 p.m. The final working of the day incurred the haulage of the 2.55 p.m. Haughley to Kenton goods. The Thursdays only diagram was almost identical except that the first working was the 5.45 a.m. ex Kenton goods to Haughley and the 7.30 a.m. return from the junction to Stradbroke or Wilby, as required. The engine and men then took up the same working as on Tuesdays. On Wednesdays, Fridays and Saturdays, the working was far less involved and incurred the 8.46 a.m. Kenton to Stradbroke goods, extended to Wilby, if required and the 9.35 a.m. ex Wilby (9.45 a.m. ex Stradbroke) return to Haughley. An early finish was assured as the engine worked the 1.10 p.m. goods ex the junction, arriving at Kenton at 2.10 p.m. On Sundays the Kenton engine was out of traffic.

In the years just before and after the grouping, it was the practice to work the line with two locomotives. Tuesdays excepted, the locomotive on Laxfield diagram 1 worked the 7.35 a.m. ex Laxfield to Haughley, arriving at 8.40 a.m. This engine then departed the junction at 9.40 a.m. to Laxfield before working the 12 noon goods as far as Aspall. After shunting, the engine returned with a goods at 2.50 p.m., relieving the mixed train of as much shunting at intermediate stations as possible. If there was a considerable tonnage of goods to be picked up at stations between Aspall and Haughley, the 12 noon goods ran through to the junction station and then returned to Laxfield at 2.55 p.m. Laxfield diagram 2 engine worked the 11.05 a.m. and 3.25 p.m. mixed trains from Laxfield, returning from Haughley with the 1.00 p.m. and 5.40 p.m. SX, 6.05 p.m. SO mixed trains. On Tuesday the principal market day in the area, the engine on diagram 1 worked the cattle and goods train from Laxfield at 3.55 a.m., returning from Haughley with a goods train at 6.15 a.m. It then worked the return 8.10 a.m. mixed train fron Laxfield, returning from the junction at 9.40 a.m. On Tuesday the afternoon goods train was cancelled. These diagrams remained in operation, except for minor timing changes, until the Second World War.

LAXFIELD DEPOT.

WEEK DAYS.

No. 1.

arr.		dep.
a.m.		a.m.
	On Duty	3 0 T O W R
	Loco'	3 45 L
	Laxfield	3 55 G T O
5 30	Haughley W.	6 5 G T O
7 50	Laxfield	8 10 T O
9 15	Haughley W.	9 48 T O
10 50	Laxfield	
	On Duty	6 40 T X
	Loco'	7 25 L T X
	Laxfield	7 35 T X
8 40	Haughley W.	9 40 T X
		noon
10 50	Laxfield	12 0 G T X
p.m.		p.m.
1 50	Aspall	2 5 G T X W R
W R 2 30	Haughley W.	3 15 W R
3 42	Aspall	{2 5 {3 42 G W R
3 20 W R 5 0	} Laxfield	L
	Loco'	

No. 2.

arr.		dep.
		a.m.
	On Duty	9 30
p.m.	Loco'	10 15 L
	Laxfield	G P 11 5
		p.m.
• 12 20	Haughley W.	1 0
2 15	Laxfield	3 25
4 45	Haughley W.	{5 40 S X {6 5 S O
S X 6 45 S O 7 10	} Laxfield	L
	Loco'	

Locomotive and Enginemen's diagrams July 1925.

In later years the locomotive allocated to the Laxfield freight diagram ran only 40 miles daily, and then only three days each week, a working which was considered to be one of the easiest in Great Britain.

From July 1924, the locomotives rostered by the LNER to work the Mid-Suffolk Light Railway services were outbased from Ipswich Motive Power Depot. Initially, three were allocated to Laxfield depot with two working and one spare. As mentioned earlier, the LNER later found this to be uneconomical and from September 1939 the number of engines outbased was reduced to two, one working the passenger diagram and the other the freight diagram. In both instances the engines were outbased at Laxfield for two or three weeks before returning to Ipswich for maintenance. Changeover was normally then effected on a Tuesday morning when it hauled either the livestock train through to the Suffolk town or after the withdrawal of this service, coaching stock being sent to Ipswich for heavy cleaning. A relief engine ran light from Ipswich to Haughley where the engine crews exchanged footplates.

The expenses incurred in the early years keeping the rolling stock of the company in running order are interesting and below are the figures for the years ending 30th June 1906 and 1907:

		30 June 1906	*30 June 1907*
		£ s. d.	£ s. d.
Salaries		20 0 0	20 11 3
Wages	Running	188 17 3	174 14 3
	Cleaning	47 6 5	45 3 2
Coal and coke		331 7 10	384 4 11
Oil and tallow		40 3 2	39 0 9
Water	Wages	44 2 1	62 7 7
	Repairs	3 18 3	23 1 7
Locomotives	Repairs	28 9 8	43 16 1
	Materials	3 13 4	18 5 5
	Boiler insurance	10 0 0	
Power supply contract		2 0 0 (R)	30 10 0
		715 18 0	841 15 0

Locomotive running expenses remained on the high side for such a small company and typical annual figures during and after the First World War were:

1914	£1679 18 5	1917	£2196 5 9
1915	£1792 15 9	1918	£2591 9 5
1916	£1834 15 8	1919	£3823 10 8

These figures included wages of drivers, firemen and cleaners, costs of coal, oil and tallow, water and running and maintenance repairs, the latter involving the costs of works attention.

LOCOMOTIVE LIVERY

During a visit to the line in 1905, the reporter of the *Suffolk Chronicle* reported that the company had recently purchased from Hudswell Clarke and Company of Leeds, a tank locomotive with 14 ins by 20 ins cylinders. The locomotive No. 1 was painted in Victorian brown livery, lined in yellow, red and black. Nos. 2 and 3 were received in the same livery. That of the Hudswell Clarke tanks was later incorrectly described as Midland crimson lake with yellow and vermilion lining. The side tanks, were, however, lettered in gilt 'MSLR' to complement polished domes, copper-capped chimneys and brass safety valve cover bases. The Midland crimson of the locomotives had been described as having a slight brownish hue by former Mid-Suffolk employees and it seems, therefore, certain that the red was slightly darker than the established Midland Railway locomotive livery. Numbers were carried on brass plates attached to the bunker side plates.

Under the LNER, No. 1 was renumbered 8316 but retained her red livery with 'LNER' lettering and numbers whilst No. 2 as 8317 was outshopped in March 1925 in unlined black livery with yellow 'LNER' and numbers shaded red and brown on the side tank but retaining her polished brass dome.

During the independent years the 'E22' class 0–6–0 tank engines loaned to the Mid-Suffolk were painted in the GER dark blue livery or post-First World War grey. After grouping the 'J65s' were painted unlined black with shaded lettering with 'LNER' and the locomotive number on the side tanks. During the Second World War the 'LNER' was replaced by a rather austere 'NE' on the side tanks. After nationalisation the title 'BRITISH RAILWAYS' was exhibited in full on the side tanks and the number located on the side of the bunker. The 'J15' class 0–6–0s were painted unlined black with 'LNER', 'NE' or 'British Railways' on the tender side plates. In the last years the BR lion and wheel emblem was displayed on the tender sides. At all times the locomotive number was displayed on the cab side sheets. For much of the time the locomotives regularly allocated to Laxfield had their brasswork and copperwork polished by the local crews.

FOOTPLATE STAFF

During the construction of the railway, Jackson employed his own driver and fireman, the former an ex-GER man, to handle *Lady Stevenson* and other hired locomotives. On opening to goods traffic the Mid-Suffolk company initially employed one driver and fireman and by early 1905 an engine cleaner was also on the establishment.

With the acquisition of the second locomotive from March 1905, a second set of men were recruited. The first occupants of these posts were driver Bennett and his fireman Sid Read as one crew, and driver Alec Boag and fireman Arthur Bowen as the second set. Boag joined the MSLR direct from the GER, apparently leaving that company after being reprimanded as a result of a collision and derailment in Trowse Yard, Norwich. Arthur Bowen started initially as cleaner and then fireman at Laxfield before varying his career by becoming the 'odd job man', carrying out minor repairs to the Mid-Suffolk Light Railway locomotives and rolling stock. Bowen received no formal training or apprenticeship, and his repairs and maintenance were of a 'make do and mend' nature until a professional job could be carried out by private firms or the GER. Finding no reason to retain the position, the LNER on take-over in 1924 re-employed Bowen as a fireman, a grade which he retained until he retired at the age of 65 in February 1949. Sid Read, after making over 50,000 journeys across the line, also retired whilst still a fireman at the age of 65.

Bowen's replacement during the first years was Cliff Bloom, son of George Bloom, the MSLR permanent way inspector, who lived in the gate house at Silver Street crossing. Cliff Bloom initially earned the princely sum of 8s 6d, of which all but one shilling went on lodging fees at Laxfield. By 1912 Bloom was eligible for promotion to driver and in October a GER motive power inspector was requested to examine him on the responsibilities of taking charge of a locomotive. For this service the main line company charged 2/6d.

Cliff Bloom's predecessor, driver Bennett, was the first driver employed by the light railway company. Unfortunately, he met with an accident in June 1905 and was registered sick for nine weeks, during which time the company paid him £1 1s 0d per week. The accident required the professional services of a doctor who charged the company 7s 6d for attending Bennett whilst the £9 9s 0d paid to the driver was recovered from the Royal Exchange Insurance Company under an arrangement the MSLR had for insuring all its staff against death or accident.

The vacancy at Laxfield filled by Cliff Bloom was caused by the transfer of driver Bennett to Kenton where he took over from an unknown driver. His regular fireman was Charlie Brunning who had originally been employed as pump attendant by the pond at Kenton, in charge of the water supply to locomotives. When the line to Westerfield was deemed semi-abandoned, Brunning was re-employed as an engine cleaner at Kenton shed, where he was required to walk along the line to the isolated building three-quarters of a mile west of the station. In 1912 Charlie Brunning became Bennett's regular fireman, a post which he retained for seven years. During the 1919 flu epidemic, driver Bennett succumbed to the illness and Brunning took over as acting driver, utilizing the services of Arthur Bowen as fireman on a temporary basis until Bennett returned to duty.

After Brunning's transfer to the position of fireman, the post of engine cleaner at Kenton was withdrawn as an economy measure. It became the responsibility of the fireman, and to a lesser degree the driver, to clean their charge. No. 2 was the engine regularly shedded at Kenton and one evening as Charlie Brunning was disposing of the engine, driver Bennett, renowned for his remarkable prowess as a poacher, arrived with shotgun in hand. Bennett advised Brunning that he was leaving the shotgun on the engine until the next day, to which his fireman readily agreed. On taking duty the following morning and after preparing the locomotive, the pair climbed into the cab where Bennett's gun was lodged against the reversing lever

Motive power staff pose in front of MSLR 0–6–0T No. 2 at Laxfield in 1923. *Left to right:* R. Tacon (odd job man); A. Bowen (fireman); A. Boag (driver); G. Bloom Jnr. (fireman); C. Bloom (driver); C. Brunning (driver); J. S. Read (fireman). *Collection G. F. Rice*

with the barrel facing up to the cab roof. Unfortunately, Bennett had left the trigger of the shotgun cocked so that when the engine vibrated and jolted on starting, the gun went off, leaving a large hole in the cab roof of No. 2 and a larger hole in the shed roof. The hole in the shed roof was never repaired and to the end of its service No. 2 retained a patch over the hole in the cab roof as a reminder of the incident. Charlie Brunning took over the driver's position at Kenton on Bennett's retirement and was transferred on the closure of the shed in 1919 to Laxfield. His service with the LNER was short for he subsequently retired in 1926.

In the final years of the 'Middy' before the closure of Kenton shed, Charlie Brunning was involved in an alarming incident whilst in charge of a returning Sunday excursion. Brunning was covering the Sunday work on this particular day in place of the Laxfield driver. The GER excursion train ran late and, in an effort to make up time, Brunning, on receiving the 'right away' from his guard, set forth with the MSLR train all speed for Laxfield. The engine forged up the 1 in 42 out of Haughley with a full head of steam, as darkness fell across the Suffolk countryside. On the approach to the second level crossing from Haughley, a sudden explosion was followed immediately by steam gushing through the firebox door and into the cab. Both driver and fireman dodged the scalding onrush and clung on to the outside of the cab as the engine rapidly lost speed. After the initial blowback of steam subsided, Brunning returned to the cab, shutting the regulator and applied the brake to halt the train. A quick assessment of the situation revealed the cause not as first suspected, a melted fusible plug, but a burst boiler tube which was leaking hot water through the end of the tube and the tubeplate on to the fire. By this time the guard arrived to enquire the cause of the stoppage and delay. Passengers were also leaning out of the window to find out when the train would continue its journey. The train crew quickly realised that there was no hope of a relief engine being sent from Laxfield as the engine was out of steam and the crew preparing the Kenton engine for the Monday service were off duty. The only hope was to either return to Haughley and leave the passengers stranded or proceed as far as Kenton where the engine based there would already have a small fire in the firebox ready for the following morning's work and hopefully steam in the boiler to allow the crew to change engines.

Brunning considered all possibilities and decided on the latter course. Provided the water level in the boiler and above the crown plate did not drop too quickly on his ailing engine, thereby melting the fusible plug and putting out the fire, he would make the changeover. The solution lay in plugging the end of the tube to prevent the water cascading across the brick arch and fire. A quick search for possible plugs proved fruitless until the guard produced his shunting pole. The implement proved ideal for the situation and after many attempts, often with the danger of being burnt, Charlie Brunning managed to ram the metal end of the shunting pole in the end of the tube. The question was whether the plug would hold once the wooden handle burnt away. The fireman made the fire up slightly and the engine and her train were juddered into motion, the firebox door being left slightly open to assist the draught across the fire to keep the pressure up. The engine and train then limped the three or so miles to Mendlesham where the coaches were detached.

While the guard and station staff consoled the passengers, Brunning and his fireman took their ailing steed on to Kenton. The handle of the shunting pole had long since disintegrated with the heat but the rammed head held in the tube end with only slight traces of water dripping through. *En route* other stations were advised of the circumstances and at Kenton the failed engine was quickly dumped as the crew luckily found that the engine in the shed was not as 'cold' as expected. Within half an hour the fire was built up with enough steam raised to make the trip back to Mendelsham and the stranded train. The passengers, by now somewhat calmed by provision of refreshments, were relieved to see an engine appear on the front of their train. After attaching, an uneventful run was made to Laxfield where arrival was made in the early hours of Monday morning, some three hours late.

Another character based at Laxfield at the time of the grouping was driver J. S. Read, who had replaced Boag. Originally he had been fireman to Bloom and Brunning. When an ex-GER locomotive inspector was sent from Ipswich to view the driving techniques on the light railway, he was not enamoured with the handling of the Hudswell Clarke tanks by the Laxfield men. The criticism was especially pertinent to the departure from the junction and the climb up the 1 in 42 out of Haughley. Driver Read, who was at the receiving end of the verbal tirade, meekly suggested that the inspector should demonstrate to the Laxfield men how the engines should be handled. The inspector readily agreed to exhibit his skill as a driver and arranged to return the following day. On the fateful morning, driver Read duly allowed the inspector to take charge of the Mid-Suffolk tank. After receiving 'right away' from the guard, our intrepid inspector opened the regulator only to find a few minutes later that the train had stalled on the bank. Permission was received to set back into the station for another go whilst driver Read and his fireman contained their mirth behind the facial mask of innocence. Several further attempts were made by the inspector to take engine and train up the bank, but each time the train stalled less then half-way to the summit. Having returned for the umpteenth time to Haughley station for a 'blow up', the red-faced and indignant inspector stomped off to the LNER station to return to Ipswich. Once he was out of earshot Read and his companion almost collapsed into fits of uncontrollable mirth. What must have been galling for the inspector was to have witnessed the Hudswell Clarke tank pounding away from the Mid-Suffolk station with its train up the 1 in 42 incline, to disappear into deepest Mid-Suffolk without the trace of a slip.

It was often rumoured by the old 'Middy' men that this incident caused the early departure of the Hudswell Clarke tanks in favour of the ex-GER 'E22', LNER 'J65' class 0–6–0 tank engines.

After his somewhat dubious career on the GER, Alec Boag settled down to become one of the most respected drivers on the light railway. He distinguished himself in November 1914 when the Mid-Suffolk directors and receiver awarded him a £2 bonus for an unspecified act. Unfortunately Boag died whilst still in the employ of the MSLR and his replacement was the aforementioned J. S. Read. When Read subsequently retired, George Rouse was transferred to Laxfield in 1932 from the most unlikely of places, Penistone, where he had been in charge of the Gresley giant class 'U1' 2–8–0 + 0–8–2 Beyer Garratt locomotive LNER No. 2395, later BR No. 69999, banking coal trains up the Worsborough incline. He was transferred to the Suffolk shed as a result of the problems encountered with the large engine. This culminated in an incident when the regulator stuck in the open position as the locomotive was banking a train. Fortunately a disaster was averted when the regulator was shut with the aid of brute force and a coal hammer. Wishing for a quieter life, Rouse moved to Laxfield where in his spare time he grew tobacco. After the necessary home treatment, he offered a tin of tobacco to the occasional visiting motive power inspector or relieving Ipswich driver. As the receiver usually turned green after inhaling two or three puffs of the potent weed, Rouse and his tobacco gained an infamous reputation in the motive power circles of Suffolk.

Although the Mid-Suffolk line was officially a light railway with a maximum speed limit of 25 mph, in practice this speed was often exceeded when trains were making up time or when officialdom was far away. Unfortunately, alleged excessive speeding finally resulted in an accident at the open level crossing near Gipping siding when a train in the charge of driver Jehu collided with a car. The locomotive sustained only slight damage but the car was a write-off and the lady driver was badly injured and later died. At the subsequent enquiry, the case against driver Jehu over the alleged speeding of the train, was nullified when it was discovered that the woman suffered a medical complaint which meant that she should not have been driving the car. This fact failed to save Jehu from disciplinary action as he had been cautioned a number of times earlier in his career for speeding. He was subsequently removed from the footplate and transferred away from Laxfield.

Cliff Bloom finally retired in 1953 having spent all but one of his years on the 'Middy'. For some while during independent days and when the LNER were operating the line, Cliff's brothers, Archie and George Junior, were employed as firemen. George in fact fired to Cliff around the 1920s. Fireman Kidby, who lived at Tuddenham, was Bloom's mate for a period in 1948/49.

In the years prior to closure, because of the reduction in the number of hours worked by footplate staff, it was often necessary for the running foreman at Ipswich Motive Power Depot to send a relief crew to Laxfield to cover for annual leave, rest days or lieu days leave taken by the Laxfield staff. The problem for most Ipswich men required to relieve at Laxfield was getting back to Ipswich after disposing of the branch engine at the rural shed. Saturday late turn was especially inconvenient as social life in the evening could be seriously jeopardised by the time taken for the driver and fireman to cycle or motor-cycle back to Ipswich or a convenient station on the Norwich main line or the East Suffolk line. Unfortunately, cycling proved exhausting after an eight hour shift and was the least popular in inclement weather. Alternatively, the men could make their way to either Halesworth or Darsham on the East Suffolk line or even Framlingham. The only problem was that trains were inconveniently timed to coincide with the signing off time at Laxfield together with the time taken for the ensuing cycle ride across country.

It was most noticeable on Saturdays whenever an Ipswich crew worked the back shift at Laxfield, the last down train from Haughley always arrived extremely early at the terminus. The engine was quickly taken to shed where the fire was thrown out and the locomotive disposed of for the weekend. The intrepid crew then cycled to the East Suffolk station of their choice to catch an earlier train back to Ipswich and home. The whole operation went undetected for some considerable time until late one Saturday afternoon shed master R. H. N. Hardy happened to be at Ipswich when the East Suffolk line train drew in to deposit two of his men on the platform at a time when they should have been departing from Laxfield. An inquest the following Monday morning revealed all.

At the time of closure of the branch, two sets of footplatemen were based at Laxfield. Driver Ernest Baker had as his fireman Ronald Thompson, whilst driver Joseph Skinner and fireman Jack Law were responsible for working the final passenger services, although all four were on the footplate of 65447 on the last run. From Monday, 28th July 1952, all four men were transferred to Ipswich Motive Power Depot. Skinner later left the railway to become a haulage contractor at Ipswich.

In the latter years of independent working, there were two sets of men located at Laxfield and one at Kenton, the first Laxfield crew signed on duty at 7.15 a.m. before preparing the engine and working the 8.15 a.m. trip to Haughley and back. After arrival at Laxfield at 6.42 p.m., the engine was disposed of before the men signed off duty at 7.15 p.m. The other Laxfield men covered any special workings and stood in for other crews on their days off. The Kenton men worked a self-contained variable roster, signing on 3.15 a.m. Tuesdays only at Laxfield, then 5.00 a.m. Mondays and Thursdays and 7.45 a.m. Wednesdays, Fridays and Saturdays at Kenton. The crew signed off at equally varying times, 11.50 a.m. Mondays only before lodging at Laxfield, 4.15 p.m. Tuesdays and Thursdays, and 2.30 p.m. Wednesdays, Fridays and Saturdays. On Sundays Laxfield men signed on at 4.15 p.m. and off at 9.30 p.m.

After grouping and with only two sets of men located at Laxfield, the early turn men signed on duty at 3.00 a.m. Tuesdays only and 6.40 a.m. Tuesdays excepted. The early starting time on Tuesday was to enable the men to work the 3.55 a.m. cattle train to Haughley, for Ipswich market, returning with ordinary goods from the junction at 6.05 a.m. One other round trip was made with a mixed train before the men signed off at 12 noon having disposed of the locomotive. On Tuesdays excepted, the men worked one round trip to Haughley with a mixed train, followed by a short goods working to Aspall and back or, if required, through to Haughley. This latter working was run to take excess goods traffic from intermediate stations and reduced the amount of shunting required to be carried out by the 3.25 p.m. mixed train ex Laxfield and 5.40 p.m. SX and 6.00 p.m. SO return ex Haughley. If the men worked through to Haughley they signed off duty at 5.40 p.m. whereas the short working to Aspall enabled them to sign off at 4.00 p.m. The second set of men had a regular diagram signing on duty at 9.30 a.m., and after preparing their engine working two round trips to Haughley and back before signing off at 7.25 p.m. SX and 7.50 p.m. SO. These diagrams remained in operation, with slight adjustments in timing, until the line closed to traffic.

During the years of LNER and BR management, Laxfield shed was a sub-shed of Ipswich Motive Power Depot. After grouping, a locomotive foreman or, as he was later titled, driver-in-charge, was appointed and he received an extra half day's pay per week for administrative duties which included the submission of drivers' tickets and coal and oil returns to the shed master at Ipswich. Under nationalisation Ipswich shed was allocated the code 32B and most locomotives working the branch under British Railways carried the shed plate bearing this code on the smokebox door.

The drivers in the independent years were somewhat ruthless towards their firemen and cleaners, especially if the engines were not spick and span. A common test was to wipe a white cloth along the footplate or on the inside of the running frame to see if the cleaning had been carried out correctly. The final polishing over was often carried out by the driver. During the coal strike of 1921, the cleaners and firemen, together with the Laxfield 'odd job man', were delegated to make briquettes from coal dust and cement to supplement the meagre coal supplies, and cut up old sleepers to light up the fire in the firebox. In addition to their normal duties, the cleaner, fireman and 'odd job man' also offloaded coal from wagons onto the coal stage. They also filled footwarmers with hot water for use in first class compartments of the coaching stock. After grouping, a cleaner was employed on regular night duties to coal and water the engines in preparation for the next day's

R. (Dick) Tacon, odd job man at Laxfield, posed for the camera at Laxfield in 1923. When the LNER took over the following year, he was appointed shed labourer and retired after World War Two.
Collection G. F. Rice

workings. The cleaner also offloaded coal from wagons on to the coaling stage.

After absorption by the LNER, a shed labourer was employed on regular day time at Laxfield, cleaning out the engine shed, unloading coal from wagons to the coal stage, and on occasion assisting with the preparation or disposal of the engines. From 1924 Dick Tacon, who was 'odd job man', was appointed shed labourer, but on his retirement after the Second World War the post was abolished. It was later reinstated and Harold Howlett served as shed labourer until the closure of the line in 1952. The night duty on shed was covered by a cleaner who, from about midnight, was preparing the engines for the day's duty. From the late 1930s it was extremely difficult to find a cleaner to work regular nights and so it was usual to outbase a cleaner from Ipswich at Laxfield. To save the expense of lodging in the town, the cleaners more often than not slept in the former MSLR superintendent's office.

Another facet of the rural depots' responsibilities was boiler washouts and tube cleaning. In independent years the Kenton engine was taken down the Debenham branch siding for boiler washout on Sundays, utilizing the water from the storage tank situated in the fork of the main line and Debenham branch. Similarly at Laxfield, boiler washouts were carried out by the pond to the east of the level crossing where water supplies were readily available all the year round. Driver Read always insisted he carried out the boiler washout on the engines when based at Laxfield. Tube cleaning was also carried out at both Kenton and Laxfield, the locomotive crews using home-made tools. After grouping, boiler washing was performed at Ipswich and locomotives were changed over regularly to ensure proper maintenance. Tube cleaning, however, continued to be carried out by footplate staff at Laxfield and usually a fireman was paid four hours Sunday rate for the work. All other maintenance and repairs to locomotives was carried out at Ipswich, although, if repairs could be easily effected, a fitter travelled down to Laxfield, sometimes lodging the night to save returning the engine to the parent shed.

After absorption by the LNER, the Mid-Suffolk drivers based at Laxfield were required to sign route knowledge sheets in accordance with the existing GER and LNER practice. Initially the men were only required to 'sign the road' between Laxfield and Haughley but in the latter years when the first up and last down services were extended to and from Stowmarket to provide a service for local schoolchildren, the men signed to Stowmarket and some through to Ipswich Motive Power Depot. This enabled them to change over engines if required. Some Ipswich men also signed the 'road' between Haughley and Laxfield to enable them to work weed-killing trains, engineers' and freight specials or engine changeovers which were normally effected at Haughley.

For a mere 19½ mile rural railway, motive power facilities on the Mid-Suffolk Light Railway were more than adequate.

The contractor originally provided a wooden engine shed at Haughley measuring some 30 feet by 12 feet which strangely straddled the main single line just south of Haugh Lane underbridge. The structure appeared to be devoid of any accommodation for staff and presumably just housed the engine. In 1904 a second engine shed, 60 ft long, was built at Haughley by A. C. Andrews for £19 6s 9d and this was located on the down or west side of the single line at the end of a 150 ft long siding, with access via points facing down trains located just north of Haugh Lane underbridge. The first shed was quickly removed but the second shed at Haughley remained until 1905. By this time it was unused, for Jackson hired the structure from 7th May to 10th June, paying the princely sum of £1 15s 0d. Lieutenant Colonel Von Donop, during his inspection in July, requested the removal of the connection from the main line and the shed was removed soon afterwards.

At some time in 1903 a second engine shed was provided at a rather inaccessible site, three-quarters of a mile west of the future site of Kenton station on the south side of the main single line. The shed was served by a single siding, 170 ft in length, with access via trailing points for down trains on the main single line. Initially the shed housed Jackson's *Lady Stevenson* during the time she was employed on the Debenham branch works trains and later for the bridge works at Brockford. After the opening of the line to goods traffic, the Mid-Suffolk outbased an engine at Kenton together with a driver, fireman and cleaner, and this arrangement certainly persisted until 1919, although the cleaner was withdrawn in 1912.

The original shed at Kenton measured 60 ft long by 12 ft wide and was large enough to house one of the tank engines. The windows were provided with shuttering whilst at the east end a pair of outward opening doors permitted the shed to be locked at night. Inside the shed an inspection pit was provided whilst a pair of buffer stops prevented an engine running off the end of the rails and through the shed end wall. The reporter from the *Suffolk Chronicle and Mercury* noted during his visit in 1905 a small workshop for the maintenance of the locomotive. The approach to Kenton shed was on a slight rising gradient which proved useful if the engine crew wished to roll the engine out of the confines of the shed by releasing the handbrake. Unfortunately, on one occasion before the First World War, some local lads visited the shed during the hours of darkness, when no staff were on duty, and, finding the shed doors open, decided to investigate further. The boys made for the cab of the engine and released the handbrake. The locomotive then rolled slowly forward down the slight gradient before coming to rest on the curve of the points leading to the main line. Fortunately a collision was averted when the driver and fireman arrived and manhandled the engine back into the short siding using pinch bars. The engine was then steamed for the day's work, with the authorities none the wiser of the incident.

Prior to the First World War the siting of an engine shed at Kenton was considered more of a hindrance than an asset to the working of the light railway and in 1912 it was decided to move the structure nearer to Kenton station. The wooden building was evidently dismantled and re-erected to the east of the station on the up side of the goods yard, and in the process it was shortened by some 30 feet. R. R. Cracknell and B. A. Fisk were involved in the operation, charging the company £3 18s 9d and £1 11s 10d respectively, although this was by no means the total cost of removal. From 1919 it was found more economical to

This cruel enlargement of the lower picture on page 56 provides a rare view of the second Kenton engine shed.
Collection G. F. Rice

work the light railway totally from Laxfield and the Kenton engine and crew were transferred. The Kenton building remained *in situ* for a further seven years when it was demolished, its useful timber being retained to repair the shed at Laxfield.

The most important shed on the Mid-Suffolk was at Laxfield where as early as January 1905 land was purchased from E. C. Hopper for £5 so that water could be obtained for locomotive use. The following year Charles Woodward was requested to arrange further water supplies to engines, charging the company £3 for the work. At first the company were content to shed their engines at Haughley and Kenton but, with the increasing goods traffic providing an excess of exports over imports, the first services were required to be worked up from Laxfield to Haughley and not down from Haughley to Laxfield. In addition to these traffic flows, the delay in opening the line beyond Cratfield and the abandonment of the Debenham line brought about a reassessment of operating practices. To this end it was decided to close the shed at Haughley and concentrate engine power at Laxfield, leaving one engine outbased at Kenton. The plan, although formulated early in 1905, was not finalised until the spring of 1907, when A. Scott completed the erection of an engine shed at Laxfield, capable of housing two locomotives, at a cost of £94 19s 0d. The wooden structure, complete with doors, engine pit and shuttered window, together with a small workshop, was located to the west of Laxfield station on the up or south side of the line. An oil storage shed was built adjacent to it in September 1910 at a cost of £8 19s 6d.

From thereon until the closure of Kenton shed, Laxfield was host to two of the Hudswell Clarke tank engines,

The wooden engine shed at Laxfield in 1923. Located to the west of the station on the up or south side of the main single line, the structure was 60 ft long with end doors at the east end. An inspection pit was located between the rails within the shed whilst the windows were equipped with shutters. Adjacent to the shed is the oil store built in 1910 at a cost of £8 19s 6d. *Collection G. F. Rice*

normally Nos. 1 and 3 with No. 2 outbased at Kenton. It was then usual for the Kenton engine and one of those at Laxfield to cover the diagrams whilst the remaining engine was retained as spare or under repair or maintenance. The spare engine took the place of that at Kenton when it required repairs or maintenance. After the closure of Kenton shed, all three engines were based at Laxfield again with two working and one spare. After absorption by the LNER, the .allocation of three 'J65' class engines was retained. As a result of rationalisation of branch workings from 1939 only two locomotives were outbased at Laxfield, any failure being substituted by a relief engine from Ipswich. When the 'J15' class took over the services, Laxfield shed was host to a Westinghouse/vacuum brake fitted locomotive for the passenger diagram and a steam brake only engine for goods workings. In 1951 Laxfield shed was damaged by a severe gale which lifted the roof off half the building. Thereafter the wooden walls were shored up with timber baulks and the building remained in this dilapidated state until demolition in 1953.

During the independent years the three Hudswell Clarke tanks travelled boiler first from Haughley to Laxfield and, in the absence of a turntable, bunker first in the opposite direction. This method was adopted to ensure the crown plate above the firebox was well covered with water when the engines were climbing the 1 in 42 away from Haughley and the 1 in 44/50 of Athelington bank. The chimneys of the engines were therefore nearest the doors of Laxfield and Kenton sheds and this way round facilitated hand coaling from the coaling stage. The LNER and BR continued this arrangement and if an engine was received from Ipswich 'wrong way round' it was turned at the first opportunity on the 42 ft diameter turntable at Haughley.

Water supplies for locomotives were available at Haughley, Kenton and Laxfield. At Haughley the water was stored in a tank situated adjacent to the coaling stage, the water being pumped from a well by a petrol-driven walking beam engine. This supply was removed when trains started using the LNER station. The water at the west end of Kenton was stored in a tank situated between the fork of the Haughley line and the Debenham branch, west of the station. The supply was pumped into the tank from an adjacent pond by another ancient petrol engine. Initially a pump man was employed but the post was subsequently

The decrepit remains of Laxfield engine shed after the structure was damaged by a severe gale in 1951. As well as ripping the doors off and the back wall out, half the roof was blown away. Thereafter the wooden walls were shored up with timber baulks. On 5th July 1952 class 'J15' 65388, fitted with steam brake only for working the thrice-weekly freight trains, is the only occupant. *G. R. Mortimer*

Study of cab fitting and footplate of 'J15' class 0–6–0 No. 65447 standing at Kenton on 5th July 1952. As the locomotive was regularly outbased at Laxfield, the local footplate crews took a pride in keeping the cab interior polished and clean. *G. R. Mortimer*

Laxfield slumbers in the early afternoon sun as 'J15' 0–6–0 No. 65447 stands at the deserted platform with the mixed train for Haughley in September 1951. Unfortunately this scene was all too familiar at stations on the line where passenger traffic was negligible, the only regular patronage being school children travelling to and from Stowmarket Grammar School. It was therefore of no surprise to many when closure was advocated. *H. C. Casserley*

abolished, the pumping of water then being the responsibility of the engine crew outbased at Kenton shed. The supply was still available for use when the line closed. Another tank was situated at the east end of the station with water pumped from a well. This supply was also available at the time of closure.

As at Kenton, the company could find no suitable site for a well to supply water at Laxfield, and early in January 1905 a plot of land, which included a pond, was purchased from E. C. Hopper for £5 and again water was pumped into a storage tank beside the main single line. On the opening of the engine shed, the pond supply was initially abandoned in favour of obtaining supplies from a small dammed stream which passed under the main single line by a wooden culvert, just west of the engine shed. The scheme was successful in winter months when the rivulet was full of water, and a petrol engine ensured that the storage tank by the shed was kept fully replenished. However, in summer months, when the stream dried up to a small trickle, difficulties were soon encountered. To rectify matters, the company transferred the petrol pump back to the pond, to the east of the level crossing and, until the stream was again flowing freely, supplies were taken from the pond. The practice continued until closure of the line, although train crews preferred to use the pond supply.

During independent years the water supply cost the Mid-Suffolk very little in capital outlay and, except for Charles Woodward making initial supply available in June 1906 for £3, the only other attention received was the repairs to Haughley well costing £5 in the autumn of 1908. The company also purchased a spare petrol pumping engine in March 1916 at a cost of £38 10s 0d.

To prevent damage to boilers from such untreated water supplies, molasses and later briquettes were dropped into the locomotive side tanks or tender tank to soften the supply.

The Mid-Suffolk Railway Company initially placed a contract with Messrs. Fosdick of Ipswich for supply of locomotive coal. Fosdick did not, however, have the monopoly, and during independent years locomotive coal was obtained from many suppliers. As early as May 1905 Phillips and Company provided a small tonnage at a cost of £6 0s 8d whilst in January 1907 J & H Girling were the regular suppliers, the company paying £40 12s 4d for one consignment. Other merchants supplying the railway included Moys, Coote & Warren and Charringtons. In the last years of independence, the MSLR more often than not received supplies from the GER, one such consignment in May 1921 costing £242 16s 7d. After grouping and until absorption, the LNER continued to supply stocks of locomotive coal to the 'Middy'. During the financial crisis the company often could not afford adequate coal supplies, and in these periods of severe economy a mixture of coal briquettes and wood were burnt in the fireboxes of the company's locomotives.

HEADCODE

The headcode carried on the engines during the independent years conformed to the Railway Clearing House standard of one white light at the base of the chimney, for stopping passenger and mixed trains but lamps were rarely carried by engines working the freight services. After grouping, the LNER introduced a white circular disc in place of the head lamp for daytime use and the stopping passenger train code of one white disc or white light under the chimney was retained until the line closed. Goods services usually ran as class K with one lamp or white disc on the lamp bracket over the right-hand buffer of the engine. As was common on many branch lines, lamps or discs were often forgotten or positioned incorrectly. It is interesting to note that on the Mid-Suffolk Hudswell Clarke tank engines, the top lamp bracket for reverse running was not located at the top of the bunker but on the cab back sheet, which in practice was often obstructed by coal. The bracket was later repositioned on the back of the bunker.

WHISTLE CODE

When enginemen at Haughley GER Junction signal box wished to shunt from the light railway to the GE sidings, the whistle code sounded was 'two short' given twice. On the light railway proper the whistle had to be sounded for 100 yards after passing the notice boards on the approach to each ungated level crossing and again before passing the cattle guards, and at Newson's crossing continuously. The whistle code for the junction was abolished after 1924 but the same instructions pertaining to the approach to level crossings remained in use until closure of the line.

CHAPTER ELEVEN

Carriages and Wagons

IN contrast to the locomotive fleet, the coaching stock of the Mid-Suffolk Railway was formed exclusively of second-hand vehicles bought from main line companies. Initially, for any special event before the commencement of passenger train operation, coaching vehicles were hired from the GER. On 23rd September 1902 for the visit of Lord Kitchener, a saloon and brake vehicle was supplied to the company to form the special train from Mendlesham to Haughley. Later other coaches were hired from time to time on a day to day basis for the conveyance of unofficial passengers.

As early as September 1904 the chairman advised shareholders that for passenger-carrying requirements the company was buying three passenger carriages with corridor connections, each with accommodation for 48 people. It was also the intention to purchase a steam railmotor to seat 50 passengers which would be used for everyday traffic, supplemented by an ordinary carriage on market and other busy days.

For the commencement of freight and parcels services from September 1904, the Mid-Suffolk initially hired goods wagons pending the purchase of its own vehicles. At the same time it was realised that a parcels van would also be required. The GER were approached and a second-hand vehicle selected for purchase. As modifications were required, immediate delivery could not be made and so in the intervening period a four-wheel passenger brake third was hired from the GER during October and November 1904 at a monthly rental of £1 15s 0d.

At the end of November the Mid-Suffolk Light Railway took delivery of their passenger brake van No. 1, a second-hand four-wheeled vehicle obtained at a cost of £40. The vehicle was originally GER brake third No. 14 to diagram 501, one of an order of thirty brake thirds supplied by the Metropolitan Carriage and Wagon Co. of Birmingham at a cost of £275 each and delivered to the main line company in September 1875. The carriage was withdrawn by the GER as a life-expired vehicle in the half year ending 31st December 1904. On 22nd October 1904 Stratford Works order No. D & P 7542 authorised 'Repairs to Brake Van No. 14 sold to the Mid Suffolk Light Railway'. The reference to repairs included the conversion of the vehicle to a full brake, not a difficult or costly operation, before delivery to the Mid-Suffolk Company.

In the Board of Trade returns, passenger brake van No. 1 was initially included in the wagon fleet statistics, rather confusingly alongside goods brake No. 1. By 1911 the vehicle was more appropriately classified in the category 'other passenger train vehicles' with horse-boxes Nos. 9 and 10. Before the introduction of the passenger train services in 1908 and delivery of goods brake van No. 2, passenger brake No. 1 was invariably used as a goods brake. Prior to the stations being fully staffed, a goods clerk used to ride in this vehicle on the goods services, handling parcels and small goods items as well as dealing with invoices. On the introduction of passenger services, this van was usually found at the tail of the mixed trains, despite the presence of one of the ex-Metropolitan brake thirds in the passenger formation. No. 1 was utilized extensively for the conveyance of milk, fruit and parcels traffic when in use on the mixed services. It was normally attached to the first up train in the morning next to the engine so that on arrival at Haughley the commodities could be offloaded easily and trolleyed to the GER station for forwarding. Conversely, the van was always located at the rear of the last down train ex Haughley in the evening.

The vehicle was fitted with oil lighting throughout its life and received extensive repairs and repainting by the GER in April 1920, the cost of the work being included in a charge of £188 14s 8d which also included repairs to a locomotive.

Being a 'life expired vehicle' even before delivery to the 'Middy', when the light railway was absorbed into the LNER the main line company found no use for the vehicle and it was very quickly withdrawn for scrapping.

Gillingwater advised in February 1905 that the company intended to acquire for passenger traffic seven carriages and a brake van, all to be painted in a Victorian brown

GER Diagram 501 4-wheel brake third. GER No. 14 was converted to full brake MSLR No. 1.

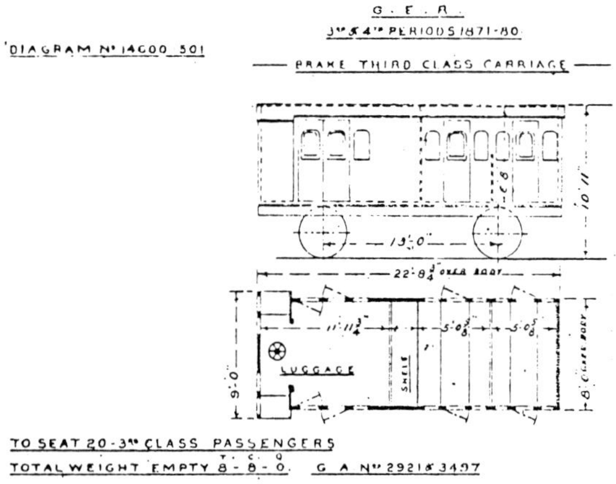

Side elevation of MSLR passenger brake No. 1 (ex-GER brake third No. 14)

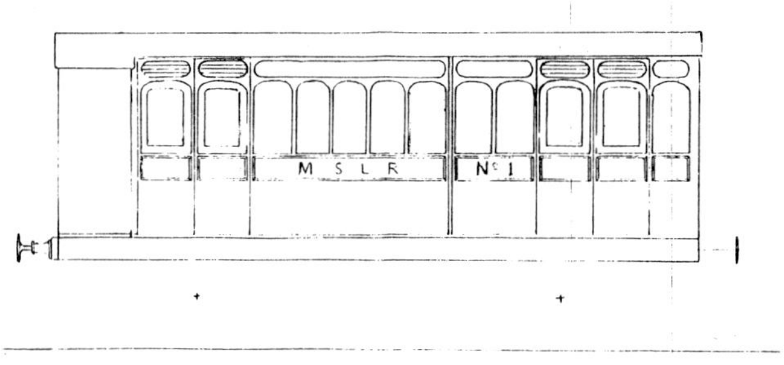

Scale 3mm to 1 foot

MSLR ex-Metropolitan 3 set close-coupled 4-compartment first, 5-compartment third, and 3-compartment brake third. Drawn by Peter Wilde based on photographs.

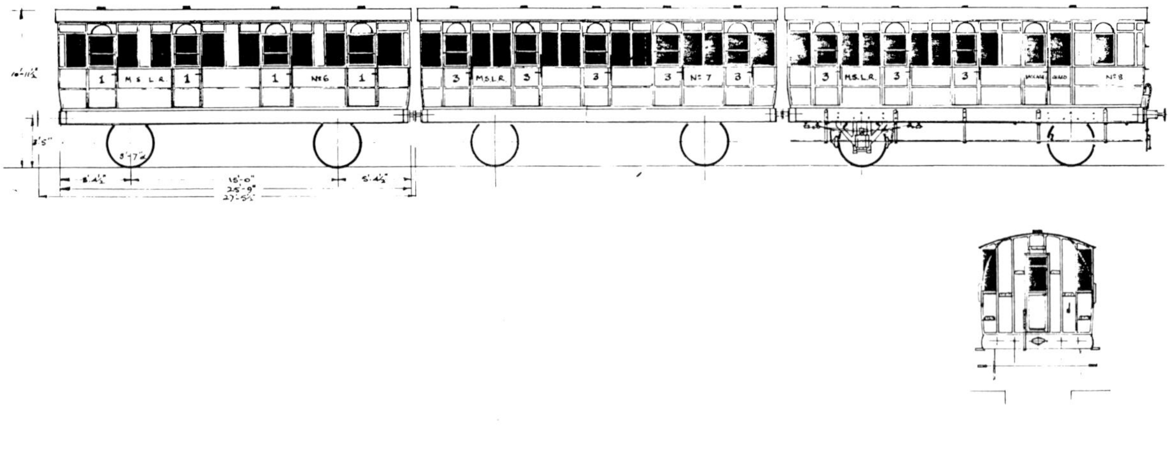

livery. First and third class accommodation would be provided with the interior comfortably upholstered. Tickets would be issued on the train by the guard and, to enable him to walk from one end to the other, the coaches would be fitted with end doors and drop plates.

For passenger-carrying requirements the Mid-Suffolk Company surprisingly ignored the GER second-hand vehicle market, probably finding nothing suitable to their requirements, and finally purchased seven four-wheel coaches from the Metropolitan Railway. The coaches selected, made surplus by the extension of electrification, were Metropolitan 'Jubilee' stock built by Cravens between 1887 and 1892 with bodies measuring 27 ft 6 ins long by 8 ft 4½ ins wide. Initially the vehicles were unsuitable for working on

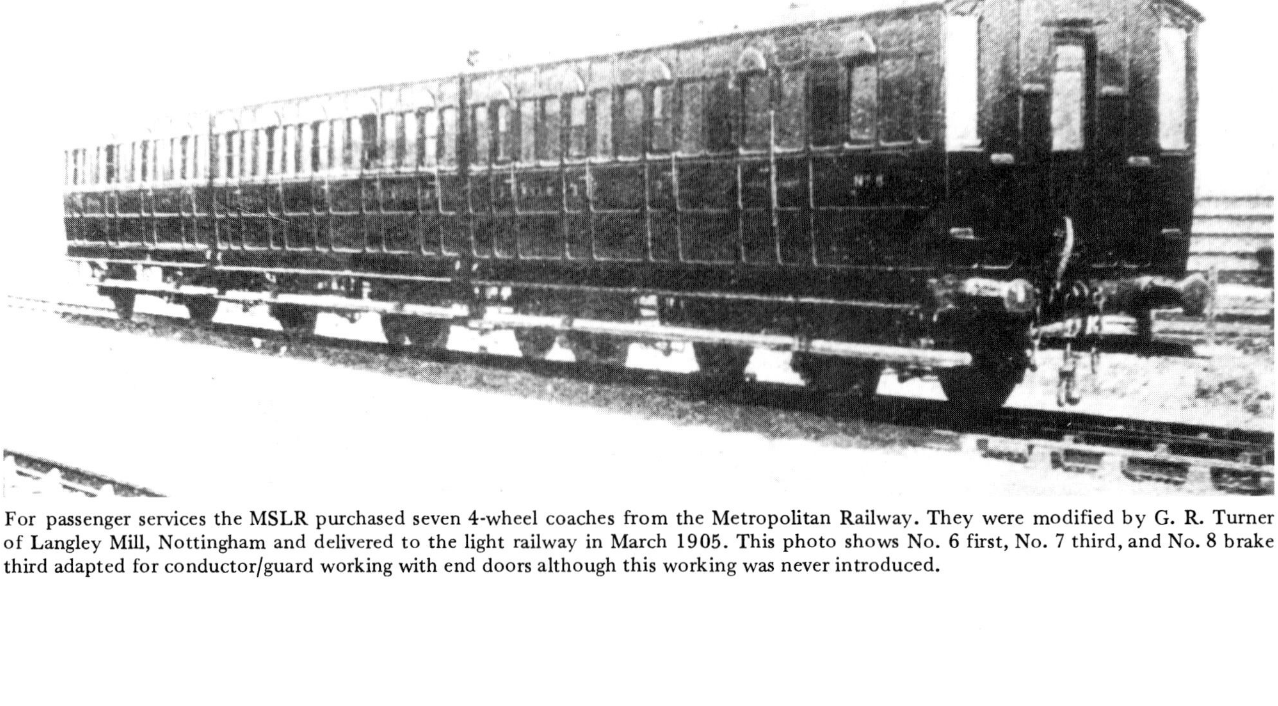

For passenger services the MSLR purchased seven 4-wheel coaches from the Metropolitan Railway. They were modified by G. R. Turner of Langley Mill, Nottingham and delivered to the light railway in March 1905. This photo shows No. 6 first, No. 7 third, and No. 8 brake third adapted for conductor/guard working with end doors although this working was never introduced.

the light railway and were sent to the firm of G. R. Turner of Langley Mill, Nottingham, for modification and renovation.

As a result of the modifications, the vehicles, three 4-wheel 5-compartment thirds, two 4-wheel 4-compartment firsts, and two 4-wheel 3-compartment brake thirds, had their compartments removed and were equipped with vestibules and gangways through the centre of the vehicle. The intermediate doors were sealed off, leaving only the end side doors available for passenger access. End doors and drop plates were also fitted to enable the guard to walk through the vehicles to collect fares. On hindsight the latter appeared an unnecessary modification, for the conductor guard method of issuing tickets, although advocated, was never adopted on the MSLR. The vacuum brake equipment used by the Metropolitan Railway was removed and Westinghouse air brake equipment substituted. Safety chains were also initially retained but during the course of the operating life of the vehicles they quickly disappeared. As part of the modification programme, one of the compartment thirds was converted to a first/third saloon with the third class accommodation occupying three compartments, and the first saloon, with a large table in the centre and seats all round, occupying the space previously taken by the other two compartments. This vehicle was often used as a VIP vehicle for important travellers on the line and was regularly utilized by Gillingwater on Tuesdays when he travelled to Haughley for Ipswich market.

The seven vehicles were purchased in the autumn of 1904, although it is unclear whether the price of £860 included the subsequent modification work. They were delivered to the Mid-Suffolk line and inspected by the GER in March 1905, well before the intended date for opening the railway to passenger traffic. The coaches were numbered as under, following on from parcels brake No. 1:

No. 2	First/third saloon
No. 3	3-compartment third/brake
No. 4	5-compartment third
No. 5	4-compartment first
No. 6	4-compartment first
No. 7	5-compartment third
No. 8	3-compartment third/brake

and were formed into two close-coupled 3-coach sets. Coaches 3, 4 and 5 formed one set, and 6, 7 and 8 the second set, leaving No. 2 as spare vehicle for special traffic or strengthening of market day trains. This arrangement also ensured that if the two sets were coupled together for excursion traffic or special workings, the brake third vehicles could be located at the outer ends of the 6-coach formation. Thus one set always worked with the brake third vehicle at the Haughley end of the train and the other set with the brake third at the Laxfield end. If the seven-coach formation was worked the first/third saloon was located as the centre vehicle between the two sets.

A month after delivery the company purchased a spare set of brake connections from the Westinghouse Brake and Signal Company for £2 10s 0d as emergency cover. The coaches were given various test runs across the line but when Colonel Von Donop refused to sanction opening, after his inspection in July 1905, the vehicles spent many months languishing in the sidings at Laxfield or Kenton. The sets were split up for a time and individual vehicles were attached to freight trains, conveying specially invited guests of the directors or parties travelling at their own risk, with the permission of the railway board.

In readiness for the second inspection and subsequent opening of the line to passenger traffic from 29th September 1908, the three car sets were reformed. Initially all seven vehicles were illuminated by rape oil lamps but in October 1911 two coaches, No. 3 and No. 4, were equipped with acetylene gas lighting. The work, which involved the fitting of two mantles in each coach and a generator at the end of each vehicle, was carried out by the Phosphor Company Ltd. at a cost of £29 5s 0d. At the same time the firm provided 2 cwt of carbide for £1 6s 6d. Because of the precarious finances of the light railway, a third vehicle, saloon No. 2, was not equipped with the new lighting until December 1912, when the Phosphor Company completed the work at a cost of £16 1s 9d. The new mode of lighting was not entirely successful as during winter months the generator on the end of each vehicle was frequently frozen so that no illumination was possible. Because of these inadequacies, the remaining coaches retained oil lighting until withdrawn from traffic. An ex-MSL employee recalled that he topped up the rape oil lamp through the hole in the roof of each coach every day during the winter months, plugging the hole afterwards with a big stopper to prevent down draughts. On some occasions he recalled the oil lamp caught fire, cracking the glass mantle and blackening the roof of the compartment before the flames could be extinguished.

As a result of these lighting modifications, the two 3-coach sets working was abandoned and the sets were split up, three-coach trains running on Tuesdays and Thursdays (Ipswich and Stowmarket market days) and two coaches at other times usually attached in a mixed train with parcels/brake No. 1 in the formation for the use of the guard.

After some nine years operation with only day-to-day maintenance at Laxfield, the light railway company requested the GER to carry out sundry repairs to the coaching stock in the autumn of 1912. The task was performed by staff travelling to Laxfield, the main line company charging £30 2s 5d for the work. Just before the outbreak of the First World War, two of the coaches were painted by the company's own staff, but lettering and lining out were left to the professional services of G. Ripper who charged the company £16 1s 9d.

The patch-up repairs made by the GE enabled the vehicles to survive the war. After the armistice, however, the passenger rolling stock was in a run-down condition, having received only minimal maintenance at Laxfield during hostilities, although the GER had carried out some tyre turning of wheels at Ipswich Carriage and Wagon shops. As with the locomotives and other rolling stock, A. P. Parker, the receiver, negotiated with the main line company which subsequently arranged a heavy overhaul programme for the coaching stock. The initial repairs were carried out between April and June 1919 at a cost of £212 13s 9d, during which time all seven vehicles received attention. It is believed that the vehicles were taken to Ipswich Carriage and Wagon shops for attention when new tyres were also fitted to the wheels of all coaches at a cost of £34 18s 8d. Having completed the initial remedial repairs, the GER then carried out a complete refurbishing of the Mid-Suffolk stock on a systematic basis over the next eighteen months and when vehicles could be released from the light railway. The work was completed by December 1920 with payment for the work being made in December 1919 £133 4s 5d, September 1920 £128 8s 8d, December 1920 £276 16s 7d and March 1921 £7 6s. 1d.

The seven passenger-carrying vehicles were considered non-standard and obsolete when the LNER took over the working of the light railway in 1924. Consequently, the new owners quickly transferred in some equally ancient GER six-wheel coaches as replacements for the Mid-Suffolk vehicles. All seven MSLR coaches were withdrawn in 1924 without being renumbered by the LNER.

The coaching stock complement of the light railway was completed by two ex-GER horse-boxes, fitted with Westinghouse brakes and numbered 9 and 10. Many of these wooden-framed vehicles were being withdrawn by the early 1900s on replacement by more modern steel-framed horse-boxes. No. 9, ex-GER No. 408, was built by the Swansea Wagon Co. in 1883 at a cost of £130 and was withdrawn from traffic on 30th June 1905. Also withdrawn on the same date was GER No. 484 built by the Birmingham Carriage and Wagon Co. in 1881 at a cost of £170, which became MSLR No. 10. The horse-boxes were purchased from the GER at a cost of £73 each and were thoroughly renovated before delivery in August 1905. During the renovation both vehicles were also provided with vacuum brake equipment for working off the MSLR and GE system and received communication cord equipment to enable them to work on passenger trains. The horse-boxes received little maintenance in the initial years when the only recorded repair was carried out to No. 9 in November 1905. They are recorded travelling off the Mid-Suffolk line to Ipswich and Colchester but other excursions are not known. After the First World War, No. 10 received an extensive renovation and overhaul at Ipswich Carriage and Wagon shops in July 1919, the GER company charging £98 7s 7d for the work. No repairs were carried out to No. 9 as in all probability this vehicle was in the better condition when originally acquired from the GER. Both were quickly withdrawn after the LNER took over the line in 1924.

Principal dimensions of the horse-boxes were:

Length over body	16 ft 0 ins
Max height	11 ft 10 ins
Max width	7 ft 8½ ins
Horse compartment length	10 ft 0 ins
Groom's compartment	5 ft 0 ins
Width interior body	7 ft 4 ins
Wheelbase	10 ft 0 ins

Maintenance and repair costs of the MSL coaching stock were initially quite moderate:

6 months ending	£	s.	d.	
31 December 1908	28	8	9	including wagons
30 June 1909	8	6	4	" "
31 December 1909	37	3	3	" "
30 June 1910	18	13	1	" "
31 December 1910	13	3	9	" "

GER horse-box to Diagram 15 (MSLR Nos. 9 & 10)

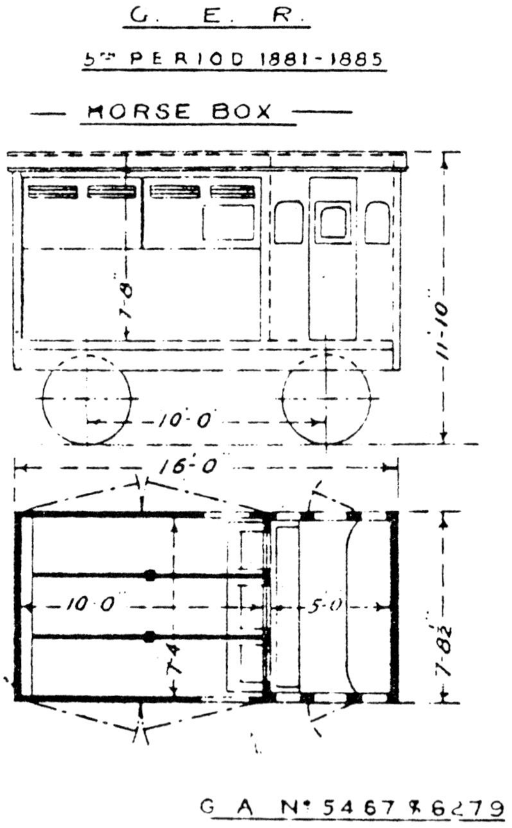

From 1st January 1911 the carriage and wagon repairs were costed separately and the coaching stock maintenance thereafter was:

6 months ending	£	s.	d.
30 June 1911	1	7	0
31 December 1911	46	7	6
30 June 1912	13	4	8
31 December 1912	33	5	9

Maintenance costs were then calculated annually:

	£	s.	d.
1913	13	16	0
1914	72	7	11
1915	186	1	6
1916	69	6	9
1917	109	5	9
1918	151	10	2
1919	594	14	4

The coaching stock of the Mid-Suffolk Light Railway was painted the same livery as the locomotives, described as Victorian Brown, but later incorrectly reported as Midland Crimson Lake, with yellow and vermilion lining. The vehicle numbers and lettering were in gilt. As with the locomotives, the Mid-Suffolk crimson was described as slightly darker than the established Midland Red containing an extra brown additive. Certainly after the First World War

Ex-GER 6-wheel coaches were transferred to the Laxfield branch from 1924. Standing in the dock road at Laxfield on 18th April 1949 are composites E63405 (ex-GE 536) and E63408 (ex-GE 539) flanking brake third E62331 (ex-GE 944). The composites dated from 1897, whilst the brake third was built in 1902. All three were withdrawn in 1951. *W. A. Camwell*

the coaches were described by an employee as more red/brown than crimson, suffering a loss of gloss as the varnish weathered.

The coaching stock allocated to the light railway after the withdrawal of the original MSLR stock, consisted mostly of ex-GER 6-wheel composites dating from 1897 to diagram 208 and 6-wheel three-compartment brake thirds to diagram 533 dating from 1901/2.

Composites to diagram 208 known to have worked on the line included:

LNER No.	*ex GER No.*	*Built*	*Withdrawn*
63390	404	April 1897	22 January 1938
63403	534	October 1897	31 December 1938
63404	535	October 1897	15 January 1952
63405	536	October 1897	24 March 1951
63408	539	October 1897	12 May 1951

The brake thirds were:

62331	944	January 1902	12 January 1951
62334	947	December 1901	4 August 1951
62338	951	March 1902	1952

The vehicles were normally formed into two coach formations, brake third and composite, with an additional composite added on Thursdays and Tuesdays, Stowmarket and Ipswich market days. All were lettered at the end of each vehicle 'Haughley & Laxfield'.

After the Second World War only three composites and three brake thirds remained in use on the branch. It was increasingly evident to the railway authorities that even with this total, the line was overstocked with vehicles. As early as 16th April 1949, composite 63405 left the branch for Ipswich but was not in fact withdrawn until 24th March 1951. The remaining vehicles remained untouched for almost two years before brake third 62331 departed for Stratford and subsequent withdrawal on 12th January 1951. Soon afterwards composite 63405 arrived at Stratford on 17th March, to follow a similar fate, whilst brake third No. 62334 was also taken to Stratford later in the same year, being withdrawn on 4th August 1951. After languishing in High Meads sidings for some months this vehicle was sent to Ilford Carriage and Wagon Shops on 29th December 1951, although its use and final scrapping date are unknown.

The last six-wheel coaching vehicles in regular use on the light railway, and indeed for passenger-carrying on British Railways, were brake third No. 62338 and composite No. 63404 which soldiered on until October 1951 pending the arrival of replacement stock. During the last months in service both vehicles suffered from leaking roofs so that passengers, notably schoolchildren, were often dampened in adverse weather by the influx of water. Ipswich Carriage and Wagon Shops sent a coachbuilder to effect repairs to the roof canvas and during the period out of traffic a bogie brake third or composite were substituted as replacement

6-wheel composite to Diagram 208.

L. N. E. R.

CODE Nº 6043.

DIAGRAM Nº 14600 - 208E — COMPOSITE CARRIAGE — BUILT 1897

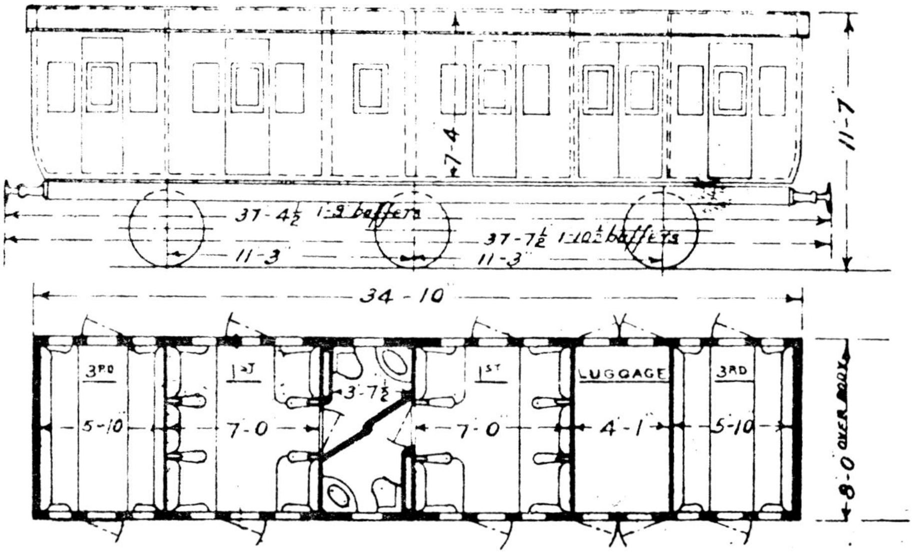

TO SEAT 10-1ST & 20-3RD CLASS PASSENGERS.

TOTAL WEIGHT EMPTY 13-19-2 (T. C. Q.) G. A. Nº 9699

FITTED WITH WESTINGHOUSE BRAKE. INCANDESCENT GAS. STEAM HEATING.

6-wheel brake third to Diagram 533.

L. N. E. R.

CODE Nº 6142.

DIAGRAM Nº 14600-533E. BRAKE THIRD CLASS CARRIAGE BUILT 1901-02.

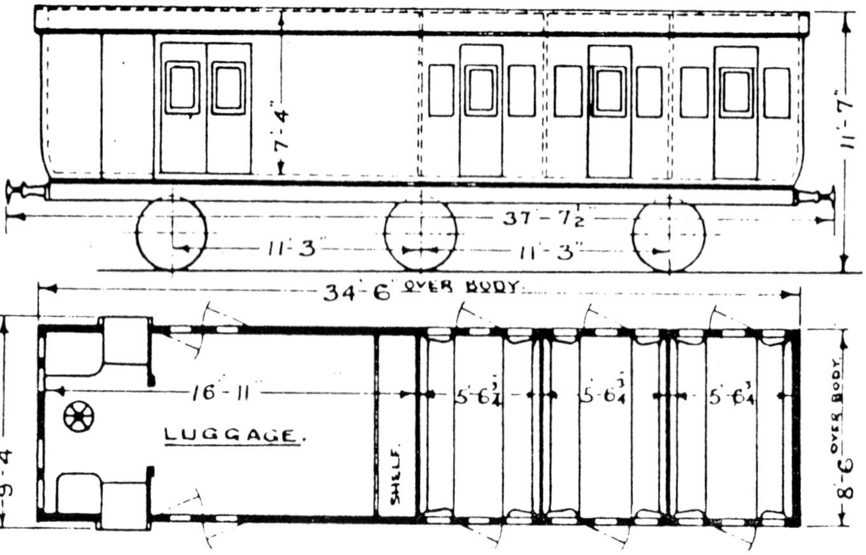

TO SEAT 30 THIRD CLASS PASSENGERS.

TOTAL WEIGHT EMPTY 12-12-3 (T. C. Q.) G. A. Nº 11636E.

" " LOADED 18-11-2 LUGGAGE LOAD 4 TONS.

FITTED WITH INCANDESCENT GAS. FITTED WITH DUAL BRAKE

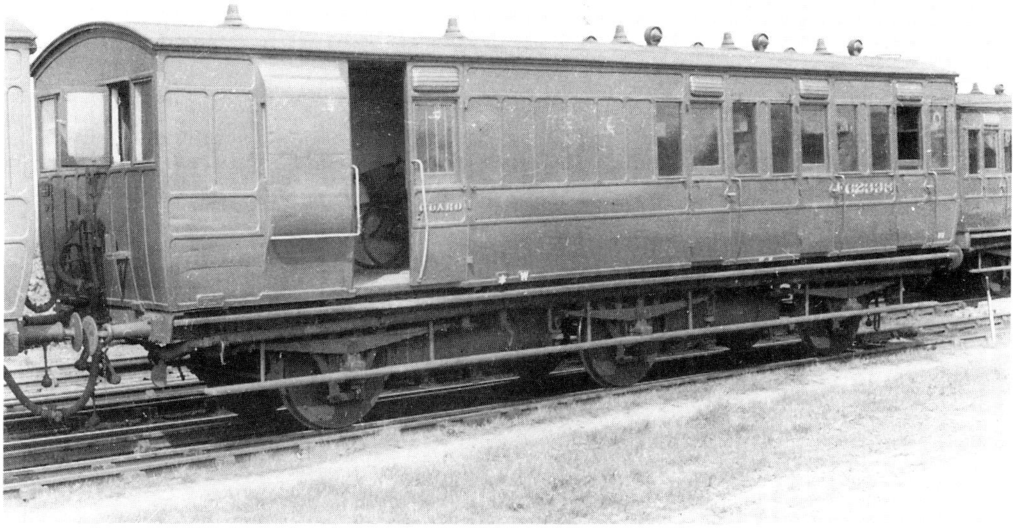

The coaching stock allocated to the light railway after the withdrawal of the original MSLR stock included ex-GER 6-wheel, three-compartment brake thirds dating from 1901/2 to diagram 533. LNER No. 62338 (ex-GE 951) at Laxfield on 18th April 1949 was withdrawn in 1952.
W. A. Camwell

vehicles. With the arrival of the Ilford suburban bogie stock in October 1951 the two six-wheel coaches were displaced and composite 63404 was withdrawn from service on 15th January the following year. Brake third No. 62338 was also withdrawn in 1952 and was later converted to a riding van before being transferred to departmental stock as No. 320112 on 28th June 1952. There are no details of its ultimate disposal.

Principal dimensions of the 6-wheel stock were:

GER Diagram	533 Brake third	208 First/third composite
Length over body	34 ft 6 ins	34 ft 10 ins
Length over buffers	37 ft 7½ ins	37 ft 4 ins or 37 ft 7½ ins
Maximum width	9 ft 4 ins over guard's lookout	8 ft 0 ins
Maximum height	11 ft 7 ins	11 ft 7 ins
Body height (internal)	7 ft 4 ins	7 ft 4 ins
Wheelbase	22 ft 6 ins	22 ft 6 ins
Seating 1st class	–	10
3rd class	30	20
Brake load	4 tons	–
Weight empty	12 tons 2 cwt	13 tons 19 cwt

The vehicles were fitted with Westinghouse brake only, steam heating and incandescent gas for lighting.

The electrification of the suburban route from Liverpool Street to Shenfield in 1949 released a considerable number of bogie compartment coaches for further use. Unfortunately the design of the vehicles severely restricted their utilization outside of the London area, as most of the cross-country and branch line services in East Anglia were worked with bogie corridor stock, enabling the guard to walk through the train to issue and check tickets. Many of the vehicles languished in the sidings at Channelsea or High Meads at Stratford as well as other locations until a suitable use could be found for them. By 1951 the condition of the six-wheel stock on the Mid-Suffolk line was giving cause for concern. From the previous year bogie coaching stock had been used as replacements when the six-wheel coaches were under repair. After the permanent way staff reported no adverse effect of the bogie stock on the Mid-Suffolk track, the railway authorities decided to withdraw the ageing six-wheelers and replace them with four of the former Ilford suburban coaches.

In October 1951 the replacement vehicles arrived on the light railway, formed into two 2-coach sets each composed of a bogie brake third and bogie composite suitably labelled Haughley to Laxfield Branch Set No. 1 and Set No. 2. The vehicles, GER bogie composite built to diagram 237 and GER bogie brake third built to diagram 542, were built by the Midland Railway Carriage and Wagon Company, Birmingham, and introduced into service in 1921.

The composites to diagram 237 were:

LNER/BR No.	*ex GER No.*	*Built*
63202	832	April 1921
63209	839	October 1921

whilst the brake thirds to diagram 542 were:

62181	1043	1921
62216	572	December 1922

Compared with the 6-wheel coaches, travelling in the straight back seats in the narrow compartments was acutely uncomfortable. The vehicles were, however, equipped with electric lighting. Again the coaches also had Westinghouse brakes. Unfortunately, the new bogie stock saw less than ten months service on the light railway and all four vehicles were used on the last passenger trains across the branch on 26th July 1952. Thus, after standing for a few weeks at Haughley, the four vehicles were worked up to Stratford for conversion to other uses, sharing the same fate as many of the other former Ilford suburban bogie stock. Subsequent modifications to the four vehicles used on the Mid-Suffolk

Bogie brake third to Diagram 542

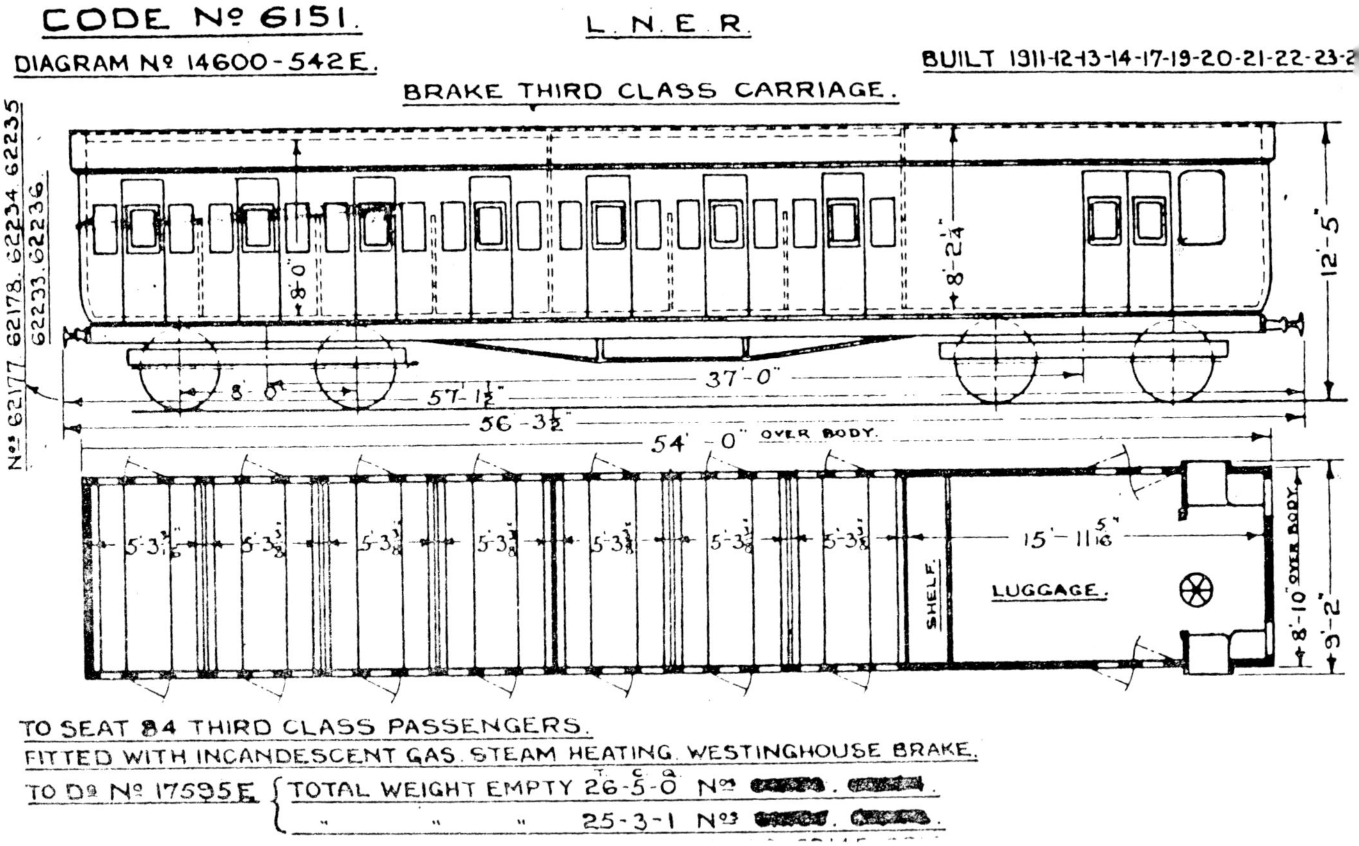
CODE Nº 6151.
L. N. E. R.
DIAGRAM Nº 14600-542E.
BUILT 1911-12-13-14-17-19-20-21-22-23-2
BRAKE THIRD CLASS CARRIAGE.
Nos 62177. 62178. 62234. 62235
62233. 62236.
8'-0"
8'-2¼"
12'-5"
8'-0"
37'-0"
57'-1½"
56'-3½"
54'-0" OVER BODY.
5'-3⅜"
15'-11 5/16"
SHELF.
LUGGAGE.
8'-10" OVER BODY.
9'-2"
TO SEAT 84 THIRD CLASS PASSENGERS.
FITTED WITH INCANDESCENT GAS. STEAM HEATING. WESTINGHOUSE BRAKE.
TO Dº Nº 17595E
T C Q
TOTAL WEIGHT EMPTY 26-5-0 Nos [redacted].
" " " 25-3-1 Nos [redacted].

Bogie composite to Diagram 237

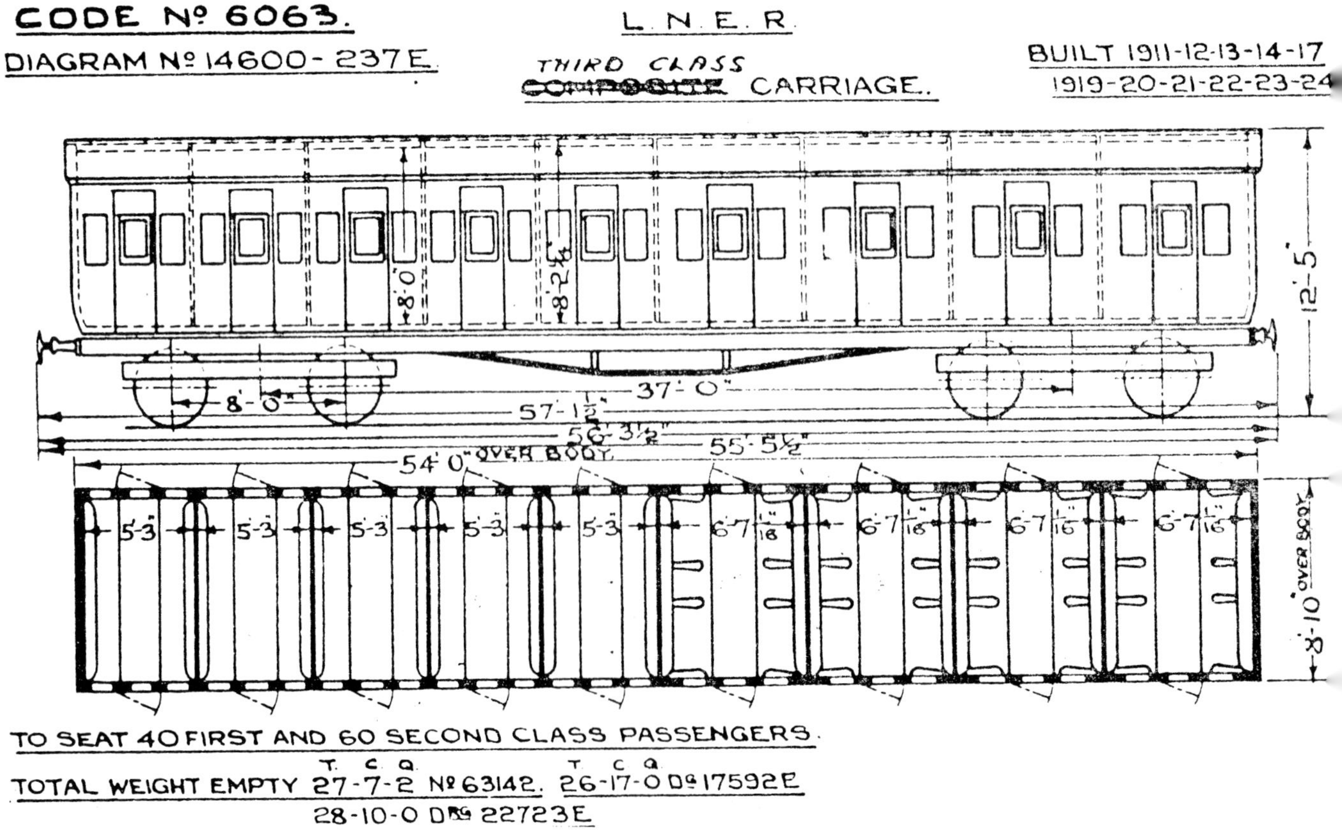
CODE Nº 6063.
L. N. E. R.
DIAGRAM Nº 14600-237E.
THIRD CLASS
COMPOSITE CARRIAGE.
BUILT 1911-12-13-14-17
1919-20-21-22-23-24
8'-0"
8'-2¼"
12'-5"
8'-0"
37'-0"
57'-1½"
56'-3½"
55'-5½"
54'-0" OVER BODY.
5'-3"
6'-7 1/16"
8'-10" OVER BODY.
TO SEAT 40 FIRST AND 60 SECOND CLASS PASSENGERS.
T C Q
TOTAL WEIGHT EMPTY 27-7-2 Nº 63142. 26-17-0 Dº 17592E
28-10-0 Dºg 22723E

In October 1951 two 2-coach bogie sets replaced the former GER 6-wheel vehicles on the Mid-Suffolk passenger services. Haughley and Laxfield set No. 1, formed of an ex-GER bogie brake third to diagram 542 and bogie composite built to diagram 237, both dating from 1921, are shown here standing in the carriage road at Laxfield on 17th July 1952. The vehicles, although only equipped with Westinghouse brake, had the luxury of electric lighting, even if the lights dimmed at every station stop. *R. F. Roberts*

line included bogie composite 63202 converted to a parcels and mail van and renumbered 6005 on 23rd April 1955, being finally withdrawn on 29th December 1962. Sister vehicle No. 63209 was converted to a parcels and mail van and renumbered 6073 on 19th May 1956. This vehicle was also withdrawn on 29th December 1962. Brake third No. 62181 was converted to a covered carriage truck (CCT) on 23rd February 1957 and was finally withdrawn from service on 29th December 1962. After laying idle for almost a year, the vehicle was reinstated on 28th December 1963 and was finally withdrawn in September 1966. Brake third No. 62216 was converted to a parcels/mail van No. 6041 in December 1955 and finally withdrawn on 9th September 1961.

The principal dimensions of the bogie vehicles were:

GER Diagram	542	237
	Bogie brake third	Bogie composite
Length over body	54 ft 0 ins	54 ft 0 ins
Length over buffers	56 ft 3½ ins or 57 ft 1½ ins	56 ft 3½ ins or 57 ft 1½ ins
Maximum width	9 ft 2 ins over guard's lookout	8 ft 10 ins
Maximum height	12 ft 5 ins	12 ft 5 ins
Body height	8 ft 2¼ ins	8 ft 2¼ ins
Wheelbase (bogies)	8 ft 0 ins	8 ft 0 ins
Wheelbase (total)	45 ft 0 ins	45 ft 0 ins
Seating 1st class	–	40
3rd class	84	60
Brake load	4 tons	–
Weight empty	26 tons 5 cwt	26 tons 17 cwt
	25 tons 3 cwt	27 tons 7 cwt

On 6th April 1952 several railway officers visited the Mid-Suffolk Light Railway to inspect the line prior to the announcement of impending closure. The group travelled in the six-wheel Norwich district inspection saloon No. 960903 which had an interesting history. The vehicle was originally built to order G24 at Stratford Works and completed in December 1889 as GER No. 14 in the inspection vehicle series, for use by John Wilson, the chief engineer of the GER, for inspection purposes. As built to Diagram 11, the coach had a 27 ft 6 ins body mounted on wooden underframes with an unusually long wheelbase of 19 ft for a 4-wheel vehicle. It was also the first GER vehicle to be fitted with electric lighting when new.

In 1897, then only 8 years old, No. 14 received extensive alterations when the body was extended to a new length of 32 ft 0 ins. A new underframe mounted on six wheels with a combined wheelbase of 22 ft 6 ins was also provided. Around 1910, in common with GER royal and other saloons and recent main line bogie stock, steam heating was installed. In the year prior to grouping, internal modifications were made to the attendant's compartment whilst a door on the corridor side of the vehicle was removed and a side door to the centre saloon sealed off. It is thought that vacuum through pipes were also fitted at this date.

Under the LNER, GER No. 14 was renumbered 68 in the GE saloon series and in 1925 was displaced from her role as civil engineer's saloon at Stratford by the conversion of royal saloon No. 5. No. 68 was then transferred to Ipswich where she served as the district engineer's saloon for some twenty years, occasionally travelling across the Mid-Suffolk line. In 1947 the saloon was renumbered 960903 but by then had been transferred to Norwich, Ipswich having acquired No. 960902, an ex-GER suburban brake third. The journey of 960903 over the Mid-Suffolk line was almost the last in her capacity of inspection saloon for soon afterwards she was displaced by DE 320042, an ex-Great Northern Railway invalid saloon No. 43087, built in 1912 and converted at Stratford in 1951 for inspection purposes. No. 960903, after use as a mobile office with the LTS and GE electrification works in the 1950s and early 1960s, was transferred to the Sheffield area before being condemned in 1973. William McAlpine subsequently purchased the vehicle for preservation and it now resides at the Rutland Railway Museum.

CLEANING

Carriage cleaning was performed by station staff at Laxfield, latterly using water stored in the ex-Midland and Great Northern Railway tender stabled in the cattle dock road at Laxfield. From 1924 heavier cleaning was performed at Ipswich every three or four weeks. To enable the vehicles to receive this additional treatment, two coaches were usually attached to the 7.25 a.m. up mixed ex Laxfield on Tuesdays. At Haughley they were forwarded to Ipswich Carriage and Wagon Shops where the interior was vacuum-cleaned and dusted whilst the exterior windows were washed. Routine maintenance was also carried out before the vehicles were returned the next day, travelling from Haughley to Laxfield on the last mixed train. When the coaches were illuminated by oil, the lamps, accessible through removable bungs in the roof, were changed at Laxfield. It was not unknown for these lamps to catch light and char the interior ceiling of the compartment. On the introduction of the incandescent gas-fitted six-wheel vehicles by the LNER, the replenishing of gas was performed either at Ipswich or Haughley. The bogie vehicles inherited from the Ilford suburban sets required no such replenishment for they were fitted with electric lighting. It was always a feature of these vehicles that lights were very dim until the train was on the move. The lights then again dimmed at station stops.

Leading porter Frank Hubbard makes light work of cleaning the side windows of bogie composite E63202 at Laxfield.

WAGON STOCK

As pointed out in chapter 2, the Mid-Suffolk Light Railway Company initially owned no wagon stock, and for the commencement of freight services in September 1904, was forced to hire vehicles from the GER. Pending delivery of a second-hand brake van from the main line company, the GE also loaned a goods brake to the 'Middy', charging the sum of £3 10s 0d for 14 days hire in September and October 1904. A brake van was again required in November for one day when the GER charged 5/-d for hire of the vehicle.

However, the company had taken steps to purchase goods stock and on 25th July 1904 Stevenson reported negotiations with the Lincoln Carriage Company for the purchase of ten 8-ton wagons and ten 10-ton wagons. Later in September 1904 the shareholders were advised that ten trucks were under construction. By the end of October the first deliveries of the new stock were made and the company reduced the number of wagons hired from the GER. Hiring was never completely eliminated and the GER, and after grouping the LNER, for a brief spell before take-over, continued to loan wagons to the light railway.

As well as hiring from the GER, the Mid-Suffolk also hired wagons from C. D. Phillips in December 1908 for £8 13s 2d, and in the same year T. Burnett loaned vehicles at a cost of £11 8s 0d.

The Mid-Suffolk stock of open wagons consisted of two types. Four 8-ton, 3-plank dropside vehicles were purchased from Jackson, the contractor, modified with ordinary buffers in place of dumb buffers and given the running numbers 1, 2, 3 and 4. With a tare weight of 4 tons 2 cwt, all were painted grey, with black ironwork and running gear. All lettering was painted in white and the vehicles were titled 'MID SUFFOLK' on each side, the lettering being placed along the top two planks of the wagon with the number and the tare weight displayed on the lower planking. The vehicles had an 8 ft wheelbase, and being utilized for ballast and permanent way work during the independent operation of the light railway company, never ventured off the system.

A variation of the 8-ton open wagons came in the form of four-plank, high-sided vehicles with slightly raised curved ends. Like the three plank dropside wagons, the brake gear was fitted on one side of the wagon only whilst the buffers had thinner shanks. With a tare weight of 6 tons and wheelbase of 9 ft, the four-plank wagons were painted in the same grey livery with white lettering, showing 'MID SUFFOLK' on the sides located on the second and half-way up the top plank. The wagons were numbered 5, 6, 7, 8, 9, 10, 11, 12, 13, 14, 15, 16, 17, 18, 25 and 26. Ironwork and

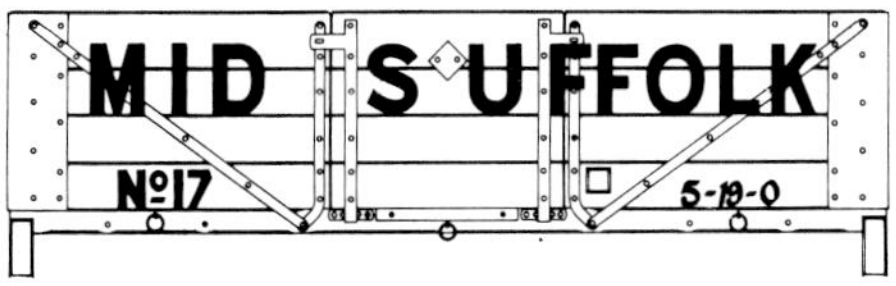

MSLR 4-plank open wagon body. Drawn by J. Watling. Scale: 4mm to 1 foot

running gear was painted black. The vehicle numbers and tare weight were carried on the lower planking. These wagons are believed to have been built by the Lincoln Carriage Company.

Unlike the three-plank vehicles, the four-plank wagons were used extensively for conveyance of goods from Mid-Suffolk stations to destinations on the GE and other railway systems. No. 17 is recorded receiving repairs by the North Eastern Railway in August 1919 at a cost of 15/11d. In April 1911 the Mid-Suffolk company paid a mileage levy on rolling stock to the Great Central Railway totalling 3/3d, whilst in May the Great Northern Railway received a similar payment of 15/5d. With the considerable mileages covered it is of no surprise that many of these vehicles received varying degrees of repairs by the GER. As early as March 1905 one of the wagons was receiving attention at a cost of £1 17s 4d. In the absence of a fully qualified fitter, the Mid-Suffolk called upon the services of various engineering firms to maintain their wagon fleet and in June 1906 Easterbrook and Company attended to truck No. 12, charging 2/6d for the minor repair.

From thereon the vehicles received little attention until just before the outbreak of the First World War. In February 1914 minor repairs to wagon No. 15 were carried out by the GER fitters for 10/2d and two months later it received some extensive repairs at Ipswich, the main line company charging £7 6s 5d for the work. During the same period four-plank open No. 7 and cattle wagon No. 19 also received attention by the GER for £12 19s 11d. The main line company gave minor attention to No. 8 for 3/6d in June 1917 and in July 1919 repaired Nos. 11, 13 and 17 at a cost of £10 18s 8d. Further repairs to unknown wagons were effected in November 1920 at a cost of £24 4s 11d and again in August 1922. There is only one recorded repainting of a Mid-Suffolk four-plank open, when No. 13 received the necessary attention from J. Vincent in July 1911 at a cost of £2 4s 0d.

No. 9, built originally as an 8-ton four-plank, high-sided open wagon, was converted in 1906 to a covered van. The modification, carried out by A. C. Andrews (Woods and Company) for £4 6s 1d, was of a hybrid nature and consisted of a box built on top of the original wagon body. The vehicle had the normal corner plates and drop doors, curved ends and horizontal planking of the open wagon, whilst the box top was equipped with flap doors directly above the drop doors. The van portion had diagonal straps running from the outer ends of the top planks to the former top planks of the open wagon portion. There was no external corner strapping on the built-up part of the van, neither were the end stanchions of the open wagon section continued on the van portion. The van carried a 6-ton tare weight, a 9 ft wheelbase and, like other unfitted wagons, was painted grey with white lettering, applied in the same position as the four-plank open wagons. After initial use as an internal user vehicle within the confines of the light railway, No. 9 was relegated to use as a sawdust store at Laxfield and subsequently rotted away over the years. The sawdust was used in cattle wagons.

Cattle traffic was always substantial in the independent years when beasts were transported to Stowmarket and Ipswich markets and to Tufnell Park for Smithfield. The Suffolk company initially hired vehicles from the GER and as late as June 1905 were still paying over £8 19s 0d, pending delivery of an order of six wagons. Three cattle wagons were in fact purchased from the GER in October 1904 at a cost of £30. The vehicles, GER Nos. 3555, 3796 and 13170 dating from 1881-1884 appear never to have been included in the MSLR capital stock for only the six new wagons were registered with the RCH and shown on Board of Trade returns. No MSLR numbers were allocated and it must be assumed that the three wagons were only utilised pending delivery of the new build and were then cannibalised for spares. The new cattle wagons, numbered 19, 20, 21, 22, 23 and 24, were supplied to the specifiction of H. R. Gillingwater, based closely on the GER design of cattle wagon and built in 1905 by G. R. Turner of Langley Mill, Nottinghamshire. The wagons, with a tare weight of 7 tons 0 cwt 2 qtrs, were through piped and equipped with screw couplings to enable them to work with passenger train stock. Like other goods vehicles, they were only equipped with the hand brake lever on one side of the vehicle. Being fitted with brake pipes, the cattle wagons were painted brown and lettered 'MID SUFFOLK' along the third planking from the floor to the left of the door, and 'TARE' and the vehicle number on the opposite side of the door, the tare figures '7—0—2' were located on the second row of planking below the word 'TARE' whilst the word 'LARGE' was situated to the right of the door on the top panel. The word 'LARGE' possibly inferred that the company intended to purchase some smaller cattle wagons but none were ever built. Certainly Gillingwater approached the board on 25th November 1905 for authority to purchase additional vehicles but no further progress was made. The six cattle wagons were in almost constant use and supplemented by hired vehicles from the GER. Like the four-plank wagons, they covered considerable distances off the 'Middy' and sustained heavy wear and tear. As early as January 1906, S. Folgate was called to effect repairs to them at a cost of £8 6s 3d. Six months later, Easterbrook gave minor attention to No. 23, charging the company 4/9d whilst in September the GER carried out tyre-turning on an unknown MSL cattle wagon at Ipswich for £2 2s 0d. In 1910 all the cattle wagons received more extensive repairs from the GER, the Mid-Suffolk paying the main line company £27 12s 6d in two instalments during June and October.

Although, as mentioned earlier, No. 19 received repairs in March 1914, by the summer of 1917 the six were showing increasing signs of lack of maintenance. Arrangements were made for the GER to provide further minor repairs at a cost of £12 16s 10d.

As the MSLR cattle wagons were similar to those of the GER, it was inevitable when replacement items were required for the light railway vehicles that GE components were supplied. Thus in later years of independent working none of the cattle wagons were identical and all were modified in one form or another, probably with parts from the GER cattle wagons.

The wagon stock of the 'Middy' was completed by two goods brake vans. Goods brake van No. 1 was an ex-Great Eastern Railway 10-ton vehicle, No. 25031, dating from 1877. Before delivery the brake was repaired and repainted by the main line company at a cost of £35. It had no corner supports on the verandah and the bulkheads were recessed into the body. The sides were built up with eight wide planks whilst the ends had six planks. The upper footsteps were fastened in the centre of the solebar whilst five stanchions supported the lower footboard. The van was also fitted with screw couplings and roof straps over the verandah. A handrail ran along the length of the body side. The body work was painted grey whilst the ironwork and running gear was black. The white lettering on the body side denoted 'MID SUFFOLK' on the fifth plank from the top and 'No. 1' on the third plank, all contained within the inverted 'V' of the side bracing of the brake. The vehicle appears to have received little attention of note when in service with the MSLR although in February 1912 the company ordered a new screw and nut from the GER at a cost of 9/3d.

Goods brake van No. 2 of 12 tons was built in 1906 by G. R. Turner of Langley Mill, Nottingham to order No. L1276 but, unlike the cattle wagons, this vehicle was based on Midland Railway design to drawing No. S753. The body of the vehicle was framed in American oak with cast iron undermembers with a screw brake inside operating all eight blocks on four wheels. It was delivered in the autumn of 1906 with screw couplings but in January 1907 a further set of screw couplings was obtained from Turner for £2 15s 0d. The vehicle was actually hired from G. R. Turner, the Mid-Suffolk paying between January 1907 and June 1910 a total of £180 17s 6d together with interest payment of £9 3s 7d for default of regular payment over the 3½ years. The final payment of £54 5s 3d and the interest payment were actually made by the courts. Being a fitted vehicle, the bodywork of brake van No. 2 was painted brown with black ironwork and running gear. It was lettered in white shaded black 'MID SUFFOLK RY' and below this in smaller lettering 'BRAKE VAN'. Centrally below this and above the side handrail was the lettering 'No. 2'.

Wagon maintenance and repair costs fluctuated considerably over the years whilst increasing traffic and shortage of vehicles made hire from the GER a necessity to conduct business. Examples of maintenance/repair costs and wagon hire charges are shown in the table alongside.

From 1913 the maintenance and repairs costs were calculated annually and were: 1913 – £24 12s 0d; 1914 – £103 10s 6d; 1915 – £35 5s 2d; 1916 – £51 6s 3d; 1917 – £156 15s 0d; 1918 – £241 14s 11d; 1919 – £123 13s 2d.

During the independent years, damage sustained by other company's wagons whilst in use on the Mid-Suffolk was the liability of the light railway company. Amongst others, the GER were called upon to effect repairs to their own horse-box No. 791 at a cost of 5/6d in December 1906, to Coote and Warren coal wagon No. 698 at a cost of £2 10s 0d in December 1915, and repair GE open wagon No. 8406 in February 1919 for 6/8d.

The wagon stock of the Mid-Suffolk line remained a constant total of 28 vehicles until after the First World War. In 1919, however, many of the vehicles were found to be requiring heavy maintenance or replacement. The company, after discussion with the receiver, decided it was easier to hire vehicles from the GER than repair or replace and therefore the worst seven vehicles were withdrawn and scrapped during the year although no individual numbers are recorded. The remaining 21 goods vehicles remained in use until absorption of the company by the LNER when all were quickly withdrawn for scrapping.

The GER, and later LNER and BR, provided a variety of non-passenger-carrying stock for branch traffic including fitted and unfitted vans for perishable produce, fruit and flowers, cattle wagons for the conveyance of livestock, horse-boxes, carriage wagons and milk vans. The great majority of wagon types consisted of five-plank or high-sided opens for general merchandise and local merchants' wagons or colliery wagons for coal traffic. These included wagons owned by Fosdick, Thomas Moy, and Coote & Warren, also Mellonie of Ipswich and Ellis & Everard, builders merchants. After nationalisation 16-ton all steel mineral wagons were used for coal and sugar beet traffic.

On the withdrawal of the MSLR goods brakes, two ex-GE and later LNER vans were allocated to the branch, each normally crewed by the same guard. After the Second World War the brake vans were often transferred between mixed trains at Kenton so that one guard worked the Haughley-Kenton section in his brake and the other worked the Kenton to Laxfield section. In the latter years LNER 20-ton Toad E brake No. E178637 was in regular use as the branch brake van with other examples of Toad B and Toad E 20-ton vehicles.

An amusing incident involving a goods brake van, which would not have been out of place in a Will Hay comedy, occurred soon after nationalisation. The new British Railways had secured an important contract for the convey-

	Maintenance/ Repair	*Wagon hire*
6 months ending	*£ s. d.*	*£ s. d.*
31 December 1907	4 16 8	24 6 3
30 June 1908	6 14 5	35 8 11
31 December 1908	*	68 17 0
30 June 1909	*	41 18 0
31 December 1909	*	21 13 0
30 June 1910	*	38 14 0
31 December 1910	*	28 16 0
30 June 1911	1 9 9	55 0 6
31 December 1911	33 14 1	61 3 0
30 June 1912	53 19 4	61 8 0
31 December 1912	3 17 0	27 13 6

* figures included with coaching stock

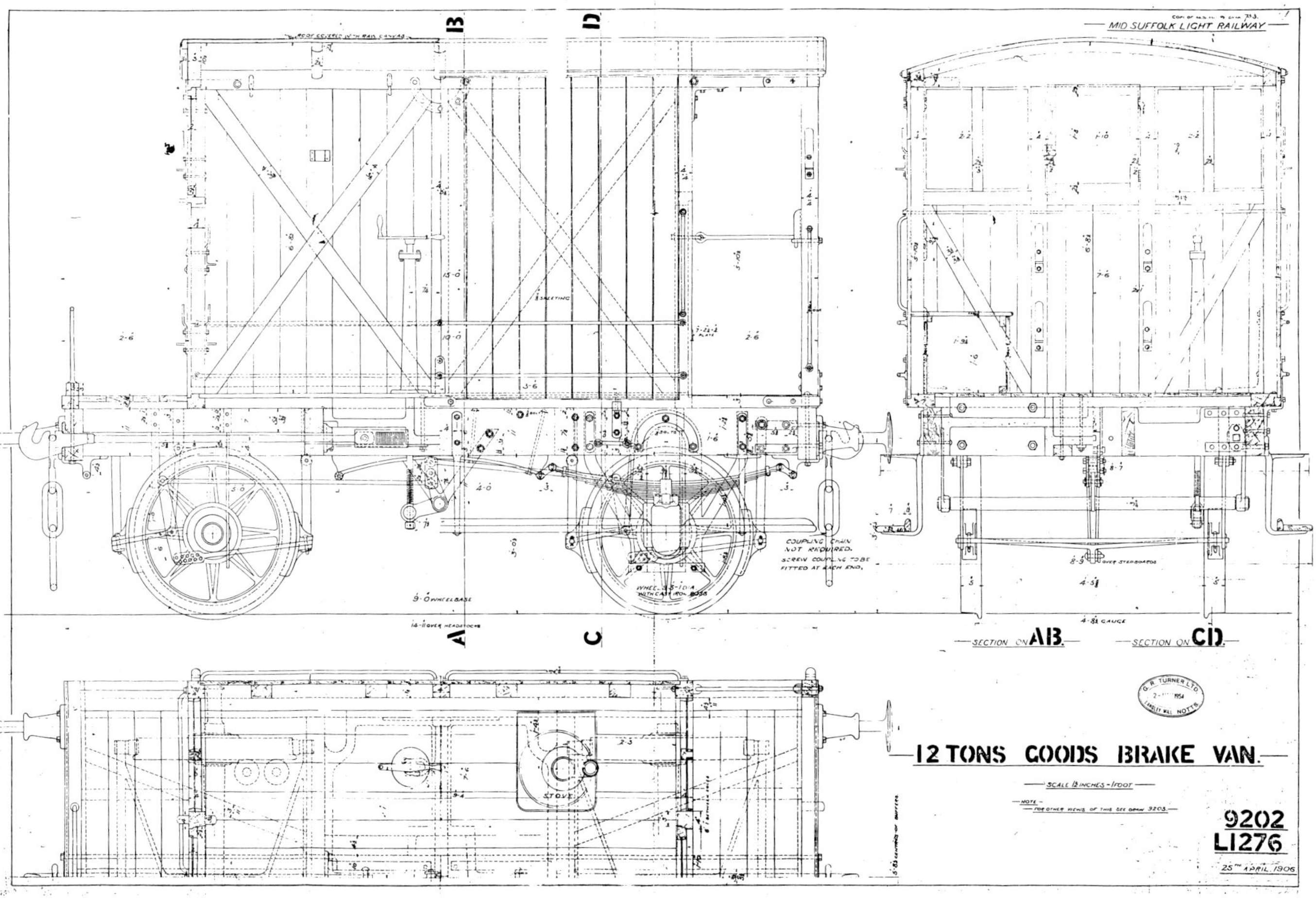

GER diagram for cattle wagons 3555, 3796 and 13170 purchased by MSLR for £30.

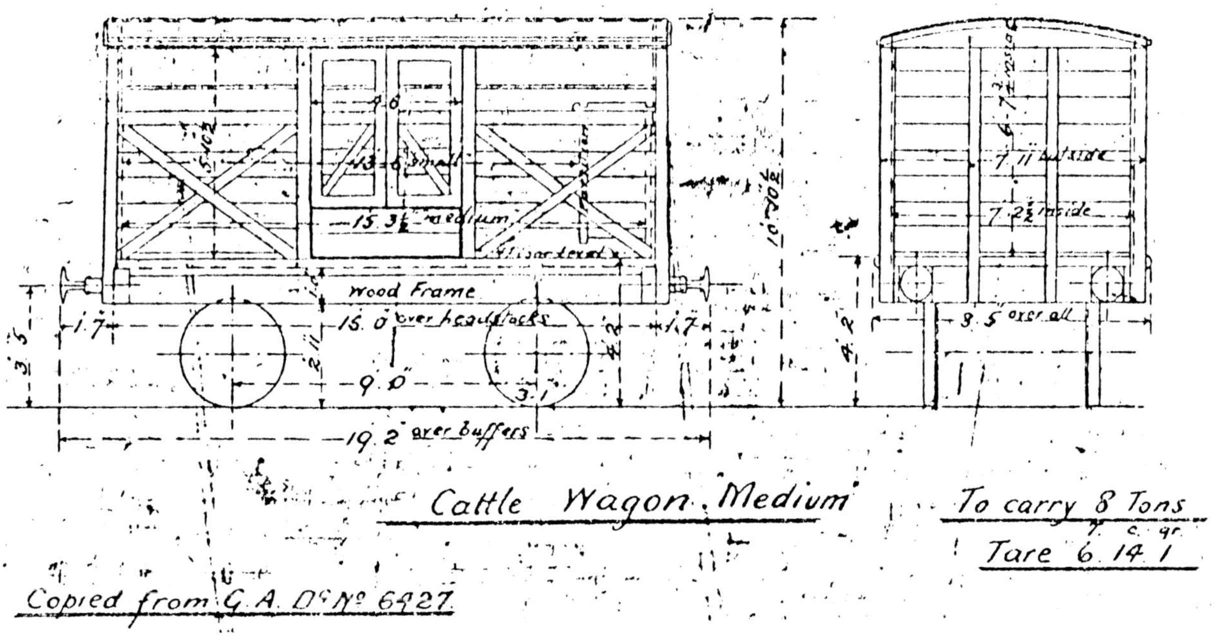

Sketch drawing of MSLR goods brake van No. 1 (ex-GER) body only.

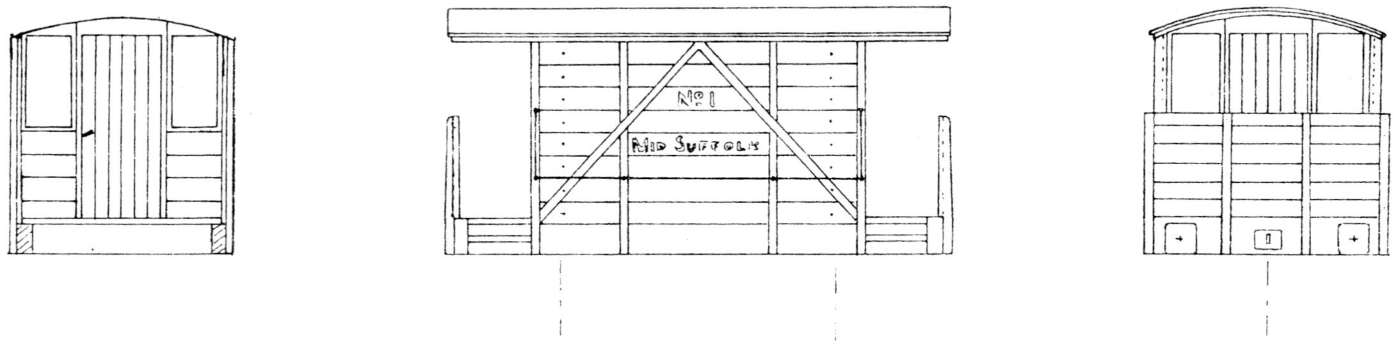

End and side views of MSLR cattle wagon (body only).

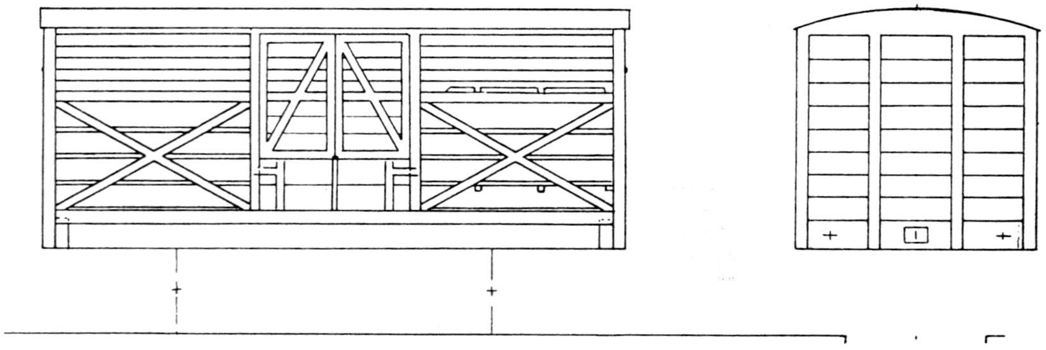

Scale: 4mm to 1 foot

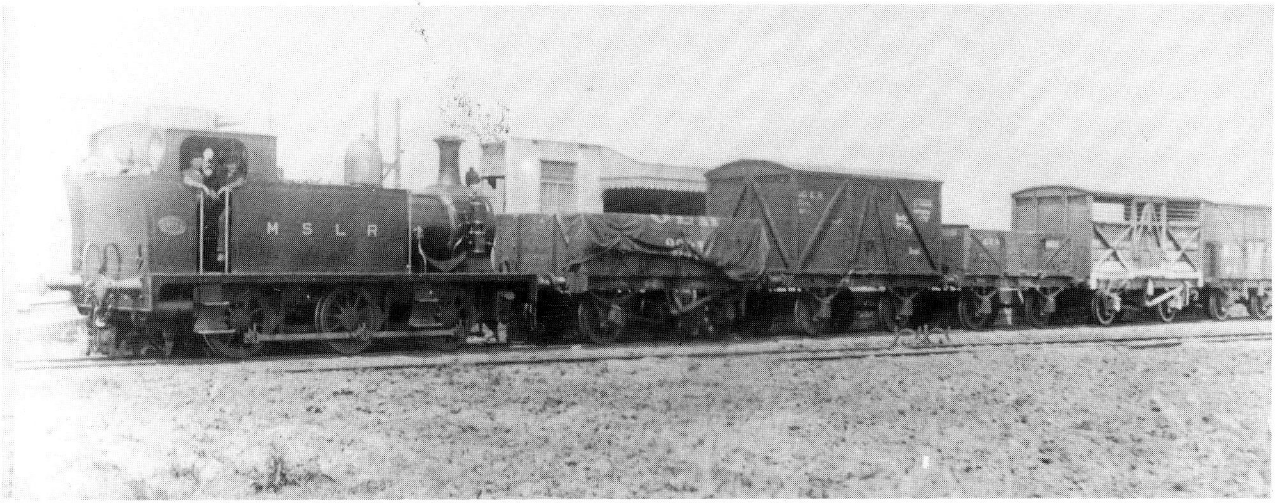

MSLR 0–6–0T No. 1 standing beside the incomplete down platform at Kenton in 1906 before the up side platform and track were installed. The train, specially placed for the photographer, is formed of three GER vehicles together with MSLR cattle wagon No. 24 and MSLR van No. 9. *Locomotive Publishing Company*

ance of freight traffic from Parkeston Quay to a destination in the Midlands. The railway authorities decided with the firm to launch the new service with due publicity and Ipswich Carriage and Wagon shops were requested to renovate, repair and repaint a goods brake van for the first working. The van duly appeared in new bauxite brown livery with shining black underframe and white walled tyres, and was given to the traffic section for a test run. The work had been completed in good time for the publicity run but as the date approached no trace could be found of the van. Searches were made in Ipswich C & W Shops and all sidings along the main line from Norwich to Manningtree, Colchester and Harwich but to no avail. Unable to find their prize brake, the railway authorities hastily prepared another vehicle and the train duly ran with the substitute at the tail. The specially prepared van was quickly forgotten until several months later when a traffic inspector made a visit to Laxfield. As the train approached the terminus, there, to the inspector's surprise, was the new painted brake van languishing in a siding. On further investigation it was found to be acting as a greenhouse for porter Hubbard who was growing geraniums and sweet peas.

When authority was brought to bear, the full story revealed that during the course of its test run, the newly painted brake van had been detached from an all stations goods train at Haughley and shunted into the yard, ready for picking up by a southbound goods for return to Ipswich and on to Parkeston. The arrival of the brake coincided with a defect which had developed with the van allocated to the Mid-Suffolk line which consequently required C & W attention. On arrival at Haughley, the branch brake was shunted into the siding and the newly painted van attached and worked back to Laxfield with the branch goods. To add to the confusion, the train crew of the up goods, only being advised to pick up the newly painted brake van, completely ignored the old branch brake van and departed Haughley without picking up the additional vehicle, thinking another train had taken the vehicle forward. The wagon examiner duly arrived to effect repairs to the branch brake which was subsequently taken forward to Laxfield with the first down mixed train the following day. Being attached to their own brake vans, the Laxfield guards soon arranged for the branch brakes to resume work on the goods and mixed services, leaving the newly painted van languishing unwanted in the siding at the terminus. No enquiries for the vehicle were made by the authorities at Haughley and Ipswich and, when no message was sent for the vehicle to be returned to the main line, porter Frank Hubbard decided to put it to good use and cultivate geraniums and sweet peas. So, proud of his horticultural prowess and his prize-winning entries in local shows, Hubbard arranged for one of the branch engines to move the brake van around the yard to shelter the vehicle and its contents from the cold winds, especially when they came from the east. Needless to say, when all was discovered, Frank Hubbard was quickly requested to remove his prize exhibits and the van returned, attached to the next up mixed train to Haughley and further remunerative service under the watchful eye of the inspector.

An interesting vehicle which served on the line in the last few years was the water tender located at Laxfield to provide supplies of water for carriage and station cleaning. The tender actually arrived on the Mid-Suffolk on 1st January 1948 and retained its faded black livery with 'LNER' on the side tanks until disposed of when the line closed. The tender was of interest being one built for the Midland and Great Northern Railway to a Midland Railway pattern dating from 1911 similar to those attached to the first two Midland class '4' 0–6–0s Nos. 3835/6. The M & GN tender differed in that the wheels were only 3 ft 7½ ins diameter compared with the Midland 4 ft 3 ins. The tender originally carried 3 tons of coal and 3,000 gallons of water and was attached to M & GN Beyer Peacock rebuilt class 'A' 4–4–0 No. 25 until the locomotive was withdrawn in May 1941. Later transferred to service stock as a water carrier, it was worked up from Laxfield on the last branch goods train on Friday, 25th July 1952, and remained at Haughley for some months. It was noted at Ipswich in 1958 and was finally scrapped in 1970.

Although the Mid-Suffolk Light Railway was nominally independent, once the LNER took over the line from 1924 the branch was almost indistinguishable from any other Great Eastern branch. This was almost wholly due to the employment of former GER locomotives and rolling stock on services, a practice which continued after nationalisation. To prove the point, 'J15' class 0–6–0 No. 65467, hauling three 6-wheel coaches and LNER goods brake, could be almost anywhere in East Anglia. It is, however, 1950 and the train is the Saturday afternoon down train passing the open level crossing where the lane leading from Monk Soham Green to Bedingfield bisected the line east of Kenton. As there was no school traffic, the train started from Haughley and, being the last working of the week, usually ran incredibly early.
Dr. I. C. Allen

CHAPTER TWELVE

Closure

SOON after taking office, the cost-conscious Railway Executive advised the railway regions of the need for further investigation into unremunerative services. Accordingly Eastern Region headquarters resurrected and dusted the documents on the Laxfield branch and enquiries resumed into the viability of the service. Since previous enquiries the number of passengers travelling daily had fallen to negligible figures and the railway appeared to all intents and purposes to be providing only a social service to the community by conveying schoolchildren to and from school.

Despite such enquiries, efforts were made to improve conditions for the few travellers on the Mid-Suffolk line. The life-expired six-wheel rolling stock, reputedly the last six-wheel coaches in regular use on passenger services on British Railways, was withdrawn in August and October 1951 to be replaced by bogie vehicles. These improvements were to be the last, for unofficial sources reported no additional money was to be spent on the line. Thus after Worlingworth level crossing gates were hit by a car and damaged in 1951, it was not thought necessary to renew the gate in view of the possible impending closure of the line. As a replacement for the shattered gate which was placed beside the track, a rope with a red flag was placed across the line. Thereafter until the withdrawal of services, each train was required to stop on the approach to the crossing so that the fireman could place the rope across the road and then open the other gate for the train to pass. After the train had proceeded over the crossing, the gate and rope were replaced across the line either by the fireman or guard before the train continued its journey. Similar conditions also applied at Mendlesham.

By the autumn of 1951 rumours of threatened closure were rife, only to be confirmed in November when the railway management officially informed members of the staff and NUR and ASLEF branches at Ipswich that proposals were actively in hand. The Railway Executive duly informed the public in December 1951 of their

Initially the GER 'Y14' class 0–6–0 locomotives (LNER 'J15') were only permitted for working ballast and permanent way trains between Haughley and Laxfield. During World War Two they worked services in an emergency and were regularly utilised hauling the ammunition trains to Mendlesham and Horham. On completion of track strengthening in 1947, the 'J15s' took control of the branch passenger and freight services until closure of the line. A particular favourite of the footplate staff at Laxfield was No. 65447 (ex-GER 647) shown at the terminus in September 1951 with fireman Law trimming the coal in the tender. *Photomatic*

Producing a minor smokescreen 'J15' class 0–6–0 No. 65447 pulls over the crossing at Mendlesham with a Laxfield to Haughley train in April 1952. Note the faggots of firewood loaded on the tender.

East Anglian Daily Press

In full cry near Gipping siding, No. 65447 has safety valves lifting as she tackles the gradient with a mixed train from Haughley to Laxfield in June 1952. The undulating gradients of the Mid-Suffolk line are evident as the railway follows the contour of the land in the far distance. The nearby open level crossing was the site of the collision between a car and the train in the charge of driver Jehu. *Dr. I. C. Allen*

proposals to close the line completely. Within days of the announcement objections to the closure were made by East Suffolk County Council and Hartismere Rural Council. Because of these objections a meeting of the Eastern Transport Users Consultative Committee was arranged, so that the objectors could state their case.

At a meeting of the Eastern Area Transport Users Consultative Committee held in London on 12th February 1952 the Railway Executive was represented by A. J. Johnson, who presented the case for closure. He claimed the retention of the branch could not be justified. Passenger traffic was very light with the only regular users being fifty or so scholars holding season tickets between the branch stations and Stowmarket. On the freight side the largest commodity conveyed was sugar beet, but only a quarter of the tonnage grown in the area was conveyed by rail. Johnson advised that arrangements had been made with the Eastern Counties Omnibus Company to provide a special bus service for scholars running at times comparable to the present train service.

A letter from Mr. G. C. Lightfoot, Clerk to the East Suffolk County Council, said withdrawal of the already attenuated services would cause inconvenience and additional expense to the local education authority for conveying children by road whilst many residents in this rural part of Suffolk would be almost completely devoid of all forms of public transport. Withdrawal of the freight service would involve transporting coal and sugar beet over narrow and tortuous roads of light construction. It was inevitable that the extra traffic would cause considerable damage.

'J15' class 0–6–0 No. 65467 working a railway officers' special between Laxfield Mill and Laxfield station on 6th April 1952. *Dr. I. C. Allen*

Mr. Johnson agreed that there should not be any increase of traffic by road but reiterated that 75 per cent of the sugar beet traffic passed that way already.

The Reverend N. L. Cribb, representing Hartismere Rural Council, reported that his committee and members viewed the proposed closure with alarming despondency. He had been informed that the reason for the number of truck loads of sugar beet conveyed on the line being less than previous years was not contracted growth, but farmers disturbed at the rumour of closure finding alternative transport for their produce.

At the conclusion of the enquiry, the committee decided to agree to recommend the proposed closure subject to the usual safeguards. After sanctioning closure, the Ministry of Transport passed their authority to the Railway Executive for action.

On 6th April 1952 a railway officers special train ran across the branch to Laxfield. 'J15' 0–6–0 No. 65467

Mid-Suffolk branch staff pose for the camera on the footplate of 'J15' class 0–6–0 No. 65447 on 23rd July 1952, a few days before closure. *Left to right:* Willis Keeble (guard); Frank Hubbard (leading porter); Ronnie Thompson (fireman); and Ernie Baker (driver). *R. E. Vincent*

hauled the single Norwich District Engineers 6-wheel saloon No. 960903 and brake van from Haughley to Laxfield and then propelled the vehicles back to the junction, enabling the officials to view the track ahead.

It was said at the time that nobody on the saloon could enjoy their lunch as they were dubious of the split staff method of working on the light railway and thought a head-on collision with a train coming in the opposite direction was always imminent.

Within a fortnight the Railway Executive issued the inevitable announcement. All train services were to be withdrawn and the line closed completely on and from Monday, 28th July. As no Sunday services were operated, the last trains would run across the line on Saturday, 26th July 1952. Some objections were again voiced, but no stay of execution was granted as buses would convey schoolchildren to Stowmarket, whilst augmented bus services from the villages served by the line to Diss, Stowmarket, Halesworth and Ipswich were considered adequate compensation for the loss of the passenger services. Farmers and growers were offered alternative facilities for wagon traffic at the various station yards on the Norwich-Ipswich main line and the East Suffolk line.

In the ensuing weeks railway enthusiasts regularly arrived at Haughley to take a last ride on the light railway and, despite the wide publicity over the closure, they were often the only passengers on the train. In the latter weeks some local people swelled the complement, some taking a nostalgic last trip to and from Ipswich market by train. On 12th July 1952 a party from the British Railways Eastern Region Staff Association visited the line to pay their last respects. The train, formed of two-coach Haughley-Laxfield bogie set No. 2, was hauled by 'J15' class 0–6–0 No. 65467. Stops were made at all stations *en route* so that the enthusiasts could take photographs of the train and buildings.

Officially the last run was to be the 3.55 p.m. down train ex-Haughley, but, because it was necessary to return

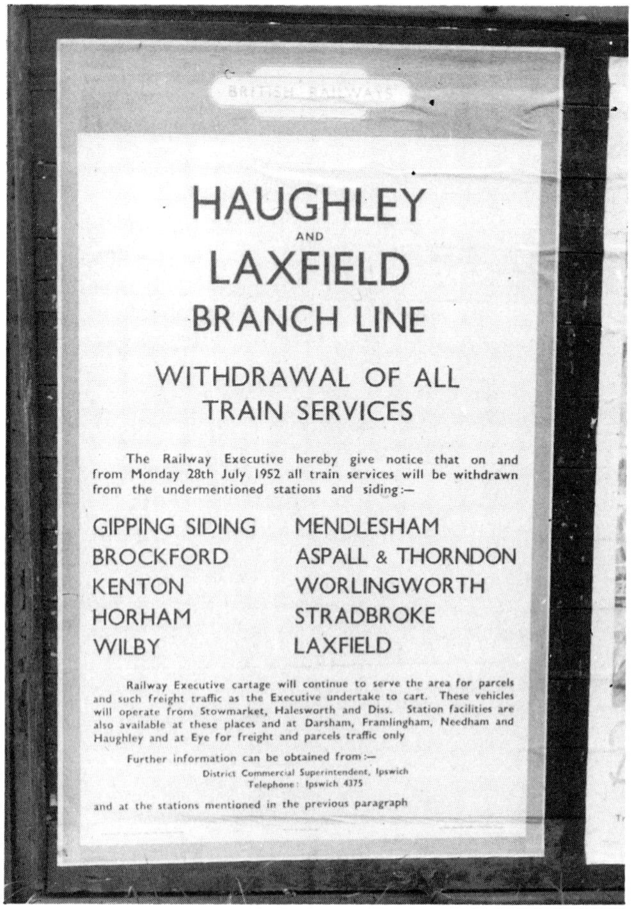

Notice announcing the withdrawal of all train services from the Haughley-Laxfield branch line on and from 28th July 1952.
B. D. J. Walsh

The last scheduled freight train from Laxfield to Haughley ran on Friday, 25th July 1952. Class 'J15' 0–6–0 No. 65388, with driver Skinner and fireman Law on the footplate, pulls into Brockford station with a heavy train, which included the ex-M & GN tender which had been attached to 4–4–0 No. 25, later converted for use as a water carrier. The vehicle used at Laxfield to hold water for carriage cleaning is the last but one vehicle on the train. *Dr. I. C. Allen*

The much overgrown main single line and Laxfield Mill siding, with class 'J15' 0–6–0 No. 65388 picking up the last wagon from the siding and propelling it back to Laxfield station. To the left of the picture in the far distance there is a glimpse of the locomotive water tank located beside the pond. *Dr. I. C. Allen*

On the last day of service 'J15' class 0–6–0 No. 65447, decorated with a wreath and garland on the smokebox, climbs away from Haughley with the 11.15 a.m. to Laxfield on 26th July 1952. Both the two coach bogie sets were utilized on the final services. *G. R. Mortimer*

the engine and passenger stock to Ipswich the same evening and also return rail enthusiasts and local people to their starting stations, railway officials arranged to run a special return working at 5.35 p.m. from Laxfield to Haughley, arriving at the junction at 7 p.m.

Saturday, 26th July 1952 dawned bright and clear and every train run on the line was filled to capacity with local people and railway enthusiasts wishing to make their last journey on the 'Middy'. So large was the complement of passengers that it was necessary to work both 2-coach sets of stock on all trains. A failure of a locomotive on a 1.30 p.m. ex-Liverpool Street main line service, which was carrying several people who wished to travel on the last down train, forced British Railways officials to hold the 3.55 p.m. departure at Haughley to await the latecomers. The fact that the Haughley station master had made special arrangements to cope with the crowds and provide a temporary refreshment room was appreciated by many.

The late running train duly arrived and passengers for the 'Middy' were quickly transferred across to the branch platform to join the 300 or so passengers jammed in the 4-coach train. At 4.49 p.m. guard Willis Keeble gave the 'right away' and 'J15' class 0–6–0 No. 65447, in the charge of driver Joseph Skinner and fireman Jack Law, eased the train out of the platform and up the 1 in 42 gradient towards Laxfield for the last time. Steady progress was made as the train halted at each crowded platform to allow more passengers to join the train. The train crew managed to make up some time on the journey and No. 65447, duly adorned with a wreath on the smokebox door and coloured ribbons tied to the boiler handrail, exceeded the official speed limit on a few sections of the line. Arrival at Laxfield, as at many other stations, was accompanied by exploding detonators and loud cheering from those on the platform.

The locomotive was quickly uncoupled and ran forward to be replenished with water. Last photographs were taken as 65447 recoupled to its four-coach train to depart at 6.17 p.m., forty-two minutes late. Among the passengers on the last up journey were a party dressed in Edwardian clothes and staff from the East Suffolk County Council offices at County Hall, Ipswich, all of whom were making the round trip from Haughley. Also travelling on the branch for the last time was A. Mayfield, a retired schoolmaster from Mendlesham, who witnessed the first train on the branch in 1902. As before, all stations were thronged with passengers and on departure from each stop, the locomotive exploded detonators to the cheers of those left on the

On the final day of services the 1.45 p.m. Laxfield-Haughley arrives at Mendlesham behind No. 65447 in the charge of driver Skinner and fireman Law. Fireman Thompson and driver Baker, extreme positions, are riding on the footplate before returning to Ipswich. The four coaches are filled with enthusiasts taking their last ride on the light railway on 26th July 1952. *G. R. Mortimer*

Crowds thronging the platform at Laxfield awaiting the arrival of the last down train from Haughley. *Dr. I. C. Allen*

Adorned with wreaths and a garland on the tender, No. 65447 stands at the head of the last special train at Laxfield. Because of the late running in the down direction, the special due to depart at 5.35 p.m. did not leave until 6.15 p.m. on the return run. As the shadows lengthen, enthusiasts take their last photographs of the train. *Dr. I. C. Allen*

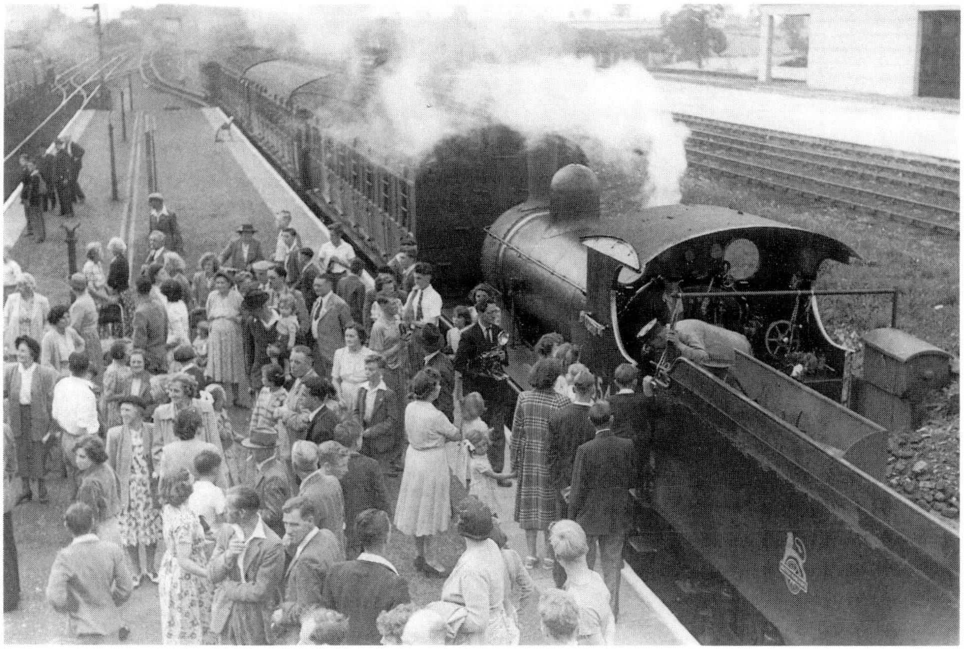

Crowds gathered round the final special train after arrival in the up bay platform at Haughley. On the footplate of No. 65447 is driver Skinner . Despite the sadness of the occasion, a 'Britannia'-hauled train in the down main platform has caused some diversion of attention. No. 65447 worked forward to Ipswich later in the evening at 8.15 p.m. after shunting the coaching stock to the up side yard. *G. R. Mortimer*

platform. The train crew again managed to make up time on the return journey, much to the relief of many who had to travel beyond Haughley. At Mendlesham a loudspeaker van was positioned at the station and played 'Land of Hope and Glory' and 'Auld Lang Syne' as the train stood at the platform and on departure, although much of the music was drowned by exploding detonators. At last the sadness of the occasion was realised by many as the train descended the 1 in 42 and eased to a halt in the platform at Haughley 25 minutes late, the 5.17 p.m. ex-Norwich making a special stop to pick up passengers. After a short duration, the crowd dispersed and 65447 worked forward light engine to Ipswich at 8.15 p.m., the passenger service on the 'middy' now only a memory after only 44 years. A log of the final runs recorded by B. D. J. Walsh is given below.

Among the passengers on the last up special run from Laxfield on 26th July 1952 was a party from the East Suffolk County Offices at Ipswich who were dressed in Edwardian clothes. A gentleman offers a helping hand to a lady as she descends from the compartment of bogie composite E63209E after arrival of the train at Haughley. *G. R. Mortimer*

MID-SUFFOLK LIGHT RAILWAY
HAUGHLEY to LAXFIELD and return.
Saturday, 26th July 1952.

J15 class locomotive No. 65447. Load: 4 bogies.

		Sch. p.m.	Act. p.m.	
HAUGHLEY	Depart	3.55	4.48½	Awaiting arrival of 1.30 p.m. ex Liverpool St.
Mendlesham	Arrive	4.07	4.59	
	Depart	4.08	5.00½	
Brockford	Arrive	4.16	5.04	
	Depart	4.17	5.06	
Aspall	Arrive	4.28	5.11½	
	Depart	4.29	5.13½	
Kenton	Arrive	4.33	5.17½	
	Depart	4.41	5.20	
Worlingworth	Arrive	4.51	5.27	
	Depart	4.52	5.29	
Horham	Arrive	4.57	5.33	
	Depart	4.58	5.35	
Stradbroke	Arrive	5.02	5.37½	
	Depart	5.03	5.41	
Wilby	Arrive	5.07	5.45	
	Depart	5.08	5.46½	
LAXFIELD	Arrive	5.19	5.52	

continued overleaf

A few days after the closure of the line, 'J15' No. 65388 was sent down the branch to collect all remaining wagons left in the goods yards. Here the return working waits to depart Laxfield on 6th August 1952. Note the engine is working boiler first in the up direction in complete contrast to the normal working preference of Laxfield enginemen.
Dr. I. C. Allen

continued from previous page

		p.m.	p.m.
LAXFIELD	Depart	5.35	6.15
Wilby	Arrive	5.46	6.20½
	Depart	5.47	6.25
Stradbroke	Arrive	5.51	6.28
	Depart	5.52	6.31
Horham	Arrive	5.56	6.33½
	Depart	5.57	6.35
Worlingworth	Arrive	6.02	6.39
	Depart	6.03	6.40½
KENTON	Arrive	6.14	6.46½
	Depart	6.15	6.48
Aspall	Arrive	6.20	6.53
	Depart	6.21	6.55½
Brockford	Arrive	6.32	7.01½
	Depart	6.33	7.03
Mendlesham	Arrive	6.43	7.09
	Depart	6.44	7.11½
HAUGHLEY	Arrive	7.00	7.22

The coaching stock remained in the up side yard at Haughley whilst over 30 wagons, some still awaiting unloading by local farmers and coal merchants, remained to be cleared from the branch stations. The wagons were finally removed from the line on 6th August 1952 when 'J15' class 0–6–0 No. 65388 ran 'light engine' from Ipswich to Haughley to pick up the empties. Considerable time was spent on the exercise and at Laxfield the tender had to be replenished with water from the local pond in the absence of water in the lineside tank.

The following day No. 65388 returned to Laxfield with the Colchester breakdown crane manned by Ipswich staff to remove the water tank adjacent to Laxfield engine shed. The signalman at Haughley junction allowed the train to enter the single line at 8.45 a.m. and expected a return by mid afternoon. Unfortunately, the task proved more difficult than planned and the railway authorities showed great concern when the train had not returned to Haughley by 6 p.m. As the lineside phones had been removed there was no way of contacting the staff working on the train, and great relief was shown when 65388 whistled up and eased round the curve and down the gradient into Haughley in total darkness at 10 p.m. The water tank was subsequently sold to the Festiniog Railway in North Wales.

The permanent way remained intact throughout the following winter and spring, the rails gathering rust, whilst the sleepers gradually disappeared under foliage and plant growth.

In the early summer of 1953 tenders were invited for the removal of the permanent way and other equipment. A site meeting was arranged between all interested parties and the District Civil Engineer when ironically all were conveyed to the various sites by road. The contract was subsequently awarded to a firm from Coatbridge, Scotland.

On 1st August the contractor delivered by road to Laxfield a small 4-wheel diesel shunting locomotive from Coatbridge. After the erection of a 22½ ton capacity rail crane, dismantling of the track east of Laxfield station commenced. Unfortunately the operation was temporarily halted when the flat bottom rail in Laxfield Mill siding collapsed under the weight of the crane. By the end of the month all track east of Laxfield had been recovered and on 30th August 1953 'J15' 0–6–0 No. 65404 hauled a train of empty engineers' wagons from Haughley to Laxfield. Where the road across the railway at Wilby had been re-metalled the locomotive pressed a path through the tar. On the return run the Ipswich District Engineer's staff loaded switches and crossings previously disconnected by the contractor's men and required for further use. Immediately after the recoverable material had been taken to Ipswich, the contractor commenced removing the track from Laxfield, working back towards Haughley with the crane lifting sleepers and rails onto wagons. J. T. Truesdale,

The Colchester breakdown crane, with mess van and assorted wagons hauled by 'J15' class 0–6–0 No. 65388, standing by the locomotive water tank east of Laxfield station on 7th August 1952. The crane subsequently recovered the tank for further use at another location.
Dr. I. C. Allen

On 7th August 1952 class 'J15' 0–6–0 No. 65388 worked to Laxfield with the Colchester steam breakdown crane (manned by the Ipswich breakdown gang) to remove the main water storage tank from beside the engine shed. The task took some considerable time to perform and the railway authorities showed great concern when the train had not returned to Haughley by 6 p.m. As the lineside telephones had been removed, there was no way of contacting the staff working on the train, and great relief was shown when 65388 whistled up and eased round the curve and down the gradient into Haughley at 10 p.m. The water tank was subsequently sold to the Festiniog Railway in North Wales.
Dr. I. C. Allen

The overgrown permanent way, platform and station buildings at Horham in 1953 before the lifting of the track. Of all the MSLR stations, Horham is the only one that remains, albeit overgrown in a private yard.
W. A. Camwell

the foreman employed by the Coatbridge firm, was in charge of the task assisted by one Scotsman and eleven local men. Over 100 tons of metal were loaded each week and 'J15' class 0–6–0s Nos. 65388 and 65404 were regularly employed removing full wagons and returning to site with empties. As the work progressed, all material was taken through to Haughley for storage before sale.

By April 1954 all work was completed and wagon loads of sleepers and rails were stored in the former MSL yard at Haughley. The rails were subsequently sold to Tyneside and South Wales collieries for re-use, iron chairs were sent to Leiston foundry, whilst many sleepers went to the Ministry of Food stores. By 1957 the site of Kenton station had disappeared under five years growth of vegetation although the nearby pillarbox still bore the inscription 'Kenton Junction'.

In the three decades which have passed since the closure and lifting of the line, all of the former trackbed and railway land has been sold. Bridge abutments at Haugh Lane and at Debenham are evidence of the former light railway, the latter surrounded by mature trees on the embankment. Nothing, however, remains of the overbridge conveying the Norwich-Ipswich road over the former railway. After the removal of the track the site was used as a rubbish tip, but in 1968 the road was slightly re-routed,

In the early summer of 1953 tenders were invited for the removal of the permanent way and other fixed assets. The contract was subsequently awarded to a firm from Coatbridge in Scotland. On 1st August 1953 the contractor delivered by road to Laxfield a small 4-wheel diesel shunting locomotive and 22½ ton capacity rail crane, and work commenced a few days later lifting the track east of the station. The small diesel locomotive stands at Laxfield prior to commencing its recovery work, with J. T. Truesdale, the foreman, in charge of Scotsmen and a local labour force.

Dr. I. C. Allen

It was obviously not all hard slog lifting the Mid-Suffolk line. The contractor's men take it easy as the diesel trundles along the branch with loaded wagons in September 1953.

Dr. I. C. Allen

the bridge demolished and the cutting filled in. The site of Mendlesham station is part of a maltings where the platform is still in use as a loading bay. There is now no trace of any of the other stations except at Horham where the corrugated iron building stands rusting and decaying in the middle of a private lorry park. A correspondent in the *East Anglian Daily Times* suggested in the spring of 1986 that the building should be preserved. Beyond the station, the former trackbed is used as a farm track. The platform at Wilby is still evident, but at Laxfield only the decaying platform lies half hidden under ever encroaching undergrowth, protected from the roadway by a rickety gate which still shows signs of LNER cream and green paintwork. Part of the station building is still in use as a pavilion on the local sports field. Beyond the erstwhile terminus the route of the former line can be traced to Laxfield Mill which still stands in use as a store. The field by Westerfield station where the cutting of the first sod was performed as so many hopes were raised, is now part of Cubitt & Gott's contractors yard.

Much of the remainder of the trackbed has disappeared under growing crops where farmers have taken the opportunity to enlarge some of their fields. In some instances shallow cuttings have been filled in or embankments levelled to provide additional arable land and the only evidence of former railway ownership is the odd glimpse of the ubiquitous post and wire fencing bordering the side of a field. Some of the deeper cuttings and embankments will, however, remain for many years to come as a reminder of the only standard gauge independent light railway to challenge the monopoly of the Great Eastern Railway in East Anglia.

The termination of the former Mid-Suffolk line at Haughley, forming a headshunt for the up yard following completion of removal work on 25th April 1954. In the foreground is the post of the uprooted outer home signal. *G. R. Mortimer*

APPENDIX – SKETCH DRAWINGS OF MSLR STRUCTURES

by Peter J. Wilde and John Watson

Not to scale unless otherwise indicated

HAUGHLEY STATION BUILDING

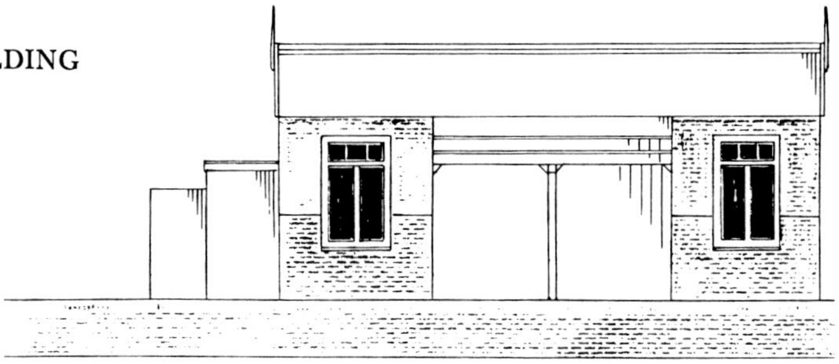

MENDLESHAM STATION BUILDING

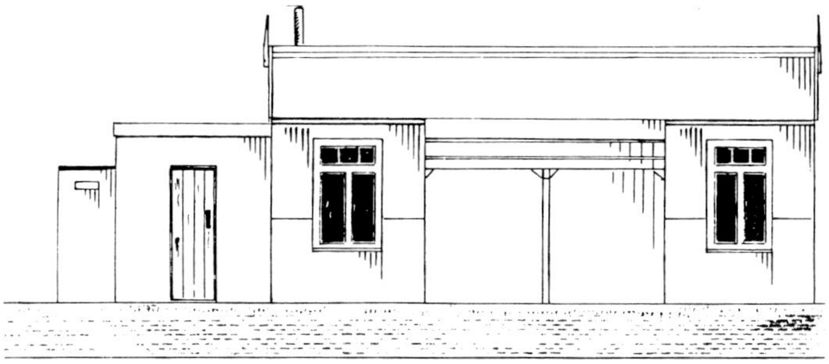

BROCKFORD STATION BUILDINGS

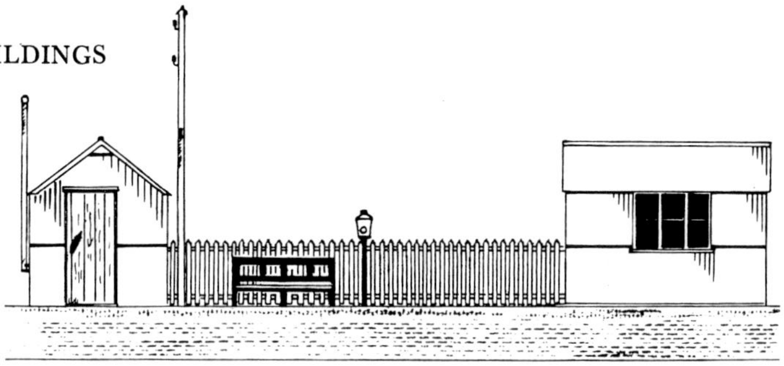

ASPALL STATION BUILDING

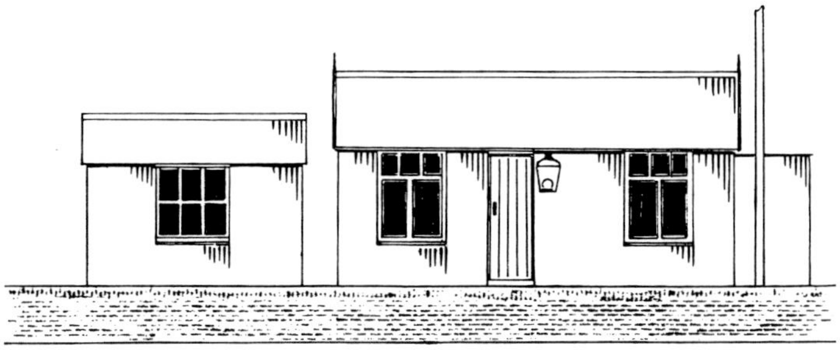

Drawn by Peter J. Wilde

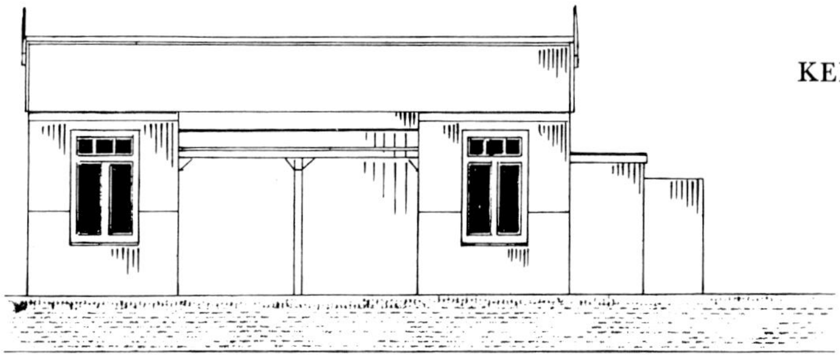

KENTON STATION BUILDING

KENTON STATION BUILDING

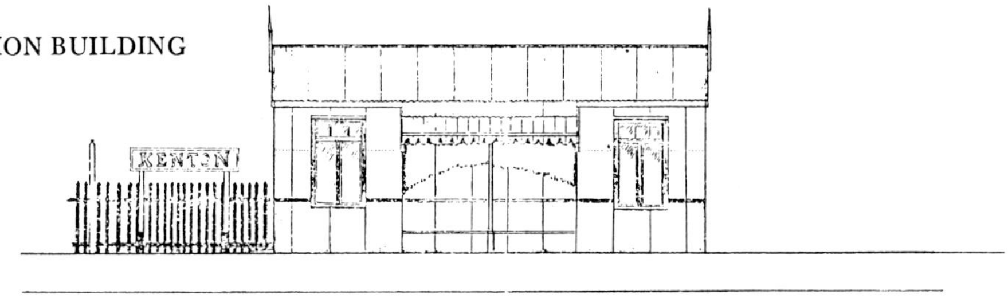

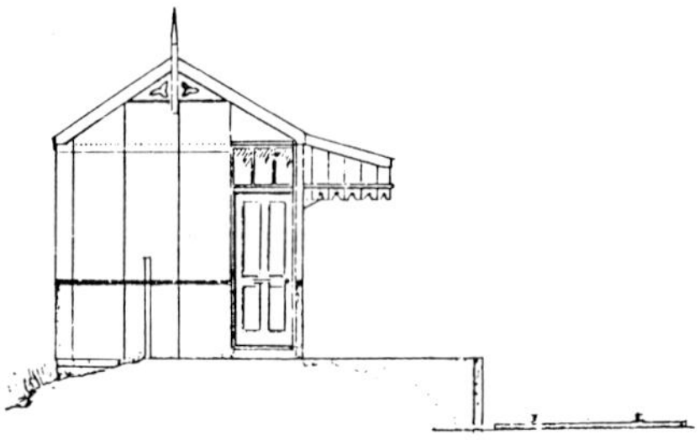

Drawn by Peter J. Wilde

DETAILS AT KENTON

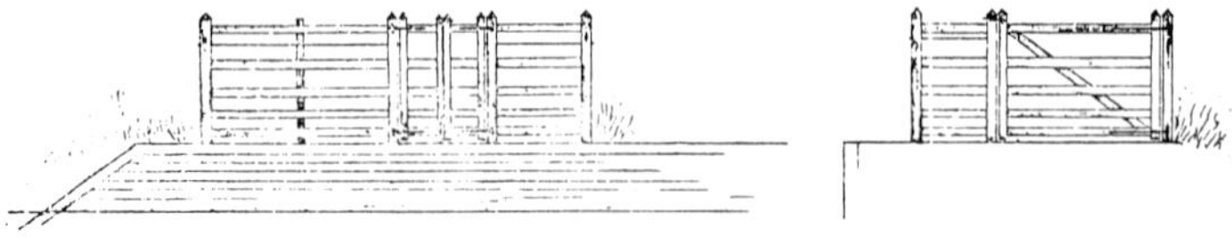

CATTLE PEN

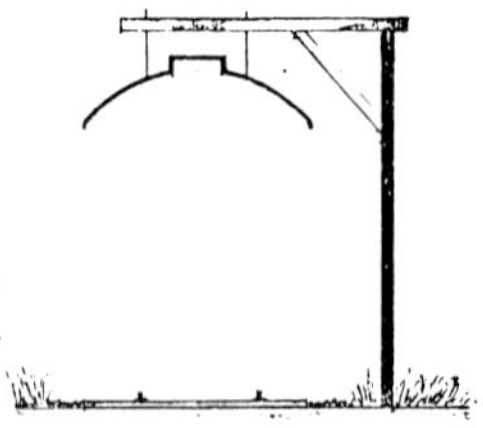

LOADING GAUGE

LEVEL CROSSING GATES (GER pattern)

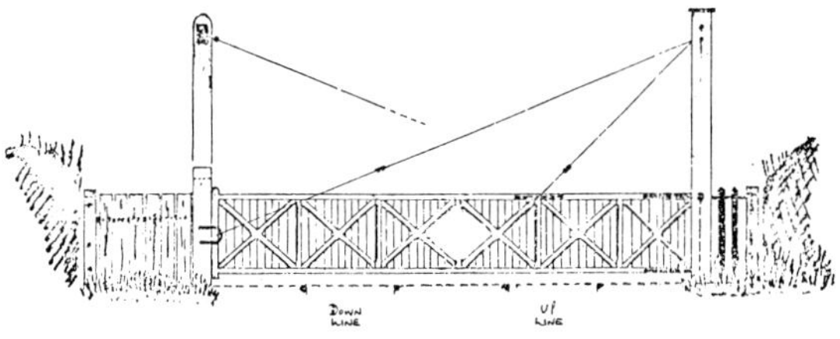

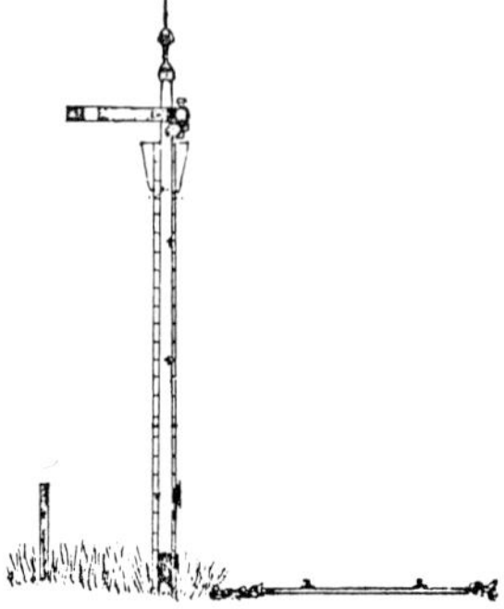

DOWN HOME SIGNAL (McKenzie & Holland)

WORLINGWORTH STATION BUILDING

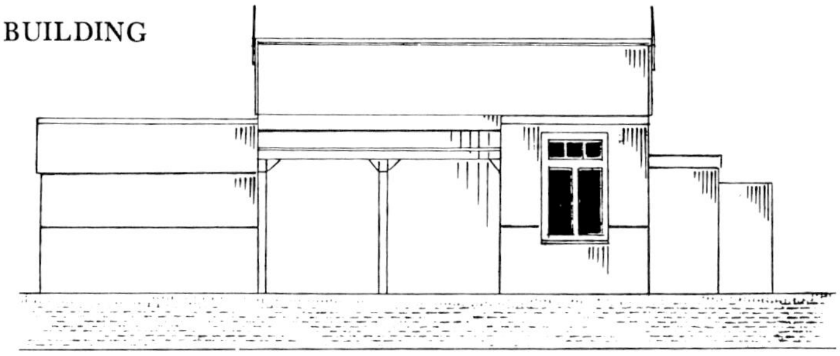

HORHAM STATION BUILDING

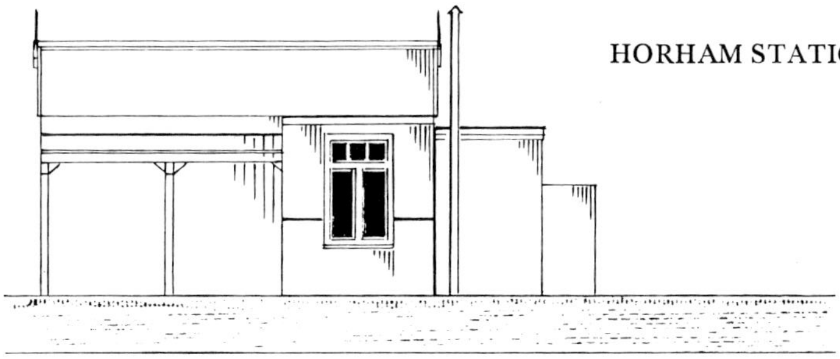

STRADBROKE STATION BUILDING

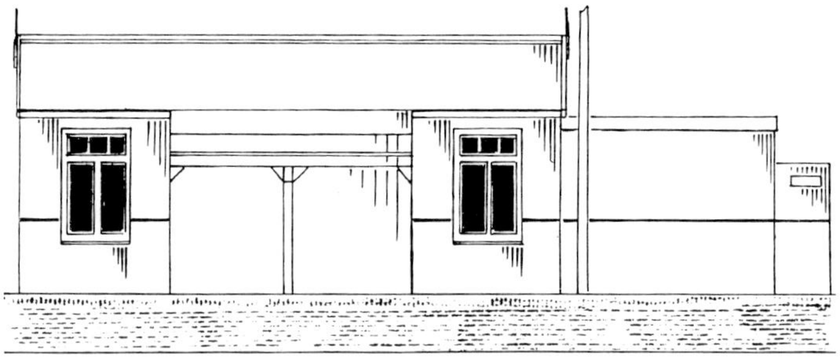

WILBY STATION BUILDINGS

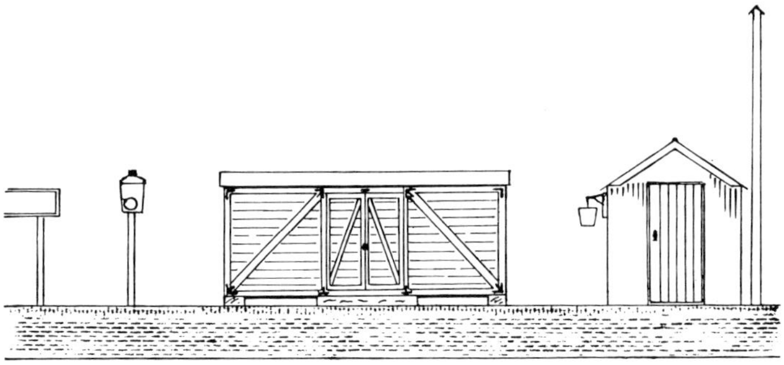

Drawn by Peter J. Wilde

LAXFIELD STATION BUILDINGS

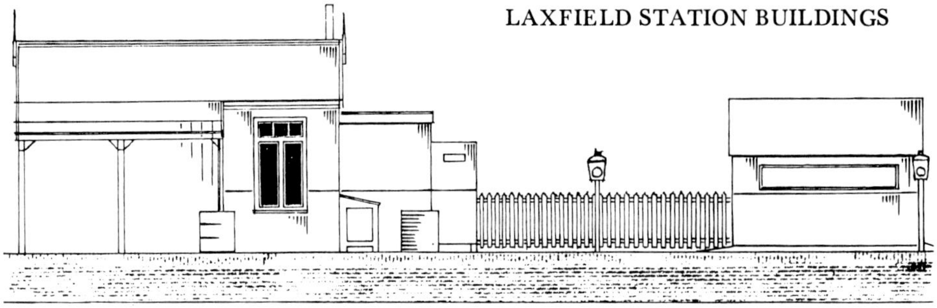

Drawn by Peter J. Wilde

LAXFIELD WAITING ROOM AND TICKET OFFICE

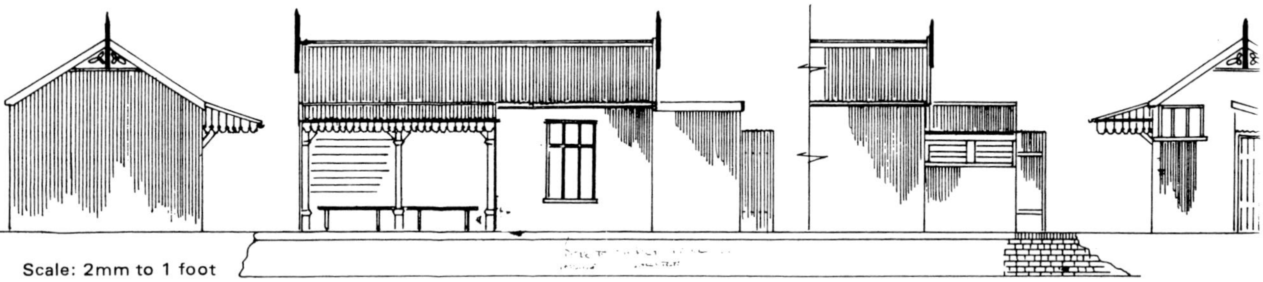

Drawn from photographs by John Watson

LAXFIELD SUPERINTENDENT OF THE LINE'S OFFICE

Drawn from photographs by John Watson

LAXFIELD SUPERINTENDENT OF THE LINE'S OFFICE AND FIRE PUMP SHED

Drawn by Peter J. Wilde

LAXFIELD TOOL SHED

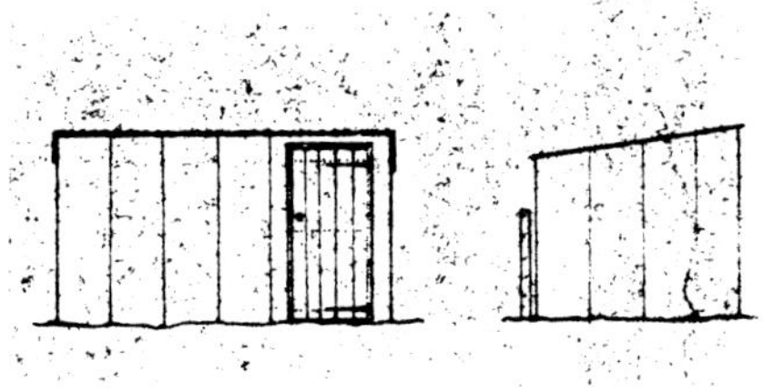

LAXFIELD P.W. HUT

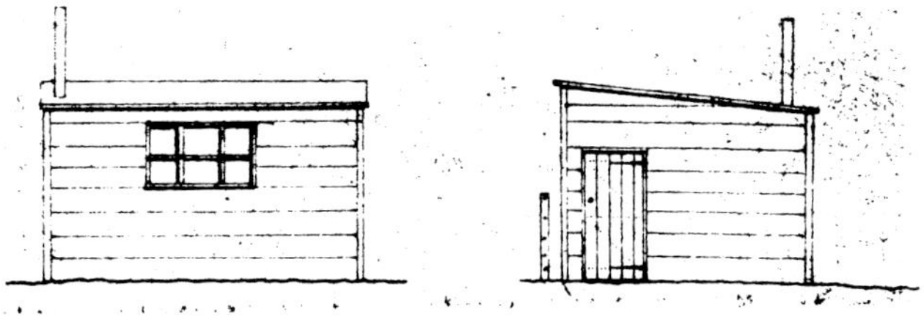

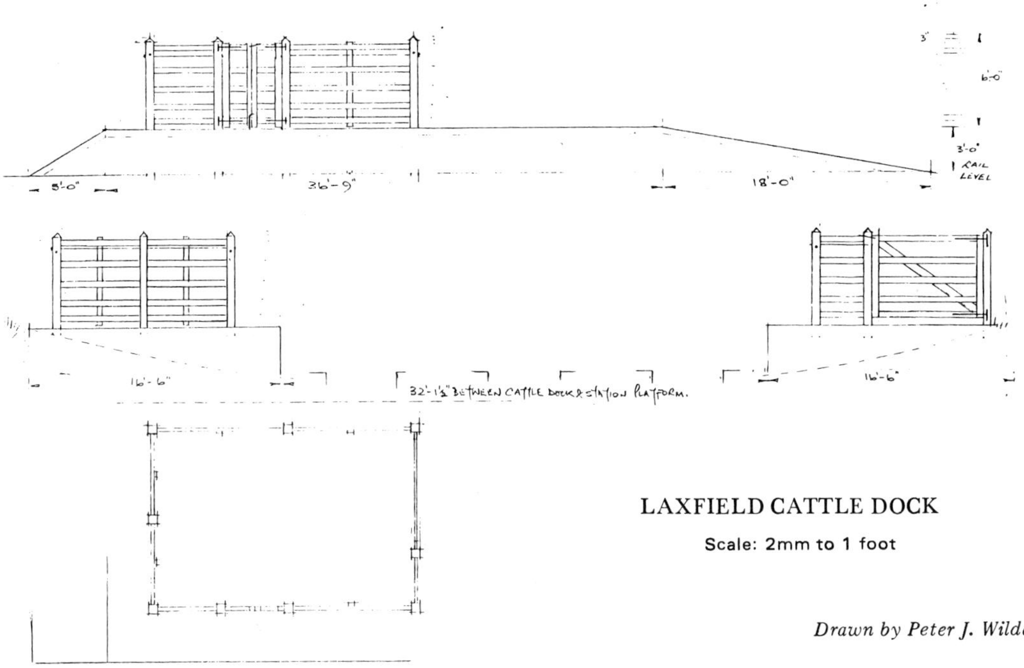

LAXFIELD CATTLE DOCK

Scale: 2mm to 1 foot

Drawn by Peter J. Wilde

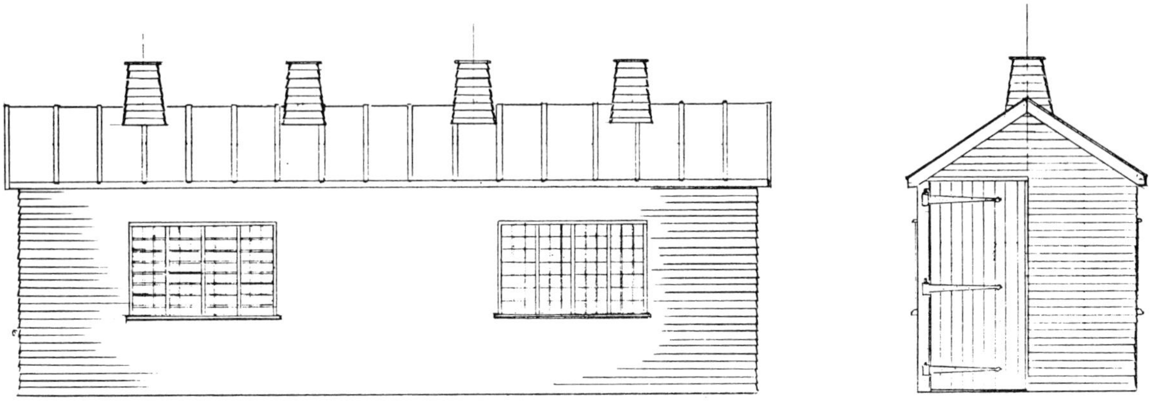

LAXFIELD ENGINE SHED

All timber construction, exterior ship-lap boarding, roof boarded, felted and battened, inspection pit running length of shed. Length to house two Mid-Suffolk locos.

Scale: 2mm to 1 foot

Drawn from photographs by John Watson

LAXFIELD WATER TANK BY THE POND (east of the station)

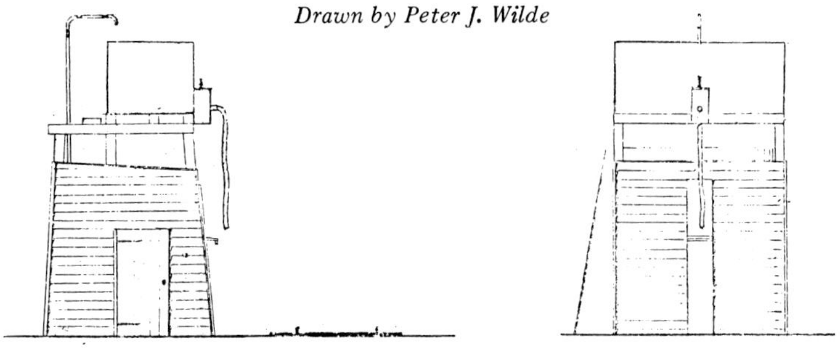

Drawn by Peter J. Wilde

ACKNOWLEDGEMENTS

The publication of this history would not have been possible without the help of many people who have been kind enough to assist. In particular I should like to thank: the late A. R. Cox, the late W. Fenton, the late G. Woodcock, B. D. J. Walsh, J. Watling, D. Taylor, G. Pember, H. C. Casserley, M. Brooks, P. Webber, R. H. N. Hardy, K. Foster, G. R. Mortimer, R. Barlow, P. J. Wilde, the late F. Bloomfield, J. Watson, C. Scholey, Rev. C. Bayes, J. King, L. Wood, and R. Kingstone.

Particular thanks must go to Geoff Rice who made a special study of the 'Middy' and allowed me access to his photographic collection. Geoff also interviewed many of the former employees of the light railway. Dr. Ian Allen passed on many reminiscences and provided a vast number of photographs of the line for the book. Harry Morling, as the Mid-Suffolk Light Railway research co-ordinator for the Great Eastern Railway Society, also placed his records at my disposal.

Grateful thanks to the staff of the former Ipswich Motive Power Depot and the many other active and retired railway staff, some of whom worked on the light railway.

Thanks are due to The Public Record Office, British Rail Eastern Region, The House of Lord Record Office, The British Museum Newspaper Library, Suffolk County Record Office, Ipswich, and the Great Eastern Railway Society.

Last but not least special thanks to Mavis Herbert for typing the manuscript.

BIBLIOGRAPHY

GENERAL WORKS

Allen, C. J.	*The Great Eastern Railway*	Ian Allan
Comfort, N. A.	*The Mid Suffolk Light Railway*	Oakwood Press
Gordon, D. I.	*Regional History of Railways of Great Britain Vol. 5 – Eastern Counties*	David and Charles
Joby, R. S.	*Forgotten Railways of East Anglia*	David and Charles
RCTS	*Locomotives of the LNER* (Various volumes)	

PERIODICALS

Bradshaws Railway Guide
Bradshaws Railway Manual
British Railways (Eastern Region) Magazine
Buses
East Anglian Magazine
Great Eastern Railway Magazine
Locomotive Carriage and Wagon Review
Locomotive Magazine
LNER Magazine
Railway Magazine
Railway World
Railway Year Book
Trains Illustrated

NEWSPAPERS

East Anglian Daily Times
Suffolk Chronicle and Mercury
Evening Star
Stowmarket Chronicle

Also Minute Books of:
Mid Suffolk Light Railway
Great Eastern Railway
London and North Eastern Railway

Working and Public Timetables: MSLR, GER, LNER and BR (ER).

Appendices to Working Timetables: GER, LNER and BR (ER).